More praise for *Grand Theft Horse*

"G. Neri and Corban Wilkin give readers a [illegible] and deliver a thrilling story full of suspense, hope, courage, and heart."
—Gigi Amateau, author of *Chancey of the Maury River*

"Greg Neri's true-life account of his cousin Gail Ruffu's efforts to save a beloved racehorse force readers to examine the difference between what is legal, what is moral, and which should win out when there's a life on the line. Neri beautifully captures the plainspoken voice and deliberate actions of his cousin Gail, whose love and concern for a racehorse will leave readers cheering."
—Crystal Hubbard, author of *The Last Black King of the Kentucky Derby*

"The Grand Theft Horse team steers us hard and true into a tale of kidnapping and escape. . . . [A] spellbinding triumph of human empathy."
—Paul Griffin, author of *When Friendship Followed Me Home*

"*Grand Theft Horse* is an original story seldom told: of a woman who sacrifices everything to the matrix of capitalism, bureaucracy, and incarceration in order to bring us closer to our humanity."—Tony Medina, author of *I Am Alfonso Jones*

"A compelling page-turner of a story that will move you to anger and tears. *Grand Theft Horse* is a graphic novel to share, ponder, talk about, and love. Neri and Wilken have crafted a thing of wonder, brilliance, and beauty."
—Andrew Smith, Michael L. Printz Honor and Boston Globe-Horn Book Award author of *Grasshopper Jungle*

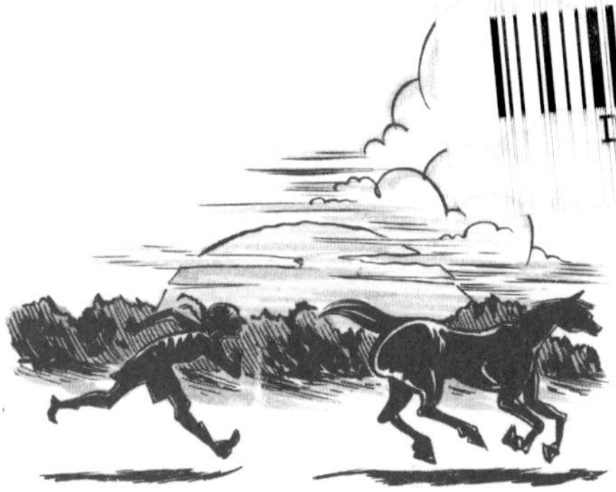

Books by G. Neri

Yummy: The Last Days of a Southside Shorty

Chess Rumble

GRAND THEFT HORSE

written by **G. NERI**

illustrated by **CORBAN WILKIN**

TU BOOKS
An imprint of LEE & LOW BOOKS Inc.
New York

This book is a second-hand memoir of Ms. Ruffu's life as reported by the writer. It reflects Ms. Ruffu's present recollections of her experiences over time. Some names and characteristics have been changed, some events have been compressed, and some dialogue has been recreated. The opinions expressed are those of Ms. Ruffu and should not be confused with those of the creators of this book.

TU BOOKS, an imprint of LEE & LOW BOOKS Inc., 95 Madison Avenue, New York, NY 10016
leeandlow.com

Manufactured in the United States of America by Worzalla Publishing Company

FSC
www.fsc.org
MIX
Paper from responsible sources
FSC® C002589

Book design by Laura Rinne and Christy Hale
Edited by Greg Hunter and Stacy Whitman
Book production by The Kids at Our House
The text is set in Cambria
The illustrations are rendered in ink
10 9 8 7 6 5 4 3 2 1
First Edition

Cataloging-in-Publication Data is on file with the Library of Congress

For Gail

G. Neri with his cousin, Gail Ruffu

INTRODUCTION

My cousin, the horse thief. Who would've thought? When I was growing up, I went to Texas once to stay on my uncle's ranch. He had thirteen kids, ten of them boys—strapping ranch hands and school wrestlers who liked to surprise-attack each other in the middle of the night out in the bunkhouse their dad built for them in the fields. To be a girl in that family, you had to be tough and willing to stand up for yourself. I could see that in my cousin Gail straight off the bat. She didn't take no guff, and she could dish it out just as hard as her brothers—maybe harder. But inside, she was thoughtful and caring, and she really loved horses.

I met Gail Ruffu only once when I was younger. Thirty-some years later, at a Christmas party at my parents' house in California, I met her again. In the intervening years, I had occasionally heard tales of her exploits. The Texas part of the family, like the state of Texas itself, was always bigger than life.

When I asked what she'd been up to lately, she paused and pulled me aside. "I'm a wanted woman, ya know," she said.

For the next hour and a half, she told me a whopper of a story of how she stole a Thoroughbred horse on Christmas Eve and became the first person in a hundred and fifty years to be charged with Grand Theft Horse—a case that went all the way to the California Supreme Court.

When she was finished, I sat there, floored. My first thought was: *That would make a great book.*

This is that book.

—G. Neri, 2018

"To live outside the law, you must be honest."
—Bob Dylan, "Absolutely Sweet Marie"

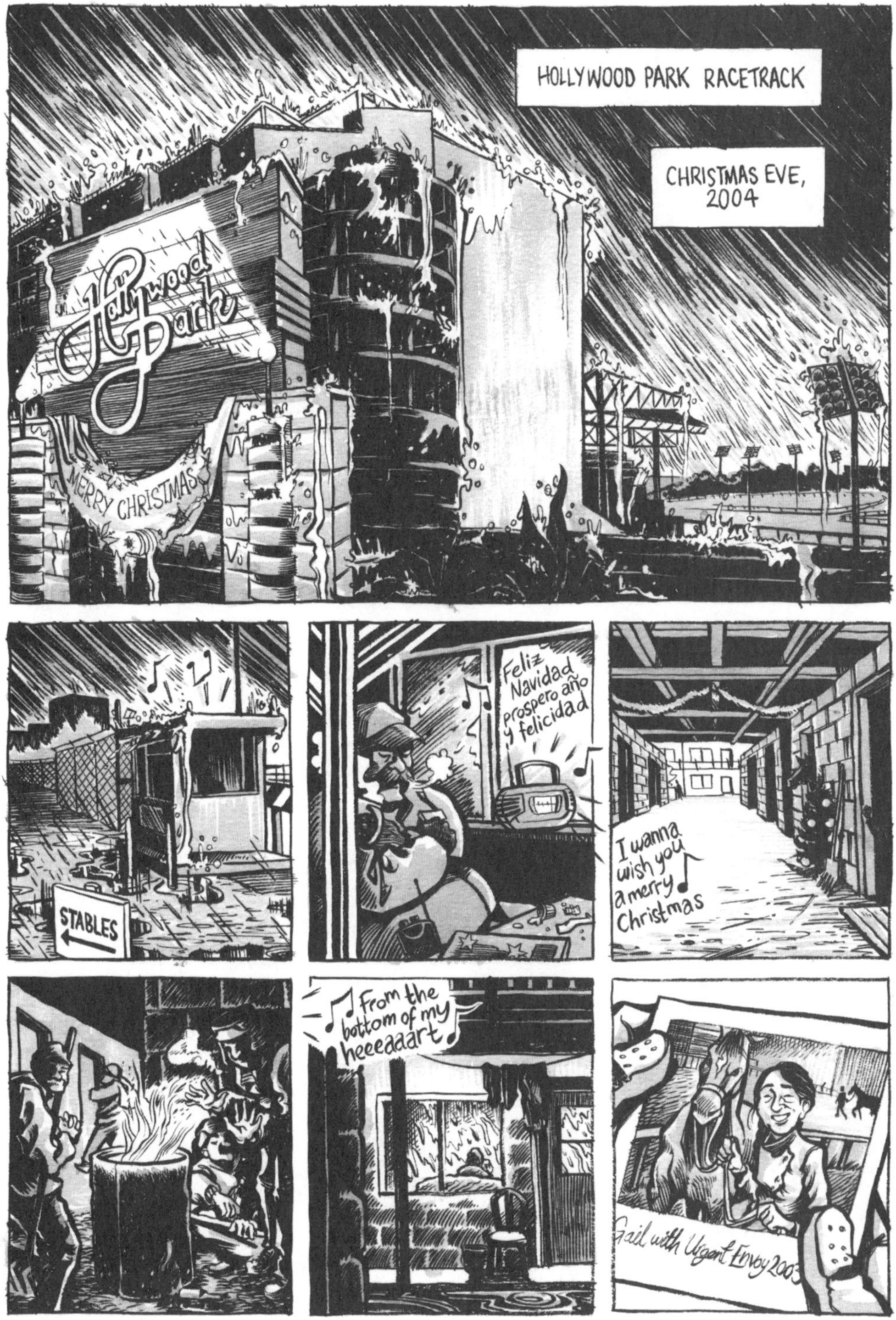
HOLLYWOOD PARK RACETRACK
CHRISTMAS EVE, 2004
Hollywood Park
MERRY CHRISTMAS
STABLES
Feliz Navidad prospero año y felicidad
I wanna wish you a merry Christmas
From the bottom of my heeeaaart
Gail with Urgent Envoy 2003

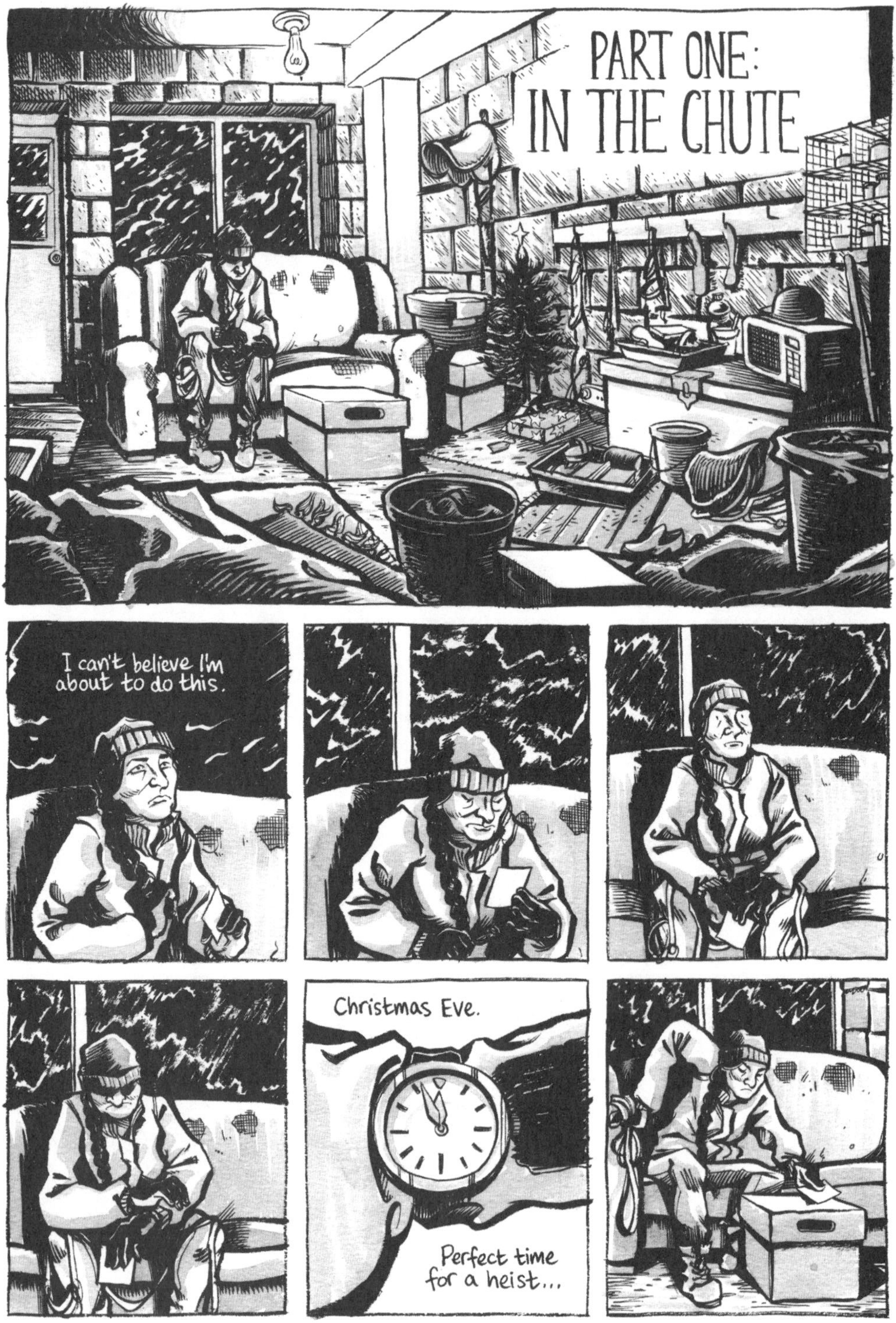
PART ONE:
IN THE CHUTE
I can't believe I'm about to do this.
Christmas Eve.
Perfect time for a heist...

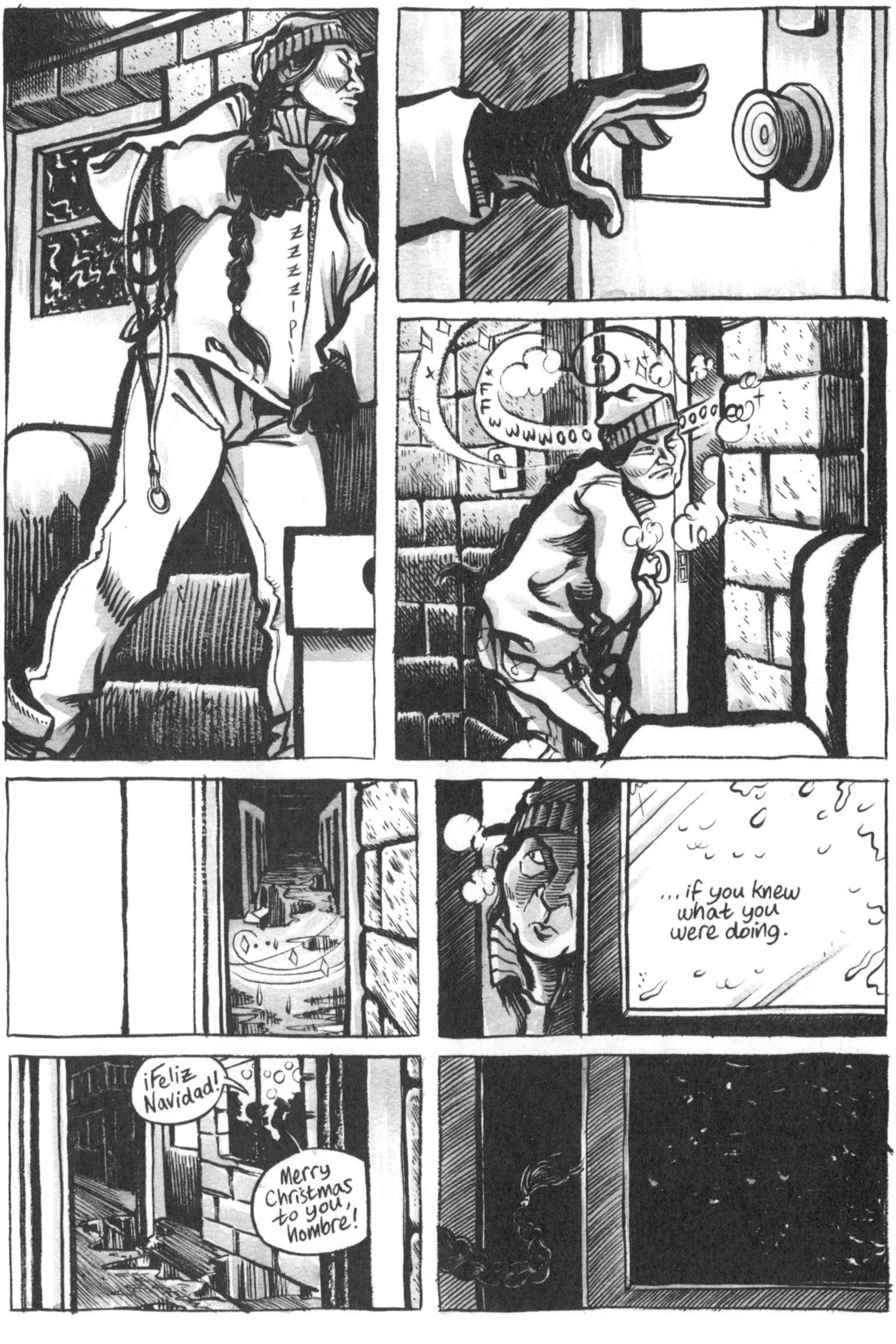
ZZZZIP!
FFWWWWOOO
...if you knew what you were doing.
¡Feliz Navidad!
Merry Christmas to you, hombre!

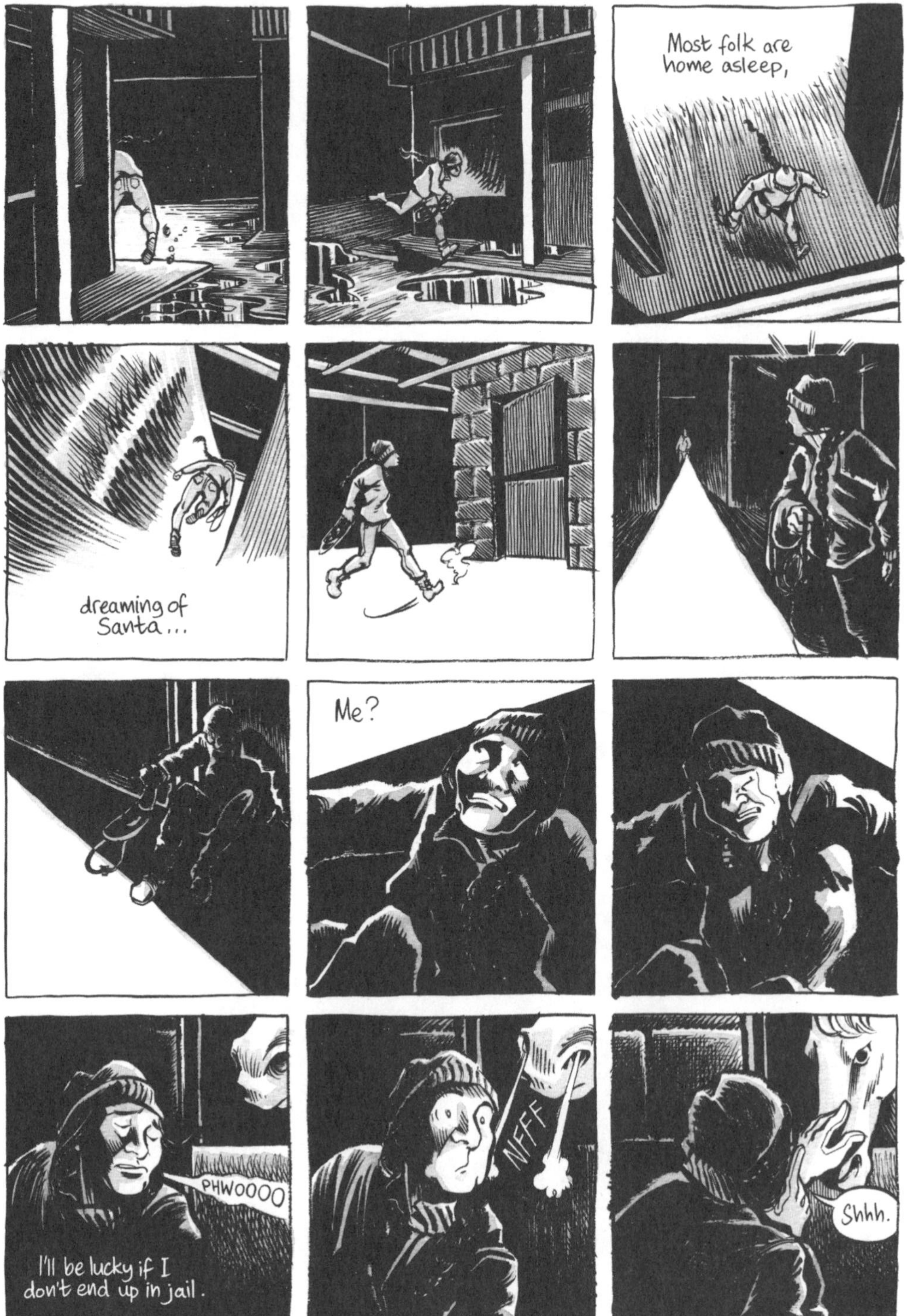

Most folk are home asleep,
dreaming of Santa...
Me?
I'll be lucky if I don't end up in jail.
PHWOOOO
NFFF
Shhh.

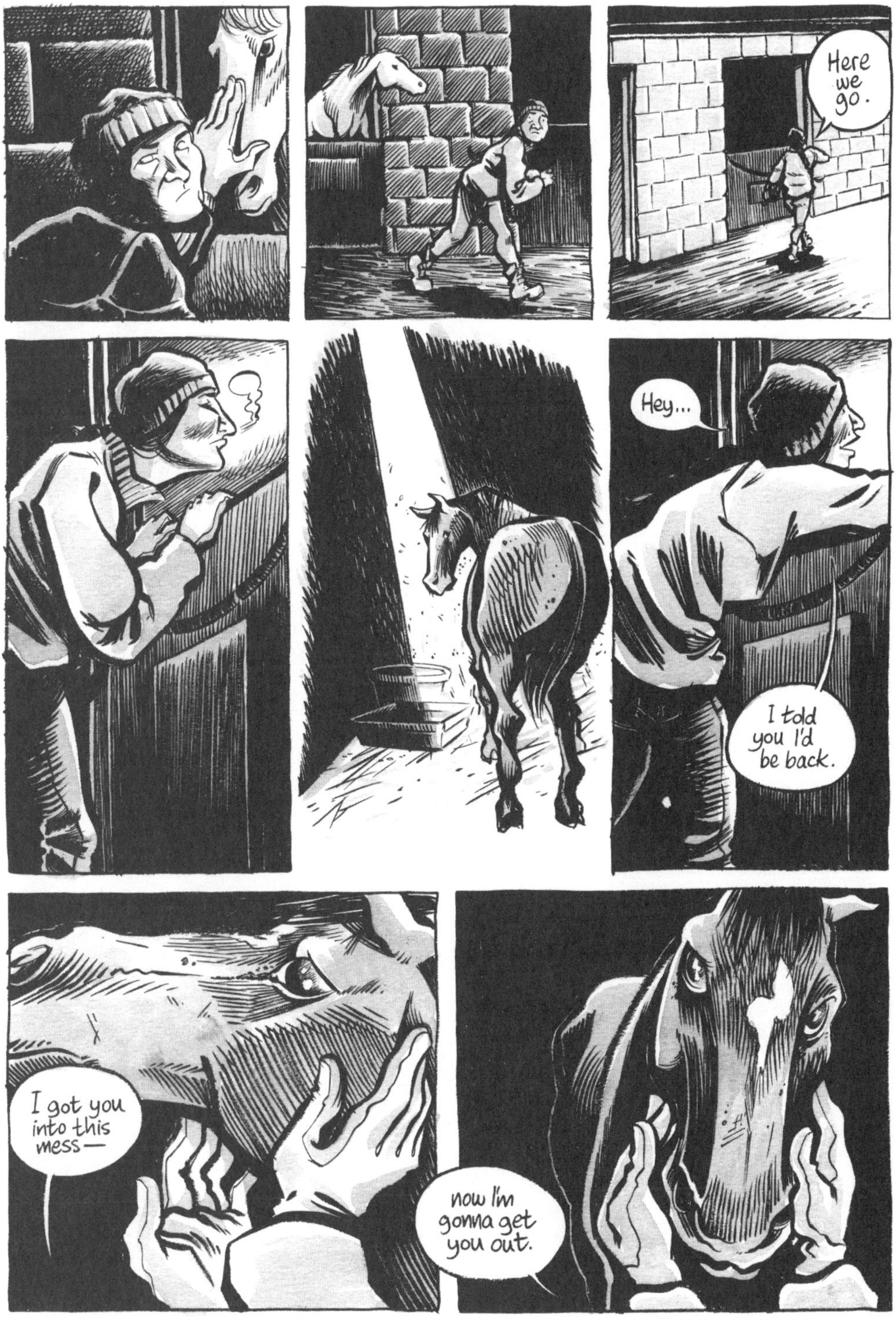
Here we go.
Hey...
I told you I'd be back.
I got you into this mess—
now I'm gonna get you out.

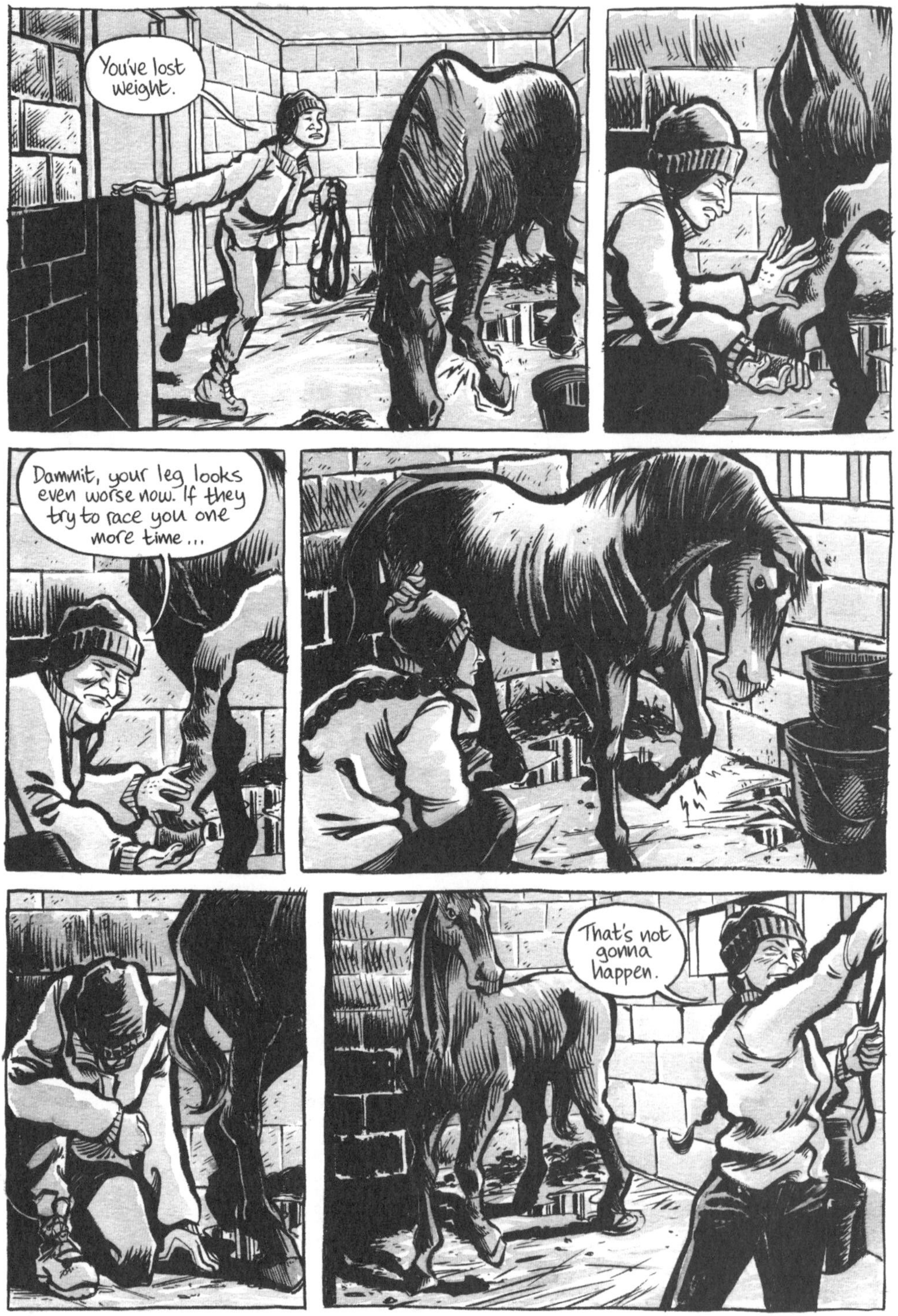
You've lost weight.
Dammit, your leg looks even worse now. If they try to race you one more time ...
That's not gonna happen.

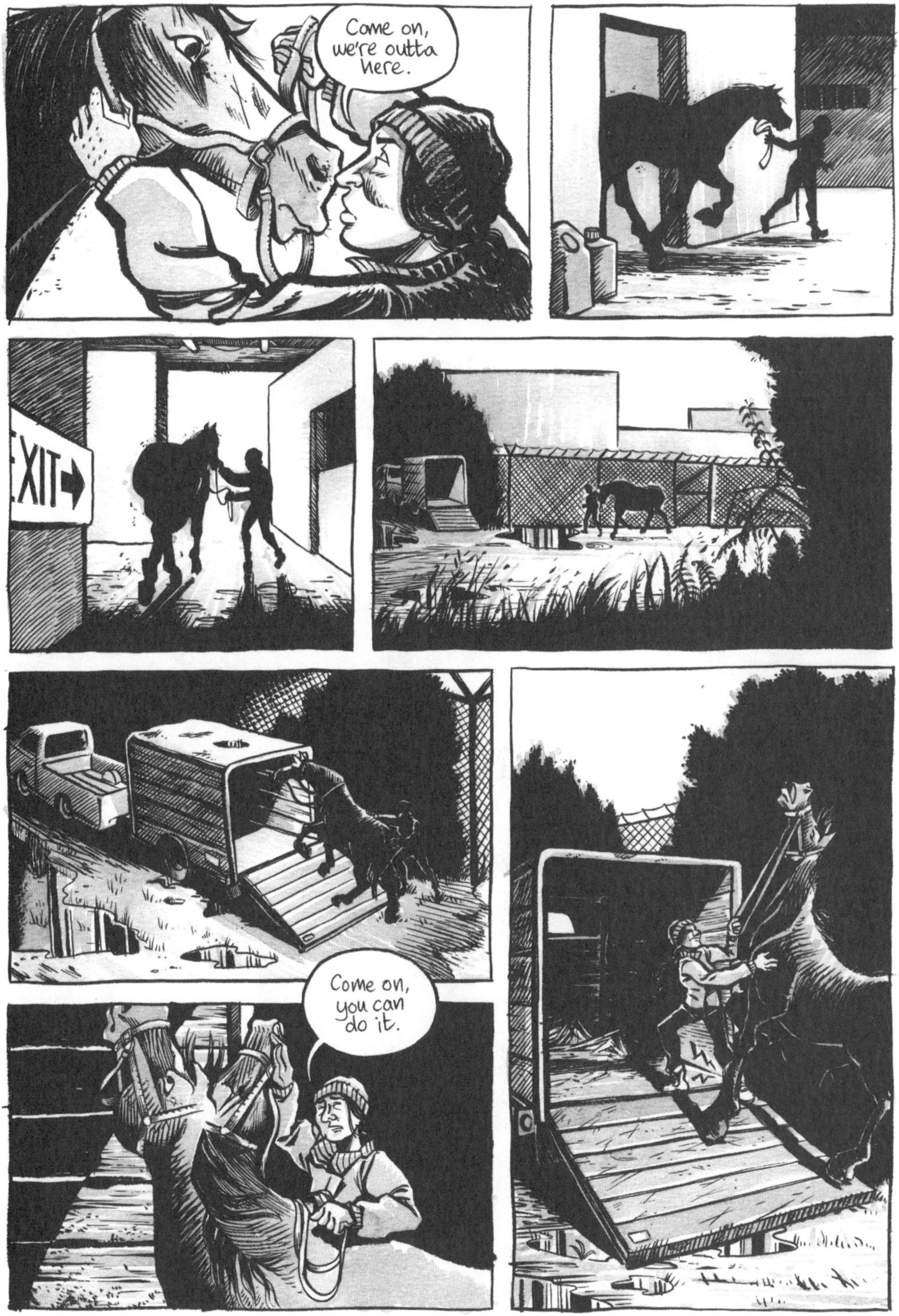
Come on, we're outta here.
EXIT
Come on, you can do it.

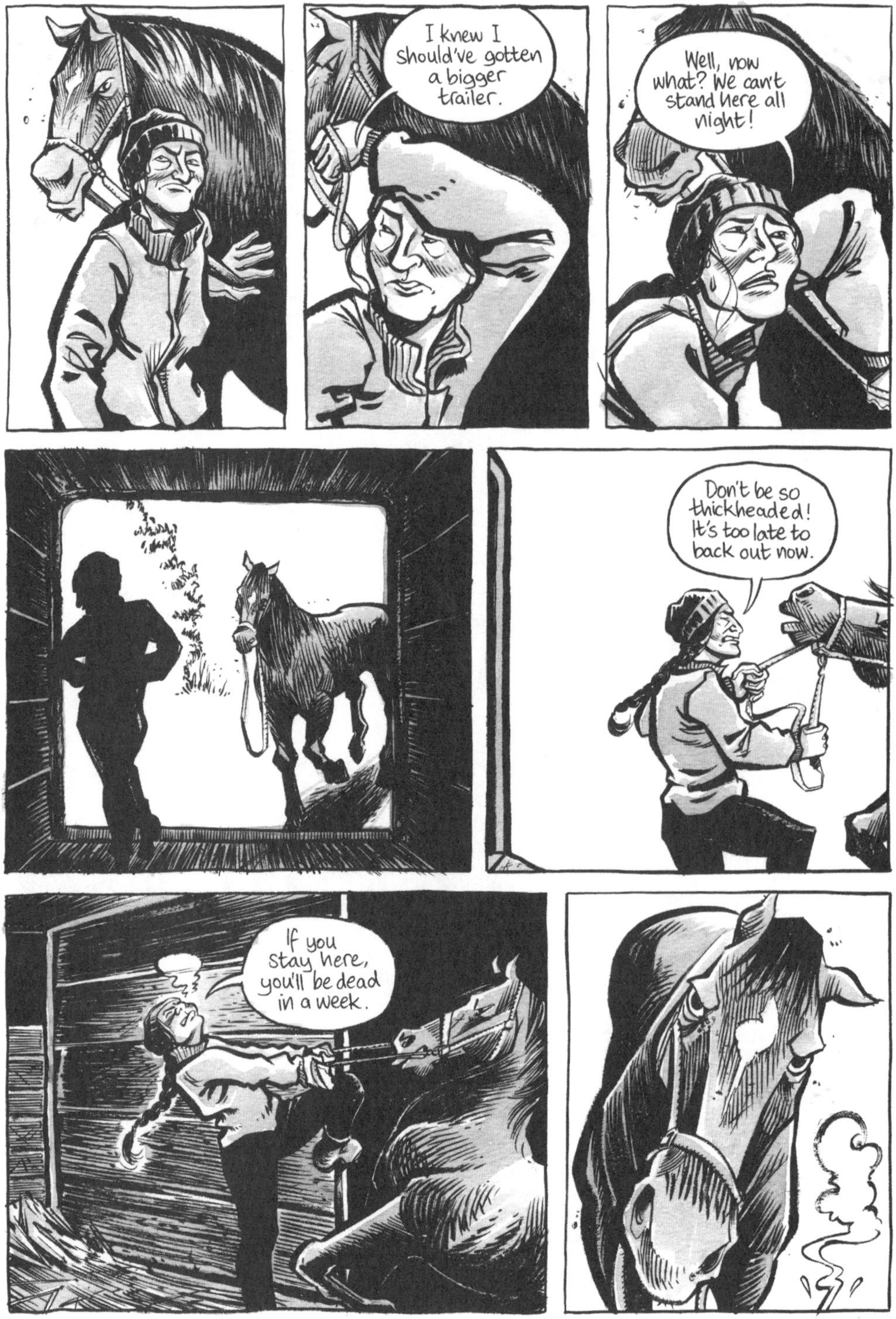
I knew I should've gotten a bigger trailer.
Well, now what? We can't stand here all night!
Don't be so thickheaded! It's too late to back out now.
If you stay here, you'll be dead in a week.

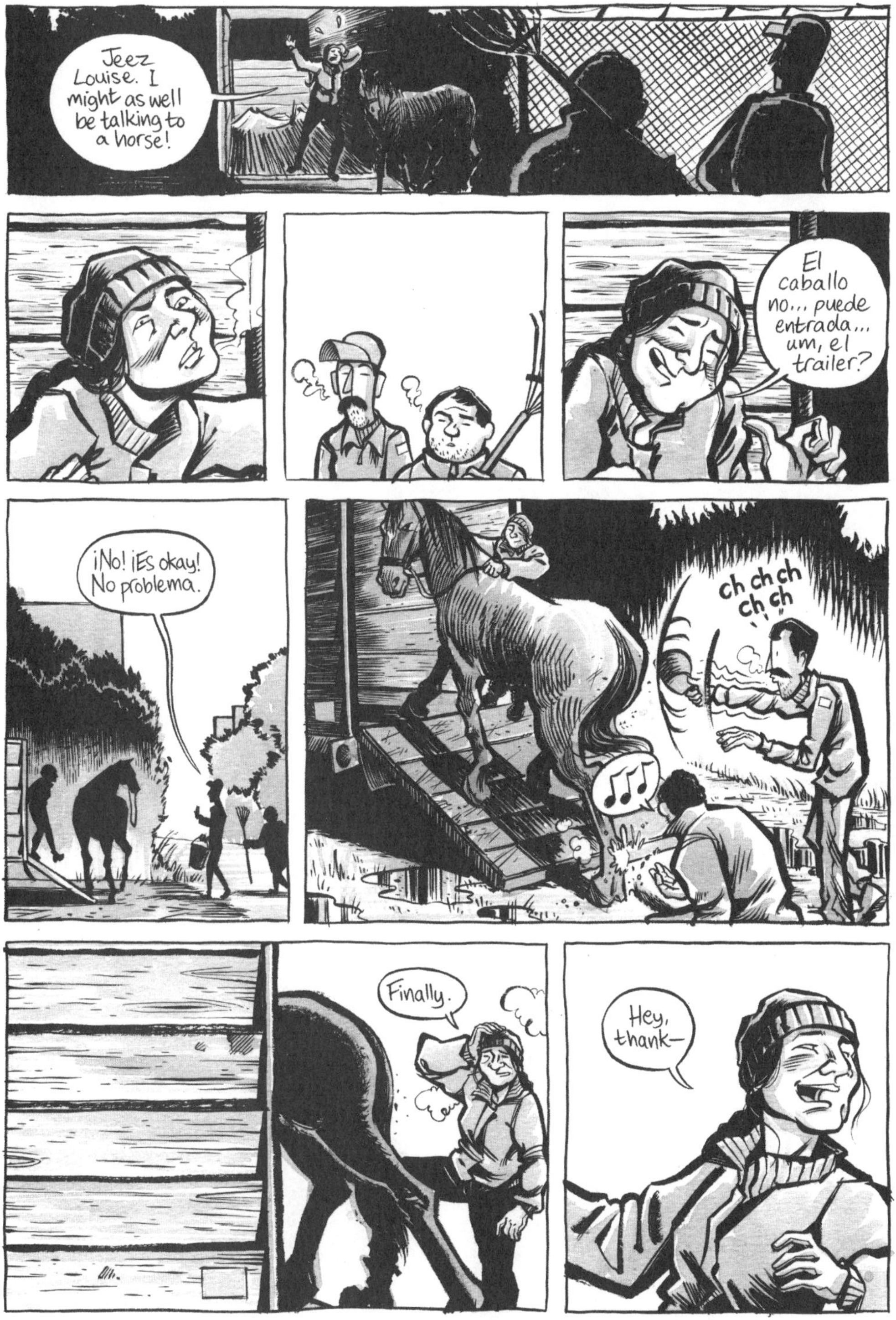
Jeez Louise. I might as well be talking to a horse!
El caballo no... puede entrada... um, el trailer?
¡No! ¡Es okay! No problema.
ch ch ch ch ch
Finally.
Hey, thank—

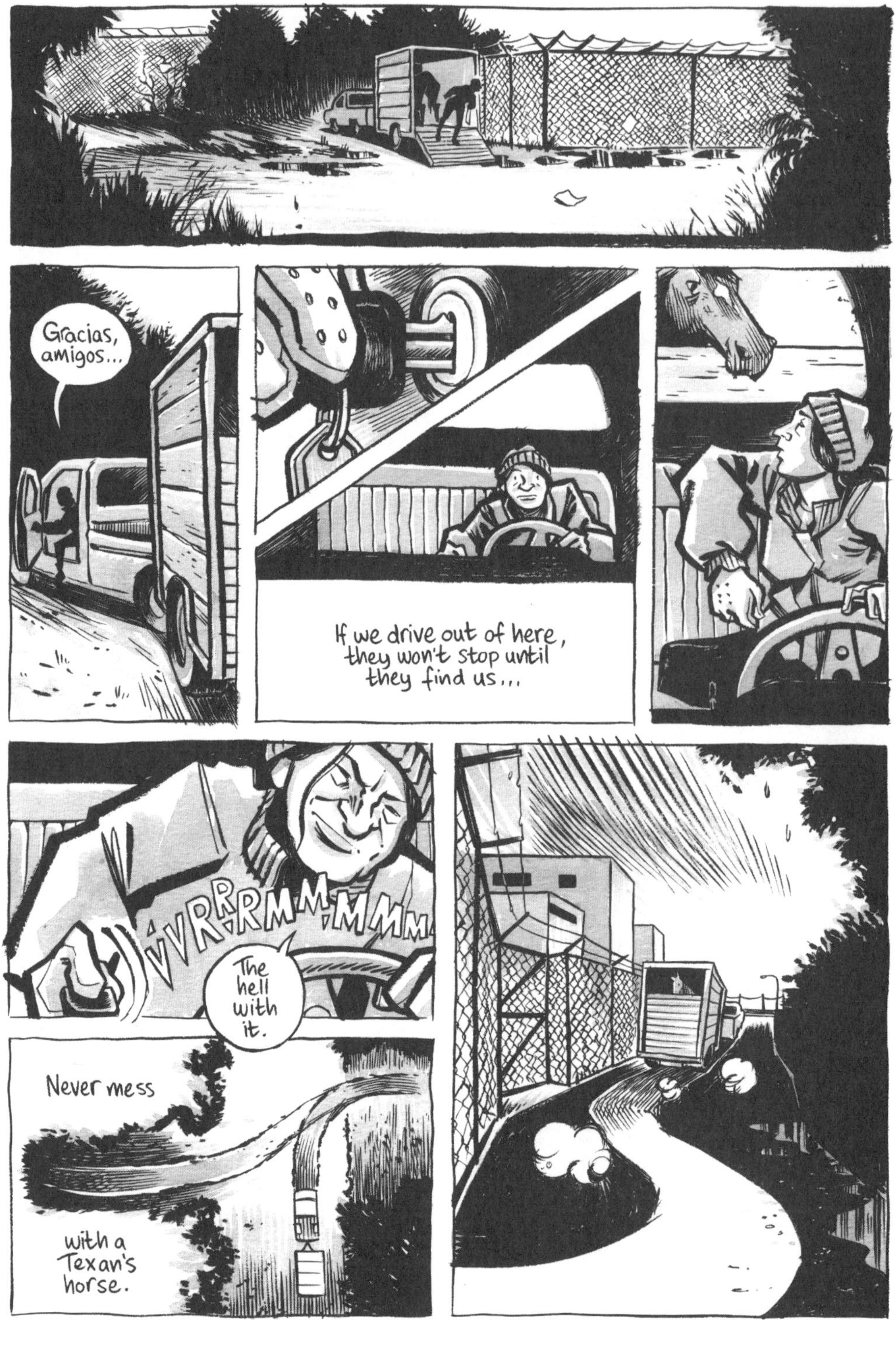
Gracias, amigos...
If we drive out of here, they won't stop until they find us...
VVRRRMMMMMM
The hell with it.
Never mess
with a Texan's horse.

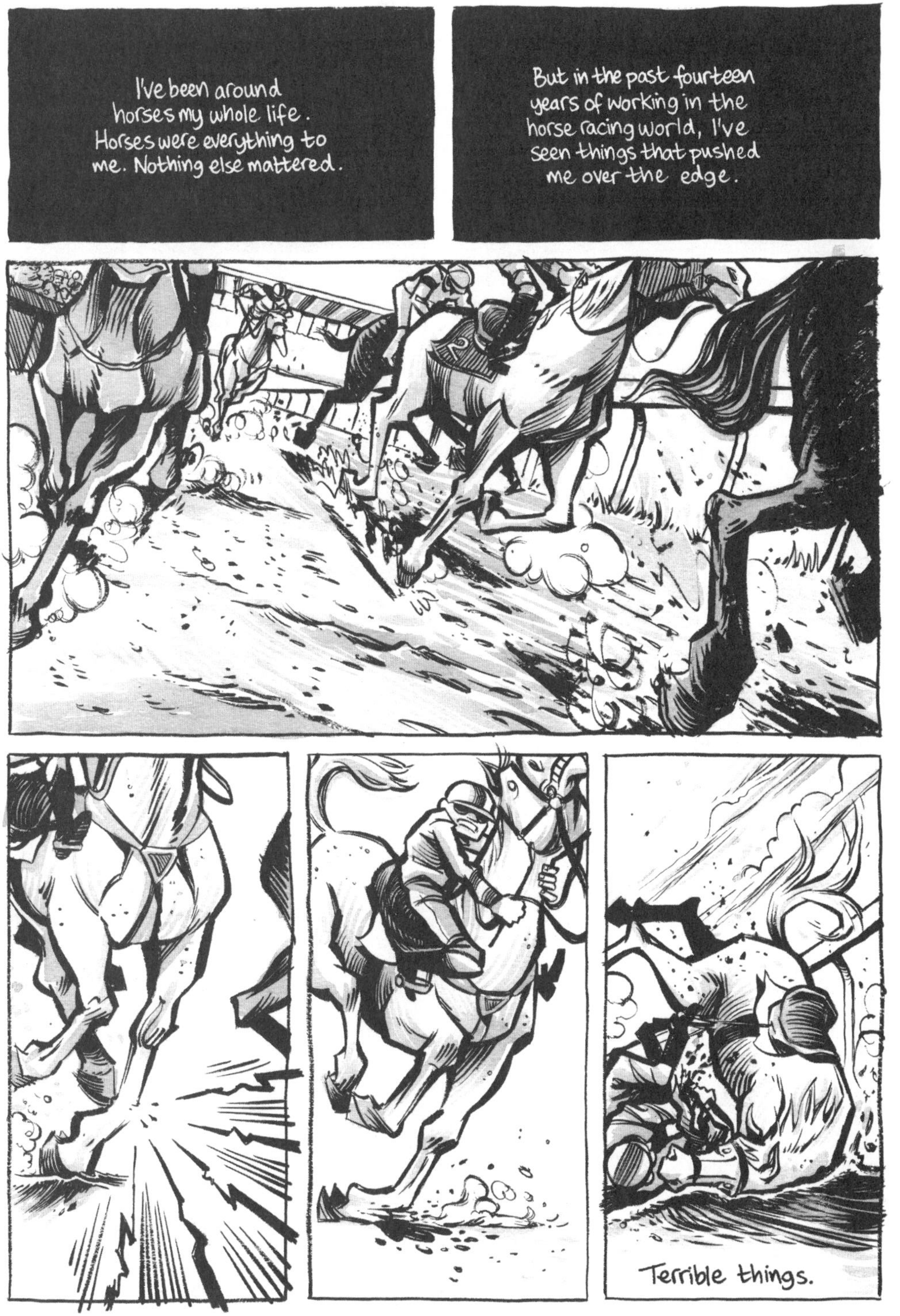
I've been around horses my whole life. Horses were everything to me. Nothing else mattered.
But in the past fourteen years of working in the horse racing world, I've seen things that pushed me over the edge.
2
Terrible things.

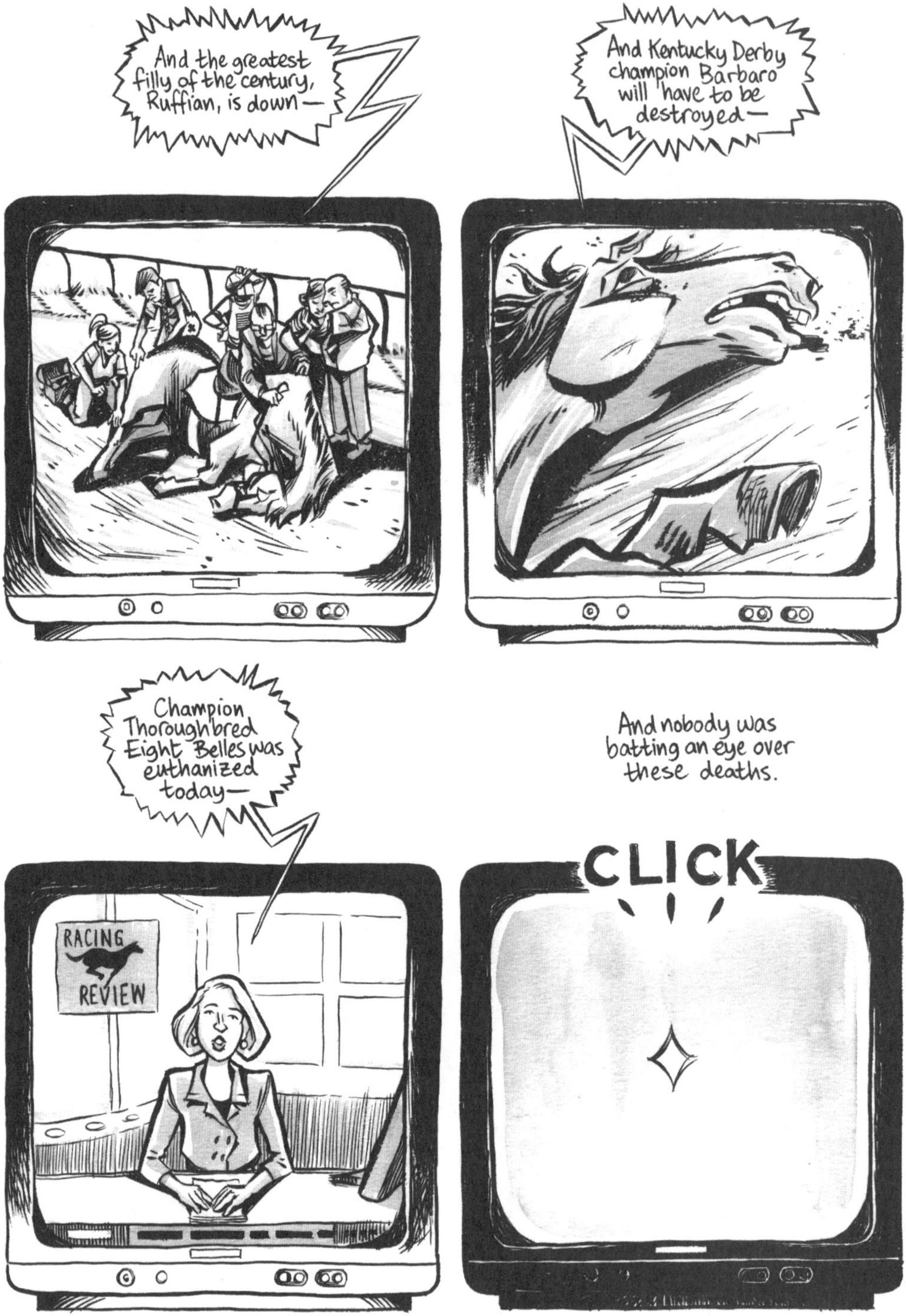
And the greatest filly of the century, Ruffian, is down—
And Kentucky Derby champion Barbaro will have to be destroyed—
Champion Thoroughbred Eight Belles was euthanized today—
RACING REVIEW
And nobody was batting an eye over these deaths.
CLICK

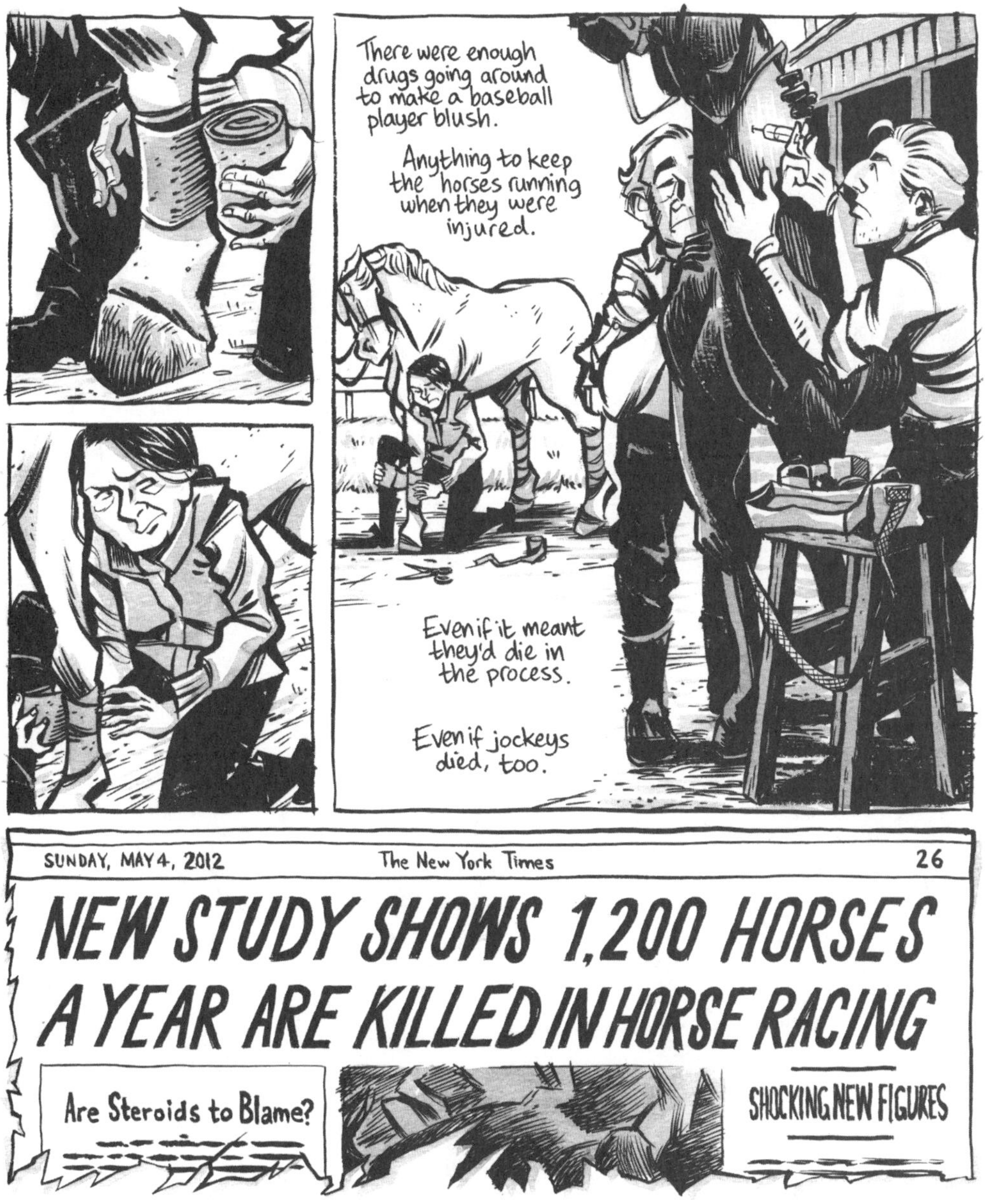
There were enough drugs going around to make a baseball player blush.
Anything to keep the horses running when they were injured.
Even if it meant they'd die in the process.
Even if jockeys died, too.
SUNDAY, MAY 4, 2012
The New York Times
26
NEW STUDY SHOWS 1,200 HORSES A YEAR ARE KILLED IN HORSE RACING
Are Steroids to Blame?
SHOCKING NEW FIGURES

And that didn't include the hundreds that were being sent to slaughterhouses after they "retired" from racing.

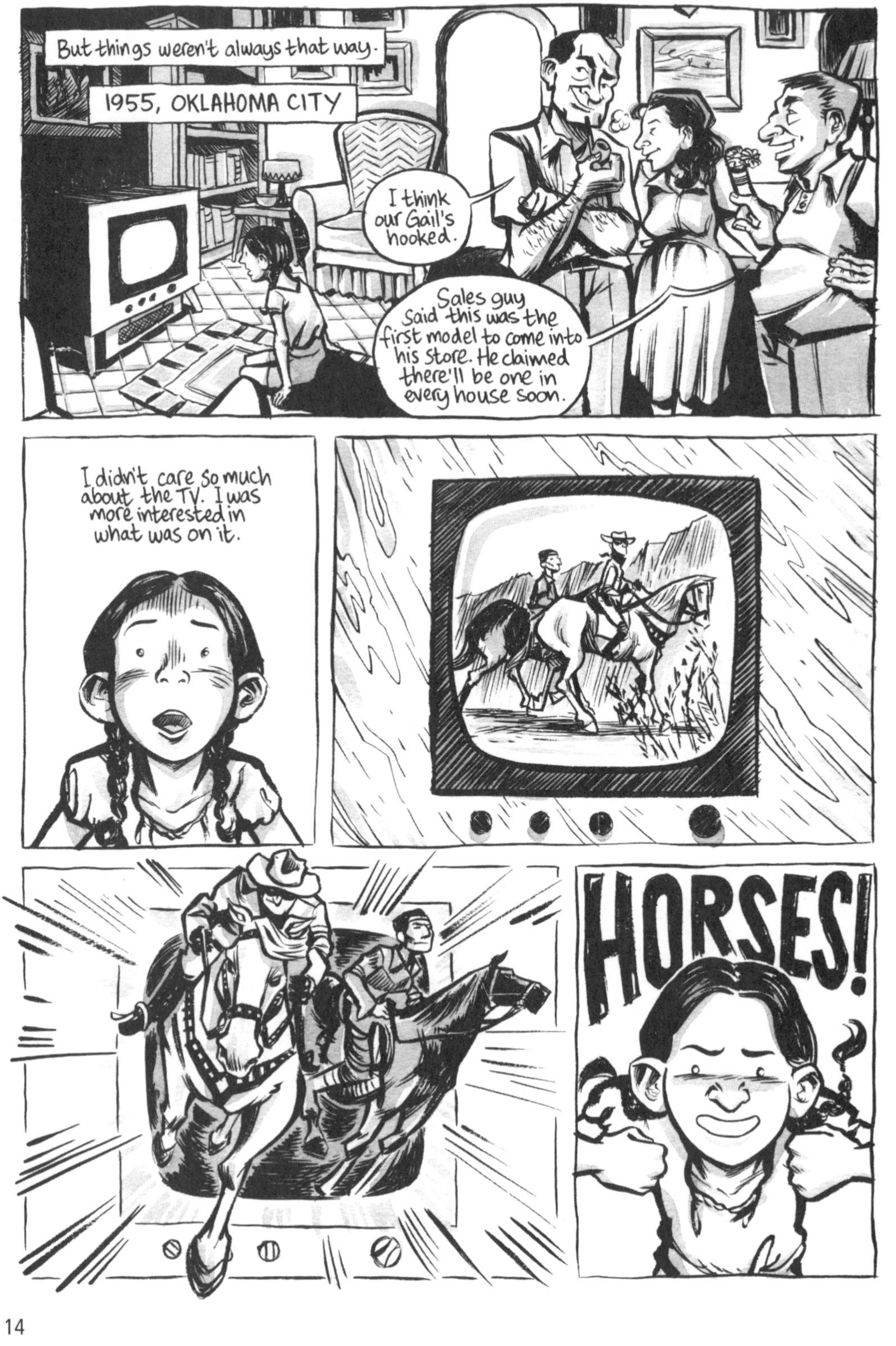
But things weren't always that way.
1955, OKLAHOMA CITY
I think our Gail's hooked.
Sales guy said this was the first model to come into his store. He claimed there'll be one in every house soon.
I didn't care so much about the TV. I was more interested in what was on it.
HORSES!

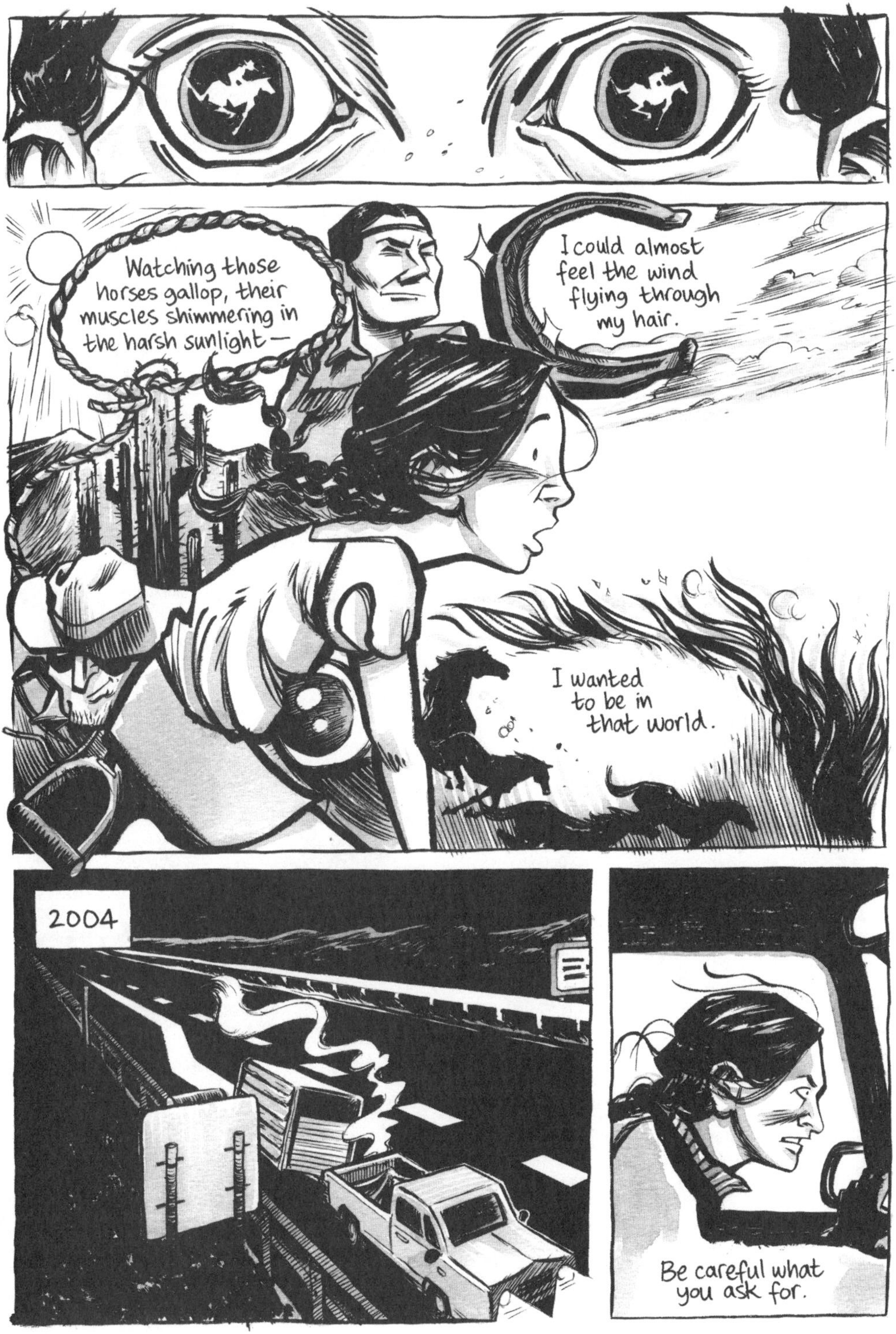
Watching those horses gallop, their muscles shimmering in the harsh sunlight—
I could almost feel the wind flying through my hair.
I wanted to be in that world.
2004
Be careful what you ask for.

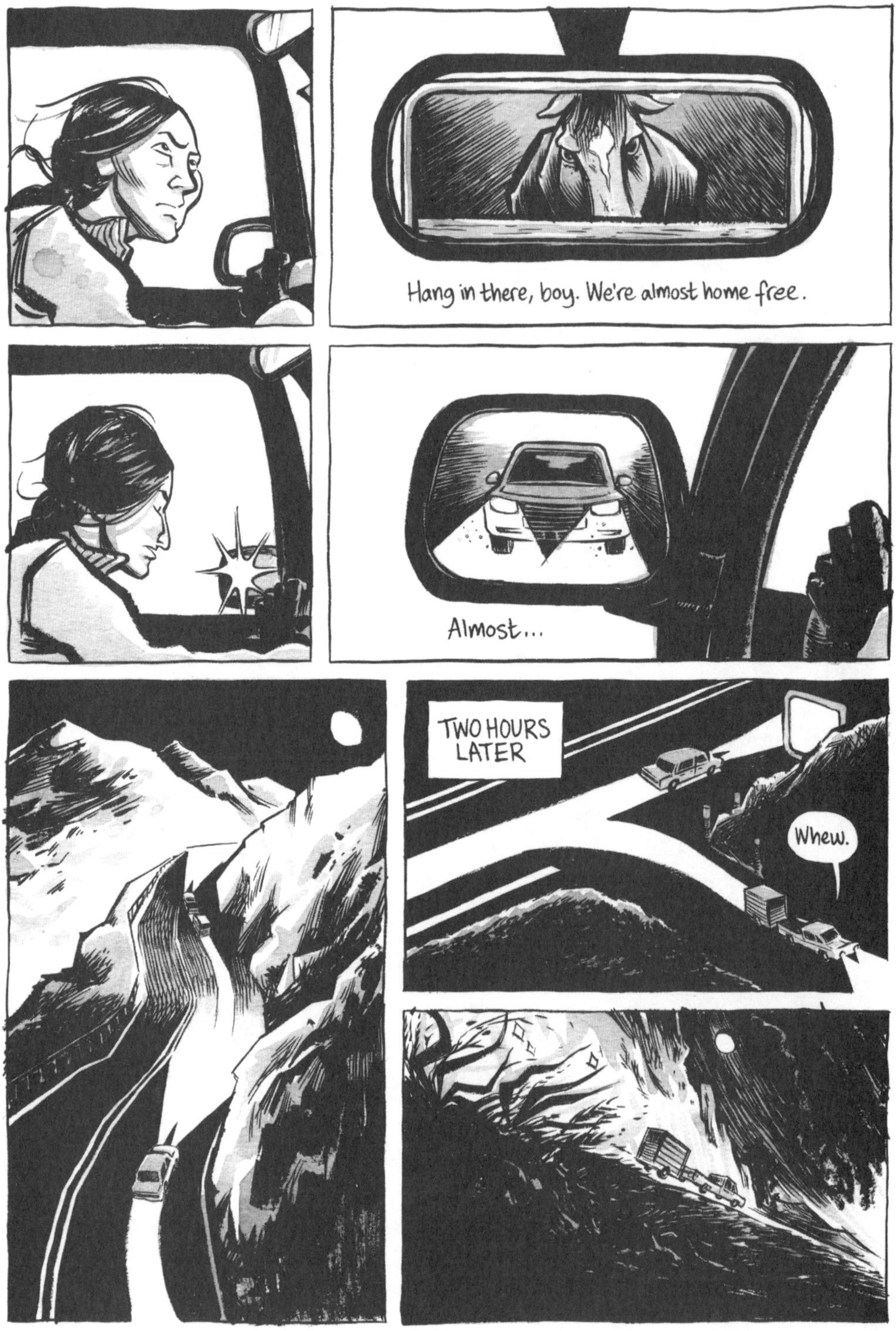
Hang in there, boy. We're almost home free.
Almost...
TWO HOURS LATER
Whew.

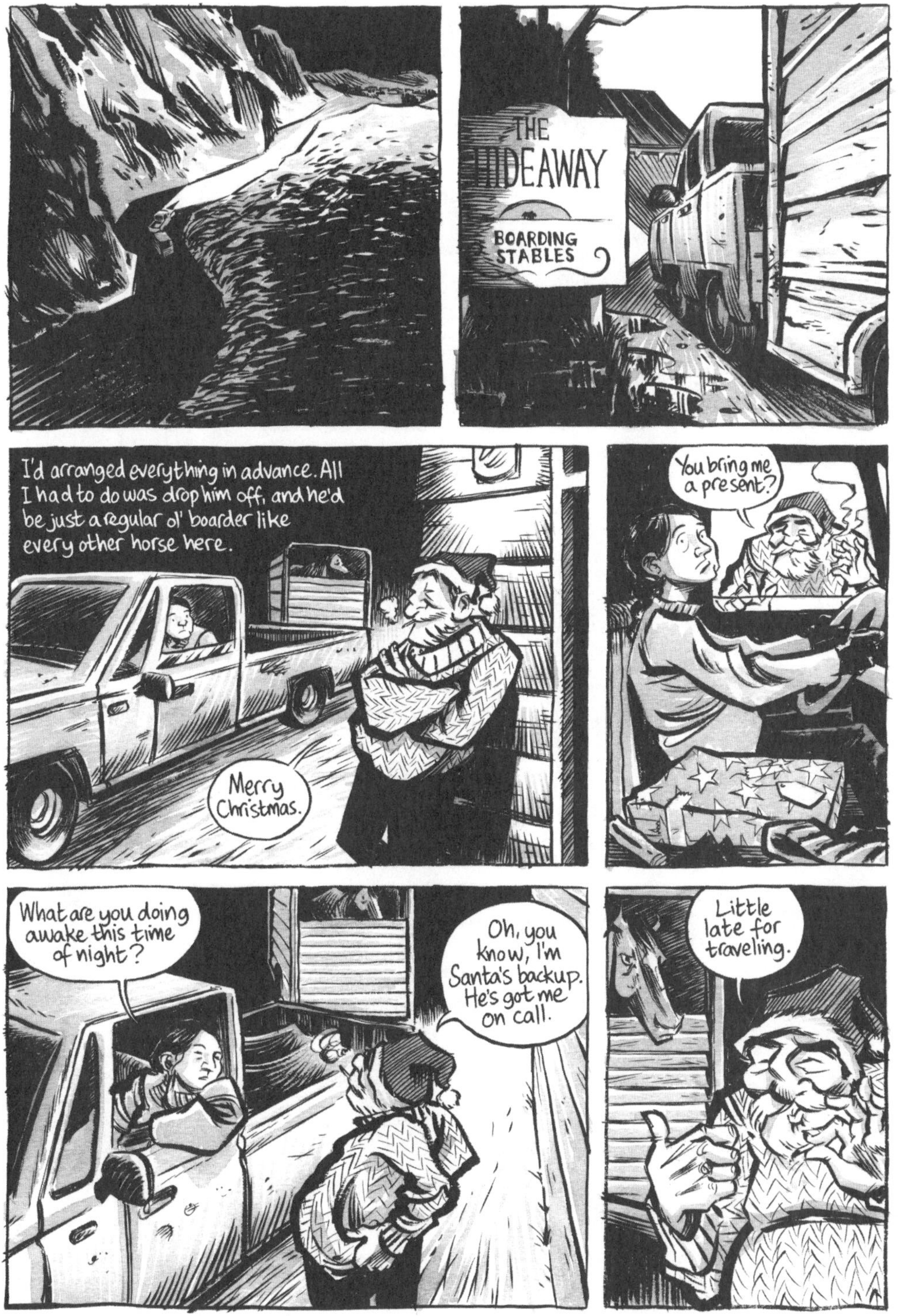
THE HIDEAWAY
BOARDING STABLES
I'd arranged everything in advance. All I had to do was drop him off, and he'd be just a regular ol' boarder like every other horse here.
Merry Christmas.
You bring me a present?
What are you doing awake this time of night?
Oh, you know, I'm Santa's backup. He's got me on call.
Little late for traveling.

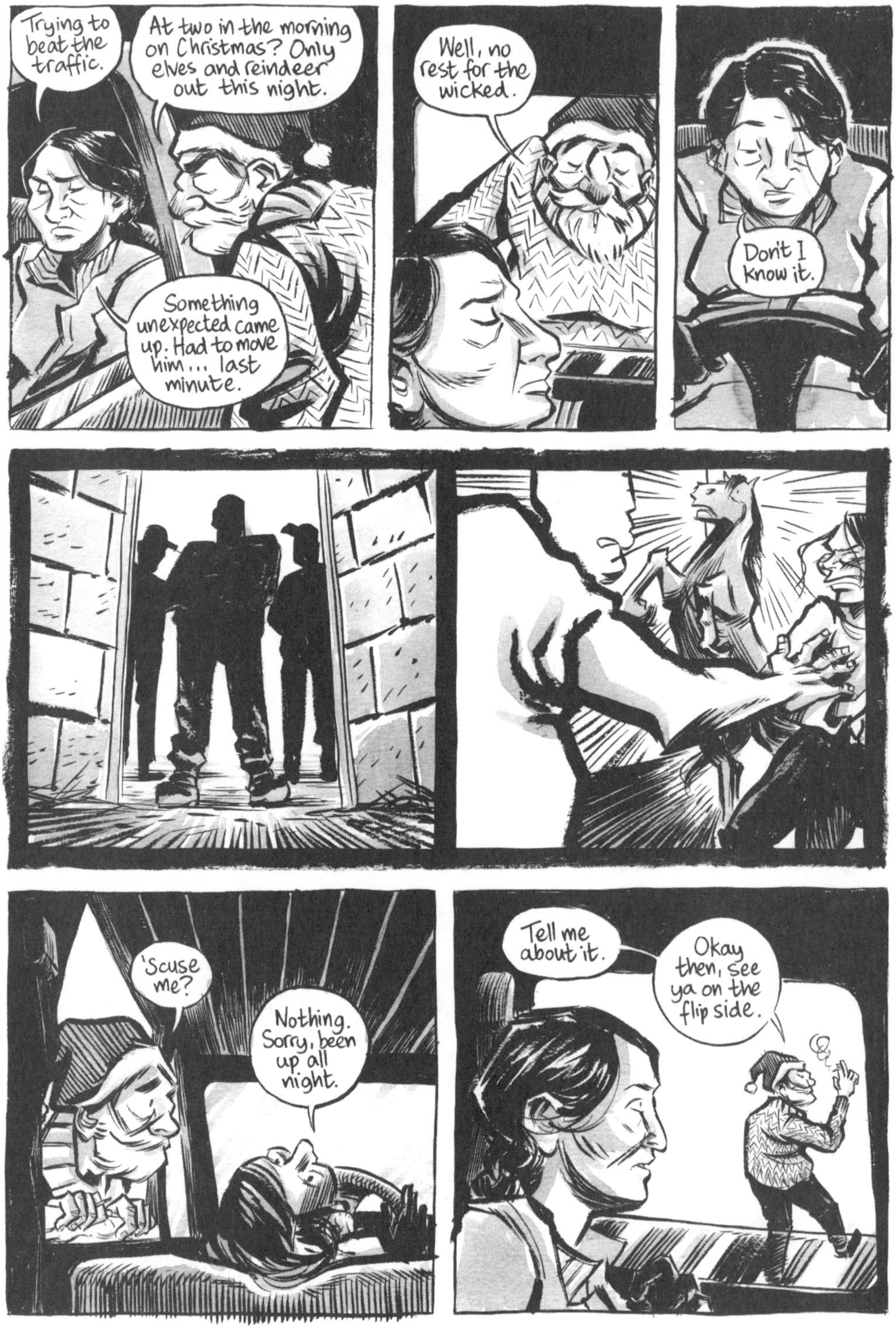
Trying to beat the traffic.
At two in the morning on Christmas? Only elves and reindeer out this night.
Something unexpected came up. Had to move him... last minute.
Well, no rest for the wicked.
Don't I know it.
'Scuse me?
Nothing. Sorry, been up all night.
Tell me about it.
Okay then, see ya on the flip side.

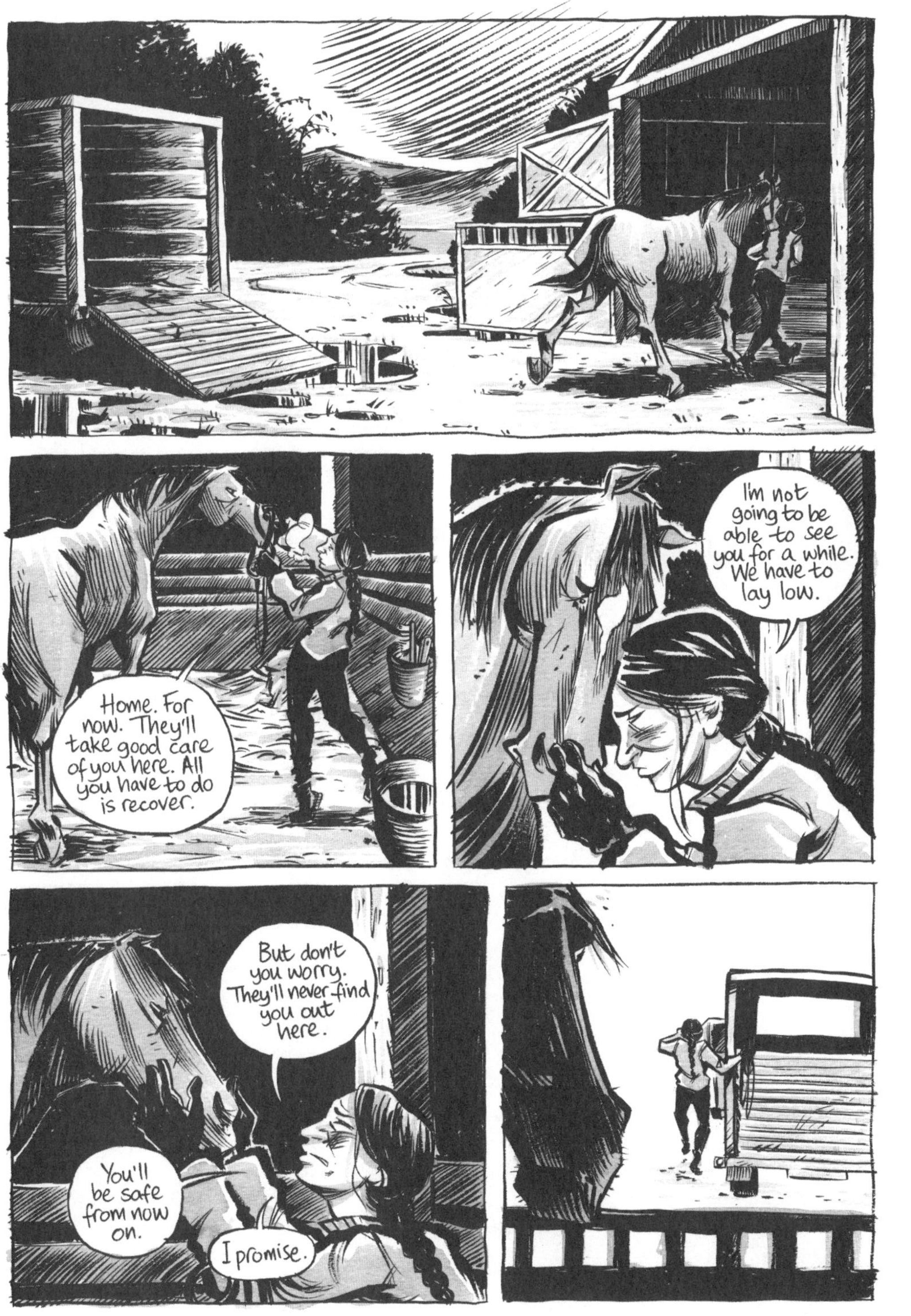
Home. For now. They'll take good care of you here. All you have to do is recover.
I'm not going to be able to see you for a while. We have to lay low.
But don't you worry. They'll never find you out here.
You'll be safe from now on.
I promise.

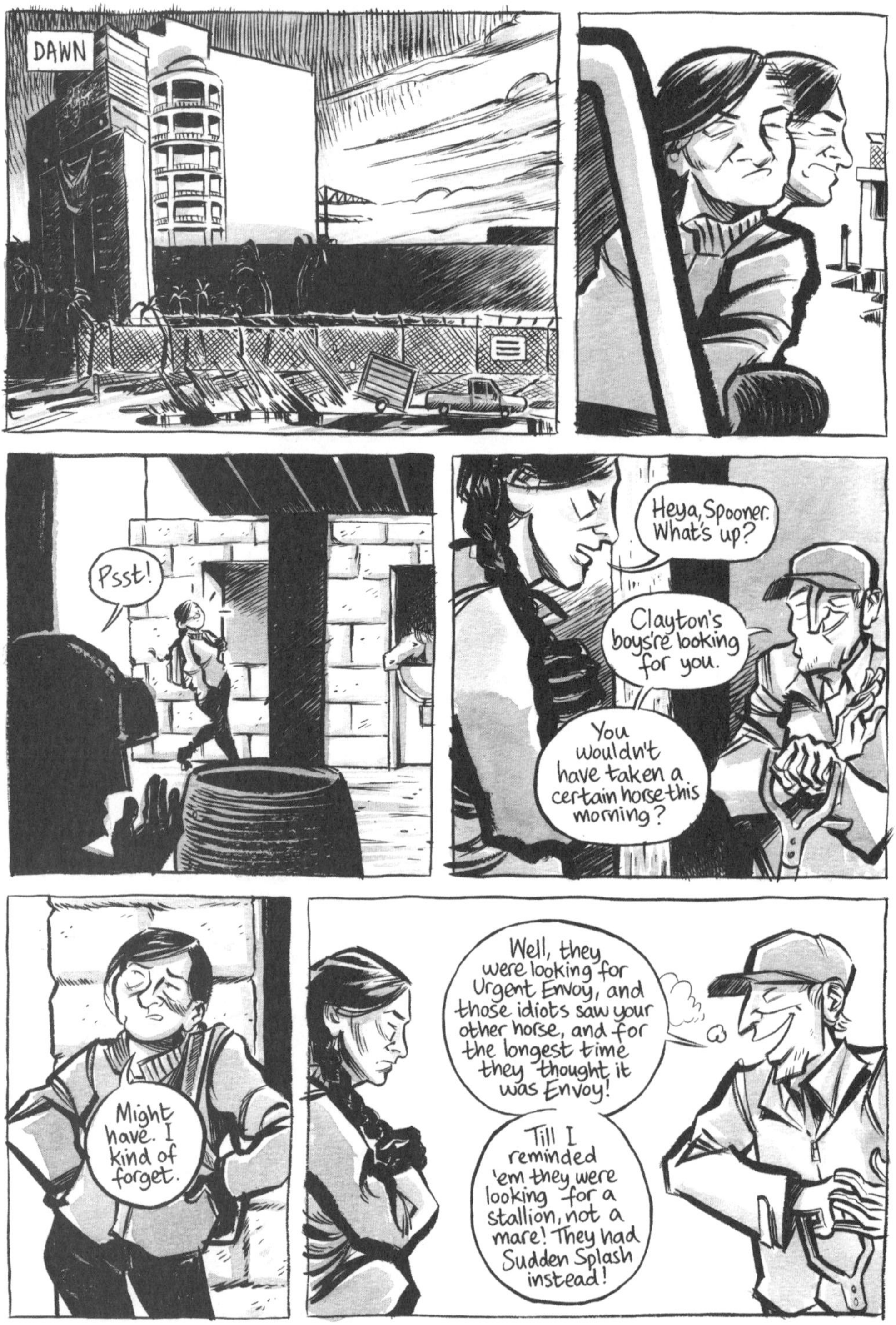
DAWN
Psst!
Heya, Spooner. What's up?
Clayton's boys're looking for you.
You wouldn't have taken a certain horse this morning?
Might have. I kind of forget.
Well, they were looking for Urgent Envoy, and those idiots saw your other horse, and for the longest time they thought it was Envoy!
Till I reminded 'em they were looking for a stallion, not a mare! They had Sudden Splash instead!

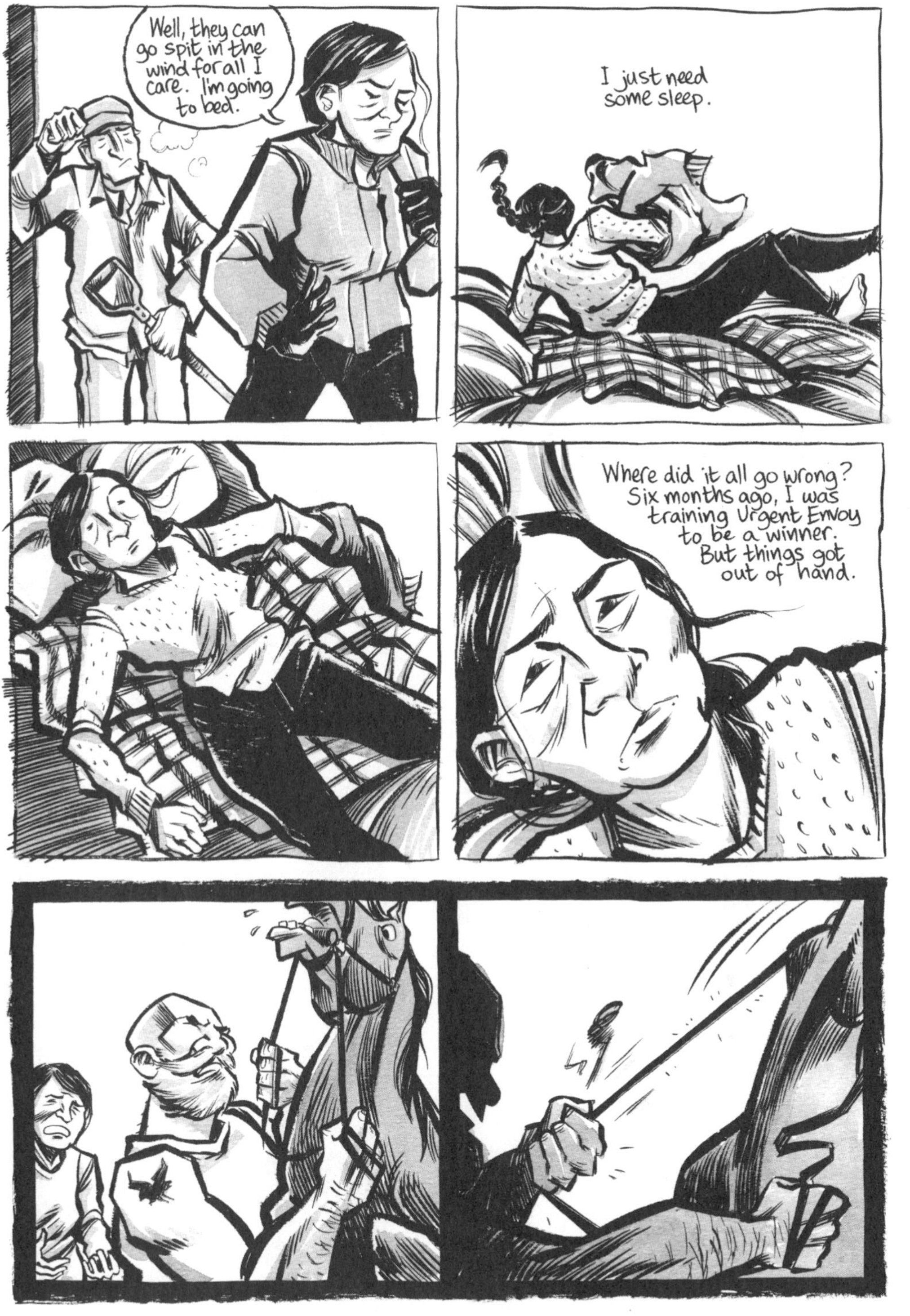
Well, they can go spit in the wind for all I care. I'm going to bed.
I just need some sleep.
Where did it all go wrong? Six months ago, I was training Urgent Envoy to be a winner. But things got out of hand.

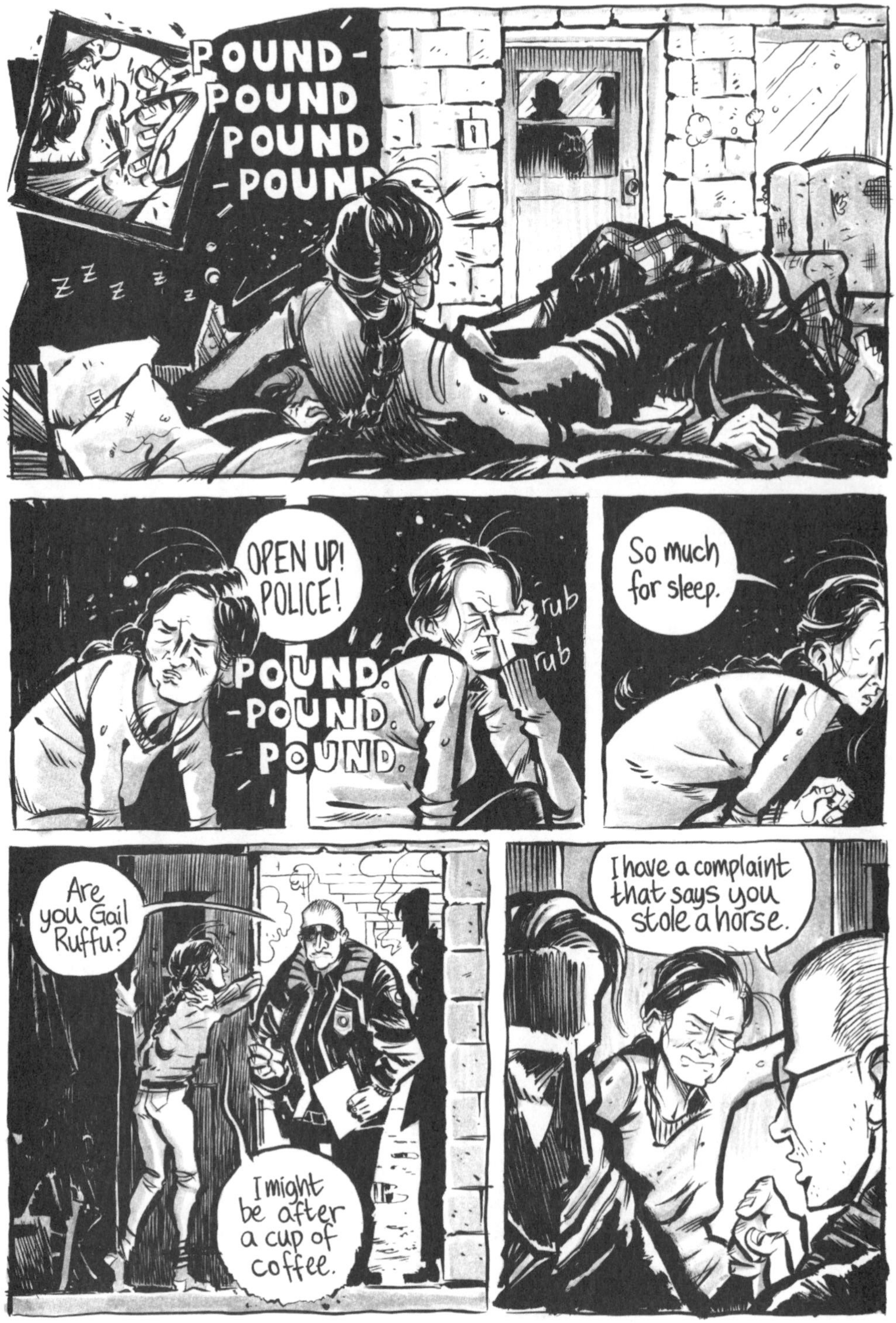
POUND-POUND POUND-POUND
Z Z Z Z Z Z
OPEN UP! POLICE!
POUND-POUND POUND
rub rub
So much for sleep.
Are you Gail Ruffu?
I might be after a cup of coffee.
I have a complaint that says you stole a horse.

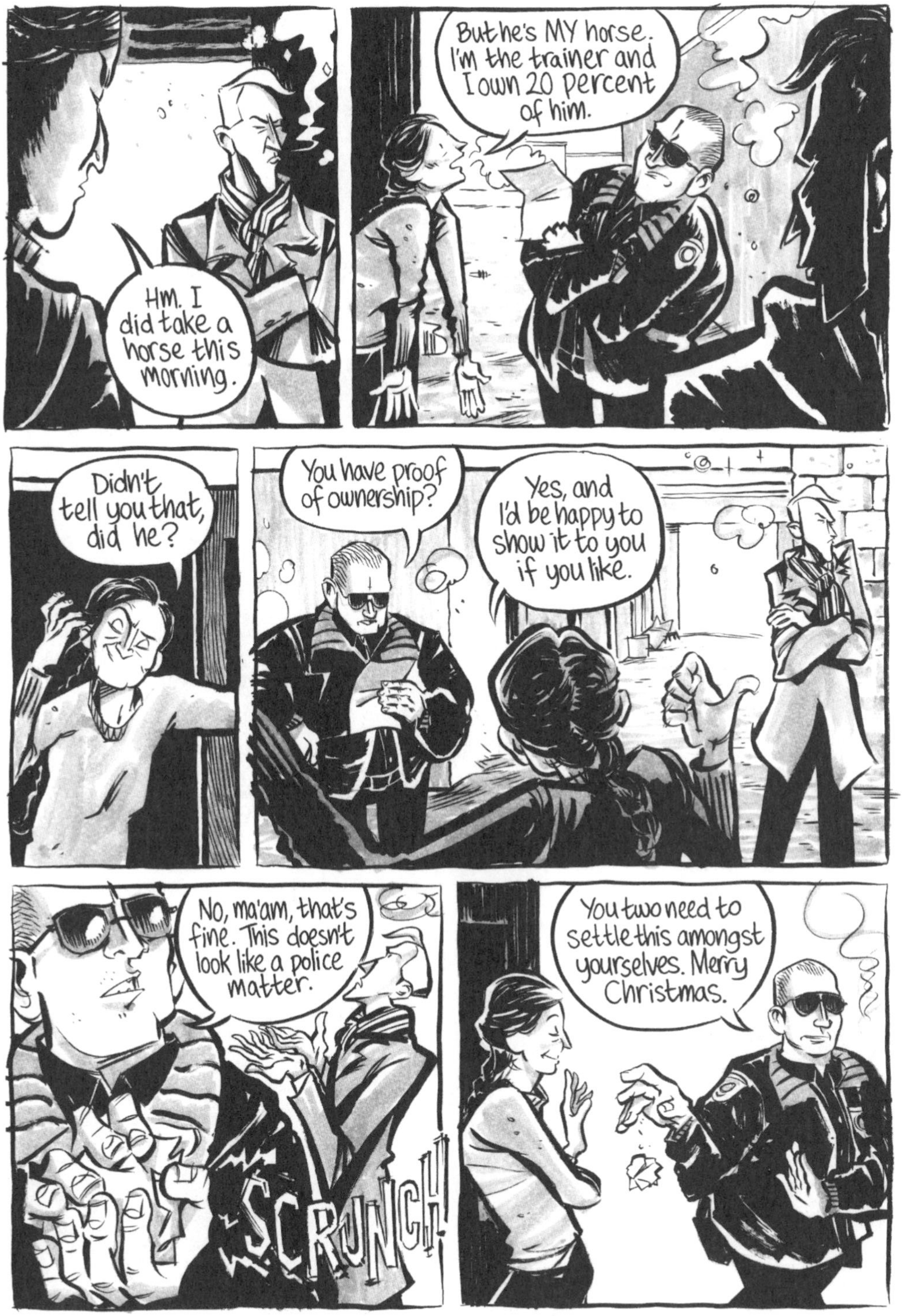
Hm. I did take a horse this morning.
But he's MY horse. I'm the trainer and I own 20 percent of him.
Didn't tell you that, did he?
You have proof of ownership?
Yes, and I'd be happy to show it to you if you like.
No, ma'am, that's fine. This doesn't look like a police matter.
SCRUNCH!
You two need to settle this amongst yourselves. Merry Christmas.

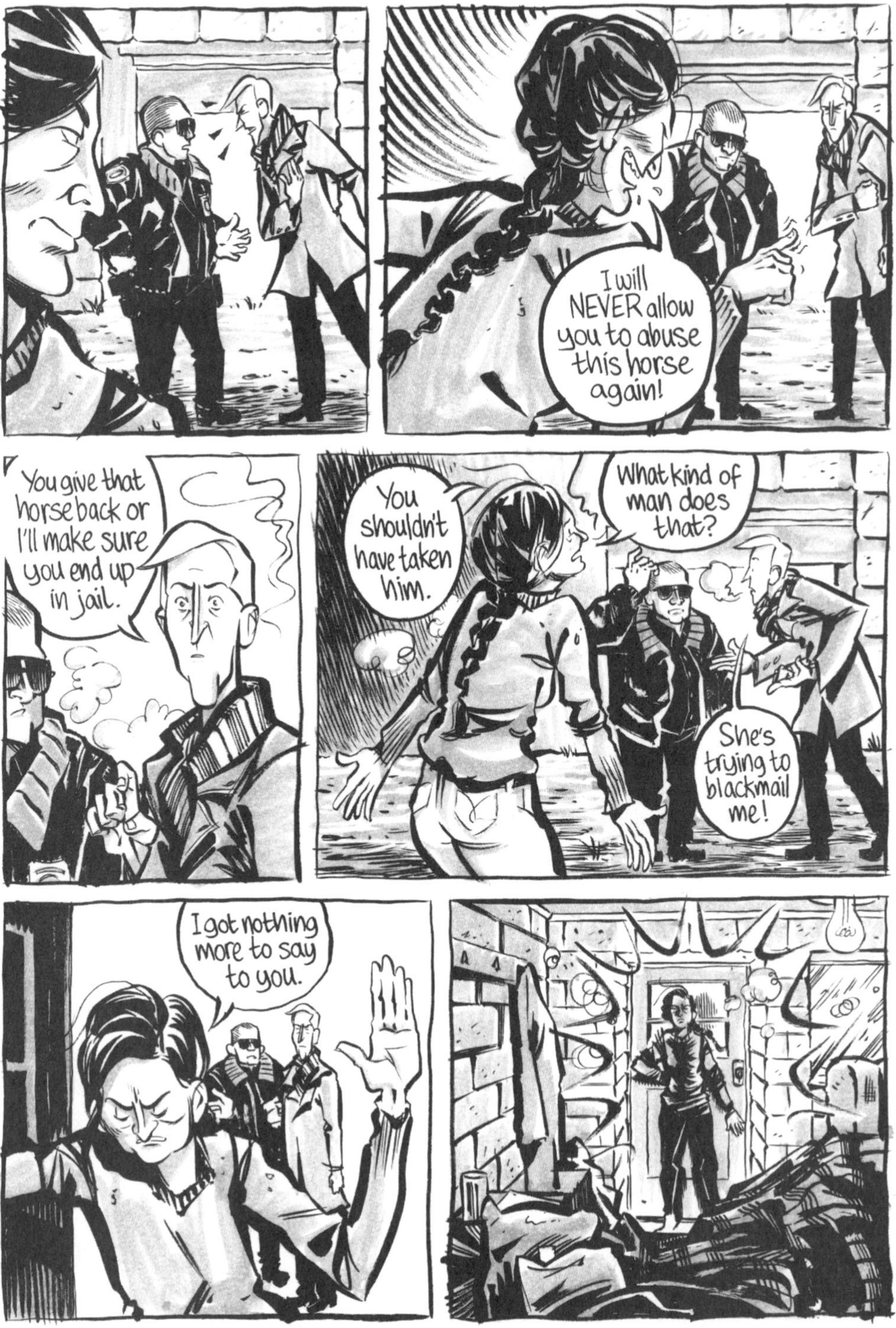

I will NEVER allow you to abuse this horse again!
You give that horse back or I'll make sure you end up in jail.
You shouldn't have taken him.
What kind of man does that?
She's trying to blackmail me!
I got nothing more to say to you.

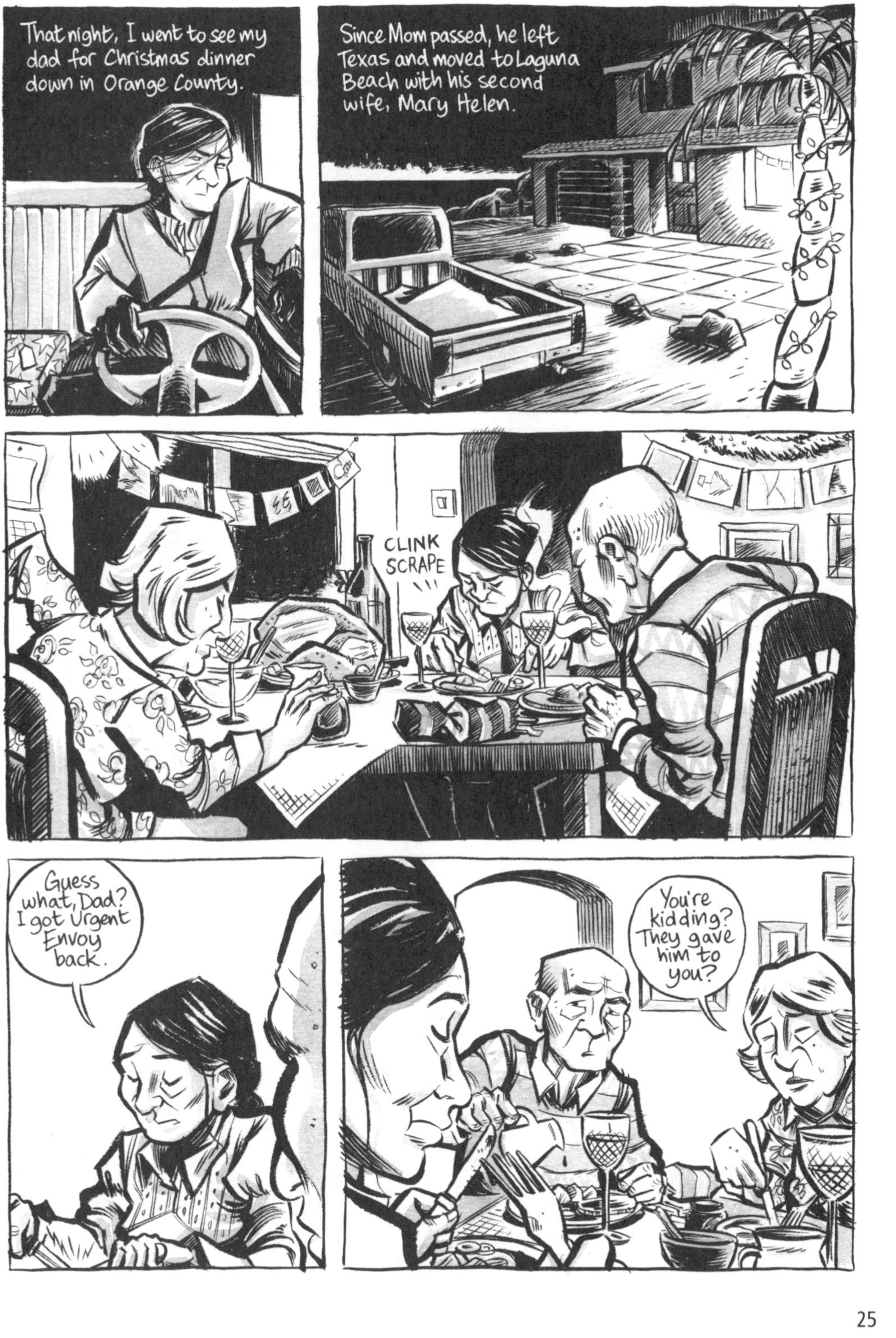
That night, I went to see my dad for Christmas dinner down in Orange County.
Since Mom passed, he left Texas and moved to Laguna Beach with his second wife, Mary Helen.
CLINK SCRAPE
Guess what, Dad? I got Urgent Envoy back.
You're kidding? They gave him to you?

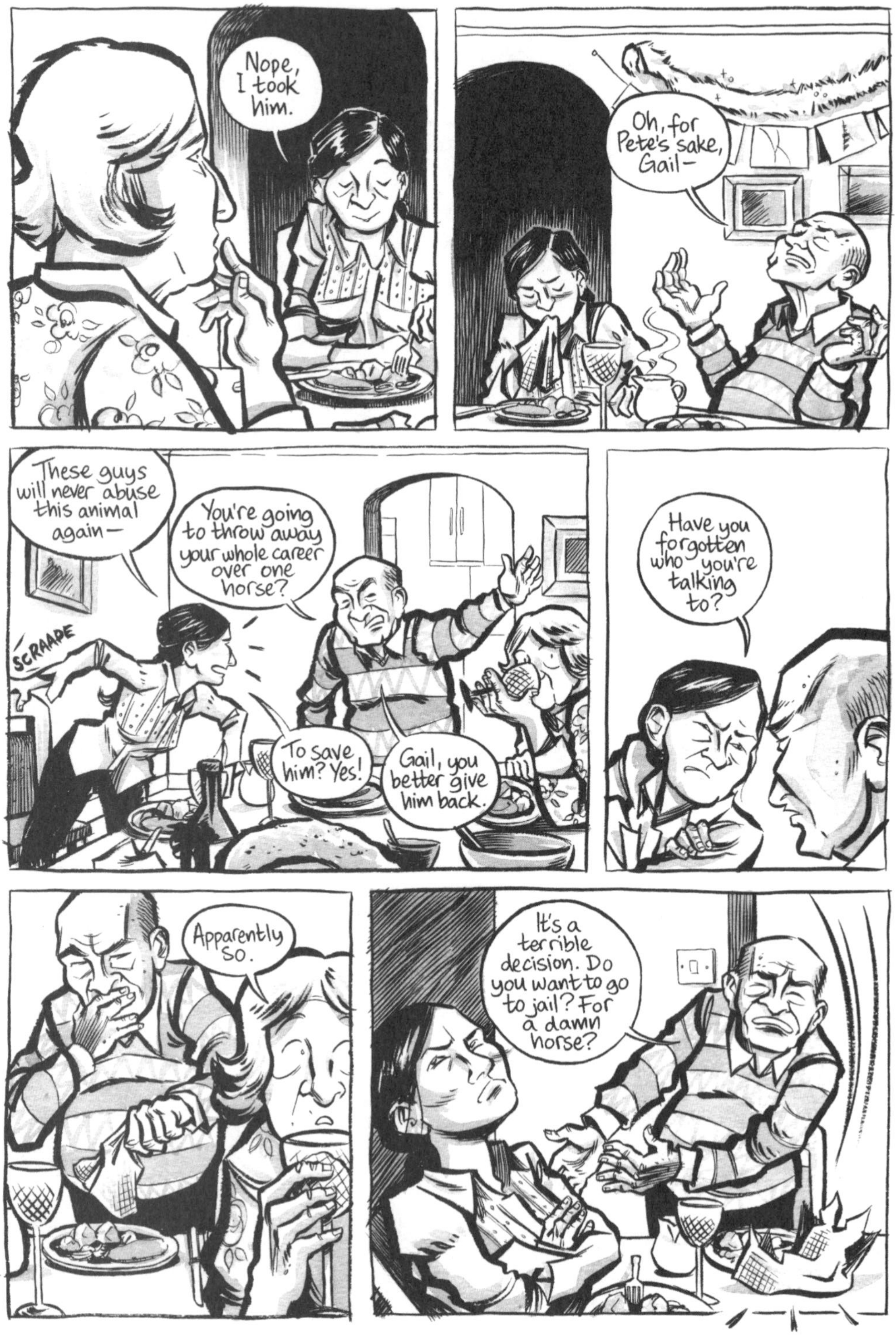
Nope, I took him.
Oh, for Pete's sake, Gail—
These guys will never abuse this animal again—
You're going to throw away your whole career over one horse?
SCRAAPE
To save him? Yes!
Gail, you better give him back.
Have you forgotten who you're talking to?
Apparently so.
It's a terrible decision. Do you want to go to jail? For a damn horse?

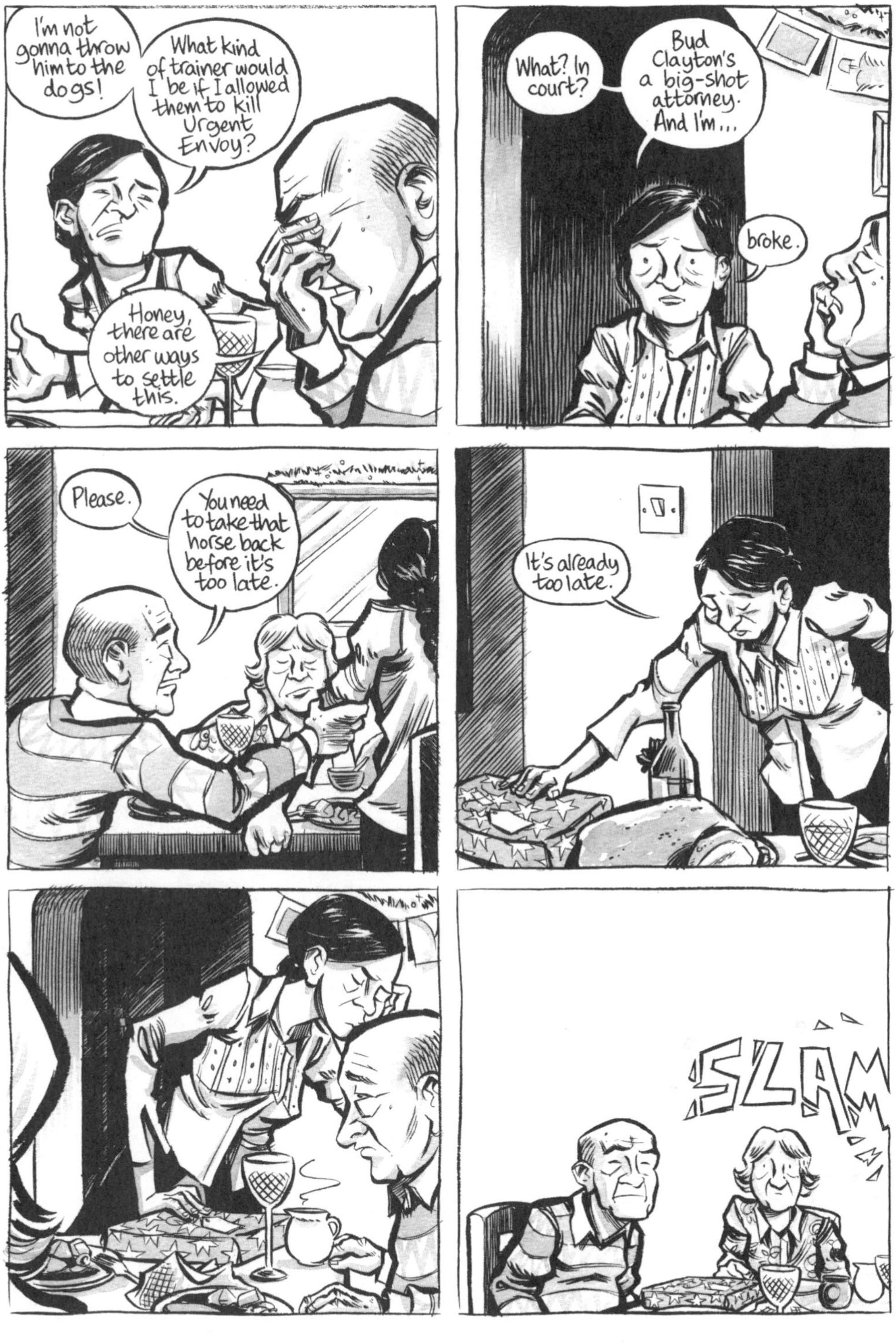
I'm not gonna throw him to the dogs!
What kind of trainer would I be if I allowed them to kill Urgent Envoy?
Honey, there are other ways to settle this.
What? In court?
Bud Clayton's a big-shot attorney. And I'm...
broke.
Please.
You need to take that horse back before it's too late.
It's already too late.
SLAM

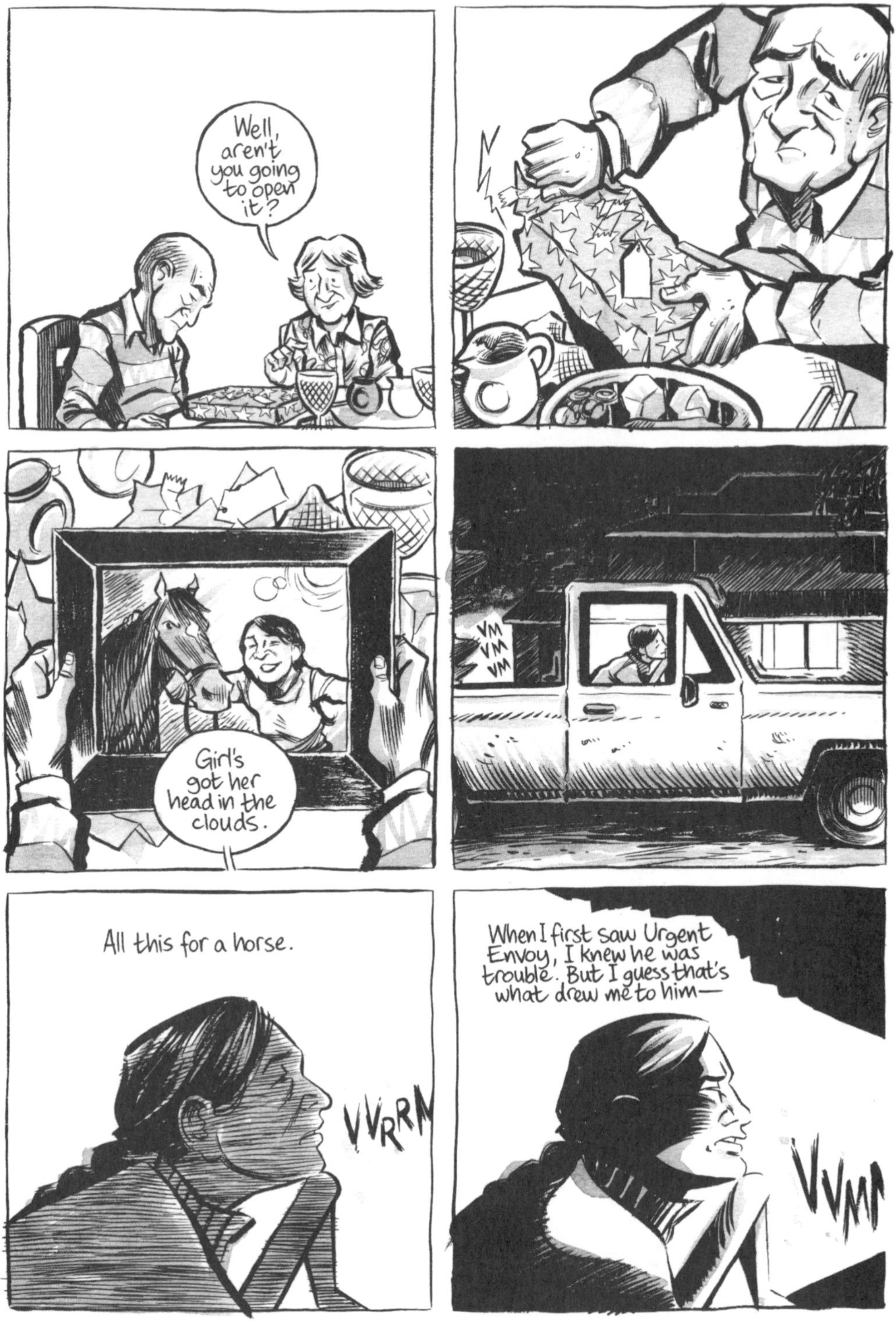
Well, aren't you going to open it?
Girl's got her head in the clouds.
VM VM VM
All this for a horse.
VVRRM
When I first saw Urgent Envoy, I knew he was trouble. But I guess that's what drew me to him—
VVM

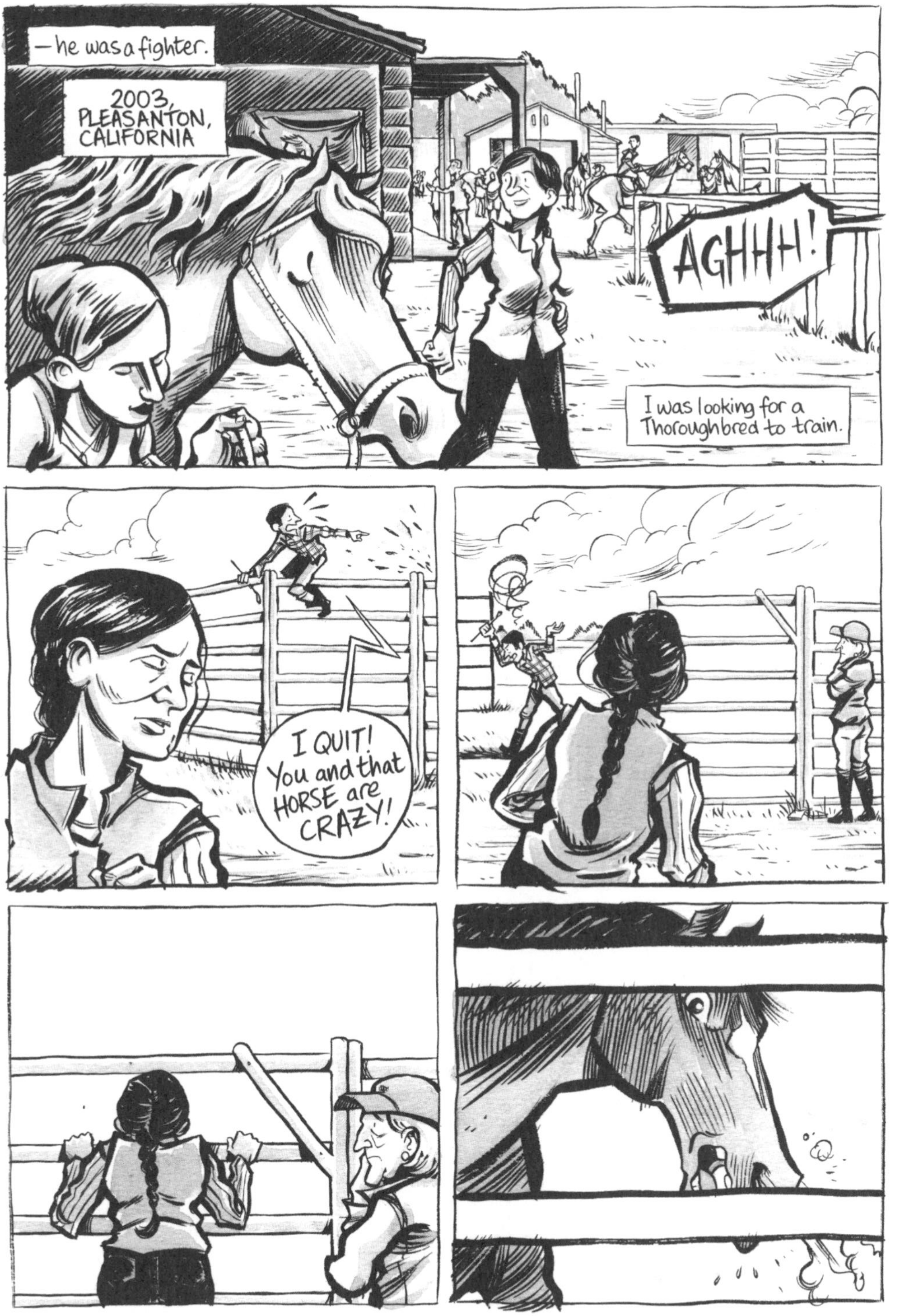

—he was a fighter.
2003, PLEASANTON, CALIFORNIA
AGHHH!
I was looking for a Thoroughbred to train.
I QUIT! You and that HORSE are CRAZY!

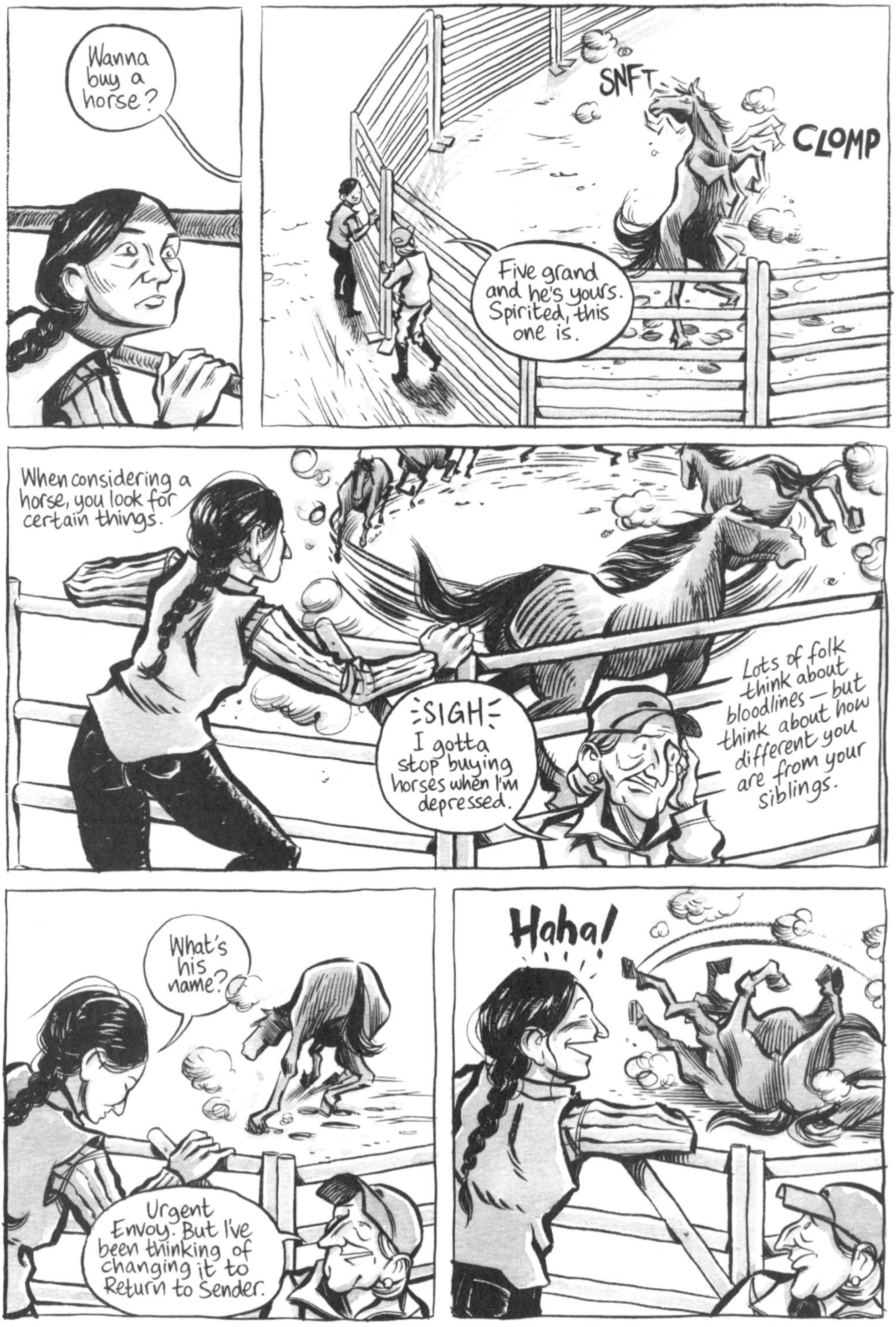
Wanna buy a horse?
SNFT
CLOMP
Five grand and he's yours. Spirited, this one is.
When considering a horse, you look for certain things.
Lots of folk think about bloodlines — but think about how different you are from your siblings.
SIGH
I gotta stop buying horses when I'm depressed.
What's his name?
Urgent Envoy. But I've been thinking of changing it to Return to Sender.
Haha!

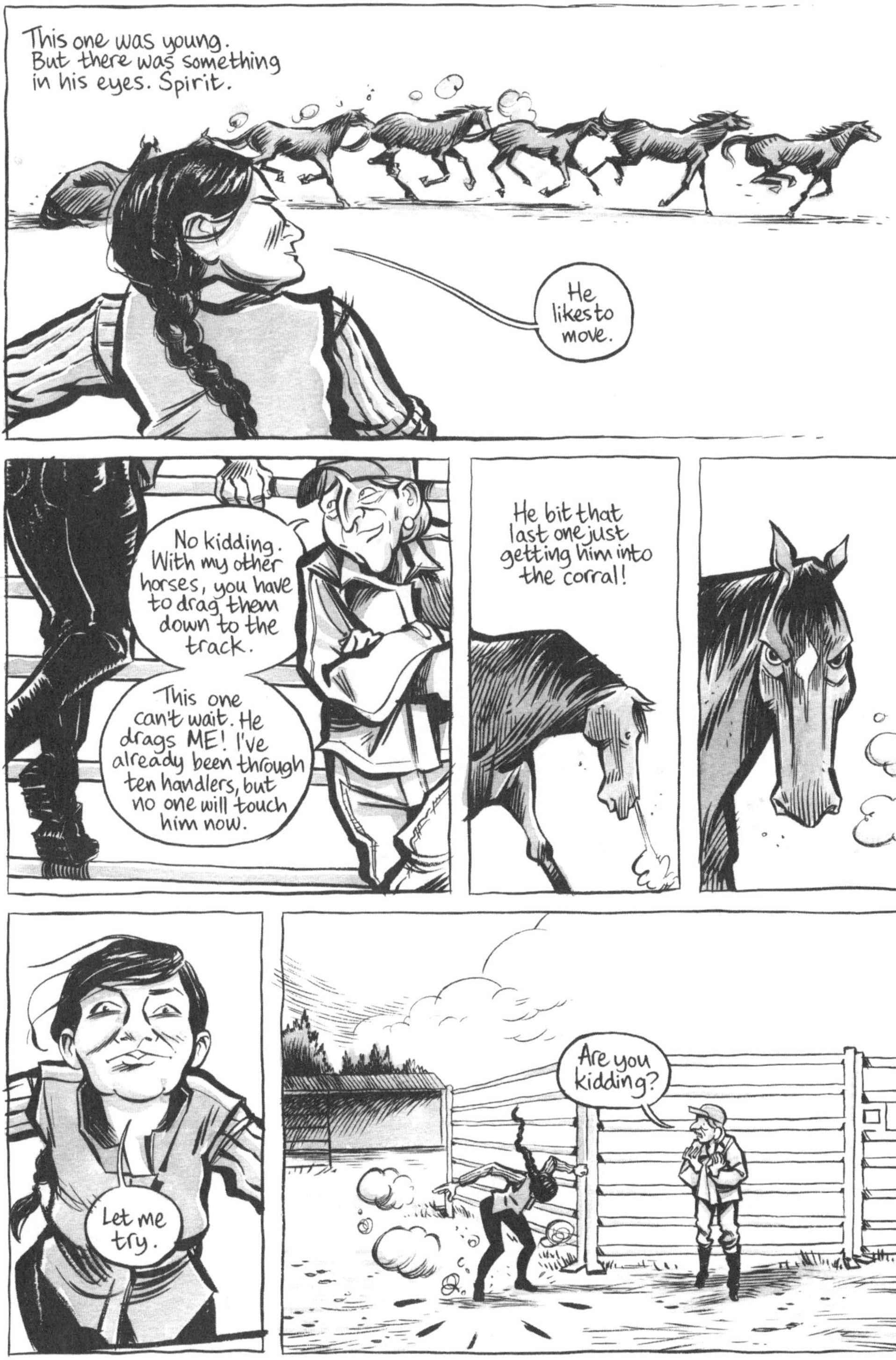
This one was young. But there was something in his eyes. Spirit.
He likes to move.
No kidding. With my other horses, you have to drag them down to the track.
This one can't wait. He drags ME! I've already been through ten handlers, but no one will touch him now.
He bit that last one just getting him into the corral!
Let me try.
Are you kidding?

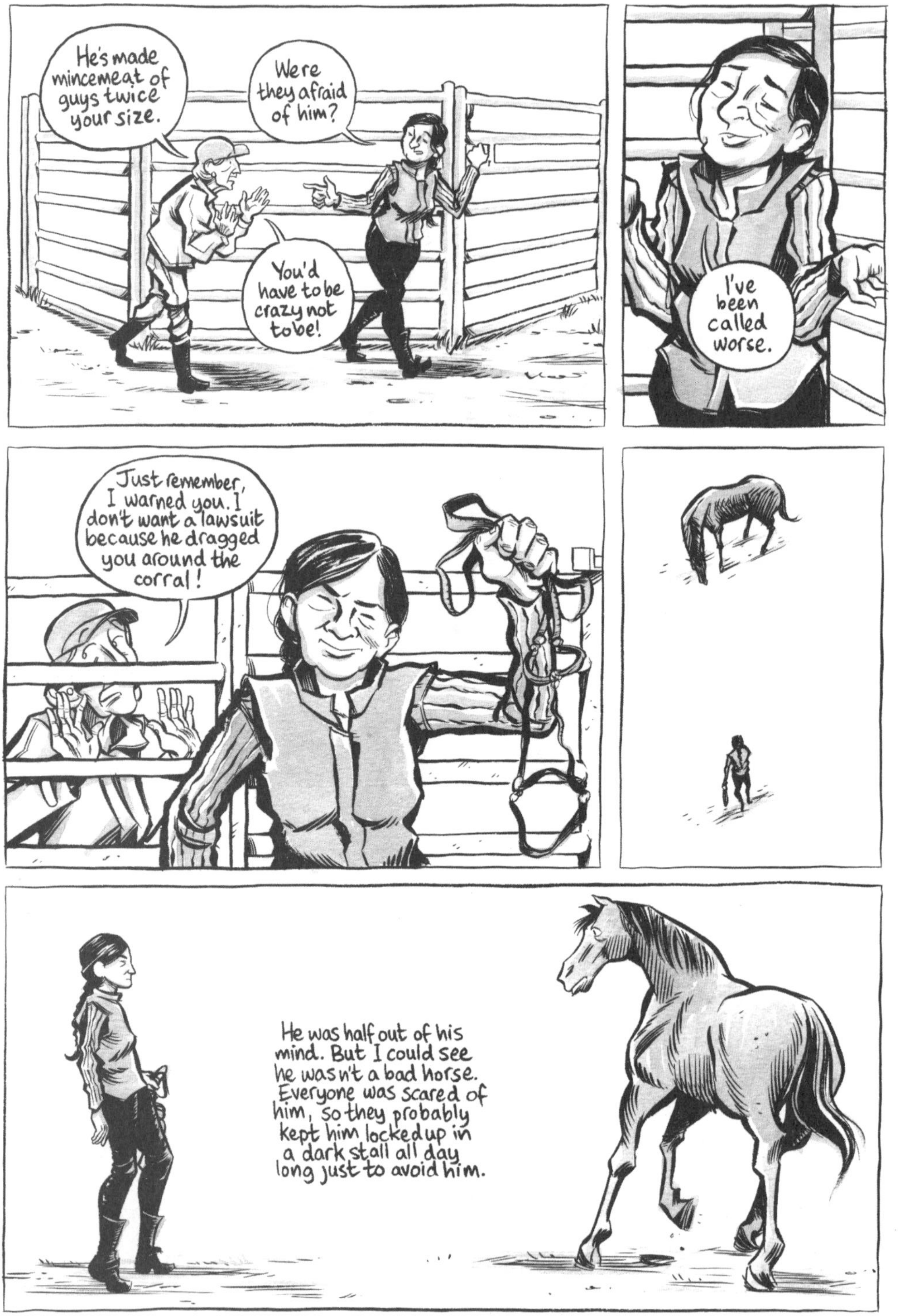
He's made mincemeat of guys twice your size.
Were they afraid of him?
You'd have to be crazy not to be!
I've been called worse.
Just remember, I warned you. I don't want a lawsuit because he dragged you around the corral!
He was half out of his mind. But I could see he wasn't a bad horse. Everyone was scared of him, so they probably kept him locked up in a dark stall all day long just to avoid him.

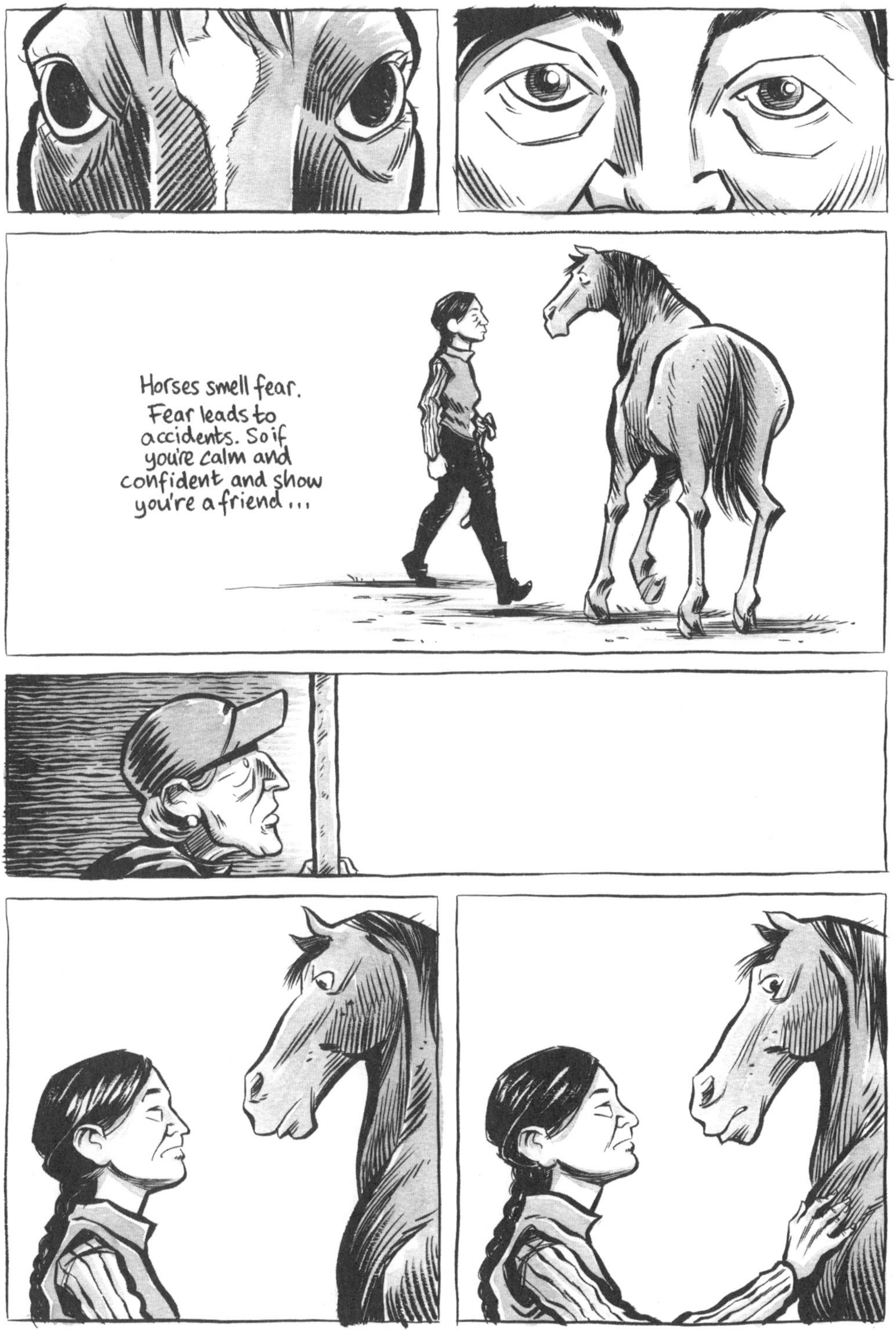
Horses smell fear. Fear leads to accidents. So if you're calm and confident and show you're a friend...

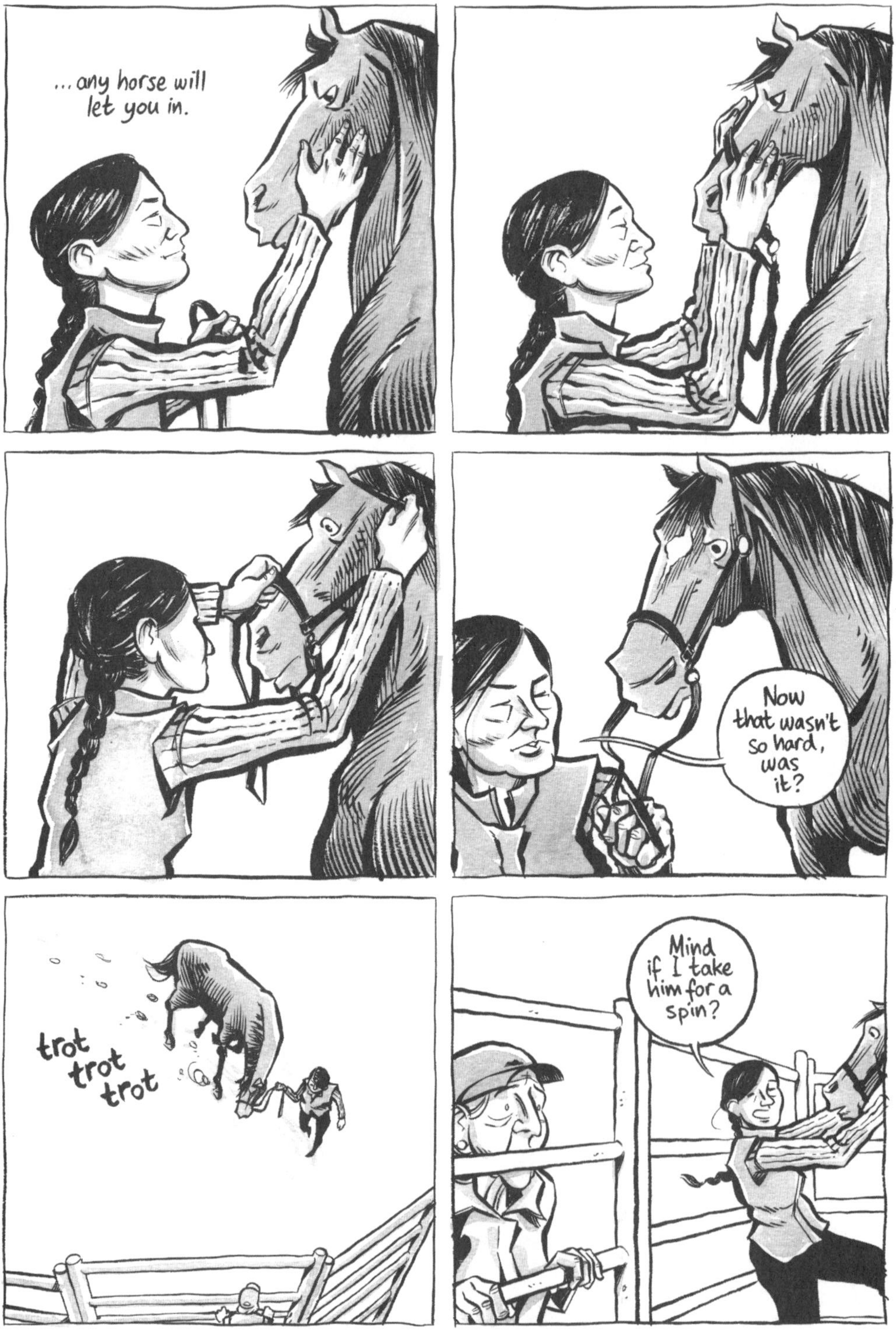
...any horse will let you in.
Now that wasn't so hard, was it?
trot trot trot
Mind if I take him for a spin?

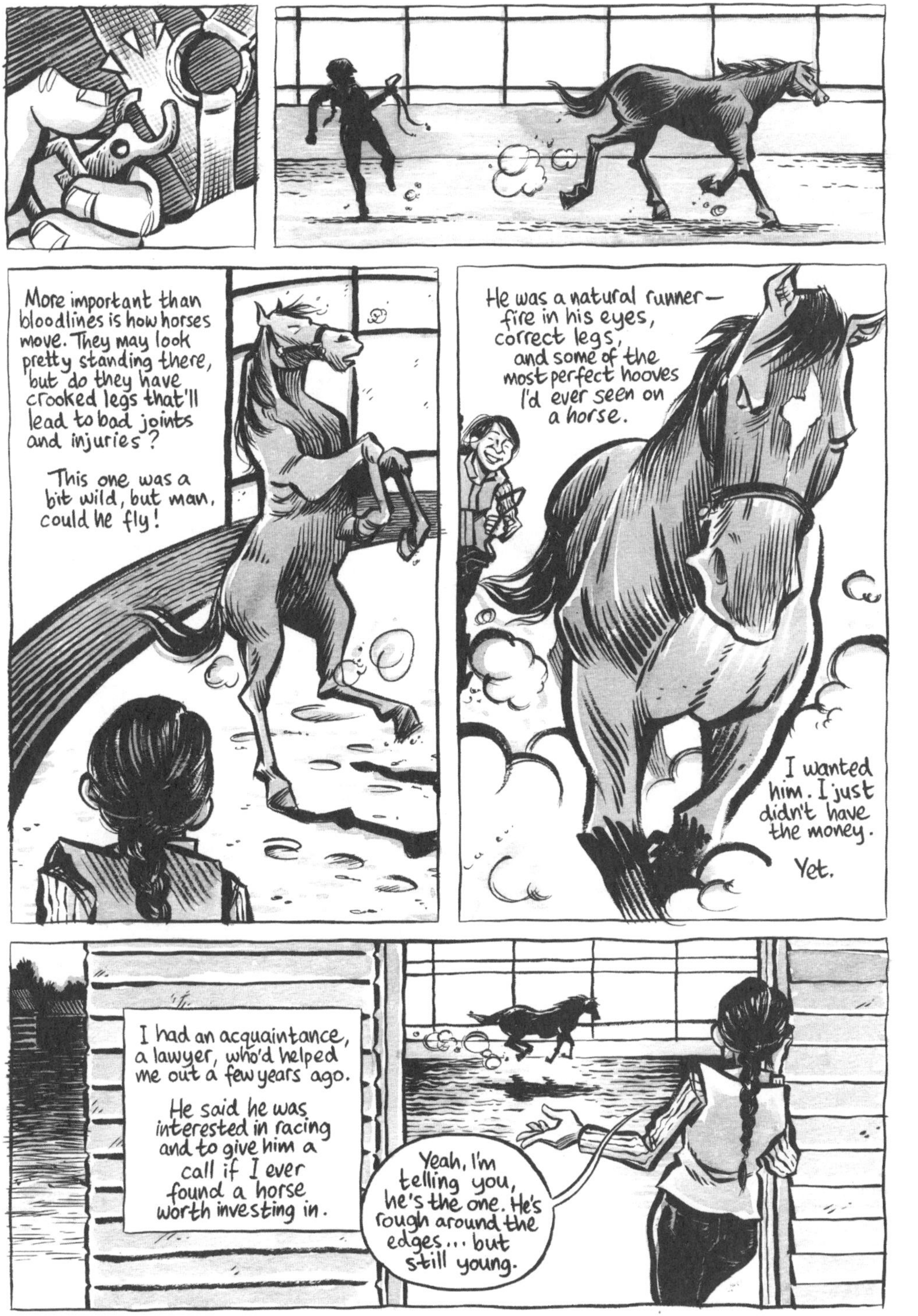

More important than bloodlines is how horses move. They may look pretty standing there, but do they have crooked legs that'll lead to bad joints and injuries?
This one was a bit wild, but man, could he fly!
He was a natural runner— fire in his eyes, correct legs, and some of the most perfect hooves I'd ever seen on a horse.
I wanted him. I just didn't have the money.
Yet.
I had an acquaintance, a lawyer, who'd helped me out a few years ago.
He said he was interested in racing and to give him a call if I ever found a horse worth investing in.
Yeah, I'm telling you, he's the one. He's rough around the edges... but still young.

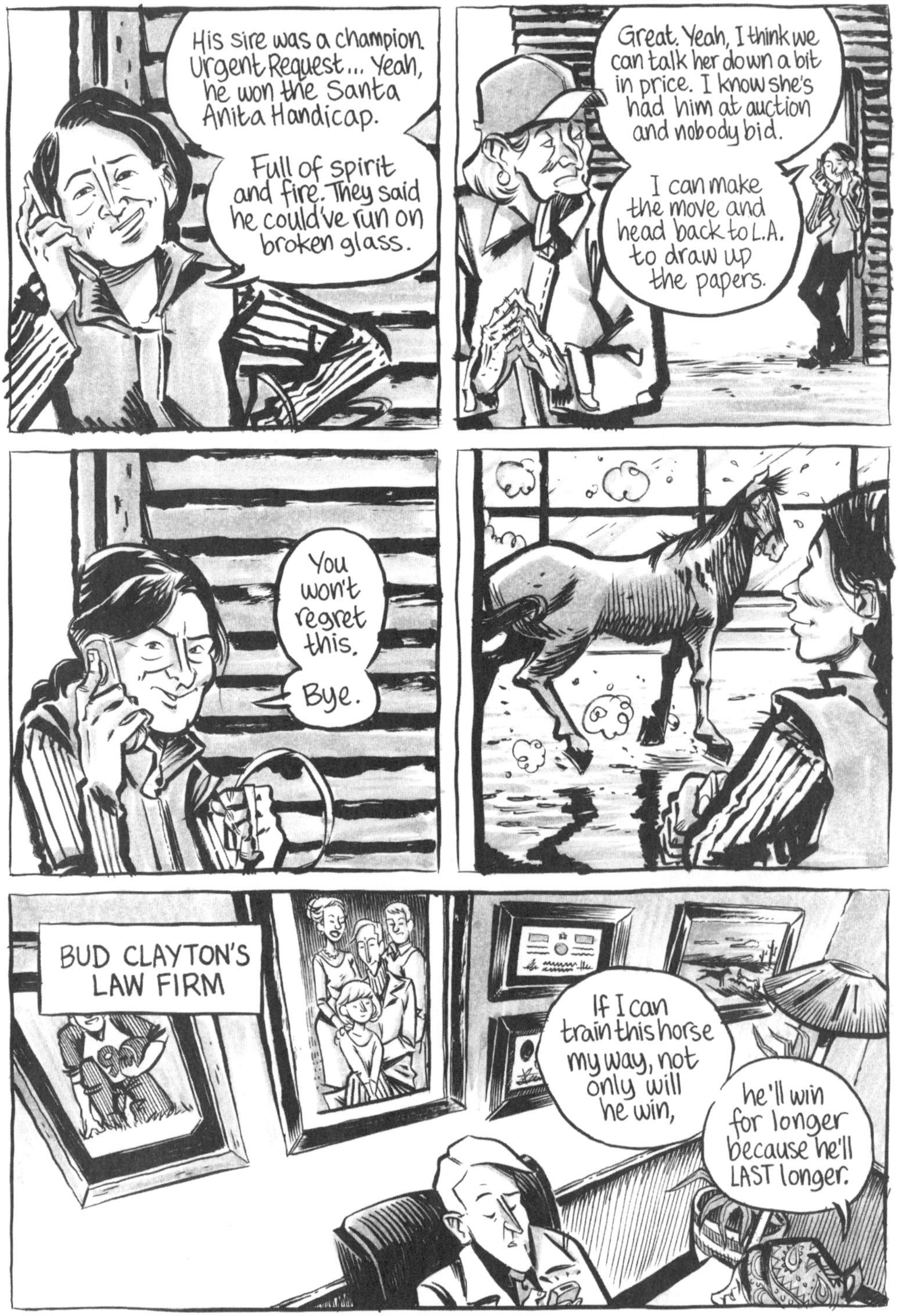
His sire was a champion. Urgent Request... Yeah, he won the Santa Anita Handicap.
Full of spirit and fire. They said he could've run on broken glass.
Great. Yeah, I think we can talk her down a bit in price. I know she's had him at auction and nobody bid.
I can make the move and head back to L.A. to draw up the papers.
You won't regret this.
Bye.
BUD CLAYTON'S LAW FIRM
If I can train this horse my way, not only will he win,
he'll win for longer because he'll LAST longer.

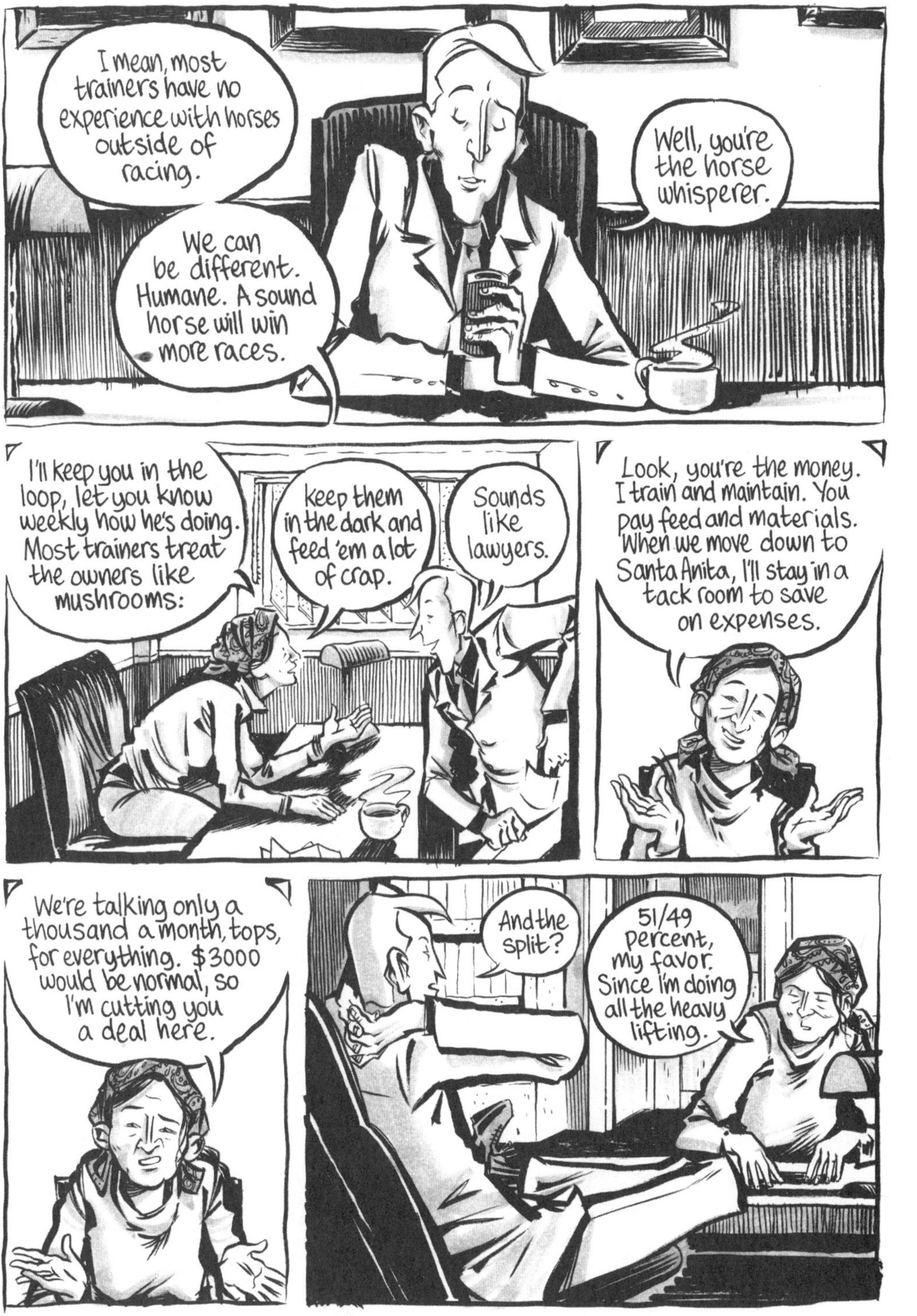
I mean, most trainers have no experience with horses outside of racing.
Well, you're the horse whisperer.
We can be different. Humane. A sound horse will win more races.
I'll keep you in the loop, let you know weekly how he's doing. Most trainers treat the owners like mushrooms:
keep them in the dark and feed 'em a lot of crap.
Sounds like lawyers.
Look, you're the money. I train and maintain. You pay feed and materials. When we move down to Santa Anita, I'll stay in a tack room to save on expenses.
We're talking only a thousand a month, tops, for everything. $3000 would be normal, so I'm cutting you a deal here.
And the split?
51/49 percent, my favor. Since I'm doing all the heavy lifting.

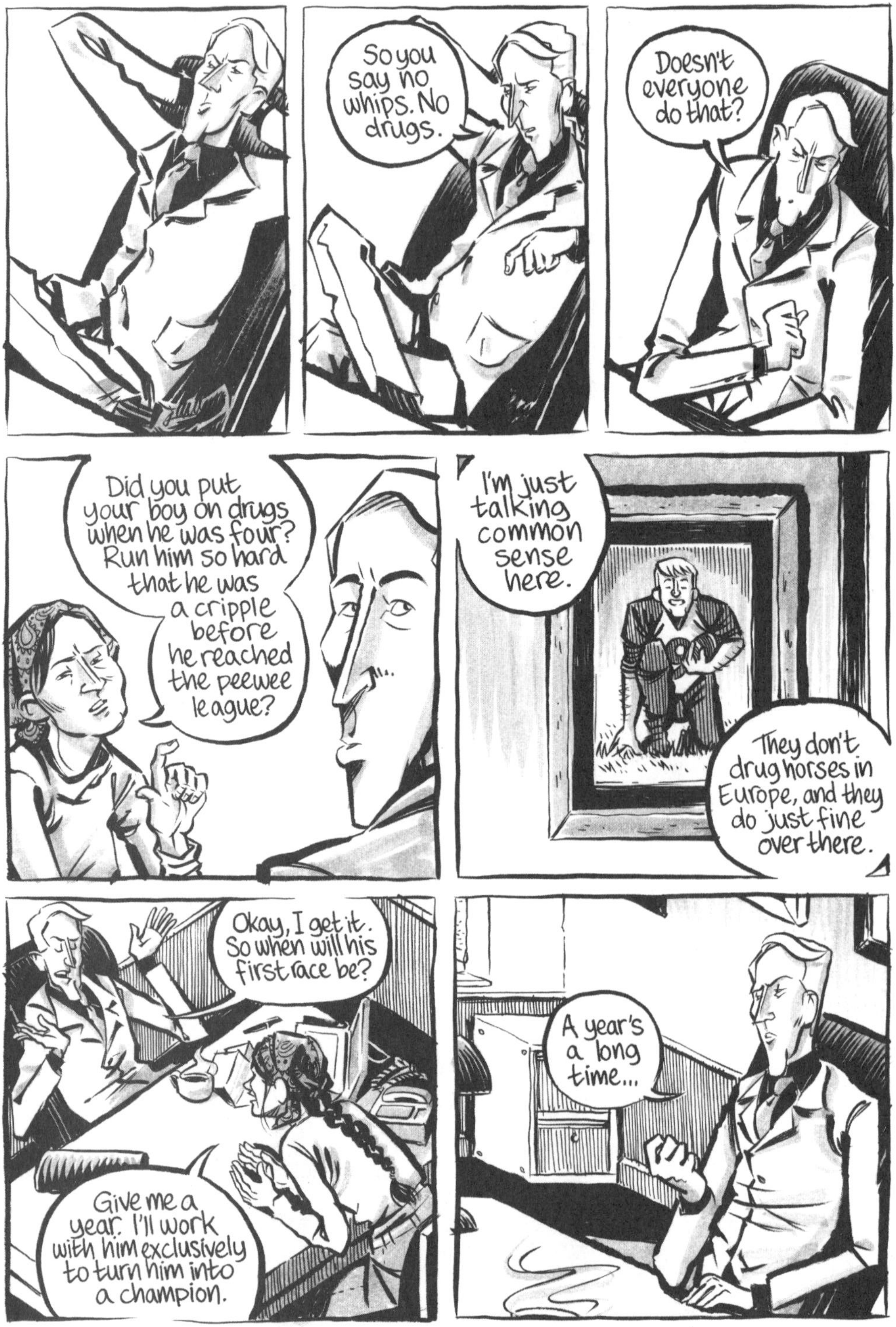
So you say no whips. No drugs.
Doesn't everyone do that?
Did you put your boy on drugs when he was four? Run him so hard that he was a cripple before he reached the peewee league?
I'm just talking common sense here.
They don't drug horses in Europe, and they do just fine over there.
Okay, I get it. So when will his first race be?
Give me a year. I'll work with him exclusively to turn him into a champion.
A year's a long time...

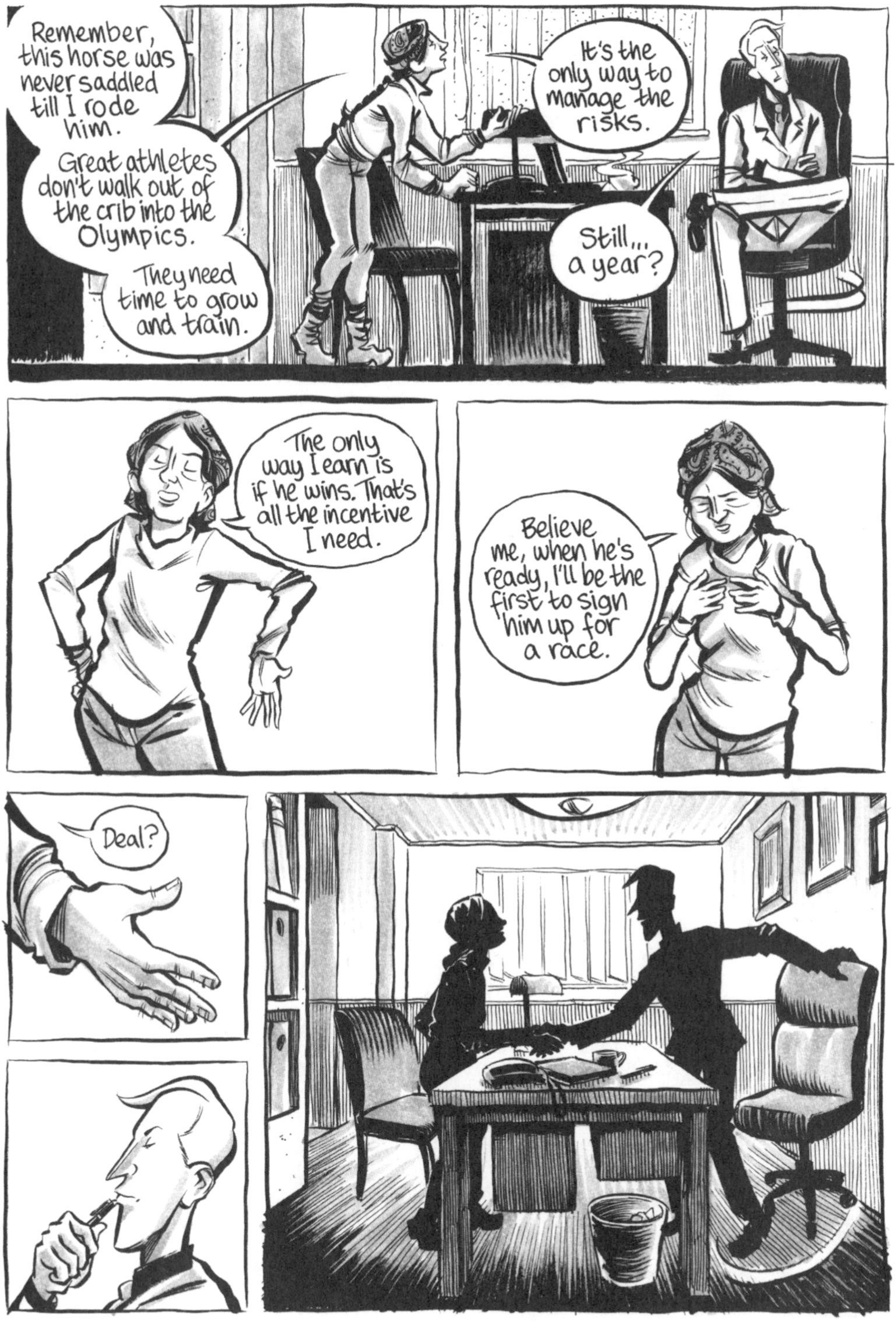
Remember, this horse was never saddled till I rode him.
Great athletes don't walk out of the crib into the Olympics.
They need time to grow and train.
It's the only way to manage the risks.
Still... a year?
The only way I earn is if he wins. That's all the incentive I need.
Believe me, when he's ready, I'll be the first to sign him up for a race.
Deal?

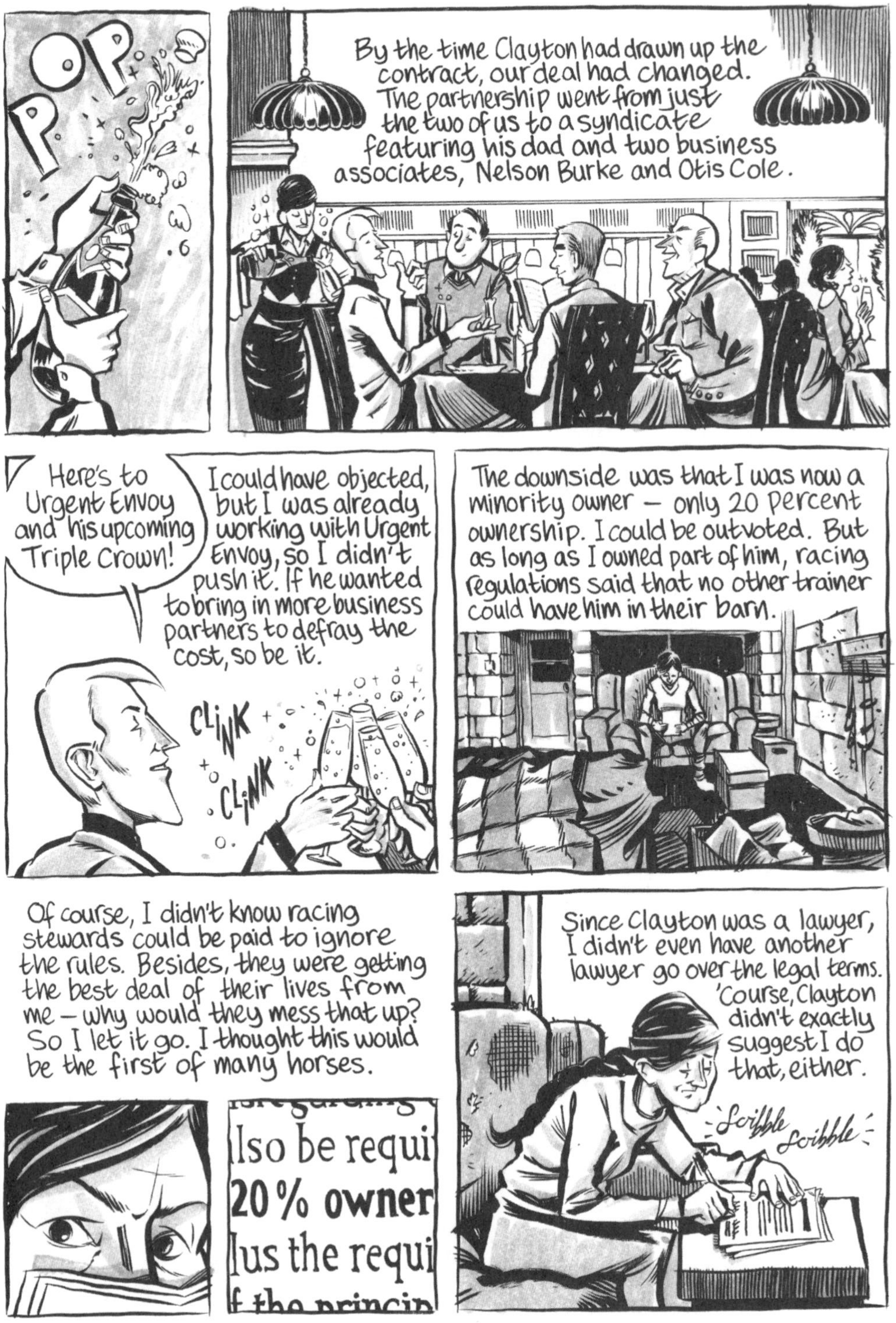

POP
By the time Clayton had drawn up the contract, our deal had changed. The partnership went from just the two of us to a syndicate featuring his dad and two business associates, Nelson Burke and Otis Cole.
Here's to Urgent Envoy and his upcoming Triple Crown!
I could have objected, but I was already working with Urgent Envoy, so I didn't push it. If he wanted to bring in more business partners to defray the cost, so be it.
CLINK
CLINK
The downside was that I was now a minority owner — only 20 percent ownership. I could be outvoted. But as long as I owned part of him, racing regulations said that no other trainer could have him in their barn.
Of course, I didn't know racing stewards could be paid to ignore the rules. Besides, they were getting the best deal of their lives from me — why would they mess that up? So I let it go. I thought this would be the first of many horses.
lso be requi
20 % owner
lus the requi
Since Clayton was a lawyer, I didn't even have another lawyer go over the legal terms.
'Course, Clayton didn't exactly suggest I do that, either.
Scribble
Scribble

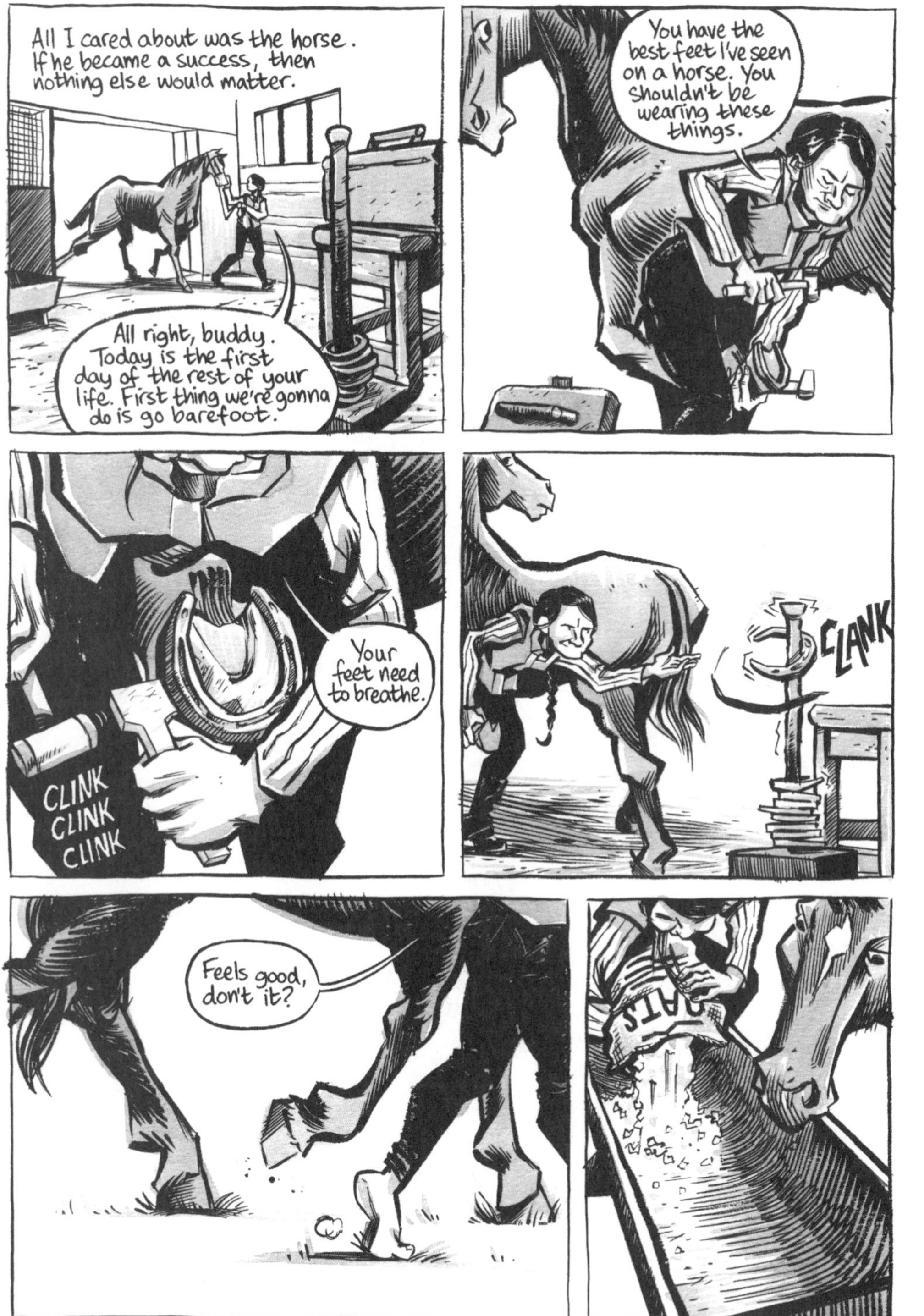
All I cared about was the horse. If he became a success, then nothing else would matter.
All right, buddy. Today is the first day of the rest of your life. First thing we're gonna do is go barefoot.
You have the best feet I've seen on a horse. You shouldn't be wearing these things.
Your feet need to breathe.
CLINK
CLINK
CLINK
CLANK
Feels good, don't it?
OATS

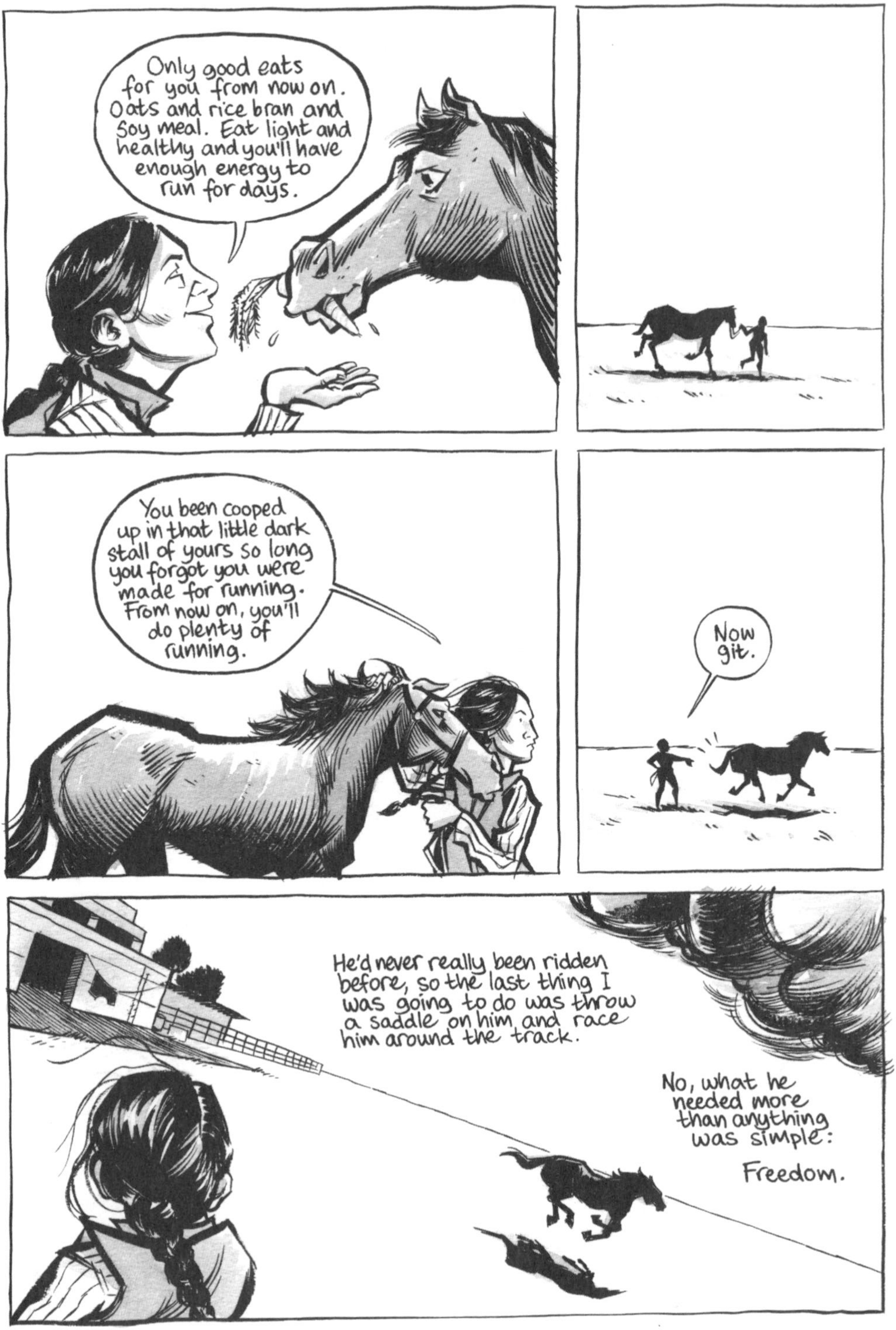

Only good eats for you from now on. Oats and rice bran and soy meal. Eat light and healthy and you'll have enough energy to run for days.
You been cooped up in that little dark stall of yours so long you forgot you were made for running. From now on, you'll do plenty of running.
Now git.
He'd never really been ridden before, so the last thing I was going to do was throw a saddle on him and race him around the track.
No, what he needed more than anything was simple:
Freedom.

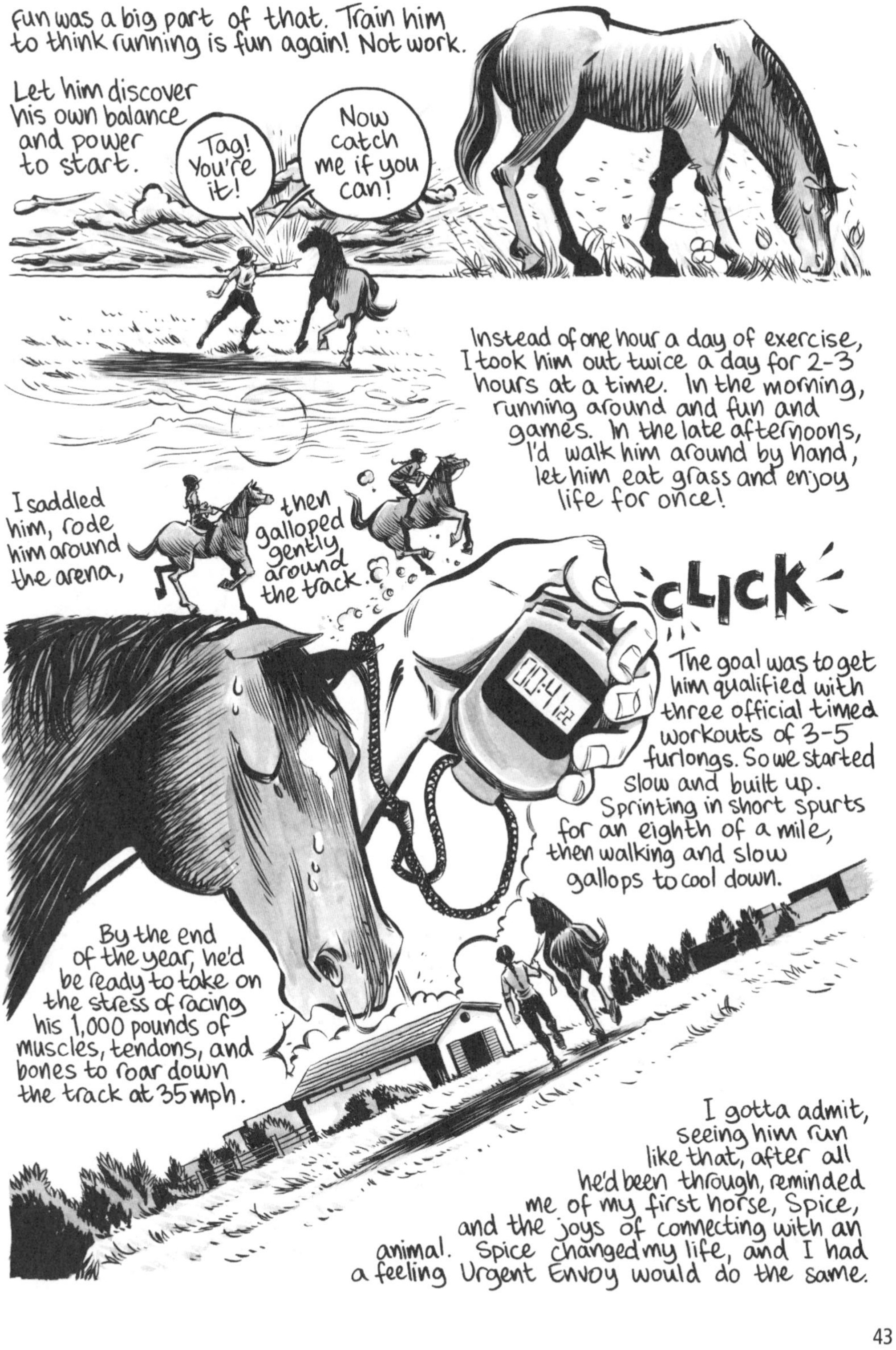
Fun was a big part of that. Train him to think running is fun again! Not work.
Let him discover his own balance and power to start.
Tag! You're it!
Now catch me if you can!
Instead of one hour a day of exercise, I took him out twice a day for 2-3 hours at a time. In the morning, running around and fun and games. In the late afternoons, I'd walk him around by hand, let him eat grass and enjoy life for once!
I saddled him, rode him around the arena,
then galloped gently around the track.
CLICK
00:41 22
The goal was to get him qualified with three official timed workouts of 3-5 furlongs. So we started slow and built up. Sprinting in short spurts for an eighth of a mile, then walking and slow gallops to cool down.
By the end of the year, he'd be ready to take on the stress of racing his 1,000 pounds of muscles, tendons, and bones to roar down the track at 35 mph.
I gotta admit, seeing him run like that, after all he'd been through, reminded me of my first horse, Spice, and the joys of connecting with an animal. Spice changed my life, and I had a feeling Urgent Envoy would do the same.

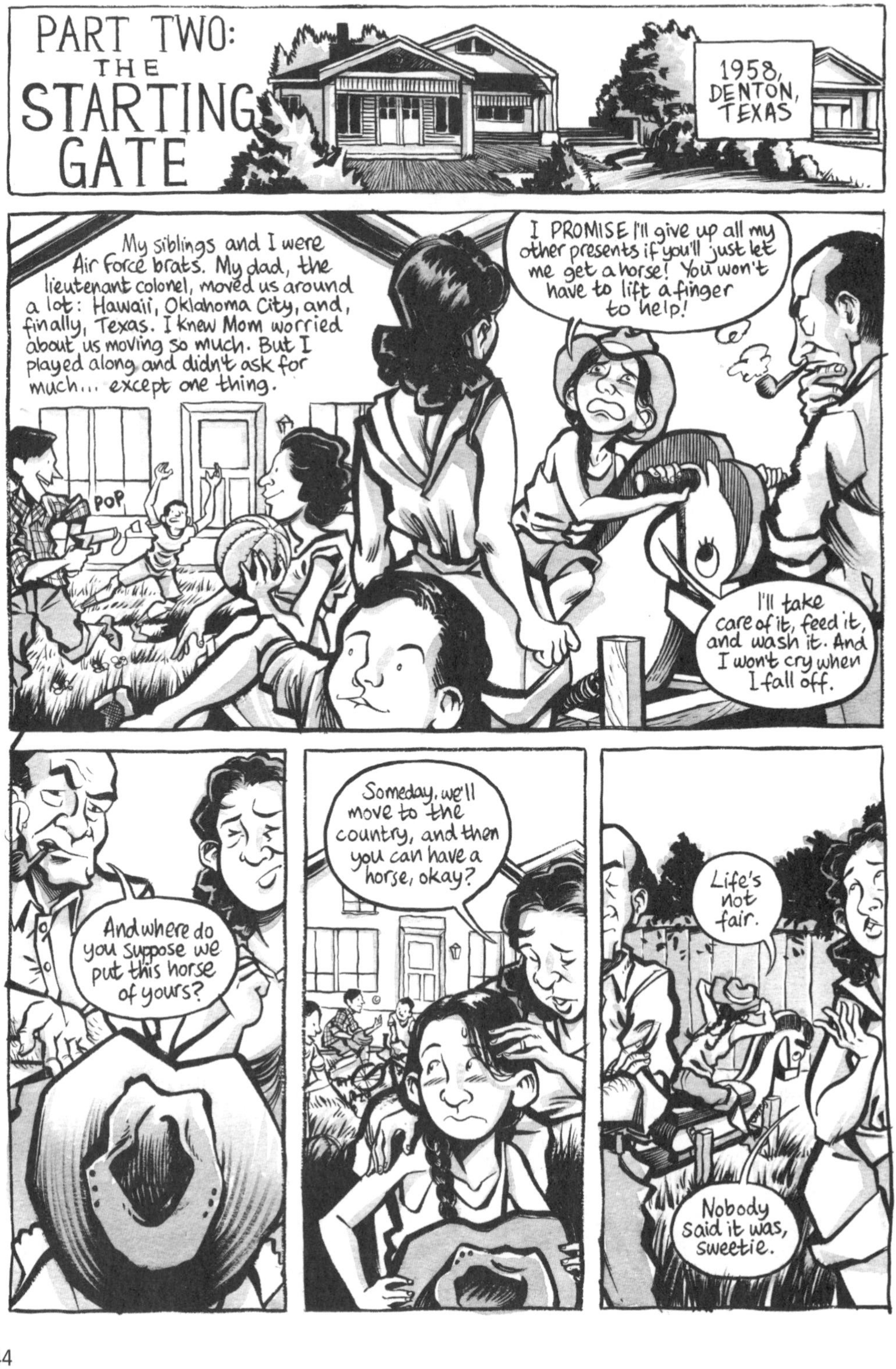
PART TWO: THE STARTING GATE
1958, DENTON, TEXAS
My siblings and I were Air Force brats. My dad, the lieutenant colonel, moved us around a lot: Hawaii, Oklahoma City, and, finally, Texas. I knew Mom worried about us moving so much. But I played along and didn't ask for much... except one thing.
I PROMISE I'll give up all my other presents if you'll just let me get a horse! You won't have to lift a finger to help!
POP
I'll take care of it, feed it, and wash it. And I won't cry when I fall off.
And where do you suppose we put this horse of yours?
Someday, we'll move to the country, and then you can have a horse, okay?
Life's not fair.
Nobody said it was, sweetie.

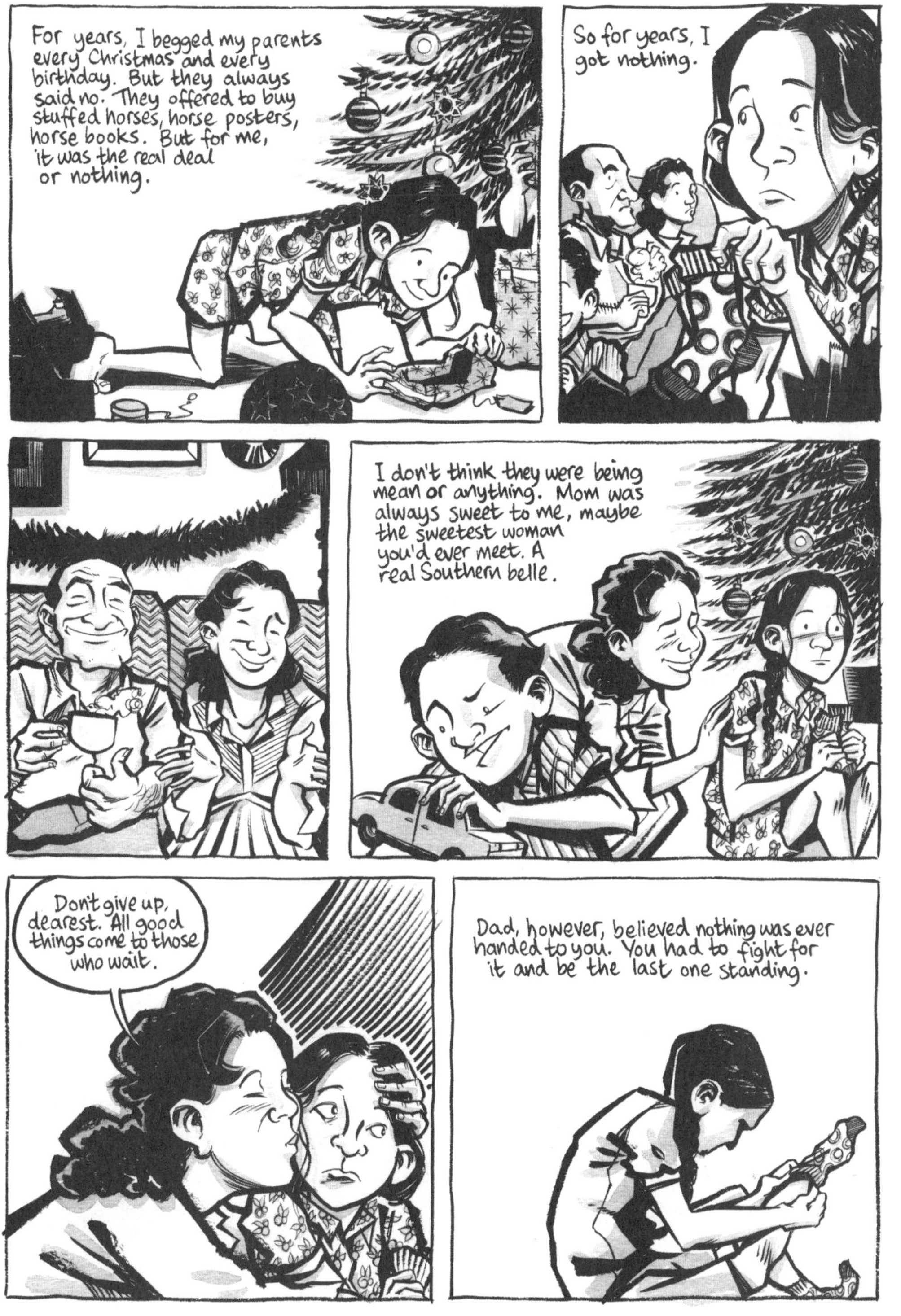

For years, I begged my parents every Christmas and every birthday. But they always said no. They offered to buy stuffed horses, horse posters, horse books. But for me, it was the real deal or nothing.
So for years, I got nothing.
I don't think they were being mean or anything. Mom was always sweet to me, maybe the sweetest woman you'd ever meet. A real Southern belle.
Don't give up, dearest. All good things come to those who wait.
Dad, however, believed nothing was ever handed to you. You had to fight for it and be the last one standing.

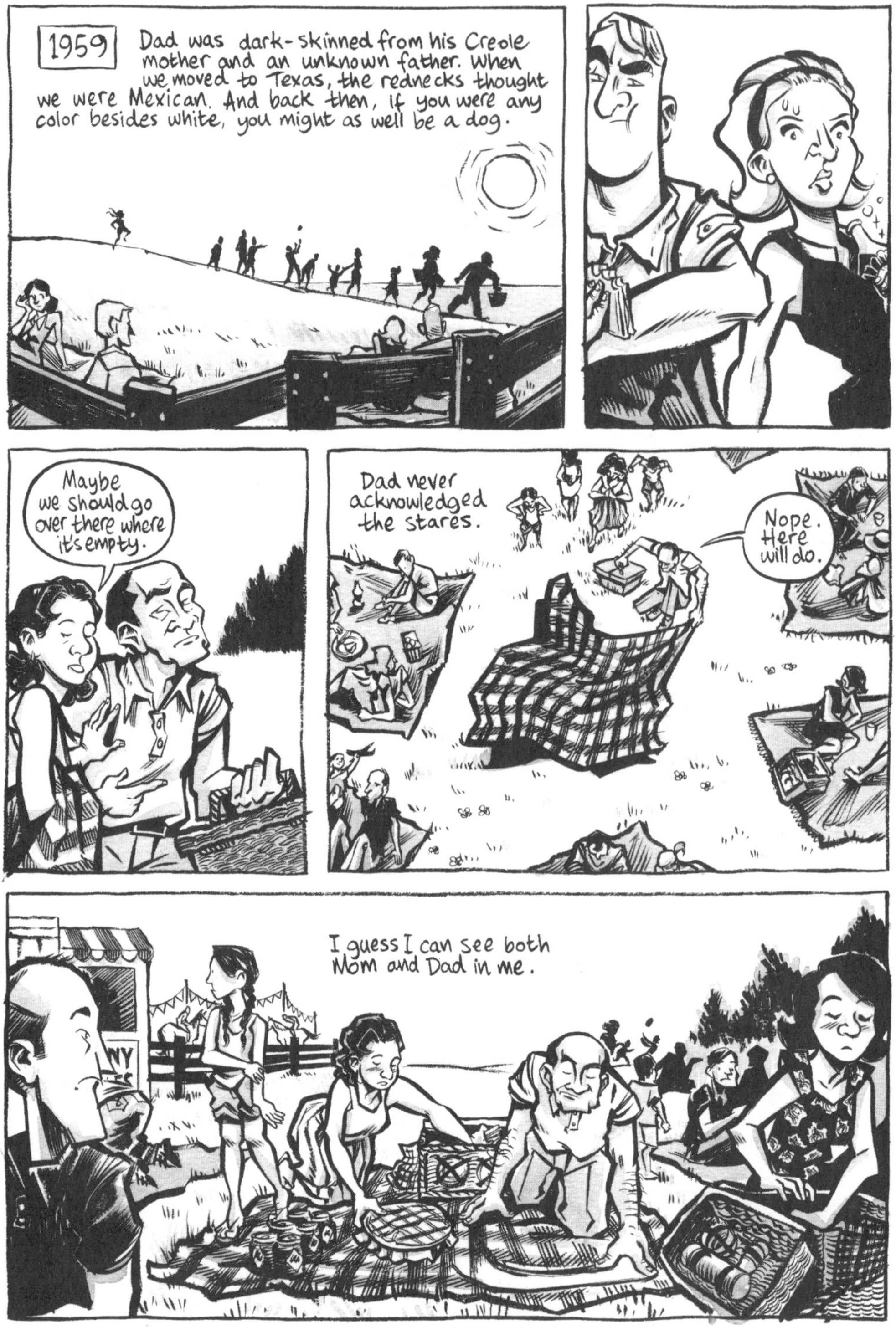
1959
Dad was dark-skinned from his Creole mother and an unknown father. When we moved to Texas, the rednecks thought we were Mexican. And back then, if you were any color besides white, you might as well be a dog.
Maybe we should go over there where it's empty.
Dad never acknowledged the stares.
Nope. Here will do.
I guess I can see both Mom and Dad in me.

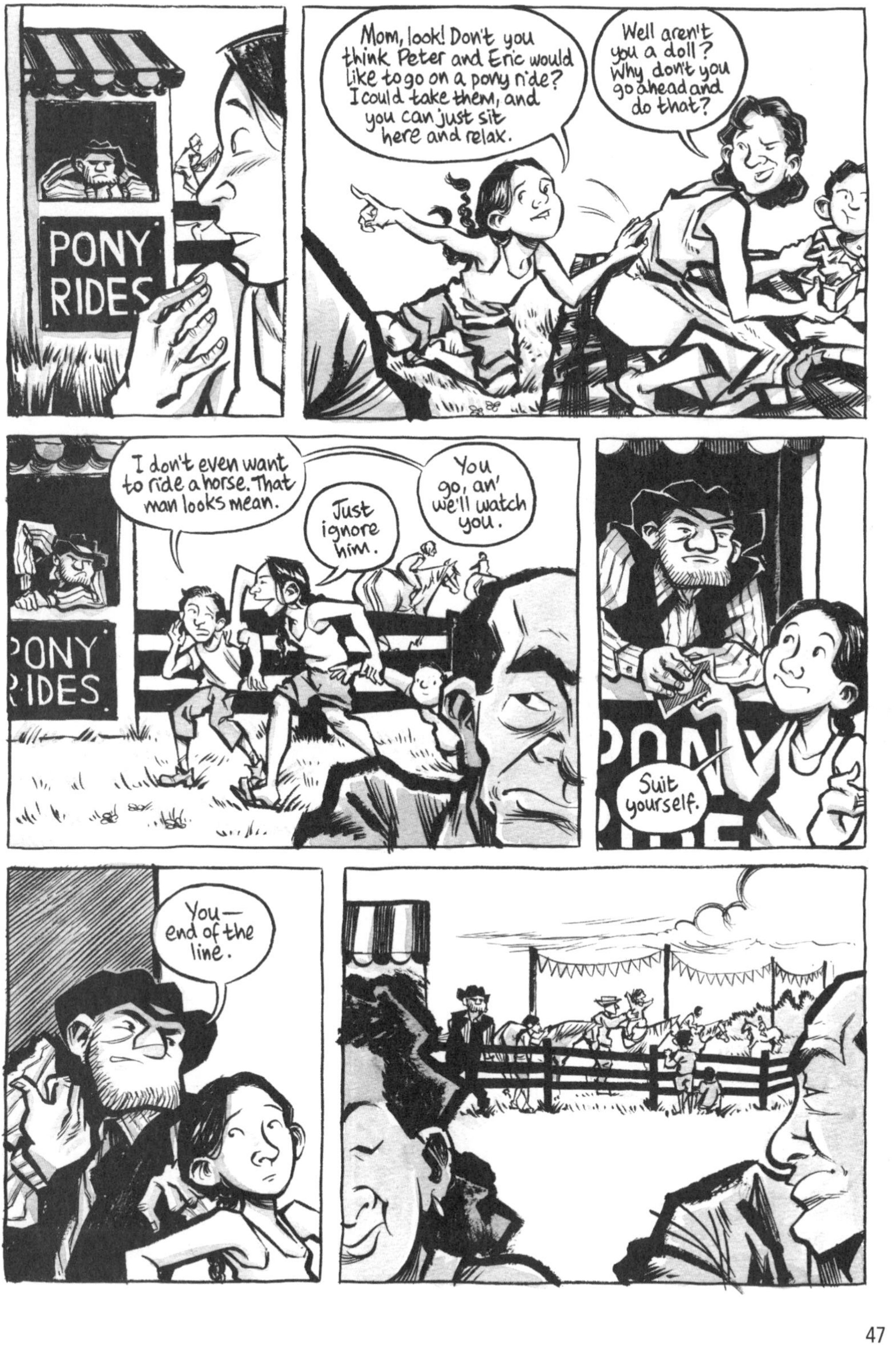
PONY RIDES
Mom, look! Don't you think Peter and Eric would like to go on a pony ride? I could take them, and you can just sit here and relax.
Well aren't you a doll? Why don't you go ahead and do that?
PONY RIDES
I don't even want to ride a horse. That man looks mean.
Just ignore him.
You go, an' we'll watch you.
Suit yourself.
You— end of the line.

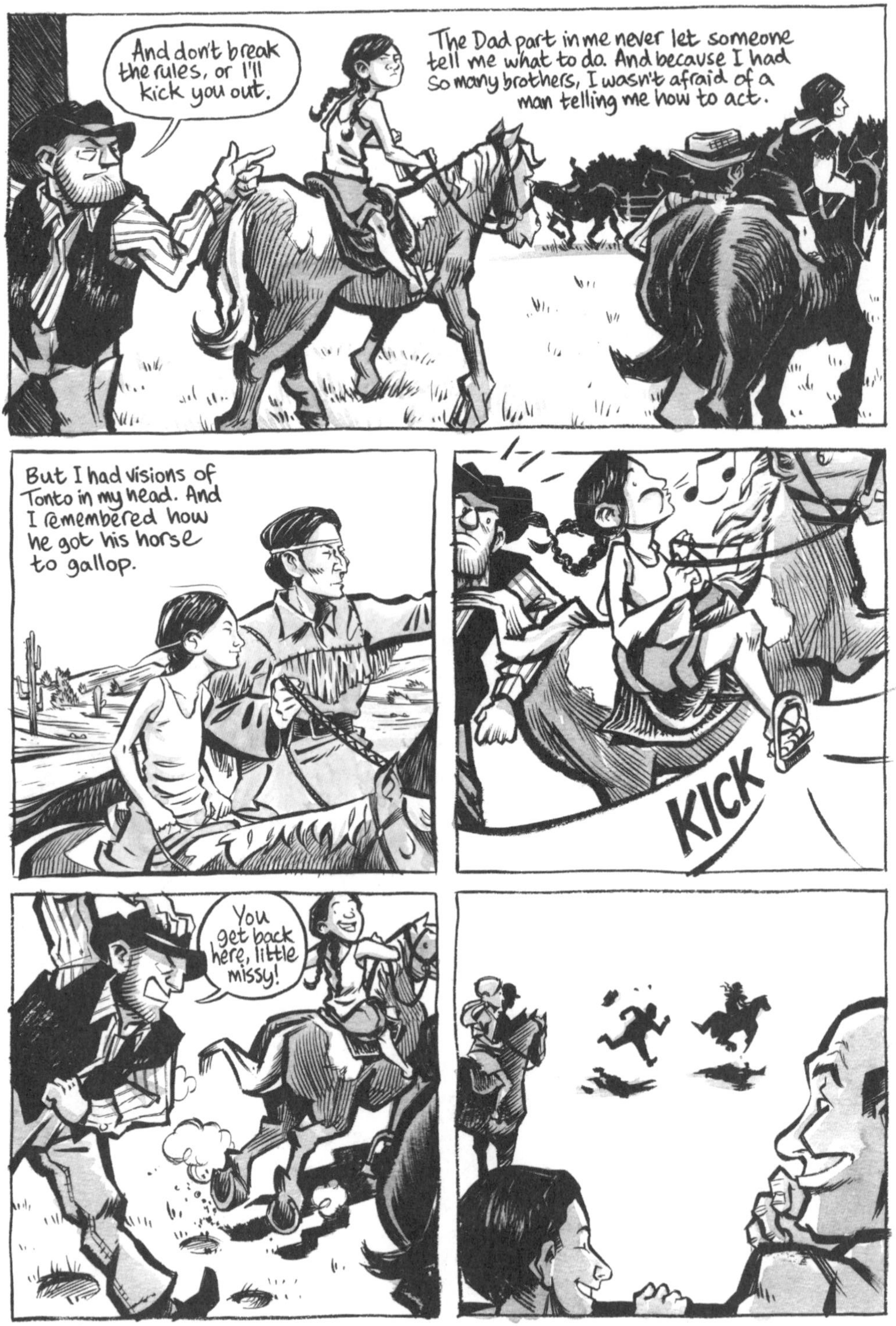
And don't break the rules, or I'll kick you out.
The Dad part in me never let someone tell me what to do. And because I had so many brothers, I wasn't afraid of a man telling me how to act.
But I had visions of Tonto in my head. And I remembered how he got his horse to gallop.
KICK
You get back here, little missy!

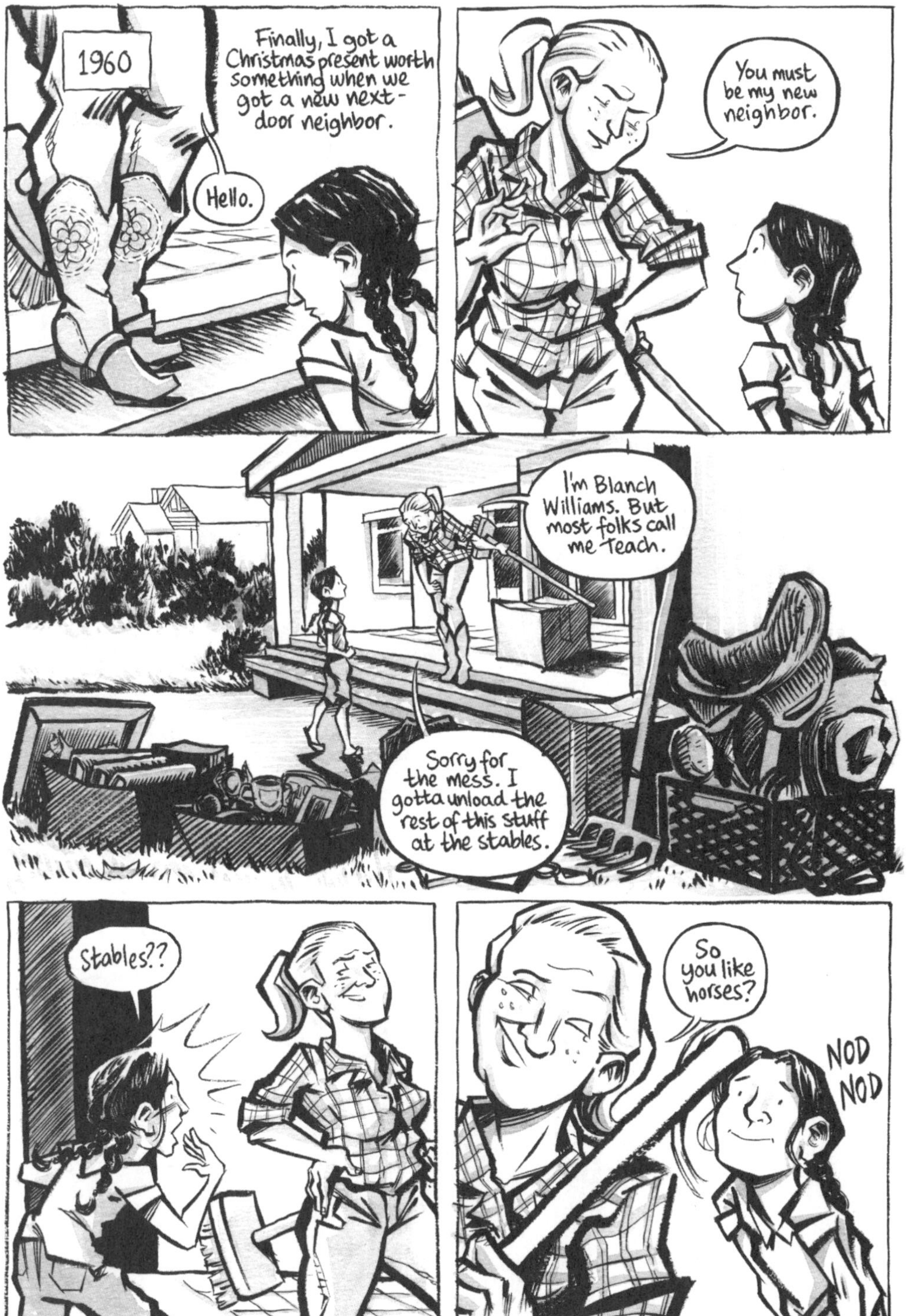
1960
Finally, I got a Christmas present worth something when we got a new next-door neighbor.
Hello.
You must be my new neighbor.
I'm Blanch Williams. But most folks call me Teach.
Sorry for the mess. I gotta unload the rest of this stuff at the stables.
Stables??
So you like horses?
NOD NOD

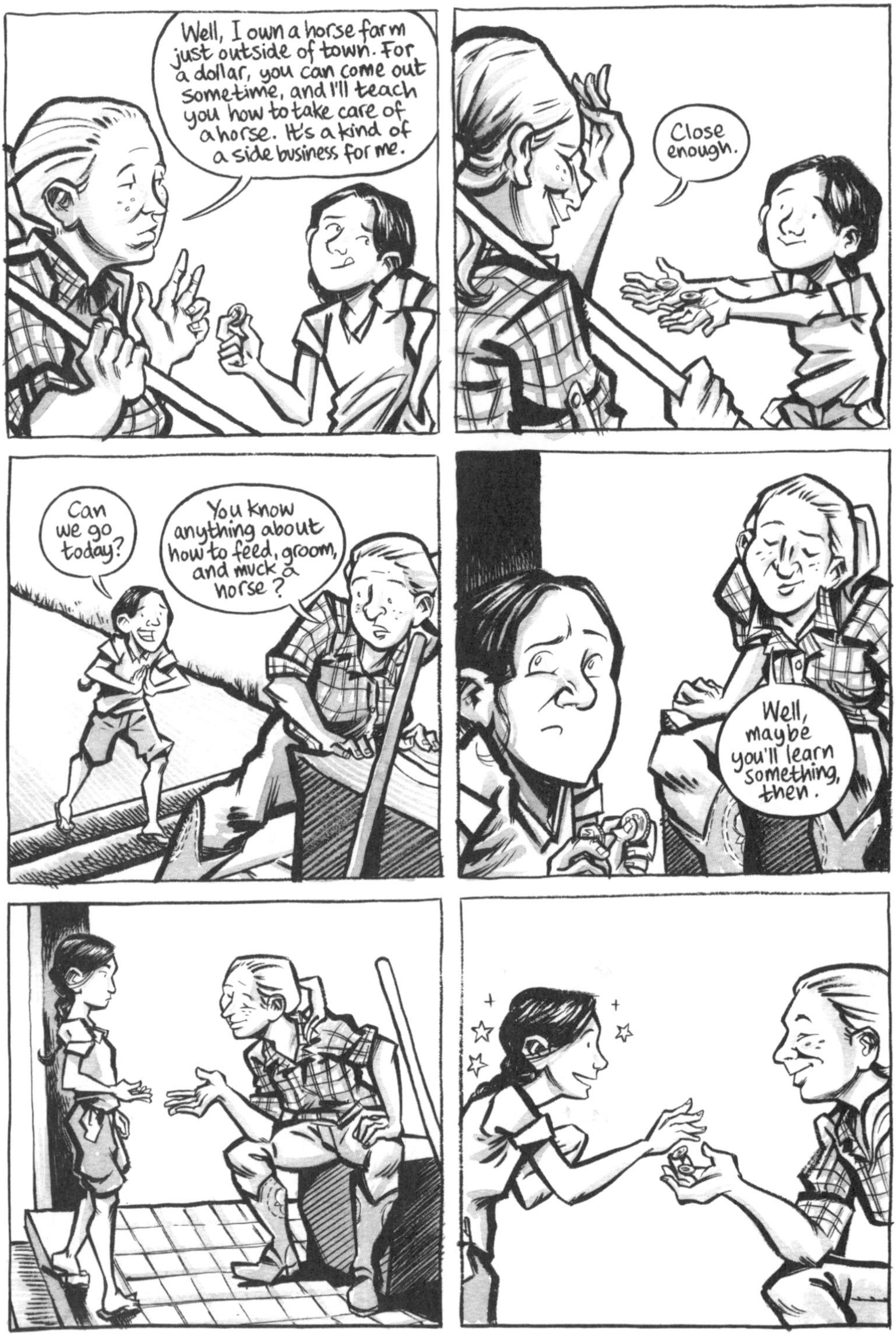
Well, I own a horse farm just outside of town. For a dollar, you can come out sometime, and I'll teach you how to take care of a horse. It's a kind of a side business for me.
Close enough.
Can we go today?
You know anything about how to feed, groom, and muck a horse?
Well, maybe you'll learn something, then.

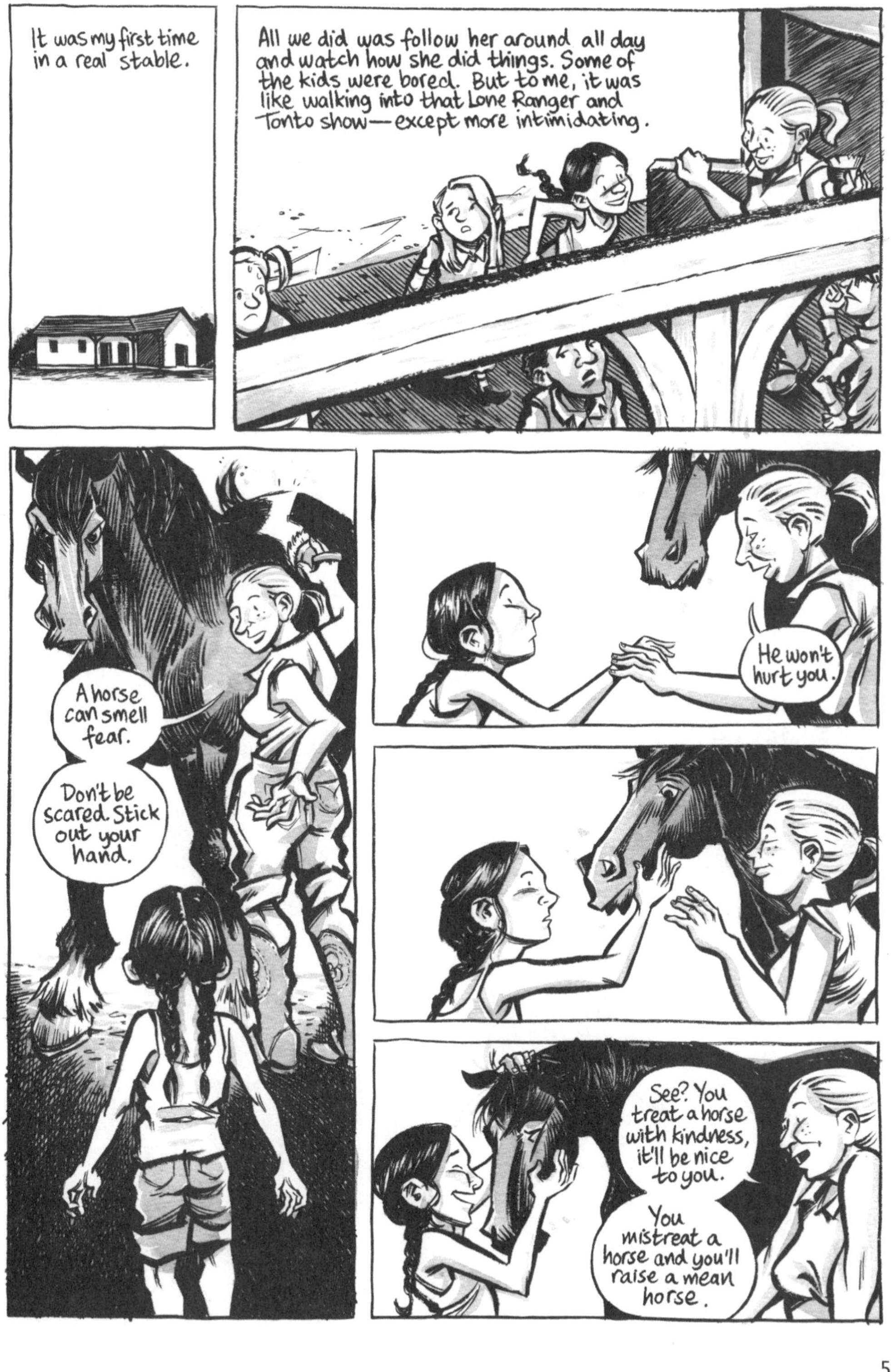

It was my first time in a real stable.
All we did was follow her around all day and watch how she did things. Some of the kids were bored. But to me, it was like walking into that Lone Ranger and Tonto show—except more intimidating.
A horse can smell fear.
Don't be scared. Stick out your hand.
He won't hurt you.
See? You treat a horse with kindness, it'll be nice to you.
You mistreat a horse and you'll raise a mean horse.

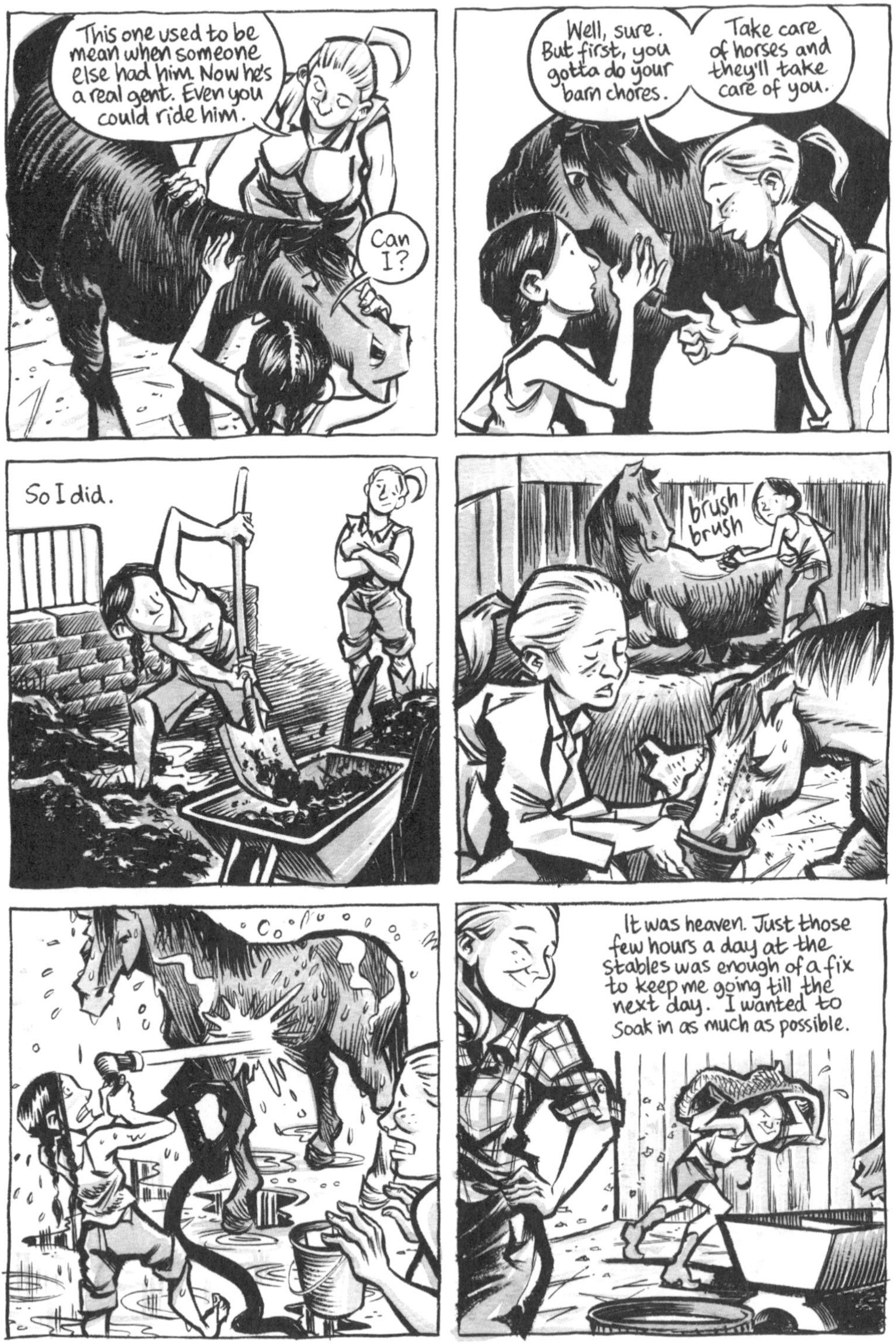
This one used to be mean when someone else had him. Now he's a real gent. Even you could ride him.
Can I?
Well, sure. But first, you gotta do your barn chores.
Take care of horses and they'll take care of you.
So I did.
brush brush
It was heaven. Just those few hours a day at the stables was enough of a fix to keep me going till the next day. I wanted to soak in as much as possible.

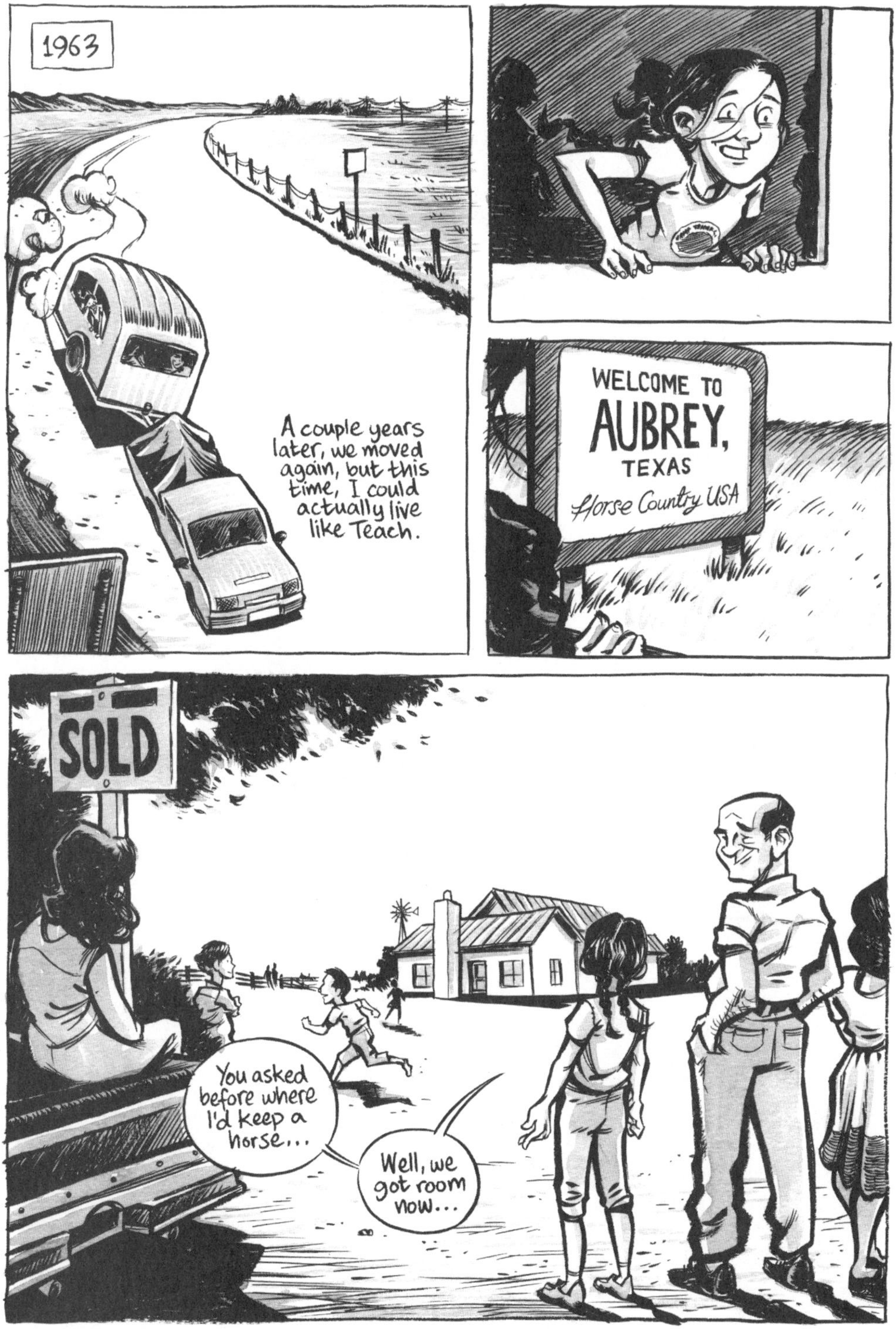
1963
A couple years later, we moved again, but this time, I could actually live like Teach.
WELCOME TO AUBREY, TEXAS
Horse Country USA
SOLD
You asked before where I'd keep a horse...
Well, we got room now...

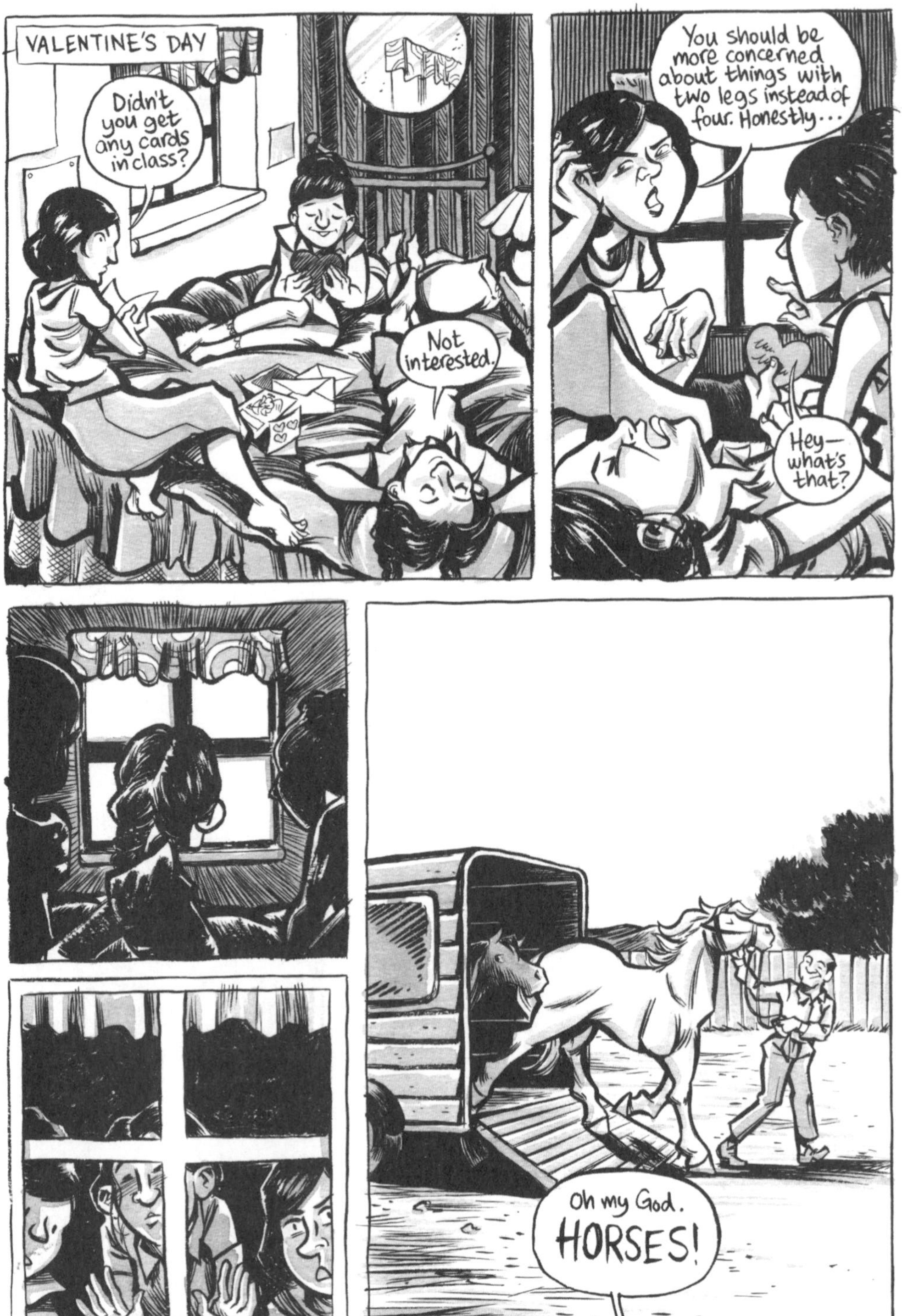
VALENTINE'S DAY
Didn't you get any cards in class?
Not interested.
You should be more concerned about things with two legs instead of four. Honestly...
Hey— what's that?
Oh my God. HORSES!

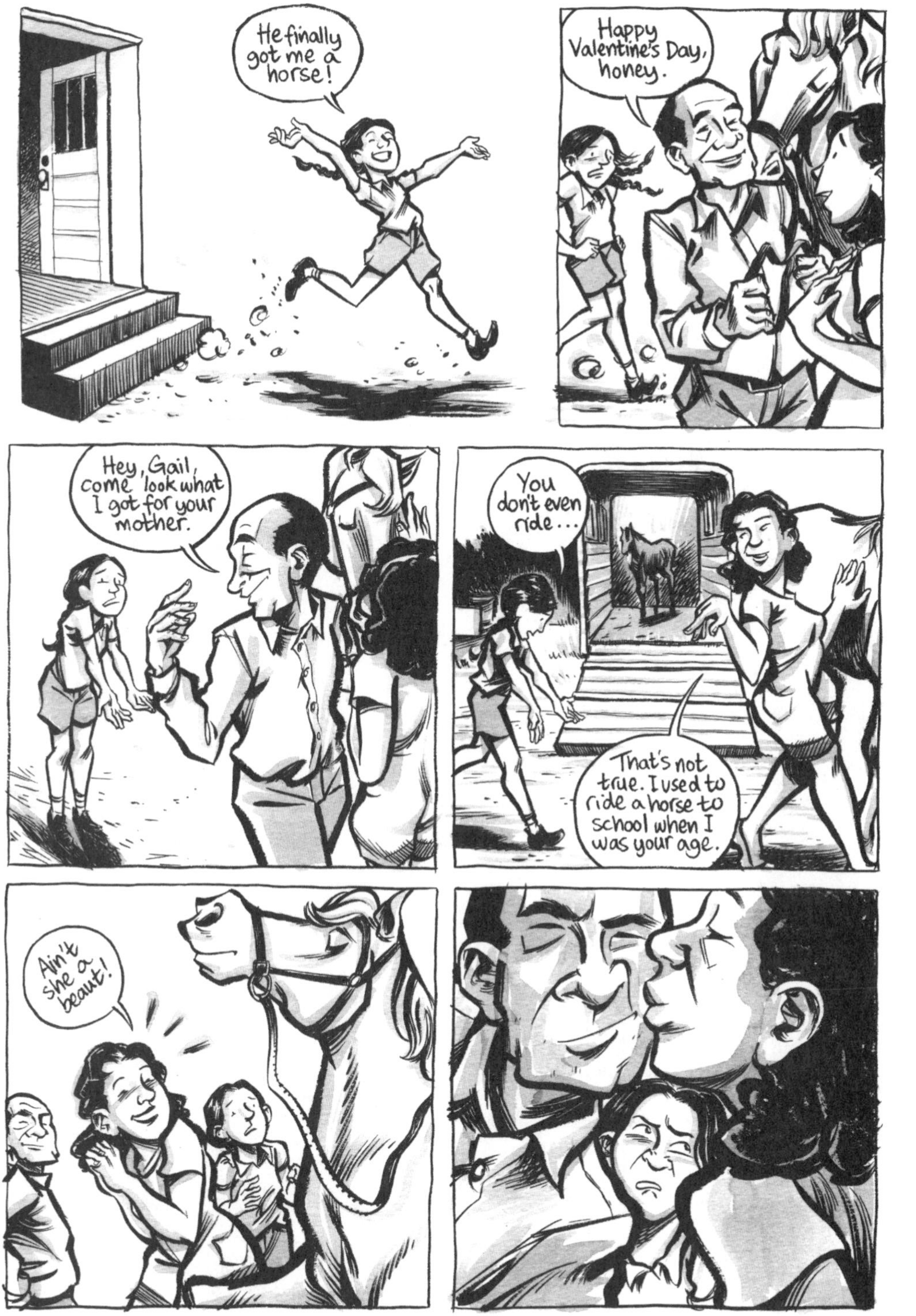
He finally got me a horse!
Happy Valentine's Day, honey.
Hey, Gail, come look what I got for your mother.
You don't even ride...
That's not true. I used to ride a horse to school when I was your age.
Ain't she a beaut!

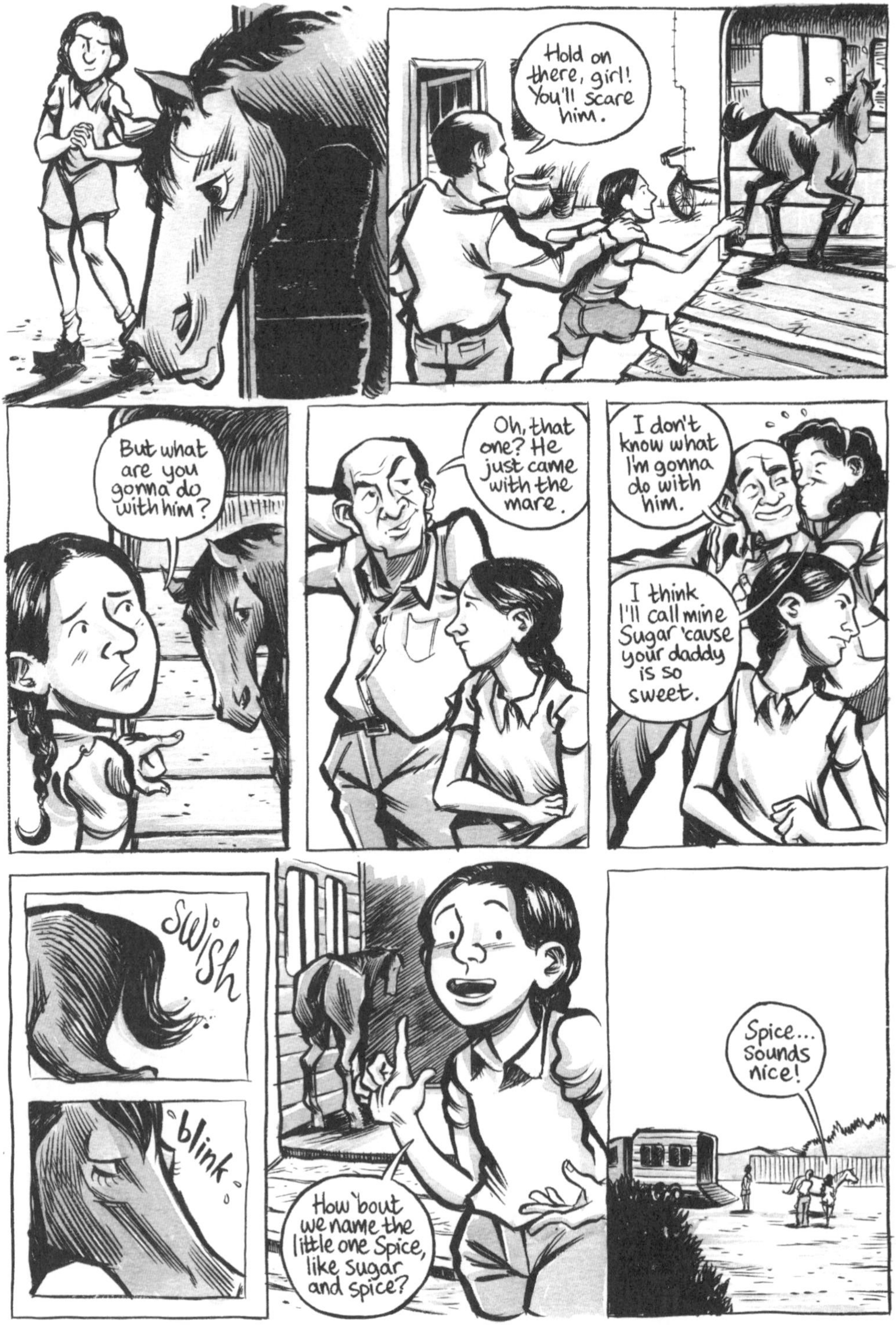
Hold on there, girl! You'll scare him.
But what are you gonna do with him?
Oh, that one? He just came with the mare.
I don't know what I'm gonna do with him.
I think I'll call mine Sugar 'cause your daddy is so sweet.
SWISH
blink
How 'bout we name the little one Spice, like Sugar and Spice?
Spice... sounds nice!

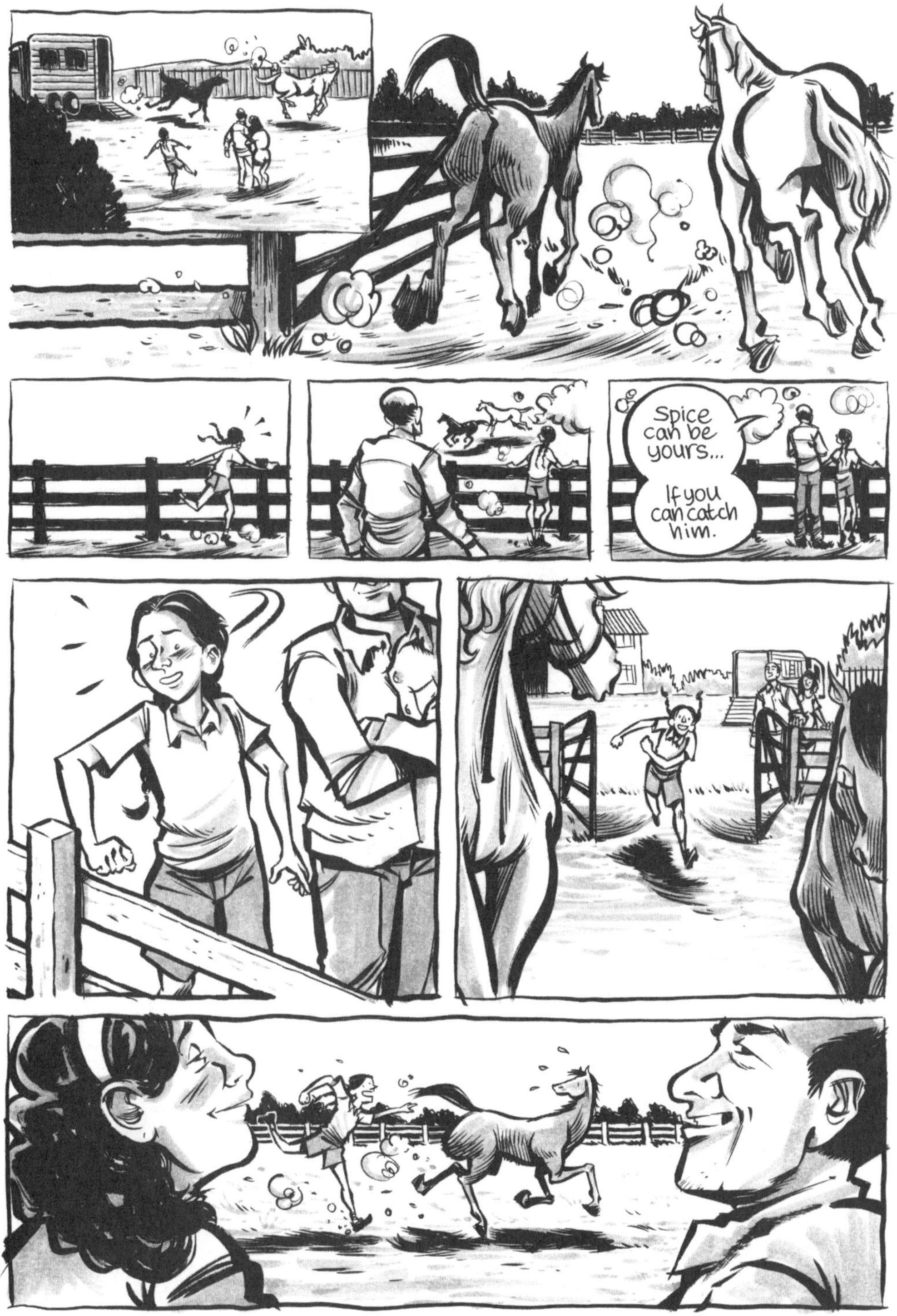
Spice can be yours...
If you can catch him.

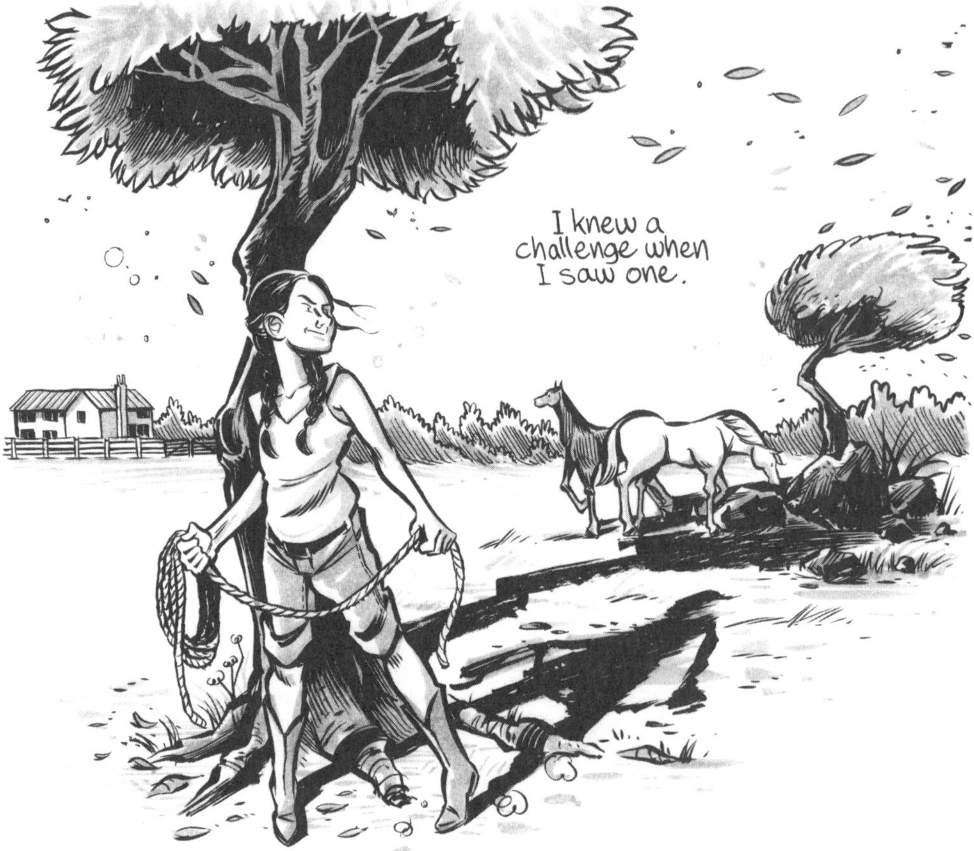
I knew a challenge when I saw one.

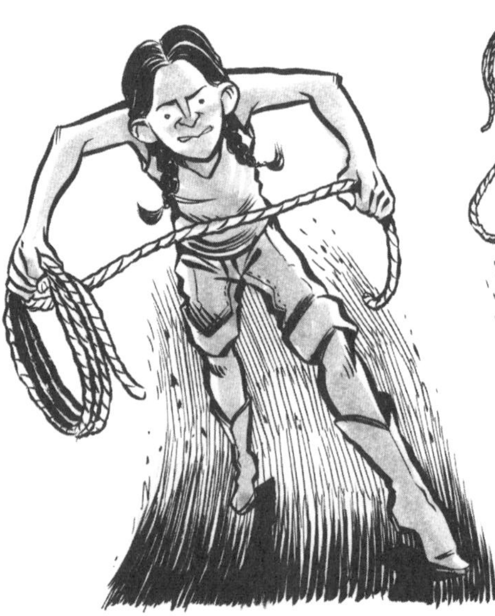

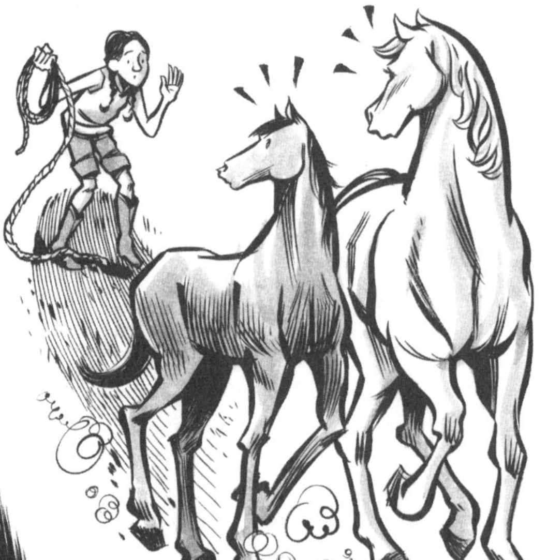

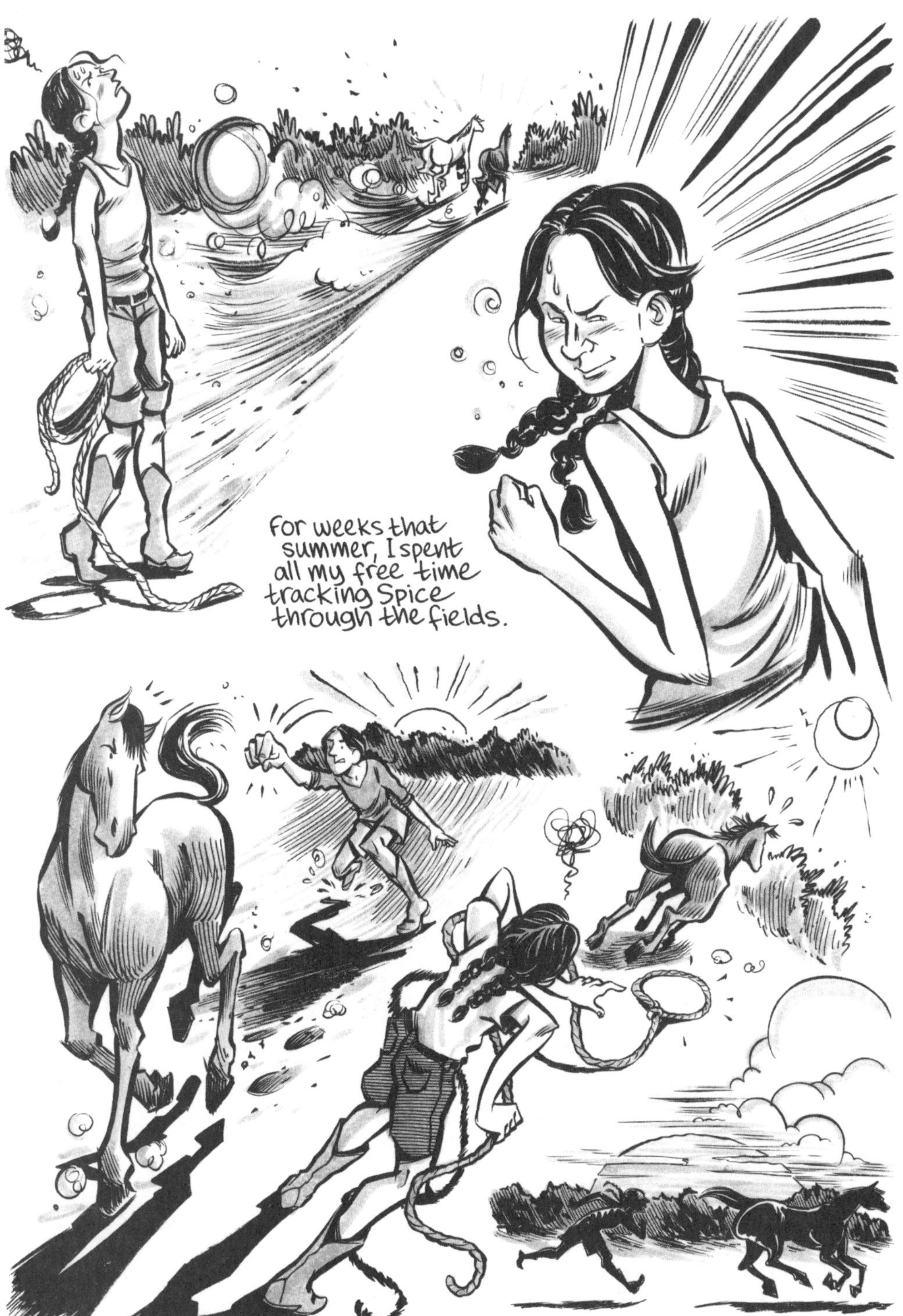
For weeks that summer, I spent all my free time tracking Spice through the fields.

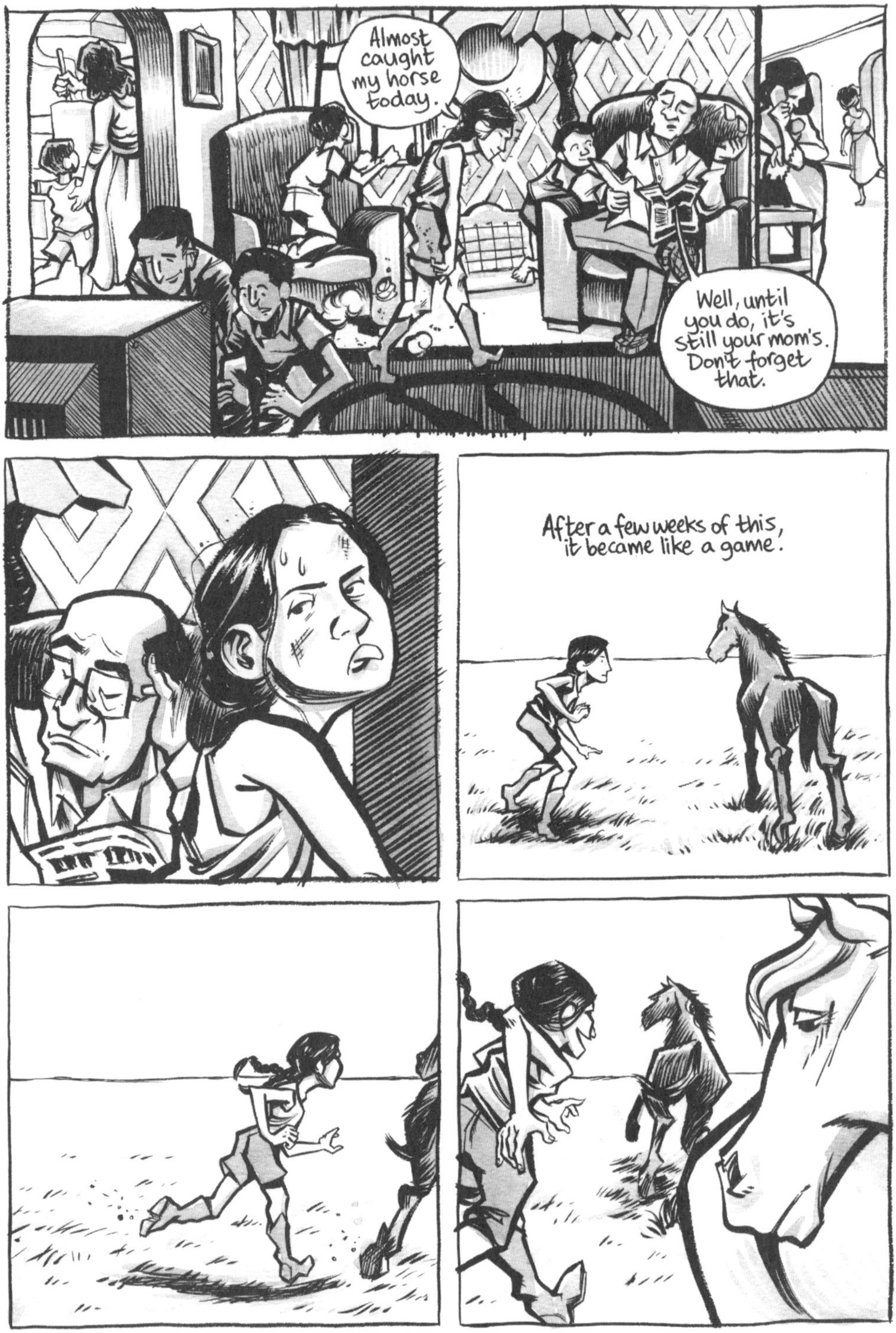
Almost caught my horse today.
Well, until you do, it's still your mom's. Don't forget that.
After a few weeks of this, it became like a game.

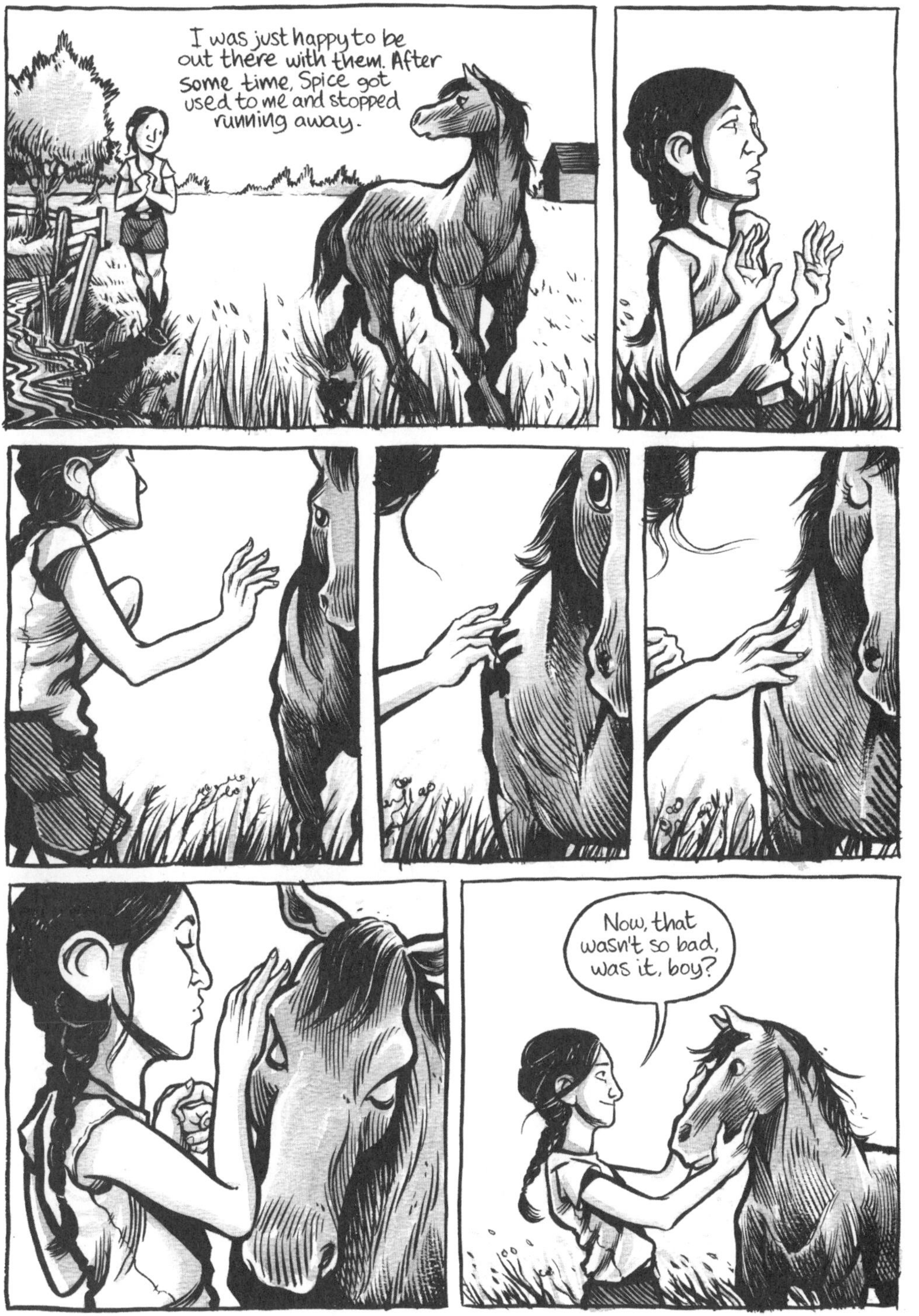
I was just happy to be out there with them. After some time, Spice got used to me and stopped running away.
Now, that wasn't so bad, was it, boy?

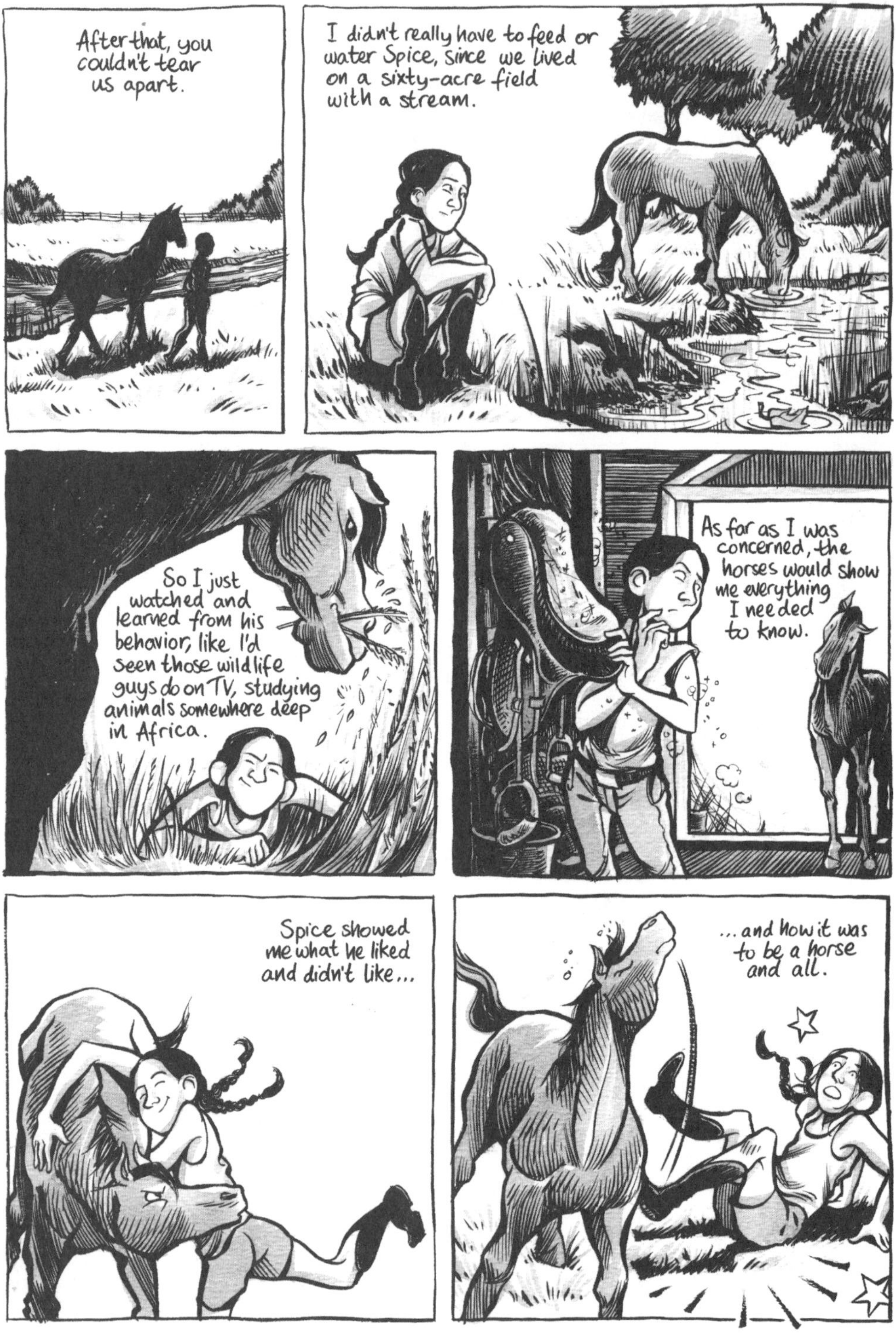
After that, you couldn't tear us apart.
I didn't really have to feed or water Spice, since we lived on a sixty-acre field with a stream.
So I just watched and learned from his behavior, like I'd seen those wildlife guys do on TV, studying animals somewhere deep in Africa.
As far as I was concerned, the horses would show me everything I needed to know.
Spice showed me what he liked and didn't like...
...and how it was to be a horse and all.

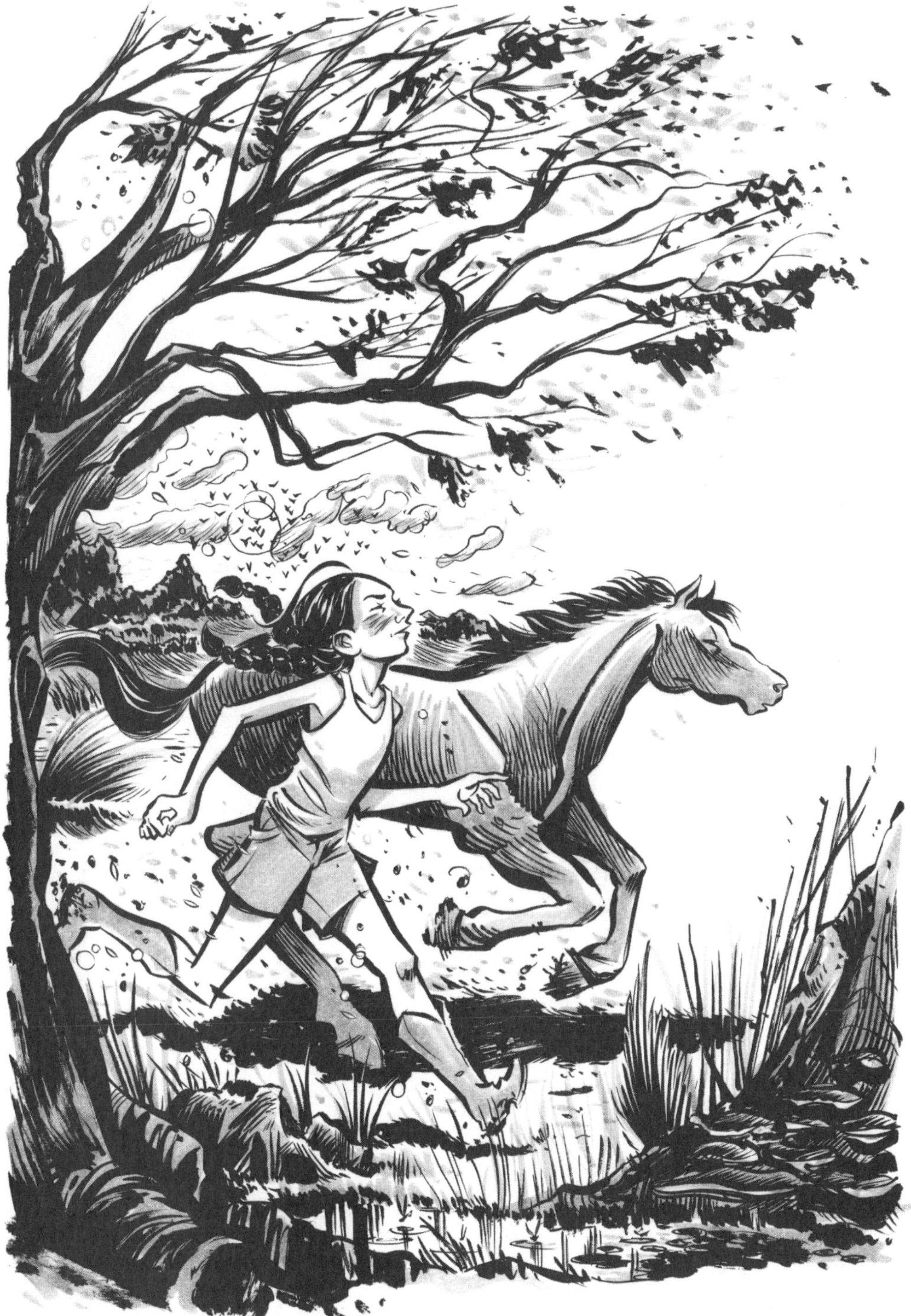

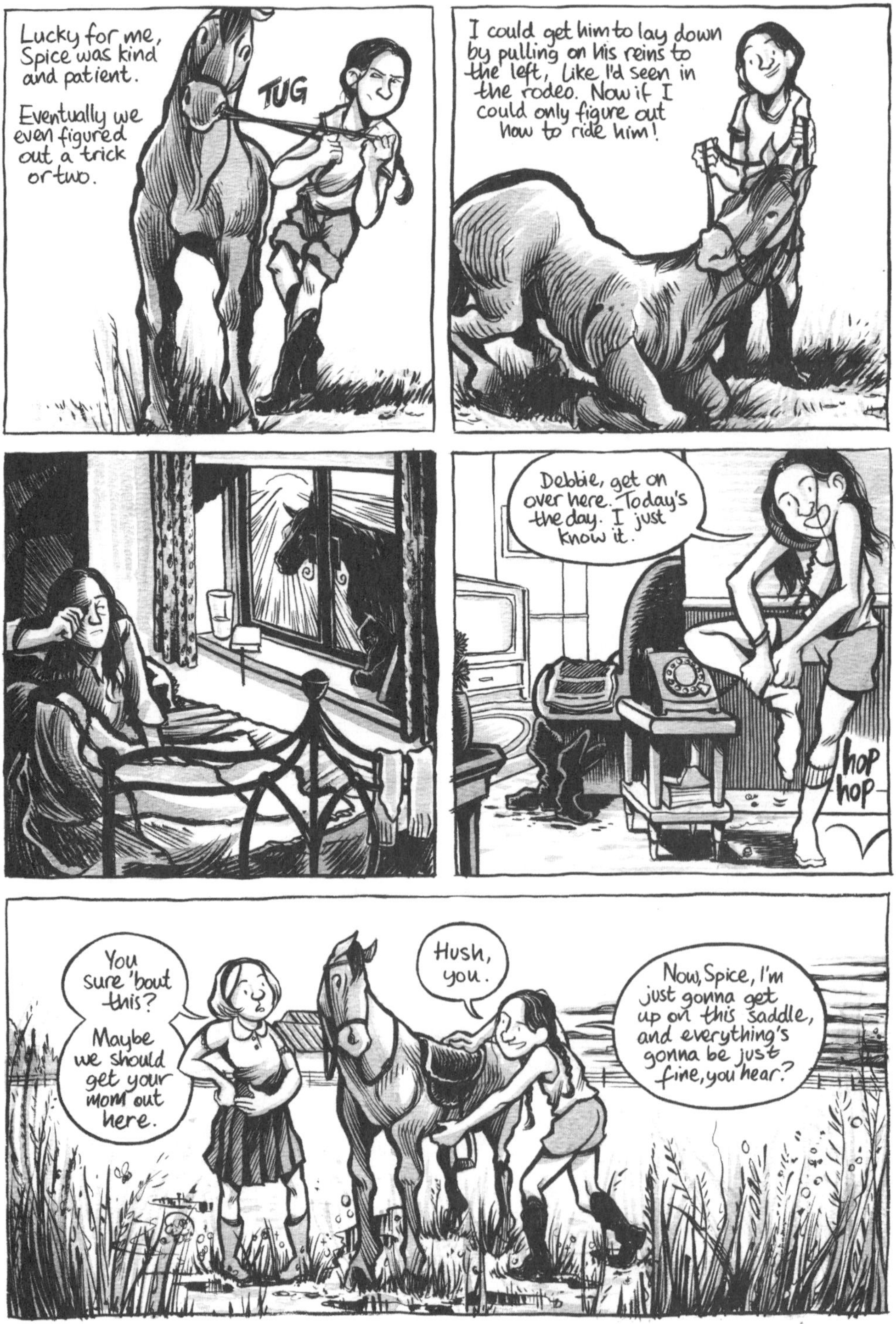
Lucky for me, Spice was kind and patient.
Eventually we even figured out a trick or two.
TUG
I could get him to lay down by pulling on his reins to the left, like I'd seen in the rodeo. Now if I could only figure out how to ride him!
Debbie, get on over here. Today's the day. I just know it.
hop hop
You sure 'bout this?
Maybe we should get your mom out here.
Hush, you.
Now, Spice, I'm just gonna get up on this saddle, and everything's gonna be just fine, you hear?

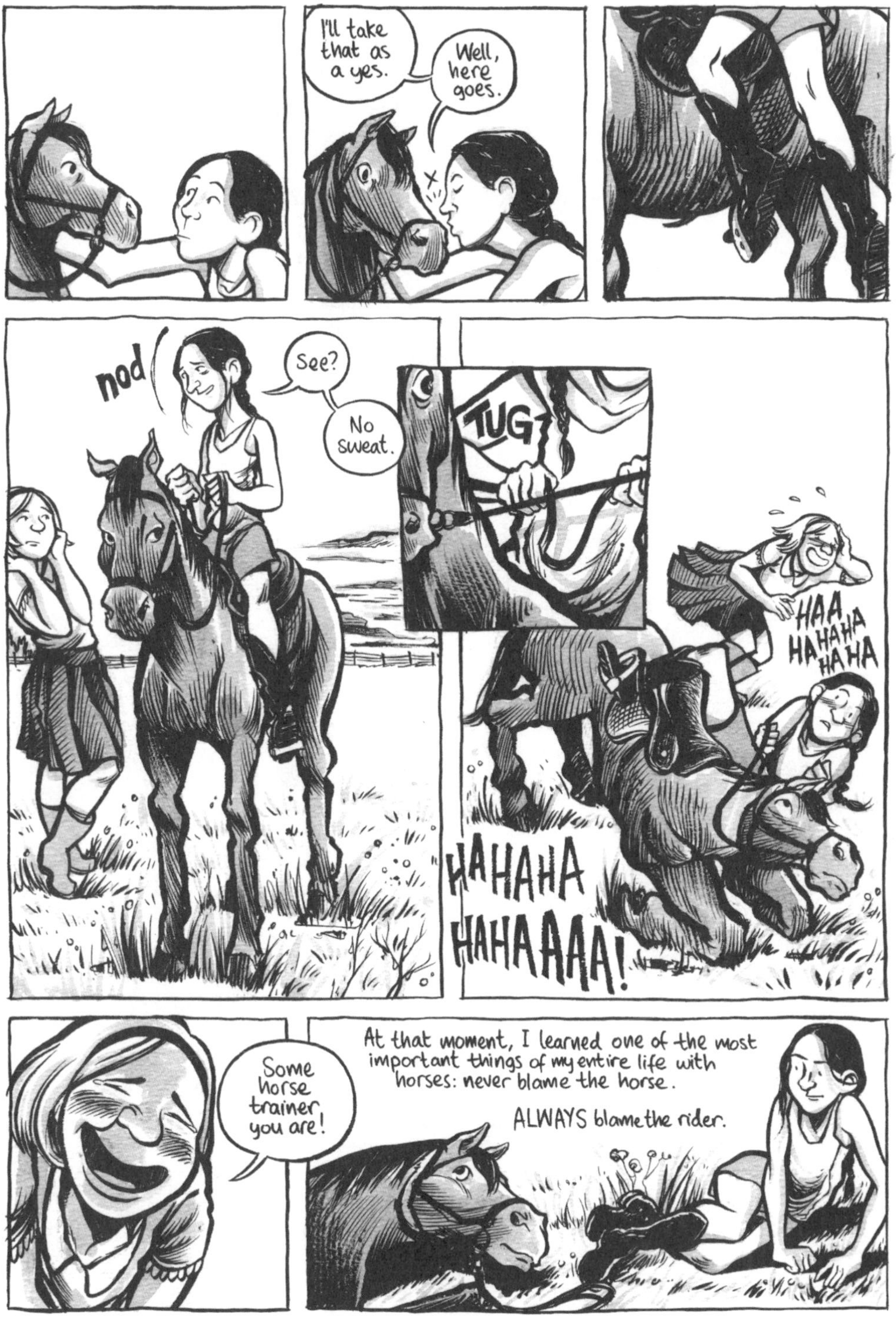
I'll take that as a yes.
Well, here goes.
nod
See?
No sweat.
TUG
HAA HAHAHA HAHA
HAHAHA HAHAAAA!
Some horse trainer you are!
At that moment, I learned one of the most important things of my entire life with horses: never blame the horse.
ALWAYS blame the rider.

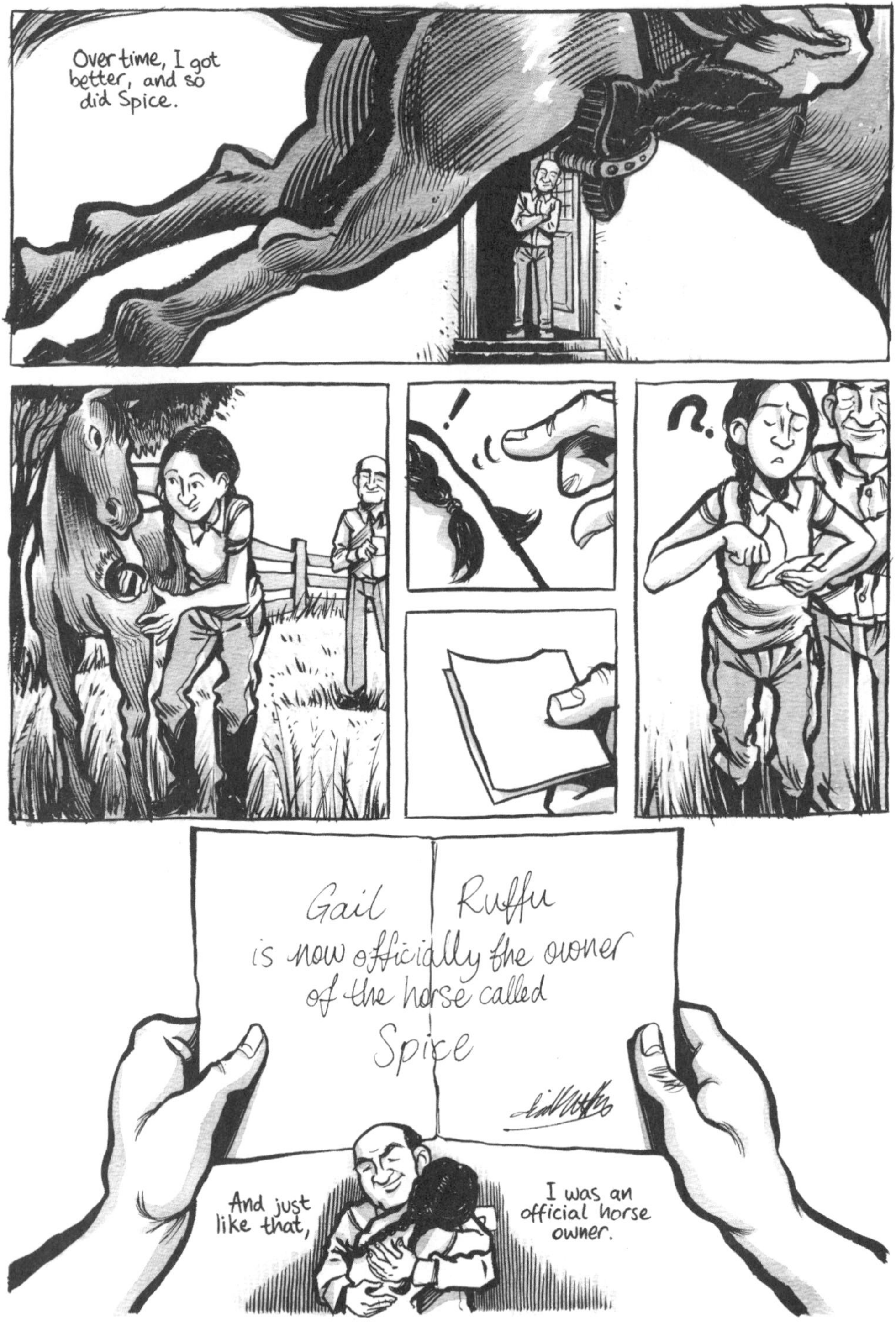
Over time, I got better, and so did Spice.
!
?
Gail Ruffu
is now officially the owner
of the horse called
Spice
And just like that,
I was an official horse owner.

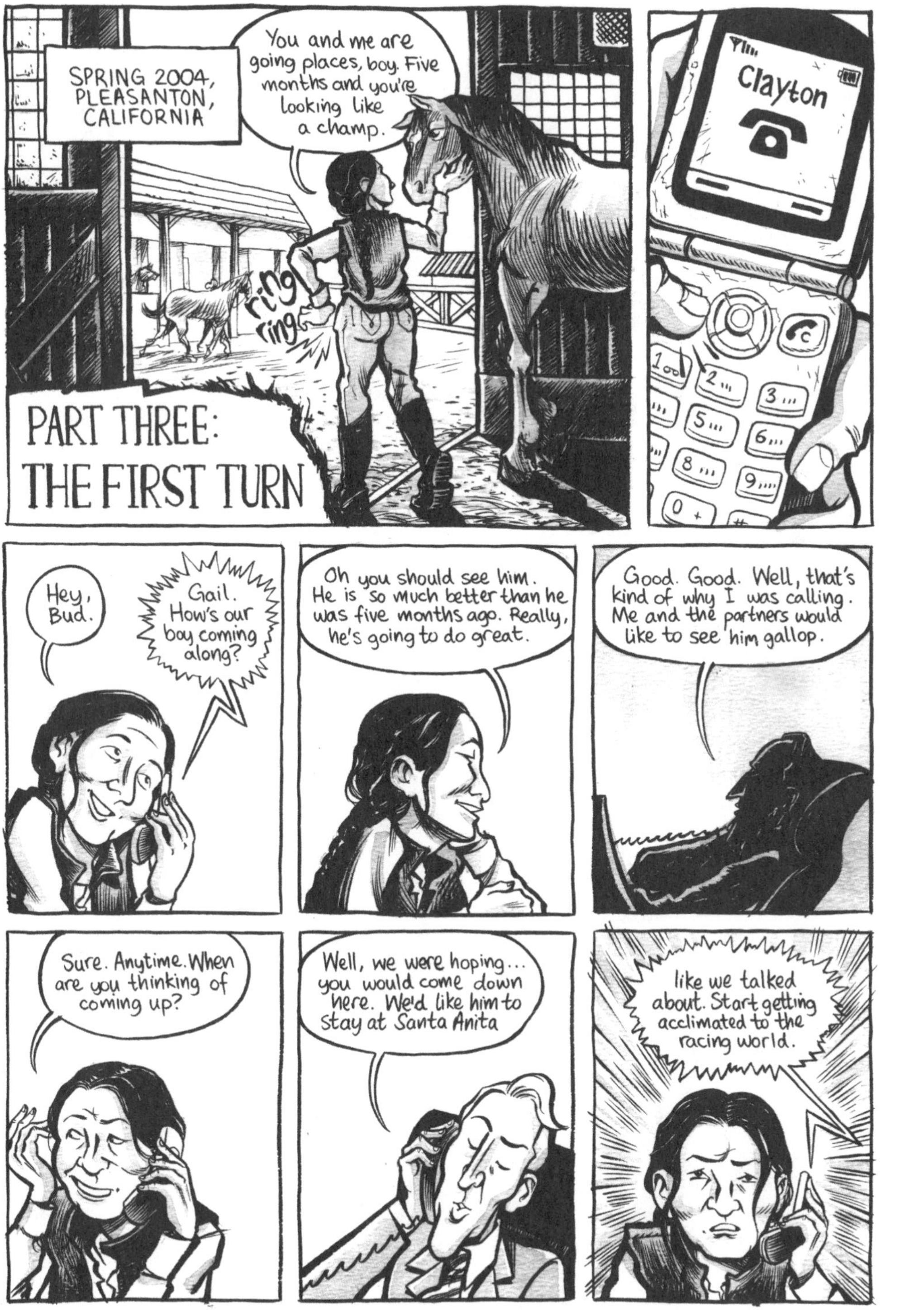
SPRING 2004, PLEASANTON, CALIFORNIA
You and me are going places, boy. Five months and you're looking like a champ.
ring ring ring
PART THREE: THE FIRST TURN
Clayton
Hey, Bud.
Gail. How's our boy coming along?
Oh you should see him. He is so much better than he was five months ago. Really, he's going to do great.
Good. Good. Well, that's kind of why I was calling. Me and the partners would like to see him gallop.
Sure. Anytime. When are you thinking of coming up?
Well, we were hoping... you would come down here. We'd like him to stay at Santa Anita
like we talked about. Start getting acclimated to the racing world.

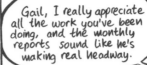

Oh. Um. Well, yeah, we were planning on coming down but not until late summer.

Gail, I really appreciate all the work you've been doing, and the monthly reports sound like he's making real headway.

That's why we're making arrangements for you two down here. We feel he's ready.

I didn't say he was ready. I said he was doing great and he was hitting my monthly projections of where he should be—

And that's great. We just want to see for ourselves. We've been talking to other people, and they say he should come down and start training on this course.

We're thinking he could run in the late spring.

But that's...

too soon.

Yeah. I know we talked about you spending a whole year with him, but really.

Isn't this enough, considering how great he's doing? I mean, that's all we've heard, right?

Right.

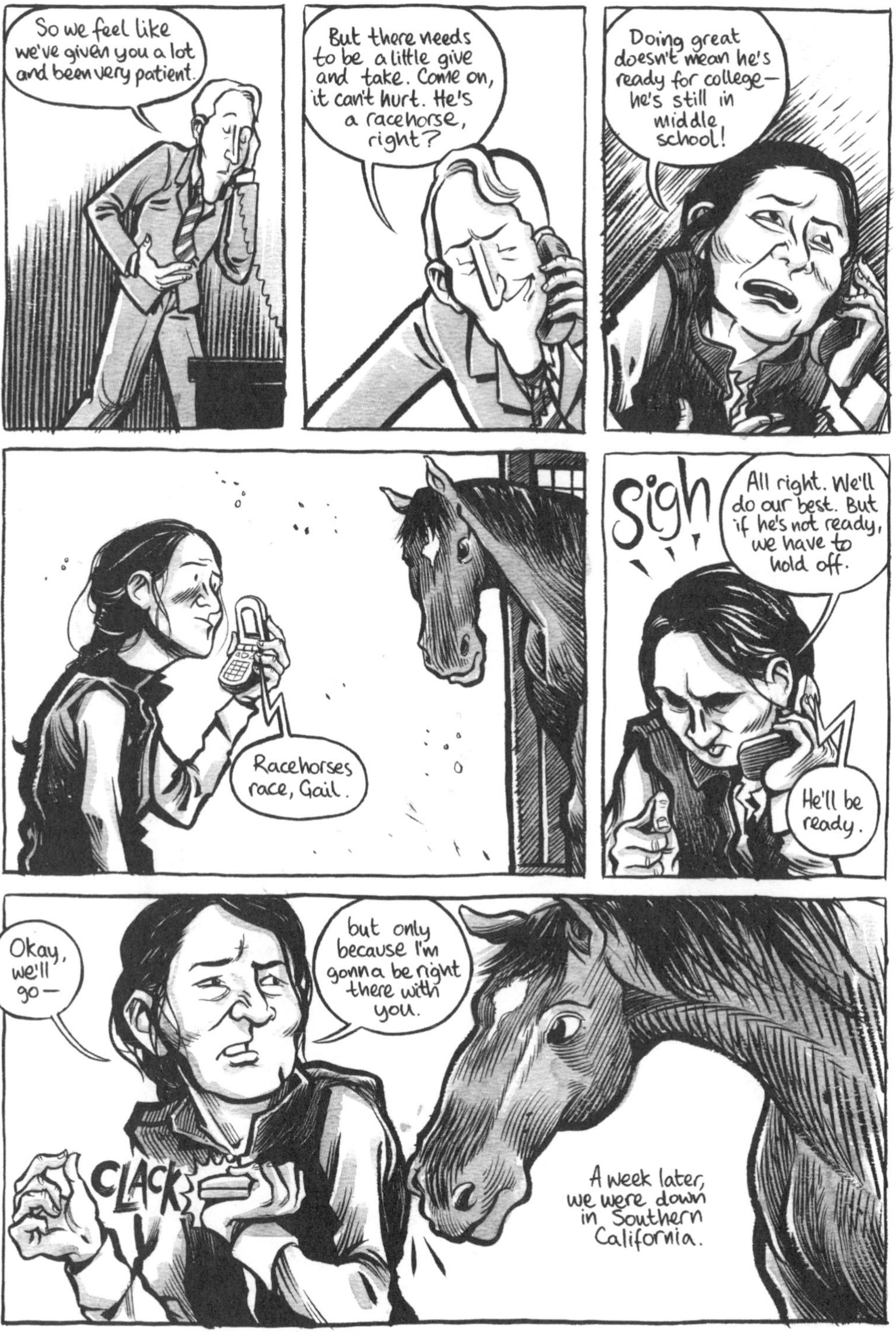
So we feel like we've given you a lot and been very patient.
But there needs to be a little give and take. Come on, it can't hurt. He's a racehorse, right?
Doing great doesn't mean he's ready for college— he's still in middle school!
Racehorses race, Gail.
Sigh
All right. We'll do our best. But if he's not ready, we have to hold off.
He'll be ready.
Okay, we'll go—
but only because I'm gonna be right there with you.
CLACK
A week later, we were down in Southern California.

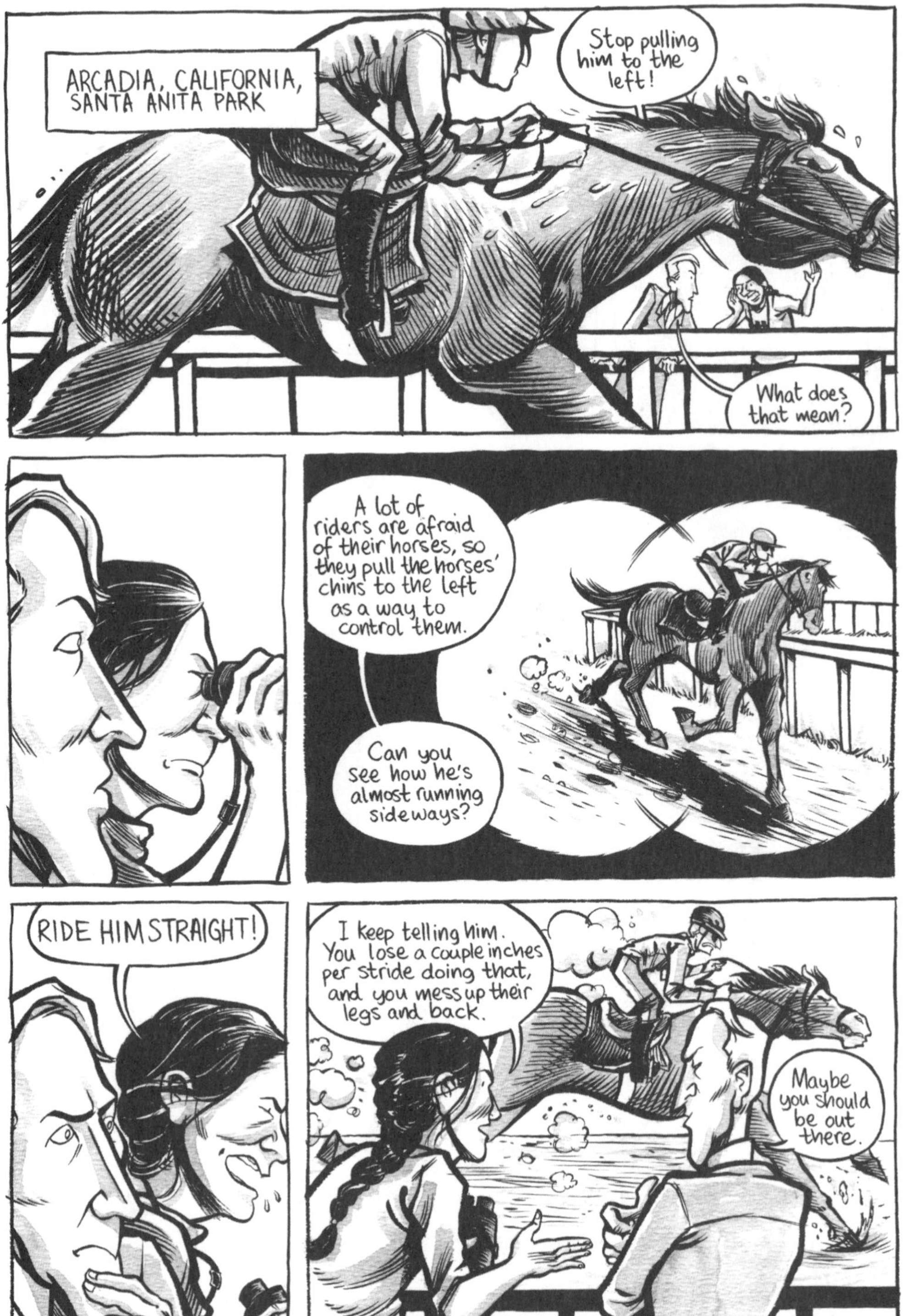
ARCADIA, CALIFORNIA, SANTA ANITA PARK
Stop pulling him to the left!
What does that mean?
A lot of riders are afraid of their horses, so they pull the horses' chins to the left as a way to control them.
Can you see how he's almost running sideways?
RIDE HIM STRAIGHT!
I keep telling him. You lose a couple inches per stride doing that, and you mess up their legs and back.
Maybe you should be out there.

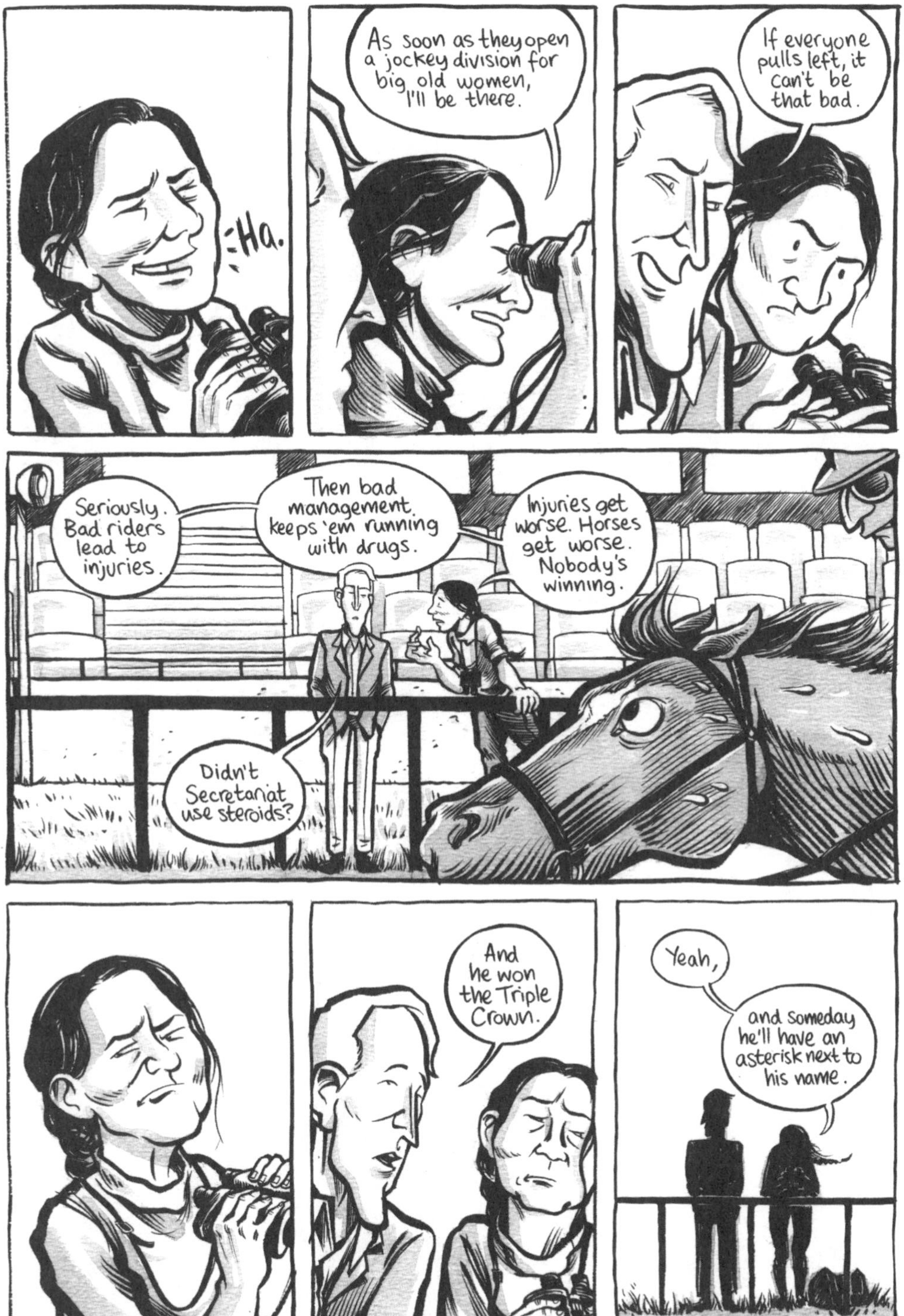
Ha.
As soon as they open a jockey division for big old women, I'll be there.
If everyone pulls left, it can't be that bad.
Seriously. Bad riders lead to injuries.
Then bad management keeps 'em running with drugs.
Injuries get worse. Horses get worse. Nobody's winning.
Didn't Secretariat use steroids?
And he won the Triple Crown.
Yeah,
and someday he'll have an asterisk next to his name.

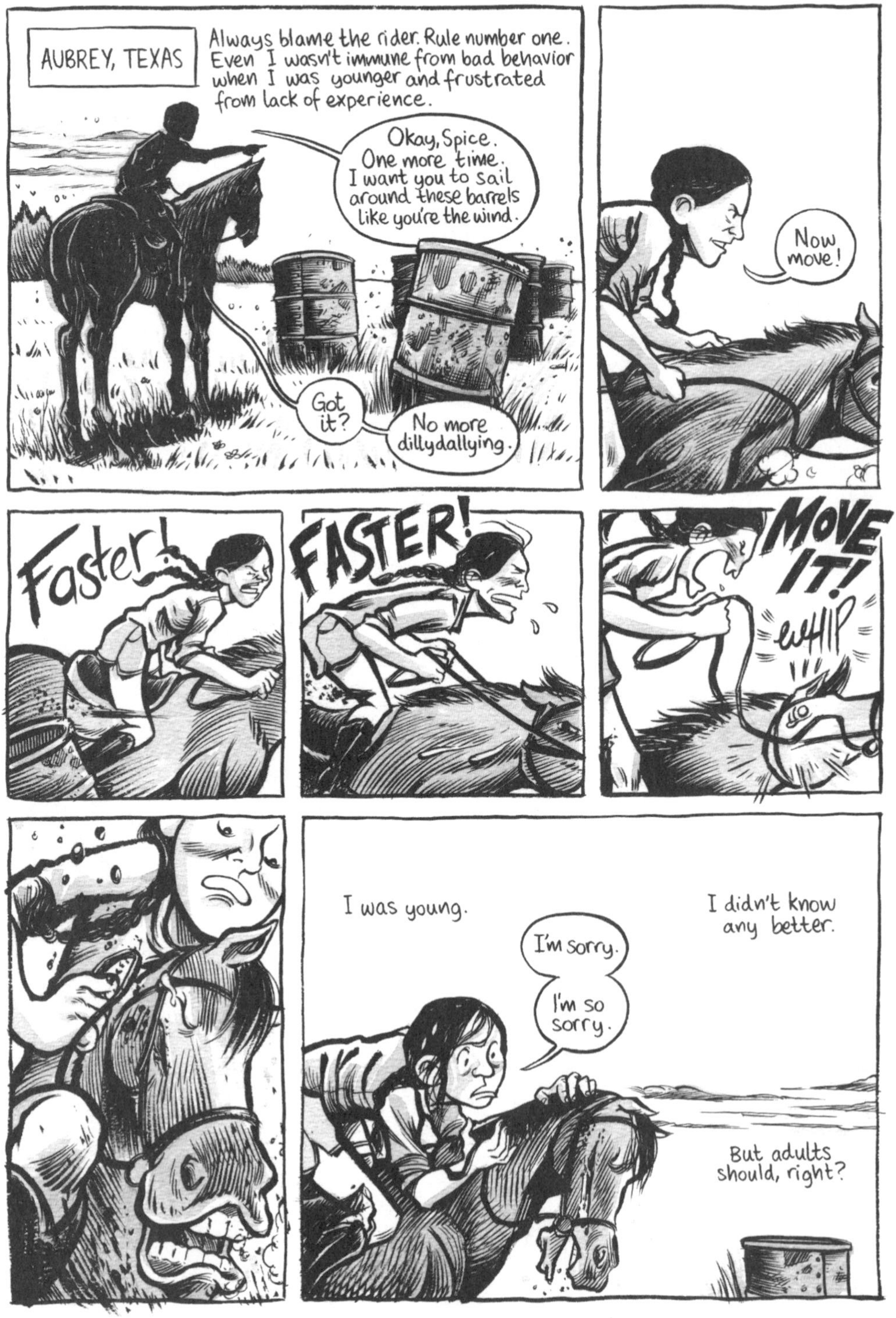
AUBREY, TEXAS
Always blame the rider. Rule number one. Even I wasn't immune from bad behavior when I was younger and frustrated from lack of experience.
Okay, Spice. One more time. I want you to sail around these barrels like you're the wind.
Got it?
No more dillydallying.
Now move!
Faster!
FASTER!
MOVE IT!
WHIP
I was young.
I didn't know any better.
I'm sorry.
I'm so sorry.
But adults should, right?

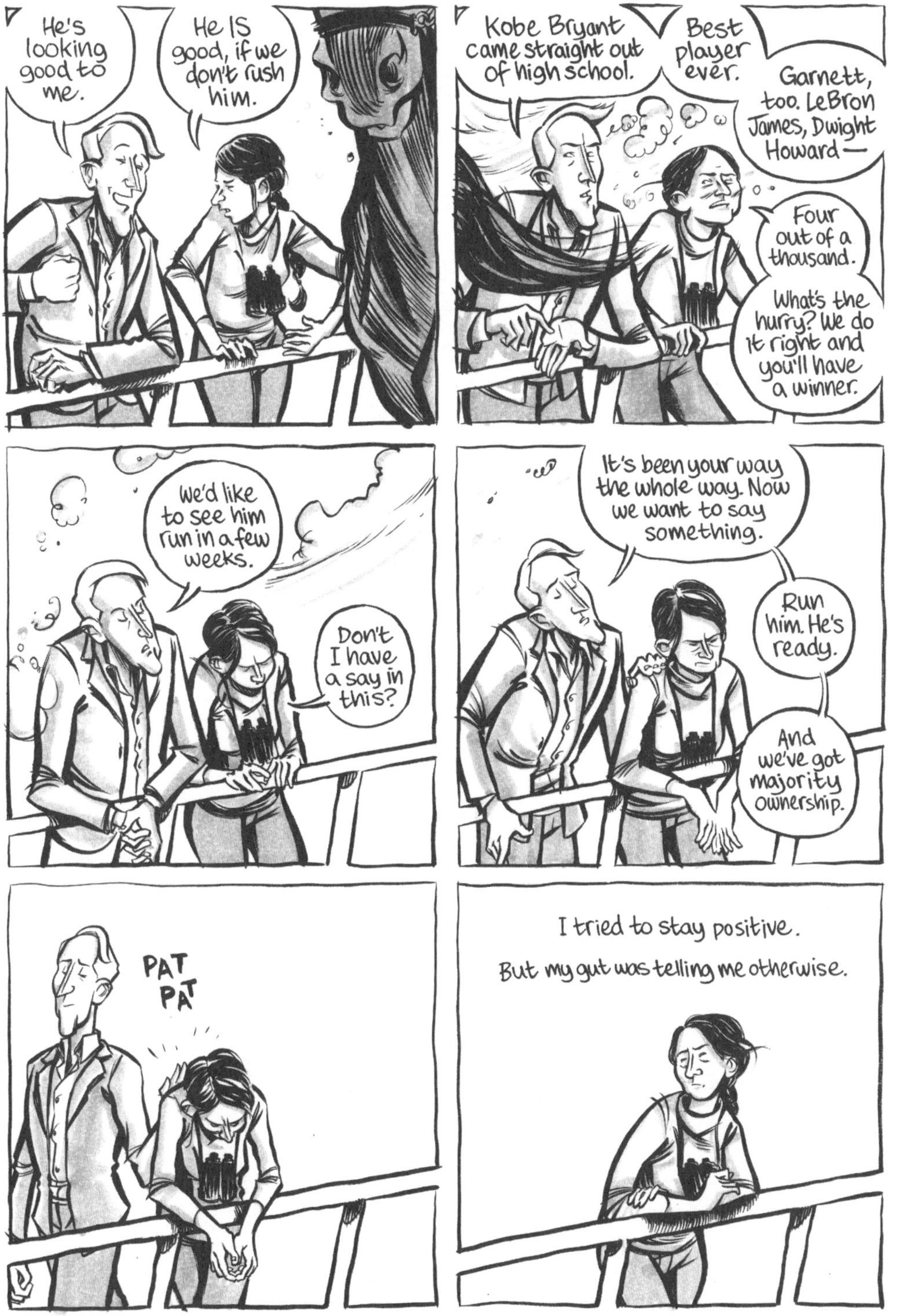
He's looking good to me.
He IS good, if we don't rush him.
Kobe Bryant came straight out of high school.
Best player ever.
Garnett, too. LeBron James, Dwight Howard—
Four out of a thousand.
What's the hurry? We do it right and you'll have a winner.
We'd like to see him run in a few weeks.
Don't I have a say in this?
It's been your way the whole way. Now we want to say something.
Run him. He's ready.
And we've got majority ownership.
PAT PAT
I tried to stay positive.
But my gut was telling me otherwise.

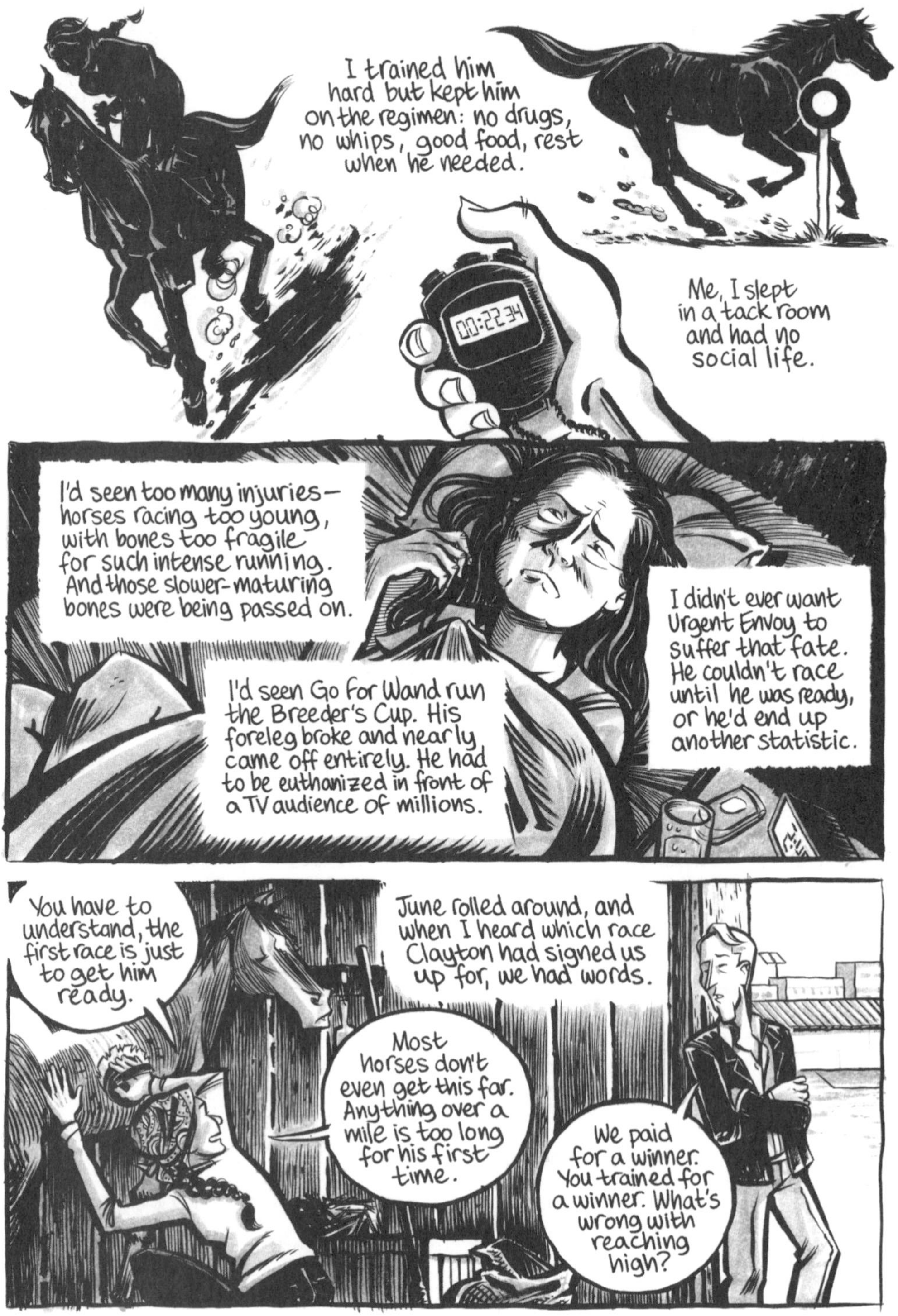

I trained him hard but kept him on the regimen: no drugs, no whips, good food, rest when he needed.
00:22.34
Me, I slept in a tack room and had no social life.
I'd seen too many injuries— horses racing too young, with bones too fragile for such intense running. And those slower-maturing bones were being passed on.
I'd seen Go for Wand run the Breeder's Cup. His foreleg broke and nearly came off entirely. He had to be euthanized in front of a TV audience of millions.
I didn't ever want Urgent Envoy to suffer that fate. He couldn't race until he was ready, or he'd end up another statistic.
June rolled around, and when I heard which race Clayton had signed us up for, we had words.
You have to understand, the first race is just to get him ready.
Most horses don't even get this far. Anything over a mile is too long for his first time.
We paid for a winner. You trained for a winner. What's wrong with reaching high?

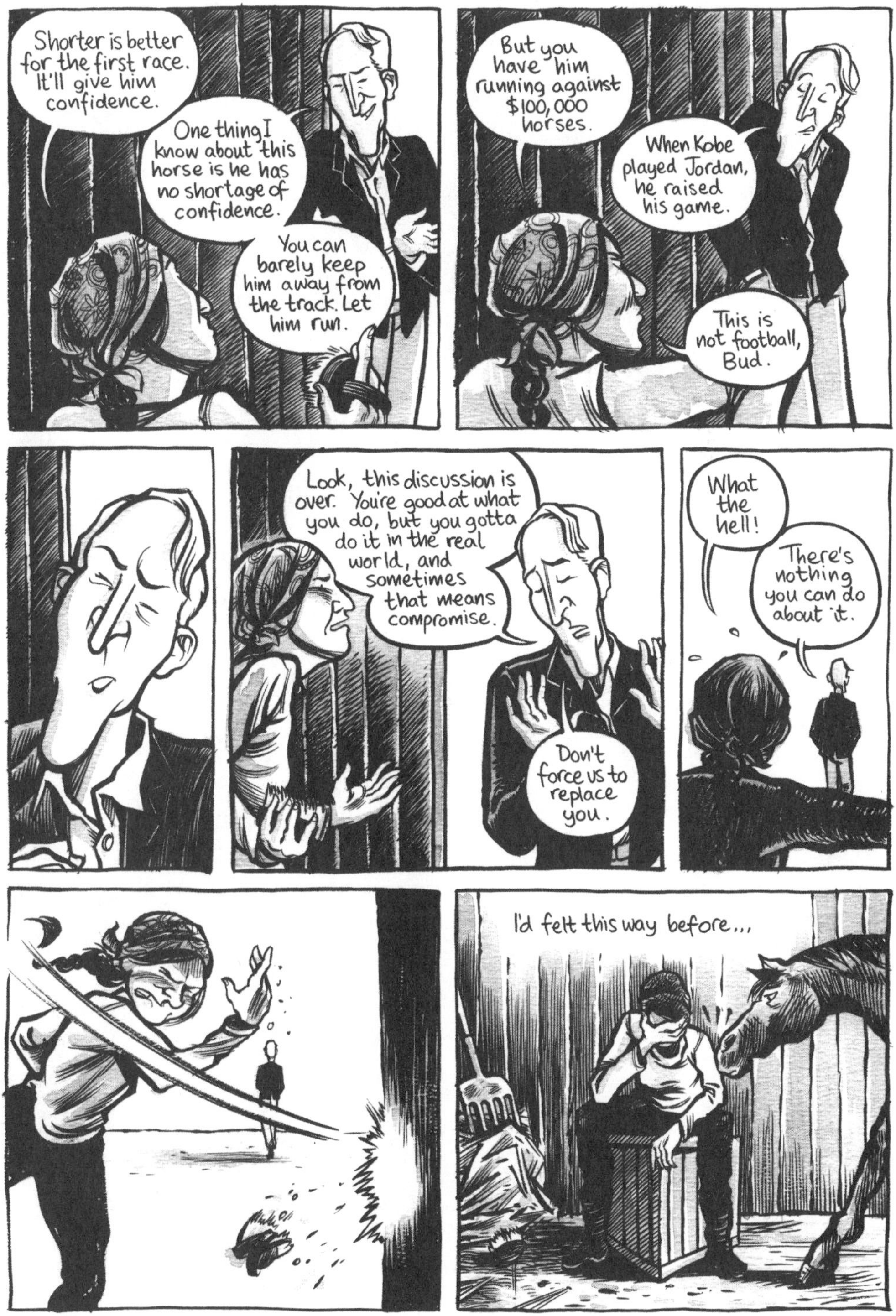
Shorter is better for the first race. It'll give him confidence.
One thing I know about this horse is he has no shortage of confidence.
You can barely keep him away from the track. Let him run.
But you have him running against $100,000 horses.
When Kobe played Jordan, he raised his game.
This is not football, Bud.
Look, this discussion is over. You're good at what you do, but you gotta do it in the real world, and sometimes that means compromise.
Don't force us to replace you.
What the hell!
There's nothing you can do about it.
I'd felt this way before...

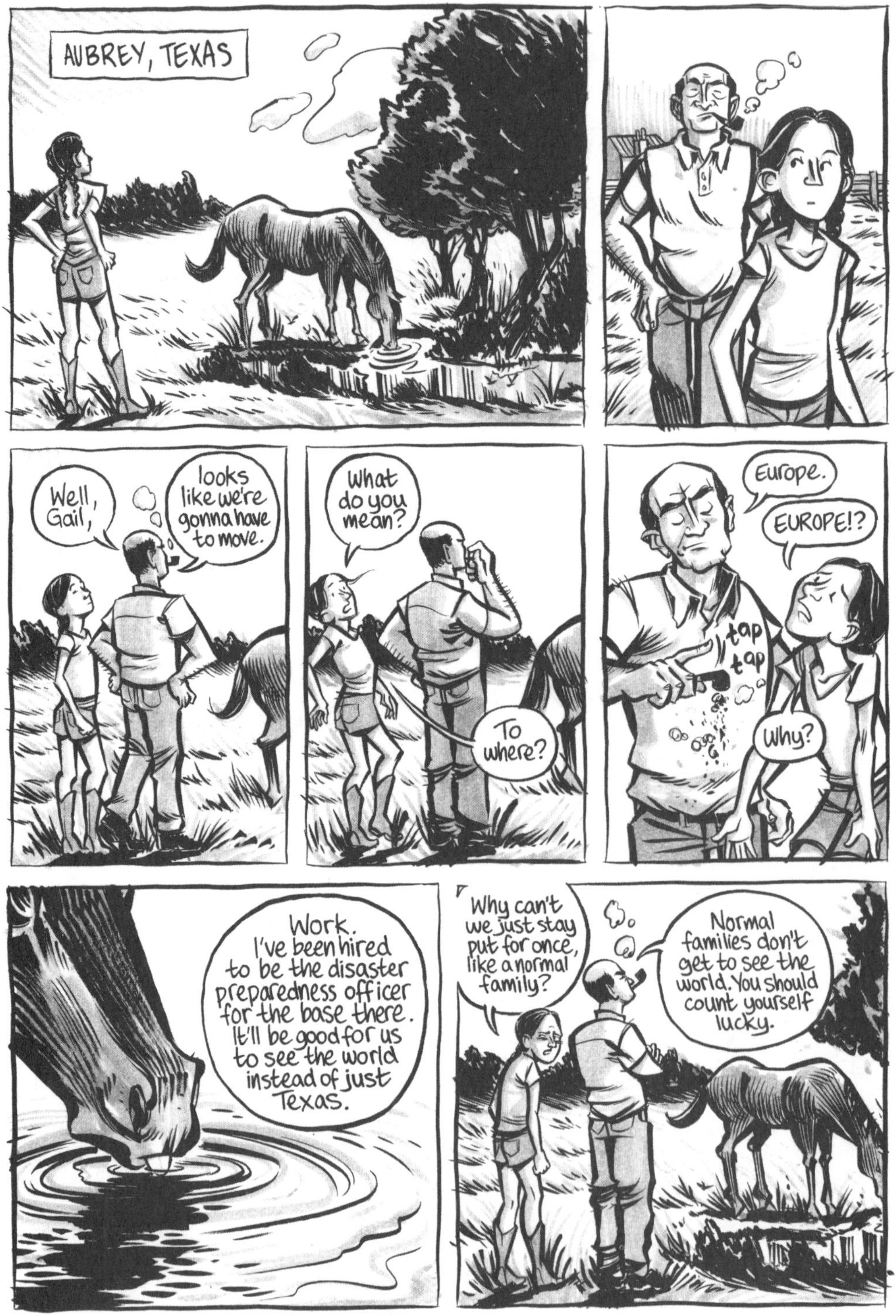
AUBREY, TEXAS
Well, Gail,
looks like we're gonna have to move.
What do you mean?
To where?
Europe.
EUROPE!?
tap tap
Why?
Work. I've been hired to be the disaster preparedness officer for the base there. It'll be good for us to see the world instead of just Texas.
Why can't we just stay put for once, like a normal family?
Normal families don't get to see the world. You should count yourself lucky.

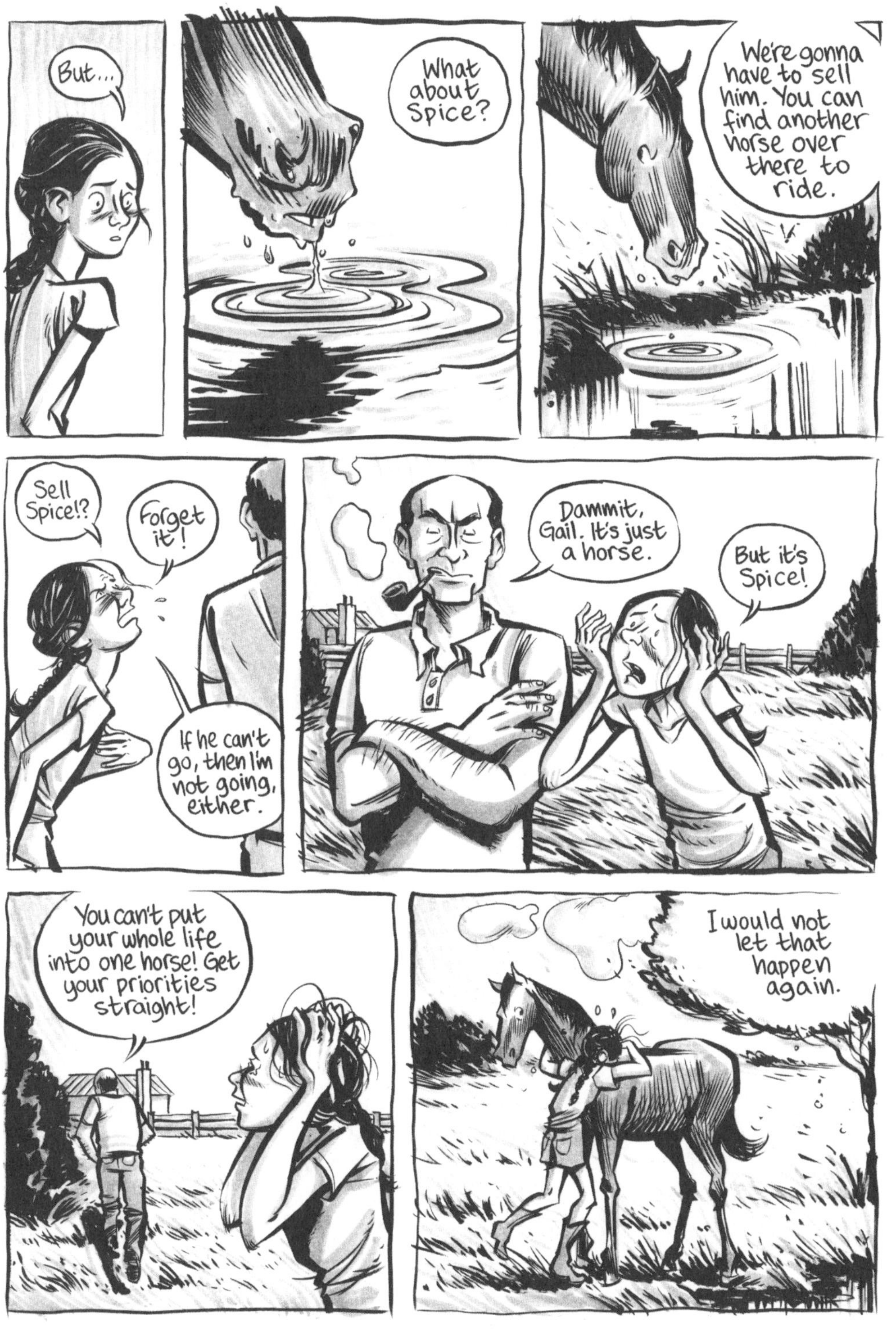

But...
What about Spice?
We're gonna have to sell him. You can find another horse over there to ride.
Sell Spice!?
Forget it!
If he can't go, then I'm not going, either.
Dammit, Gail. It's just a horse.
But it's Spice!
You can't put your whole life into one horse! Get your priorities straight!
I would not let that happen again.

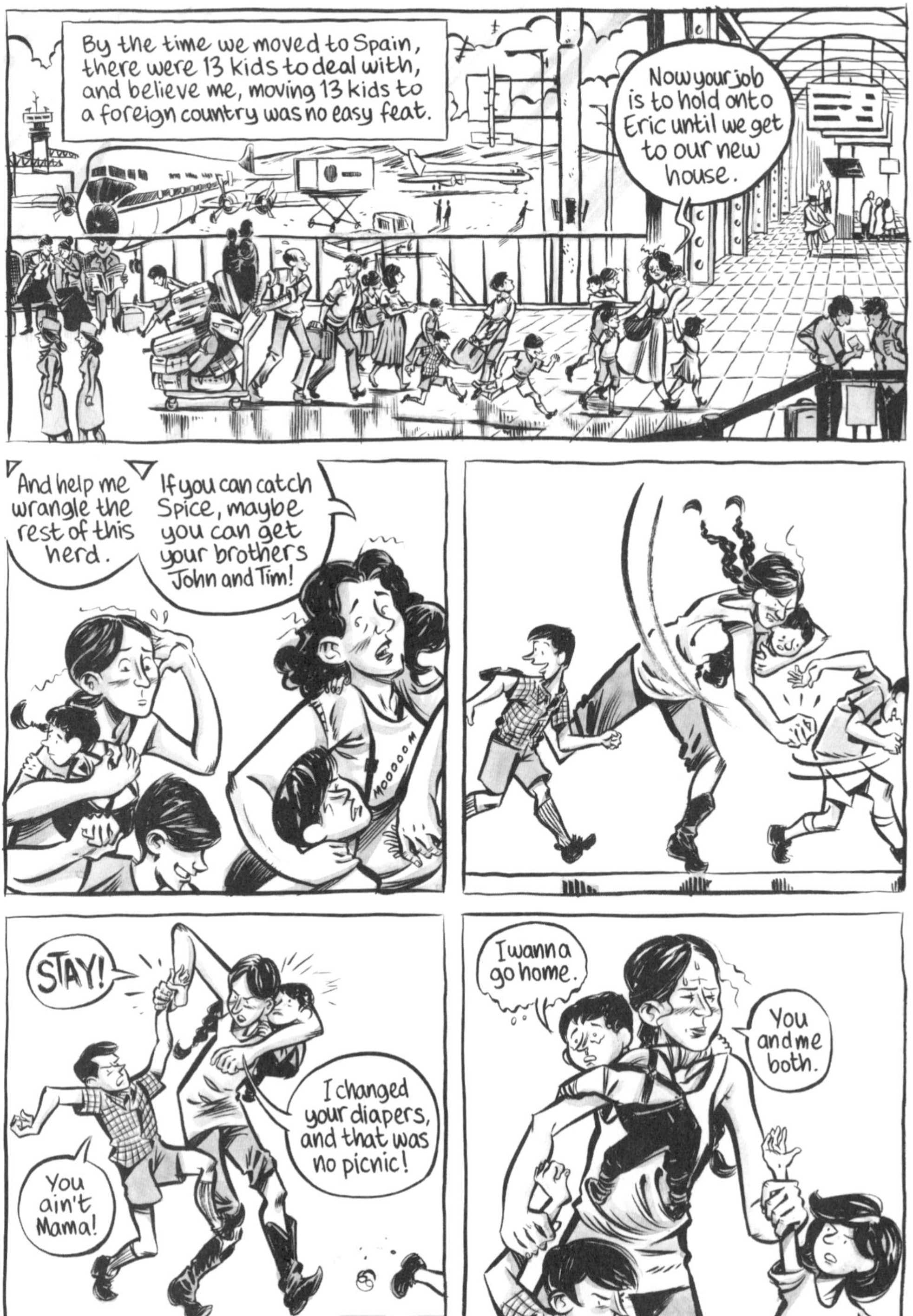

By the time we moved to Spain, there were 13 kids to deal with, and believe me, moving 13 kids to a foreign country was no easy feat.
Now your job is to hold onto Eric until we get to our new house.
And help me wrangle the rest of this herd.
If you can catch Spice, maybe you can get your brothers John and Tim!
MOOOOOM
STAY!
I changed your diapers, and that was no picnic!
You ain't Mama!
I wanna go home.
You and me both.

LONDON, ENGLAND — 1967

CARNABY STREET WELCOMES THE WORLD

I spent my teen years living in Spain, then Germany, and in the summers I would escape on my own to England.

Things were happening there. The world was changing. Music and art were changing.

STREET RECORDS

BEATLES

JOIN THE PROTEST STOP THE WAR

NO NUKES

GET STERE IN YOUR CAR

JIMI HENDRIX EXPERIENCE

LIVE AT THE ASTOR

It seemed every teen was rebelling. Peace and free love were in; the old ways I'd grown up with were out.

Me? I was headed another direction. If I was gonna do my own thing, I had to know what I was doing. So I started learning dressage and stable management.

ACADEMY OF DRESSAGE

I'll admit, exchanging my cowboy boots and jeans for jodhpurs and proper riding boots was not easy.

Ugh.

They said I had natural ability as a rider. No fear, good balance, a connection to horses.

But—

What you need are the fundamentals.

If Western riding was like country line dancing, then English riding was classical ballet. It was Shakespeare. Dressage was the foundation to everything horses. In fact, dressage basically means "training" or "schooling."

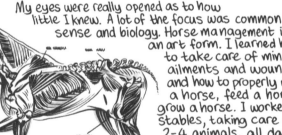

My eyes were really opened as to how little I knew. A lot of the focus was common sense and biology. Horse management is an art form. I learned how to take care of minor ailments and wounds, and how to properly ride a horse, feed a horse, grow a horse. I worked in stables, taking care of 2-4 animals, all day, every day.

See, a horse is made of 6 basic elements: heart, lungs, muscles, tendons, ligaments, and bones. Bones take the longest to train. If horses race too fast before their bones are ready to support their weight under duress, then bones break.

I realized how different things were in Europe compared to the US. And when I got my British assistant instructor degree, I wanted to take that knowledge back to the States.

But then, I got sidetracked...

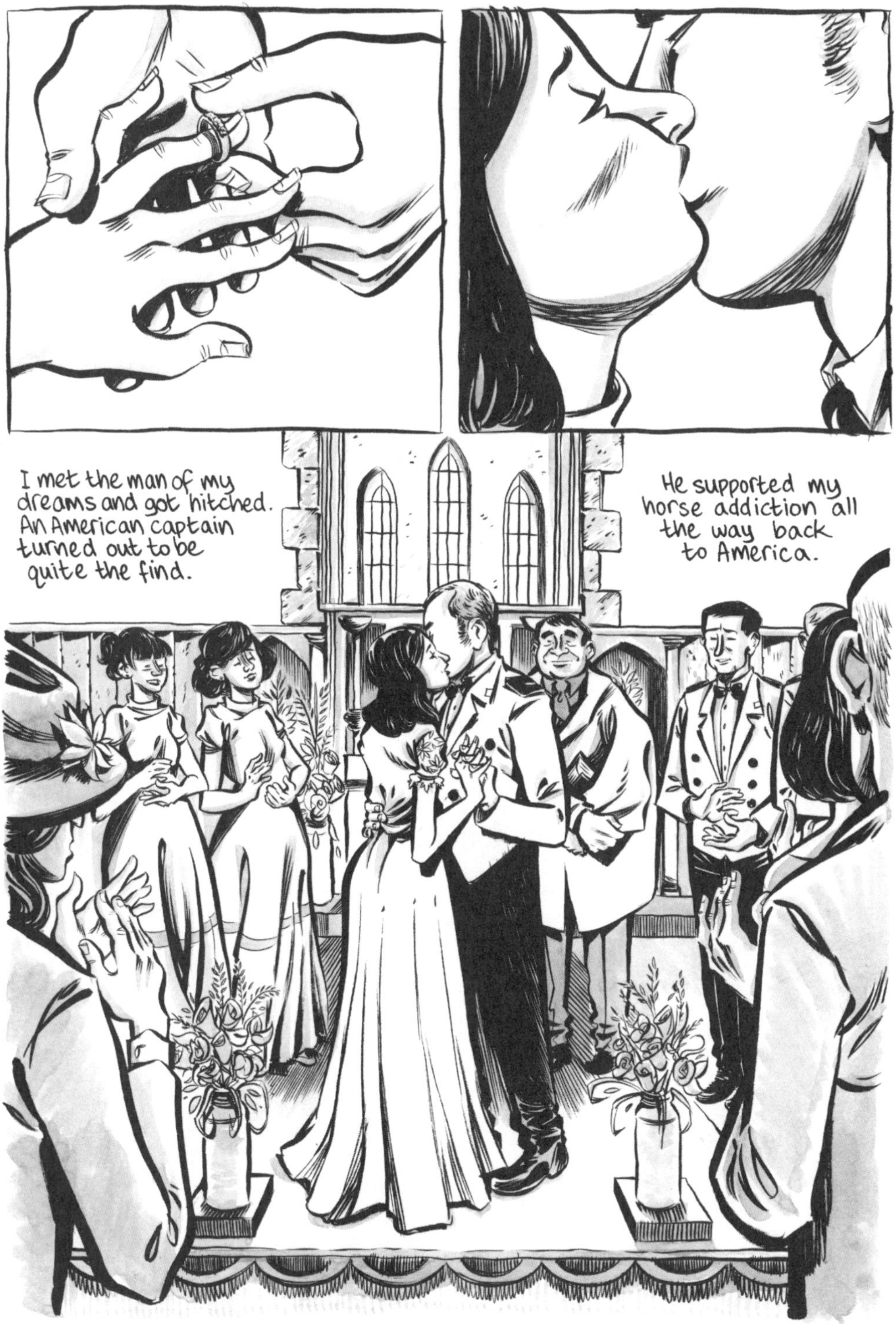
I met the man of my dreams and got hitched. An American captain turned out to be quite the find.
He supported my horse addiction all the way back to America.

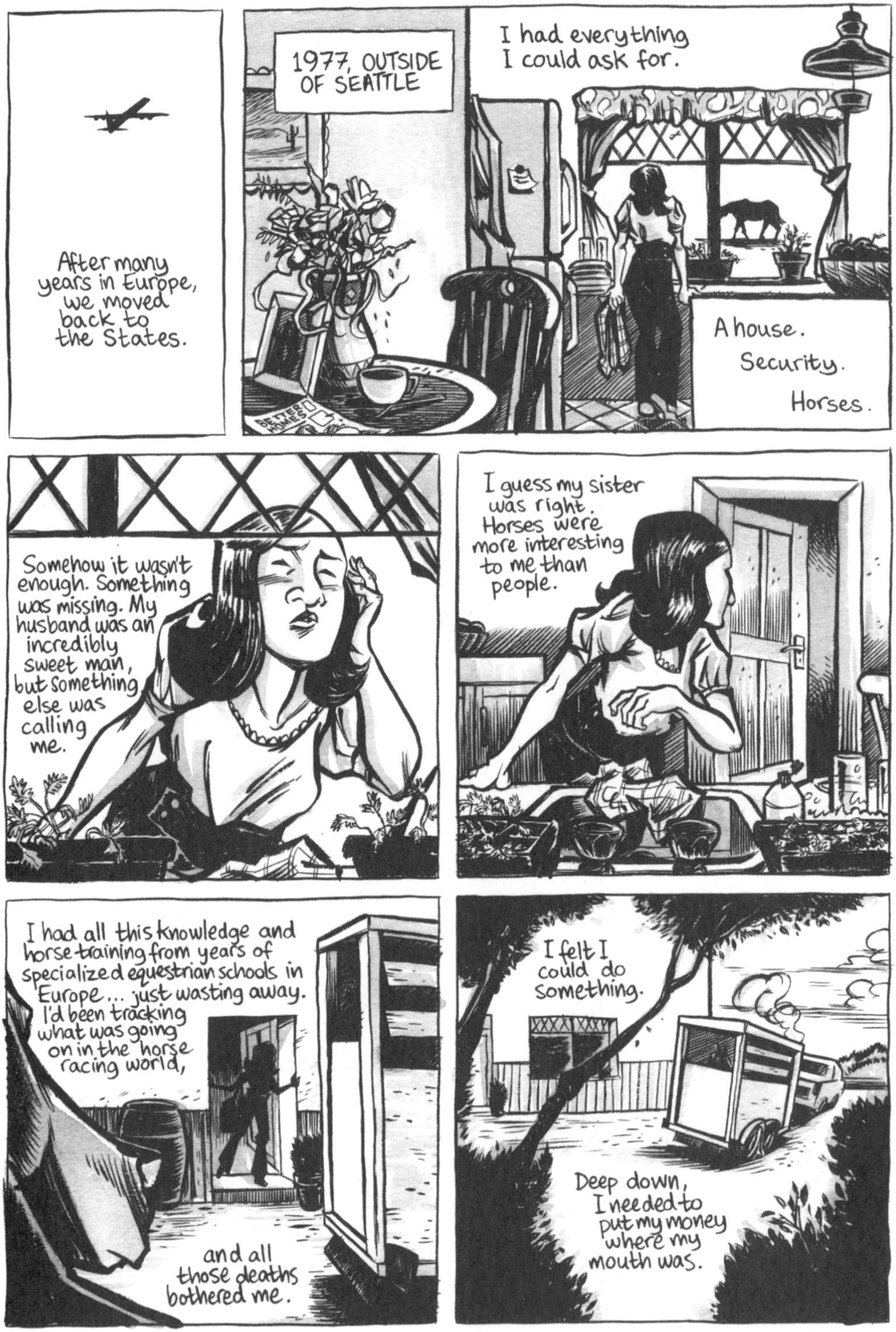
After many years in Europe, we moved back to the States.
1977, OUTSIDE OF SEATTLE
BETTER HOMES
I had everything I could ask for.
A house.
Security.
Horses.
Somehow it wasn't enough. Something was missing. My husband was an incredibly sweet man, but something else was calling me.
I guess my sister was right. Horses were more interesting to me than people.
I had all this knowledge and horse training from years of specialized equestrian schools in Europe... just wasting away. I'd been tracking what was going on in the horse racing world,
and all those deaths bothered me.
I felt I could do something.
Deep down, I needed to put my money where my mouth was.

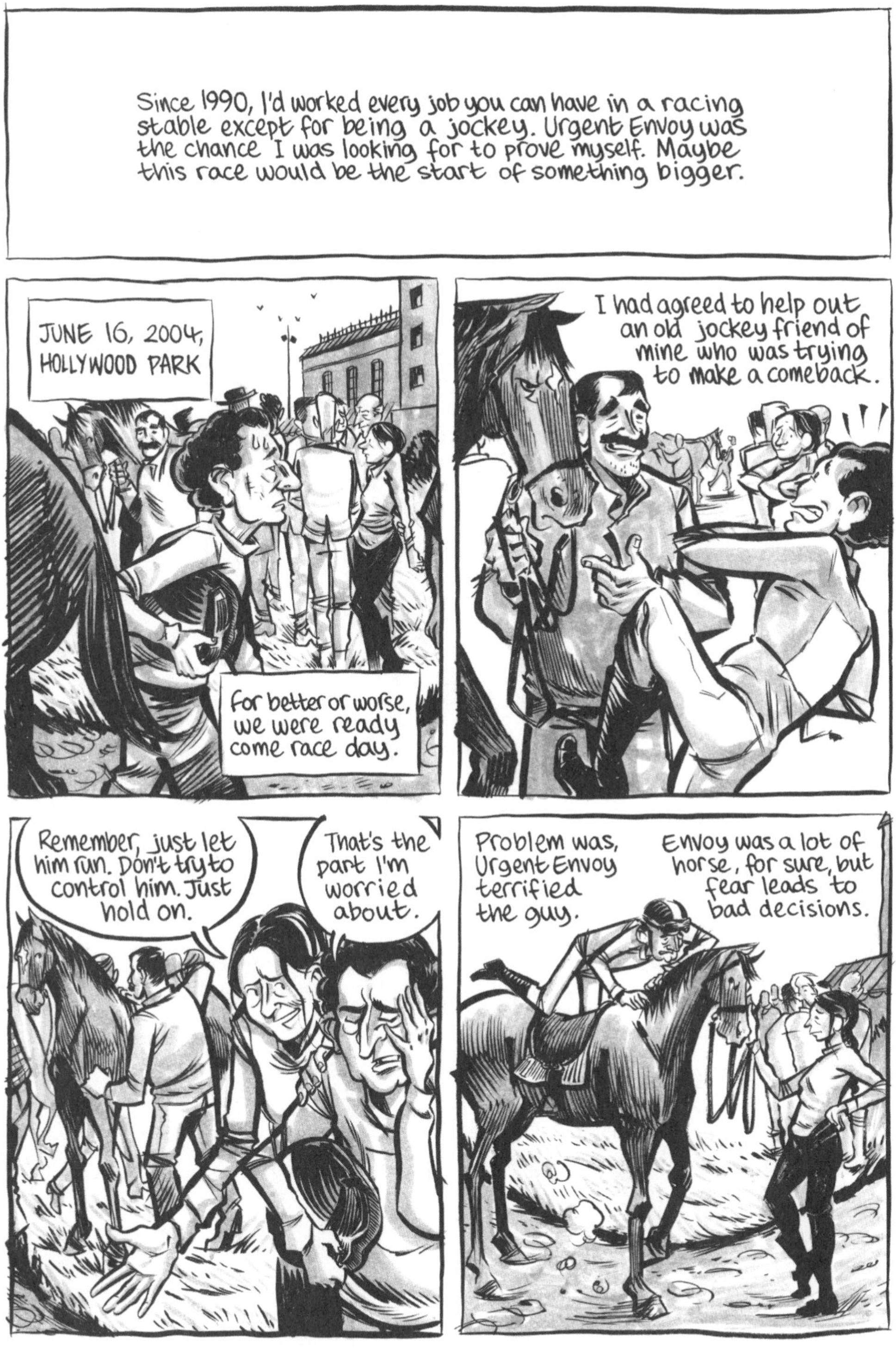
Since 1990, I'd worked every job you can have in a racing stable except for being a jockey. Urgent Envoy was the chance I was looking for to prove myself. Maybe this race would be the start of something bigger.
JUNE 16, 2004, HOLLYWOOD PARK
For better or worse, we were ready come race day.
I had agreed to help out an old jockey friend of mine who was trying to make a comeback.
Remember, just let him run. Don't try to control him. Just hold on.
That's the part I'm worried about.
Problem was, Urgent Envoy terrified the guy.
Envoy was a lot of horse, for sure, but fear leads to bad decisions.

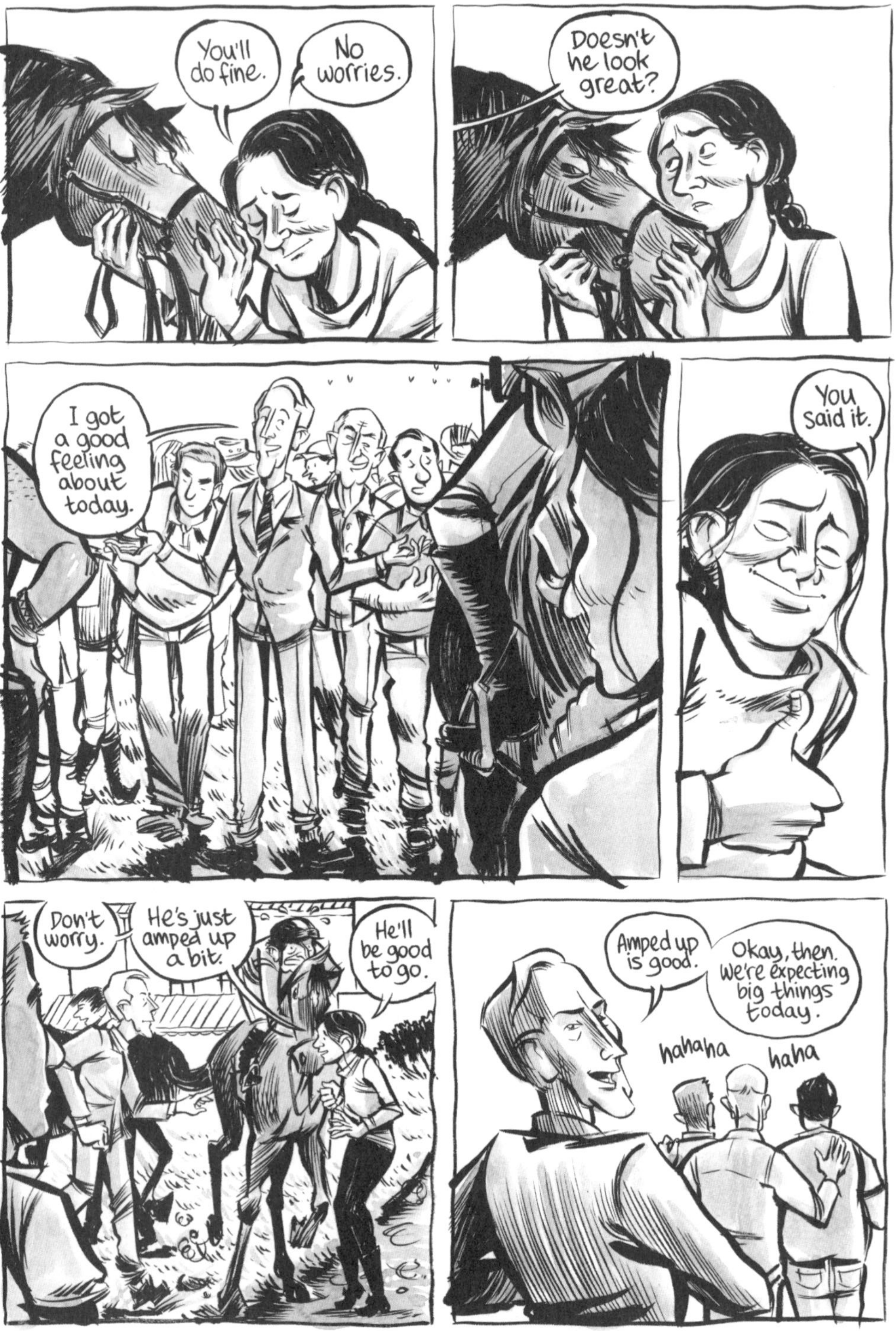
You'll do fine.
No worries.
Doesn't he look great?
I got a good feeling about today.
You said it.
Don't worry.
He's just amped up a bit.
He'll be good to go.
Amped up is good.
Okay, then. We're expecting big things today.
hahaha
haha

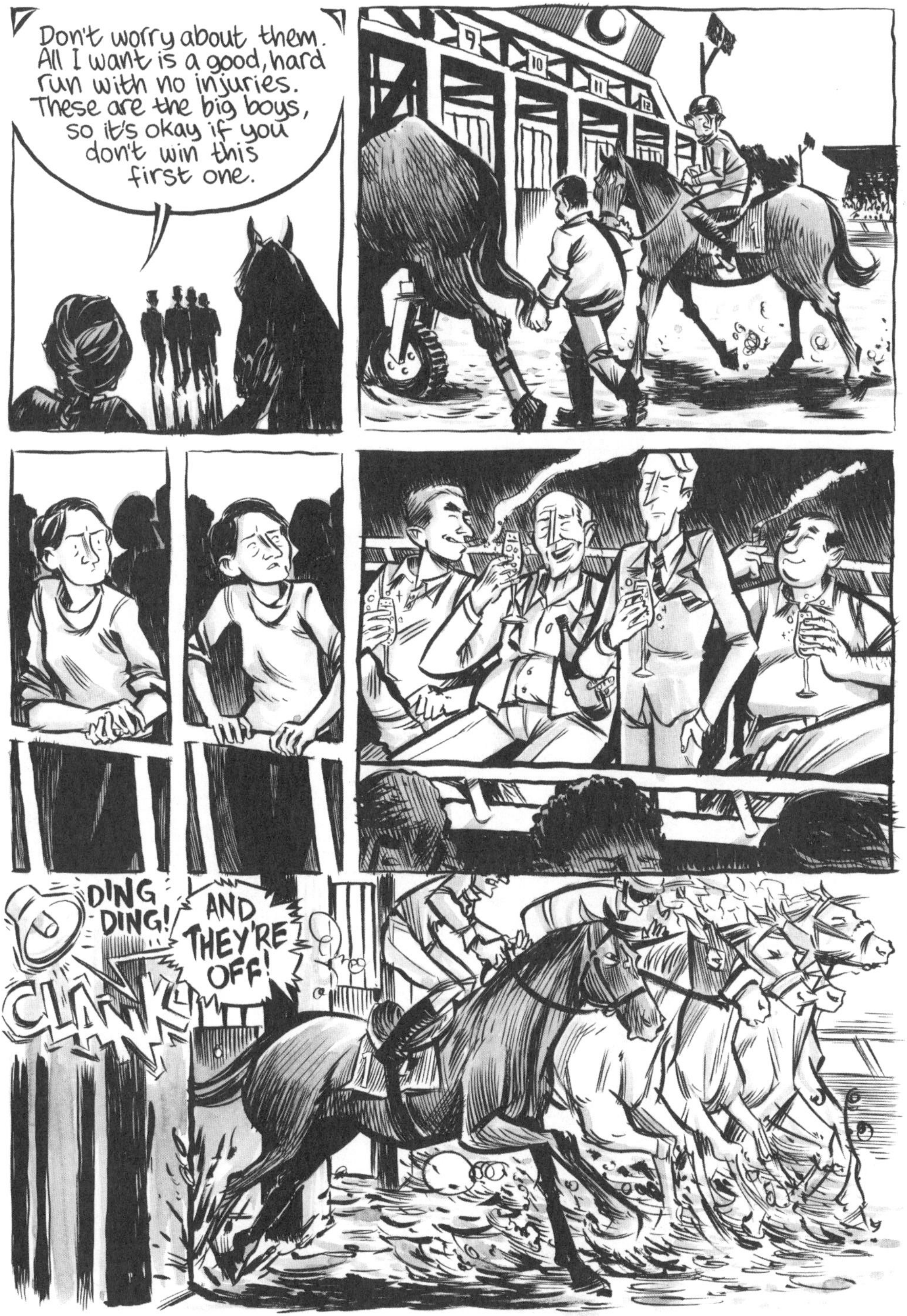
Don't worry about them. All I want is a good, hard run with no injuries. These are the big boys, so it's okay if you don't win this first one.
DING DING!
CLANK!
AND THEY'RE OFF!

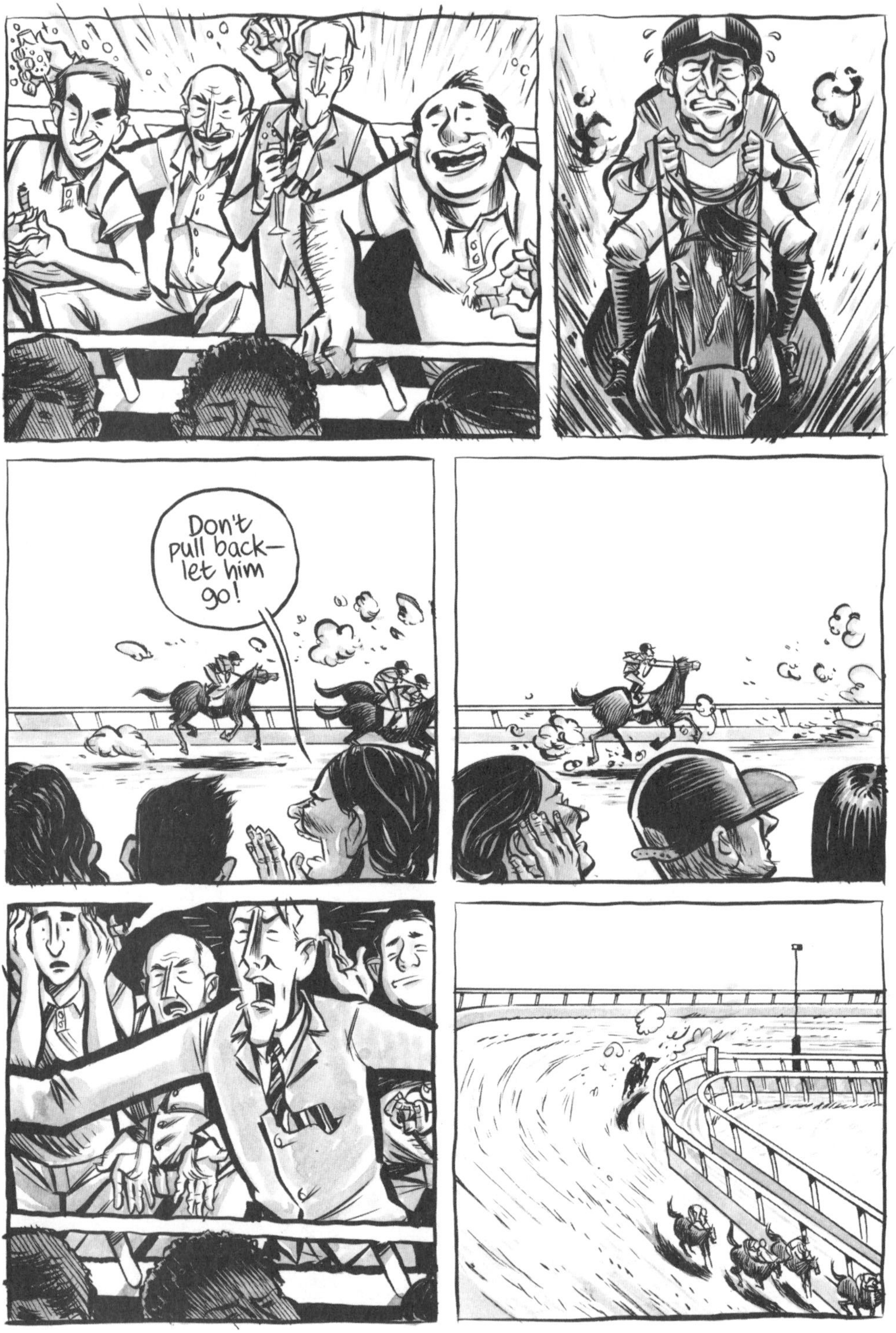
Don't
pull back—
let him
go!

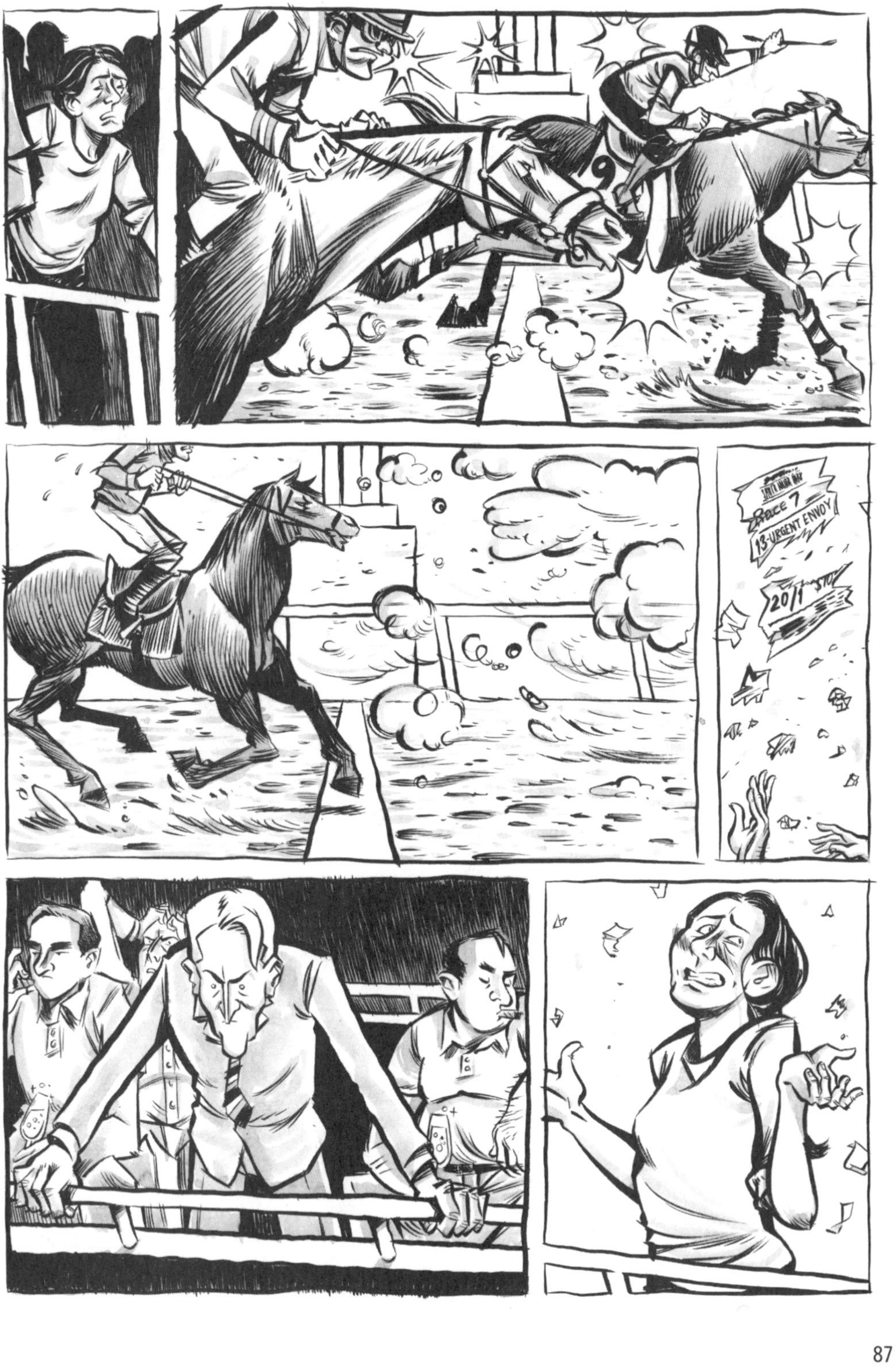

Race 7
13-URGENT ENVOY
20/1

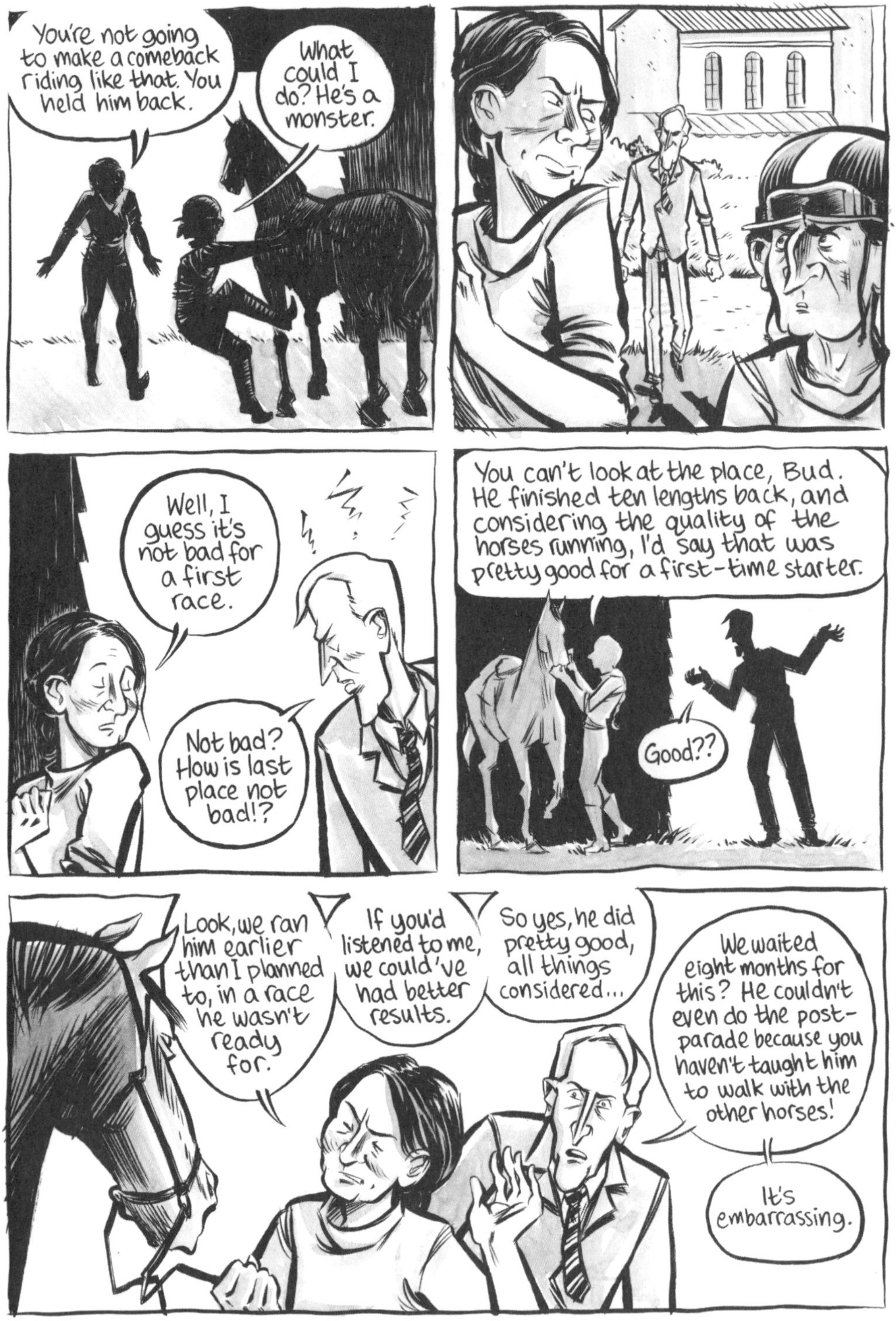
You're not going to make a comeback riding like that. You held him back.
What could I do? He's a monster.
Well, I guess it's not bad for a first race.
Not bad? How is last place not bad!?
You can't look at the place, Bud. He finished ten lengths back, and considering the quality of the horses running, I'd say that was pretty good for a first-time starter.
Good??
Look, we ran him earlier than I planned to, in a race he wasn't ready for.
If you'd listened to me, we could've had better results.
So yes, he did pretty good, all things considered...
We waited eight months for this? He couldn't even do the post-parade because you haven't taught him to walk with the other horses!
It's embarrassing.

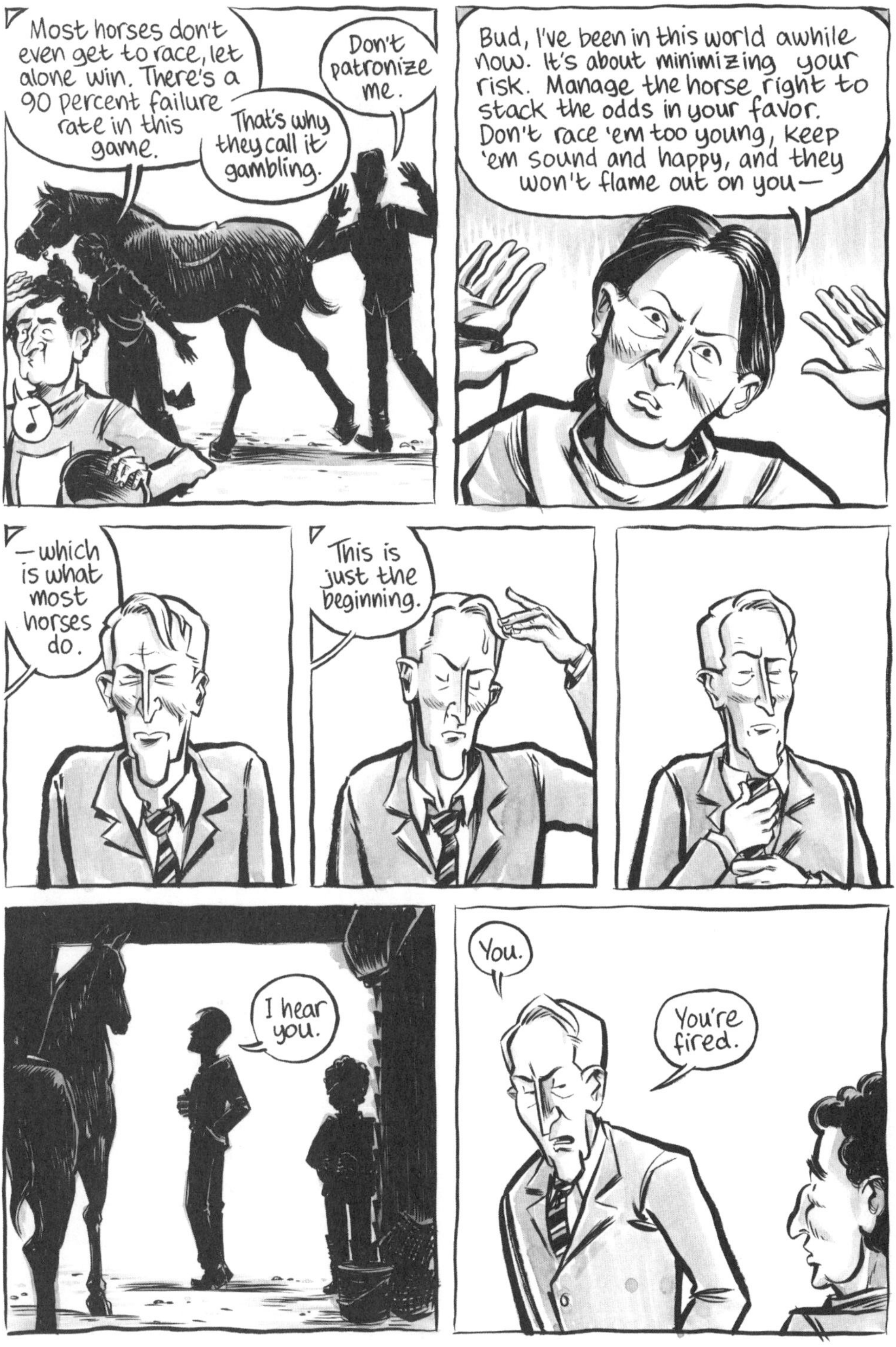
Most horses don't even get to race, let alone win. There's a 90 percent failure rate in this game.
That's why they call it gambling.
Don't patronize me.
Bud, I've been in this world awhile now. It's about minimizing your risk. Manage the horse right to stack the odds in your favor. Don't race 'em too young, keep 'em sound and happy, and they won't flame out on you—
—which is what most horses do.
This is just the beginning.
I hear you.
You.
You're fired.

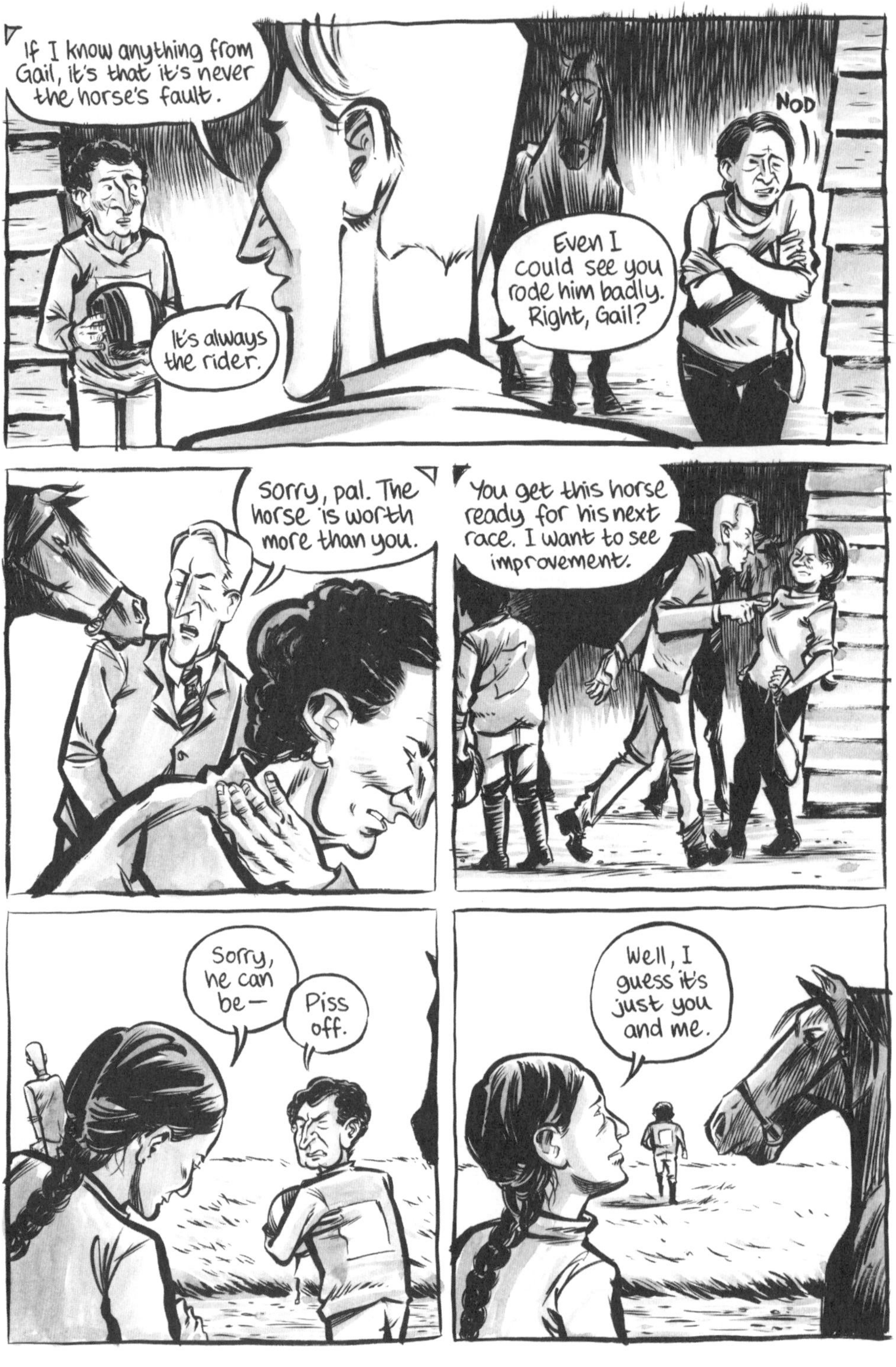
If I know anything from Gail, it's that it's never the horse's fault.
It's always the rider.
Even I could see you rode him badly. Right, Gail?
NOD
Sorry, pal. The horse is worth more than you.
You get this horse ready for his next race. I want to see improvement.
Sorry, he can be—
Piss off.
Well, I guess it's just you and me.

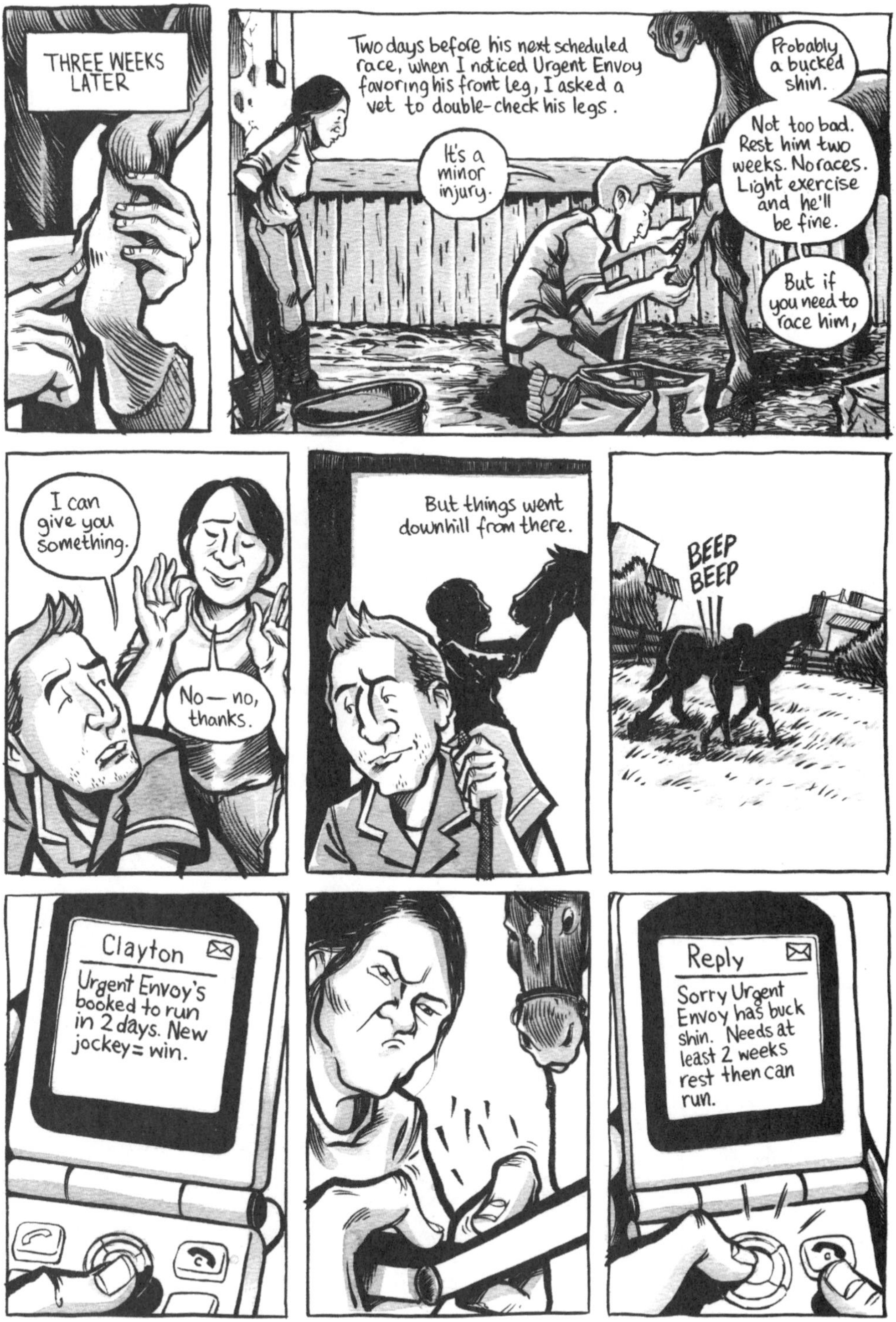
THREE WEEKS LATER
Two days before his next scheduled race, when I noticed Urgent Envoy favoring his front leg, I asked a vet to double-check his legs.
It's a minor injury.
Probably a bucked shin.
Not too bad. Rest him two weeks. No races. Light exercise and he'll be fine.
But if you need to race him,
I can give you something.
No—no, thanks.
But things went downhill from there.
BEEP BEEP
Clayton
Urgent Envoy's booked to run in 2 days. New jockey= win.
Reply
Sorry Urgent Envoy has buck shin. Needs at least 2 weeks rest then can run.

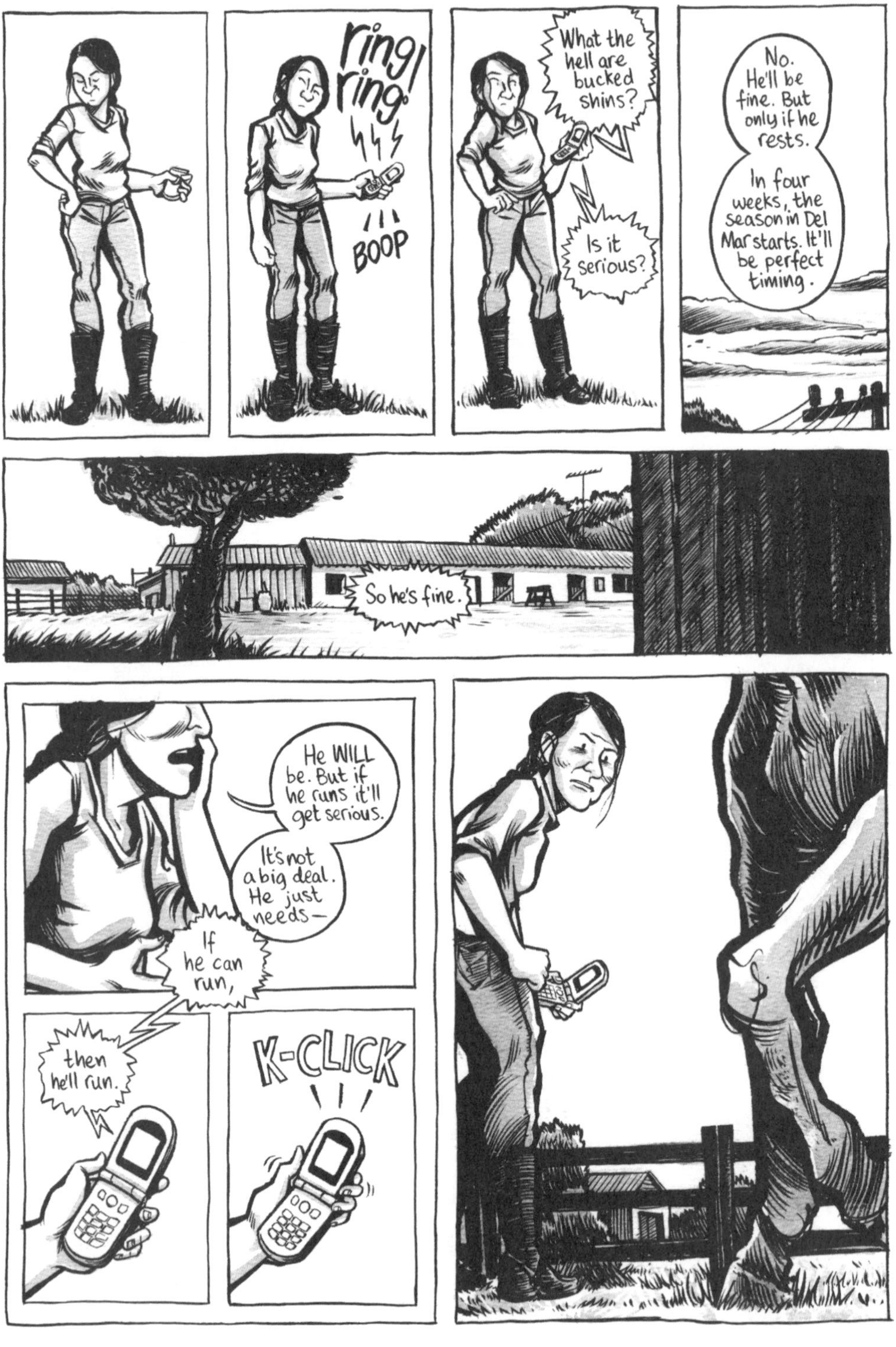
ring! ring!
BOOP
What the hell are bucked shins?
Is it serious?
No. He'll be fine. But only if he rests.
In four weeks, the season in Del Mar starts. It'll be perfect timing.
So he's fine.
He WILL be. But if he runs it'll get serious.
It's not a big deal. He just needs—
If he can run,
then he'll run.
K-CLICK

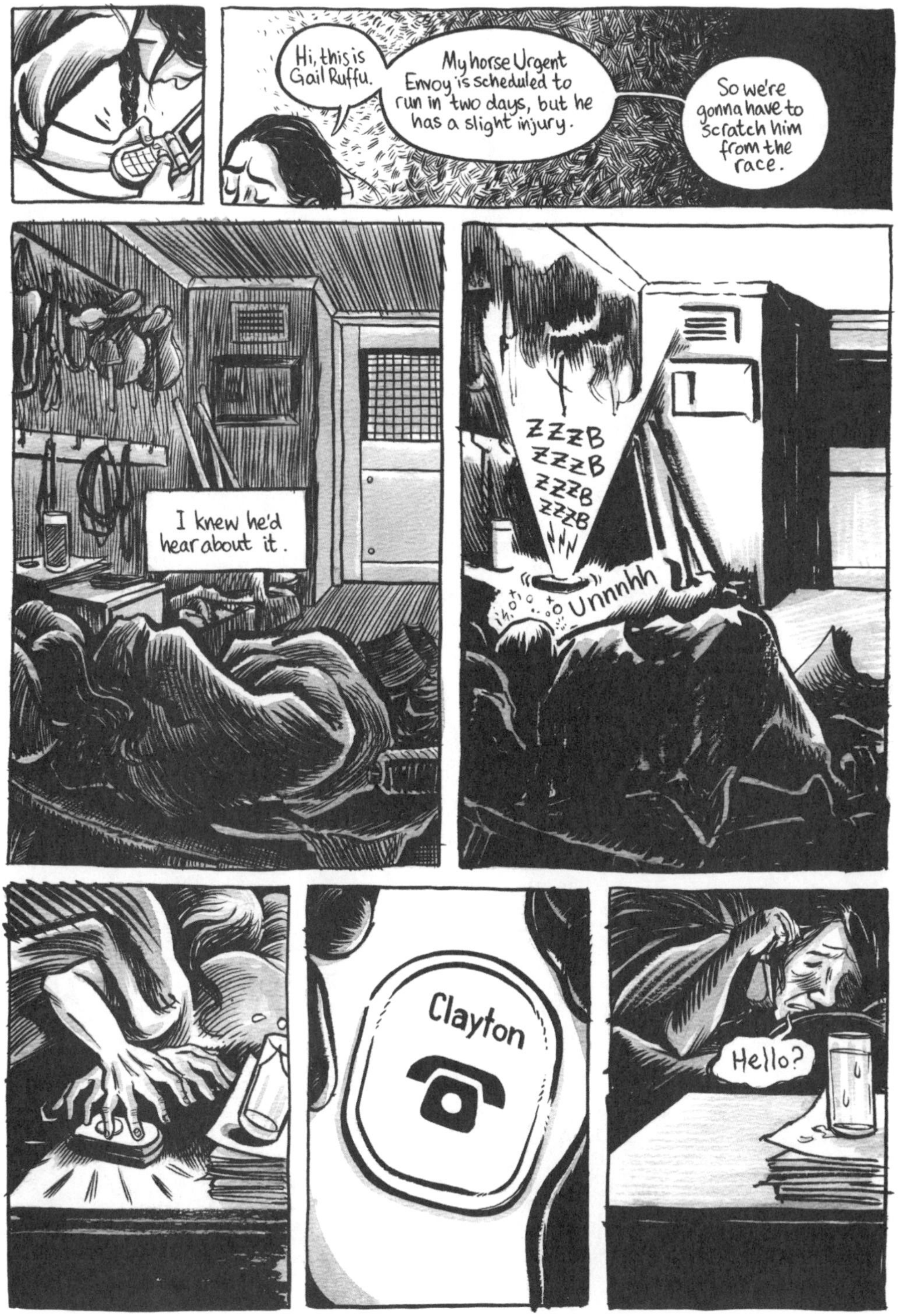
Hi, this is Gail Ruffu.
My horse Urgent Envoy is scheduled to run in two days, but he has a slight injury.
So we're gonna have to scratch him from the race.
I knew he'd hear about it.
ZZZB ZZZB ZZZB ZZZB
Unnnhh
Clayton
Hello?

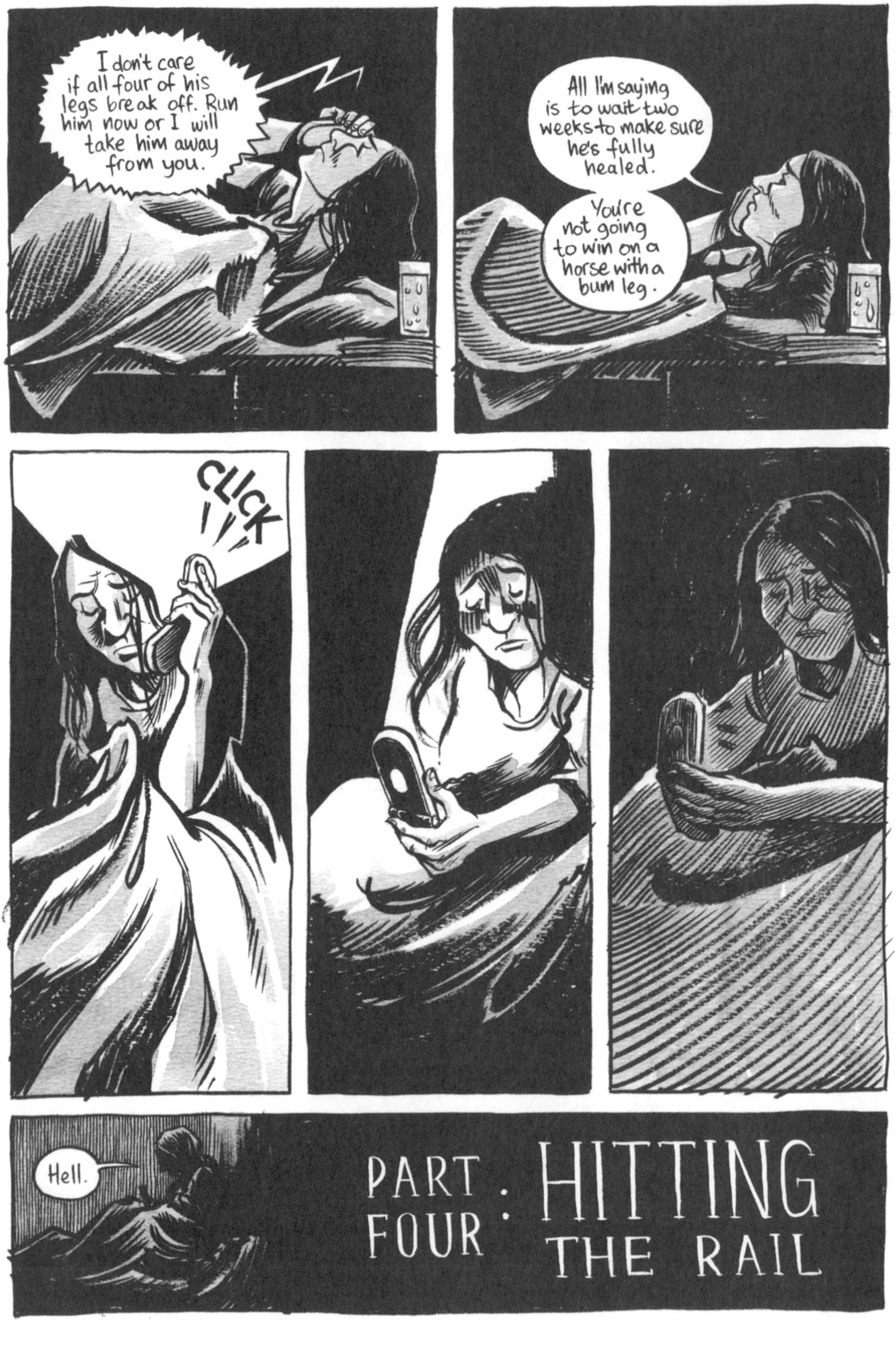
I don't care if all four of his legs break off. Run him now or I will take him away from you.
All I'm saying is to wait two weeks to make sure he's fully healed.
You're not going to win on a horse with a bum leg.
CLICK
Hell.
PART FOUR: HITTING THE RAIL

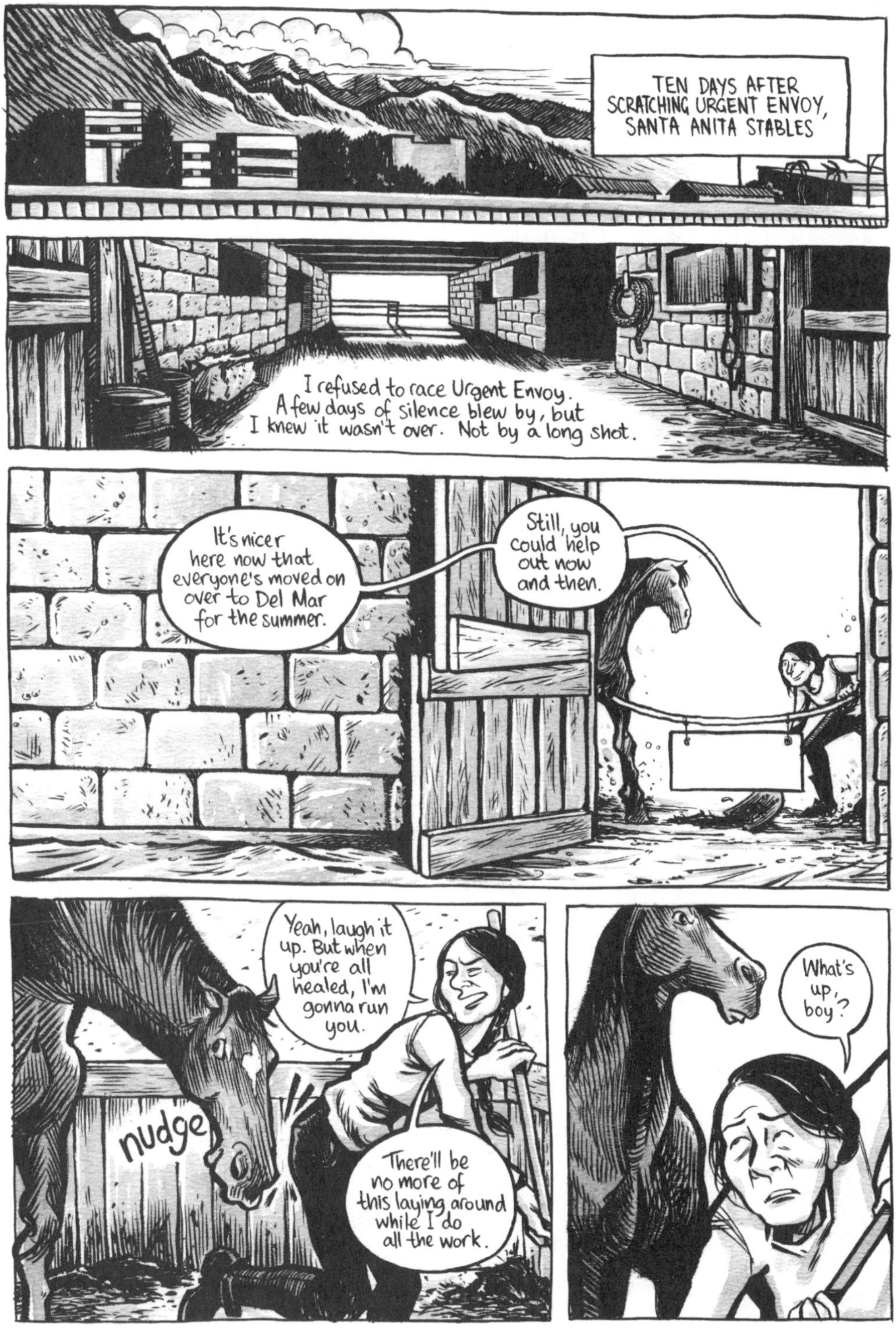
TEN DAYS AFTER SCRATCHING URGENT ENVOY, SANTA ANITA STABLES
I refused to race Urgent Envoy. A few days of silence blew by, but I knew it wasn't over. Not by a long shot.
It's nicer here now that everyone's moved on over to Del Mar for the summer.
Still, you could help out now and then.
Yeah, laugh it up. But when you're all healed, I'm gonna run you.
nudge
There'll be no more of this laying around while I do all the work.
What's up, boy?

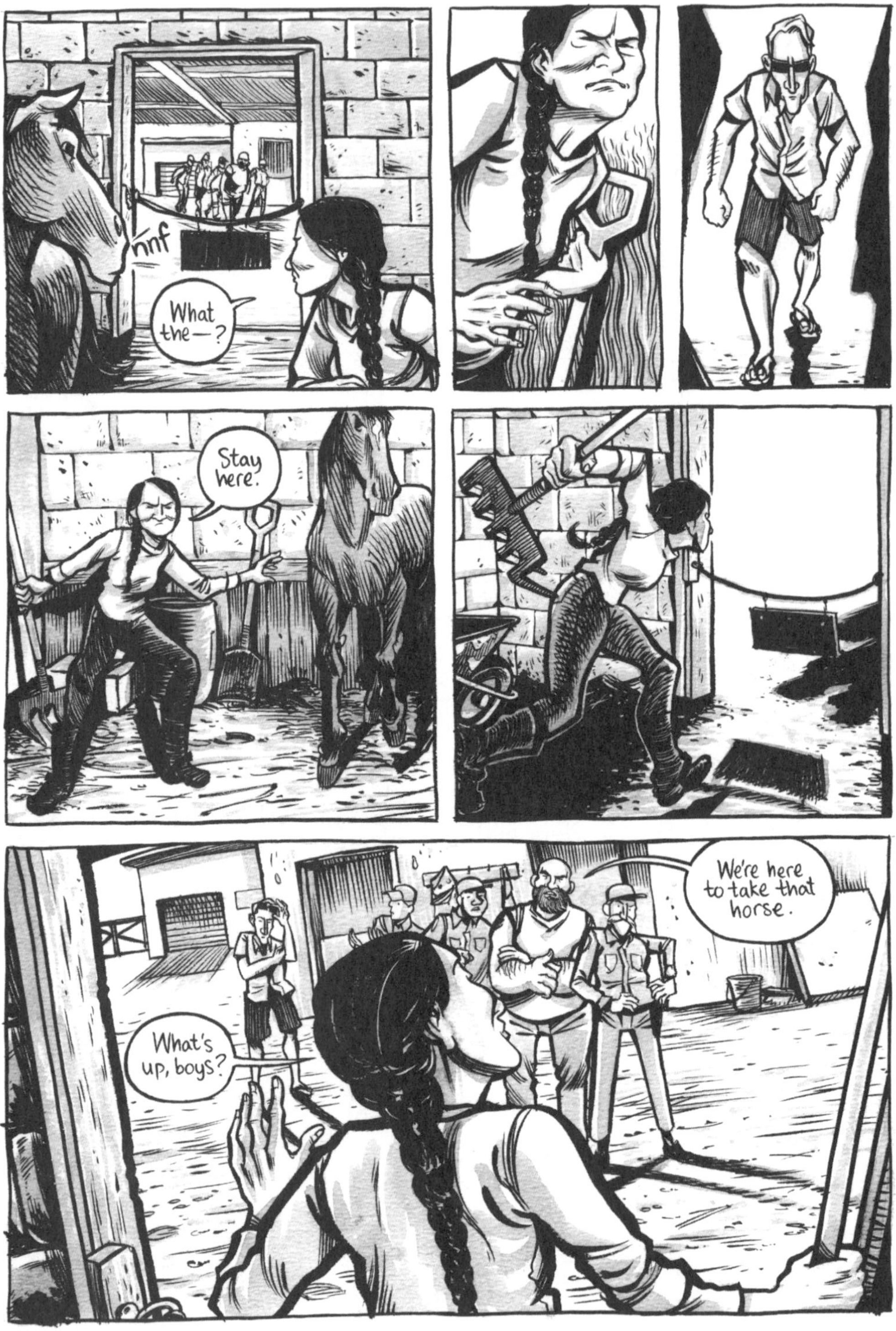
nnf
What the—?
Stay here.
We're here to take that horse.
What's up, boys?

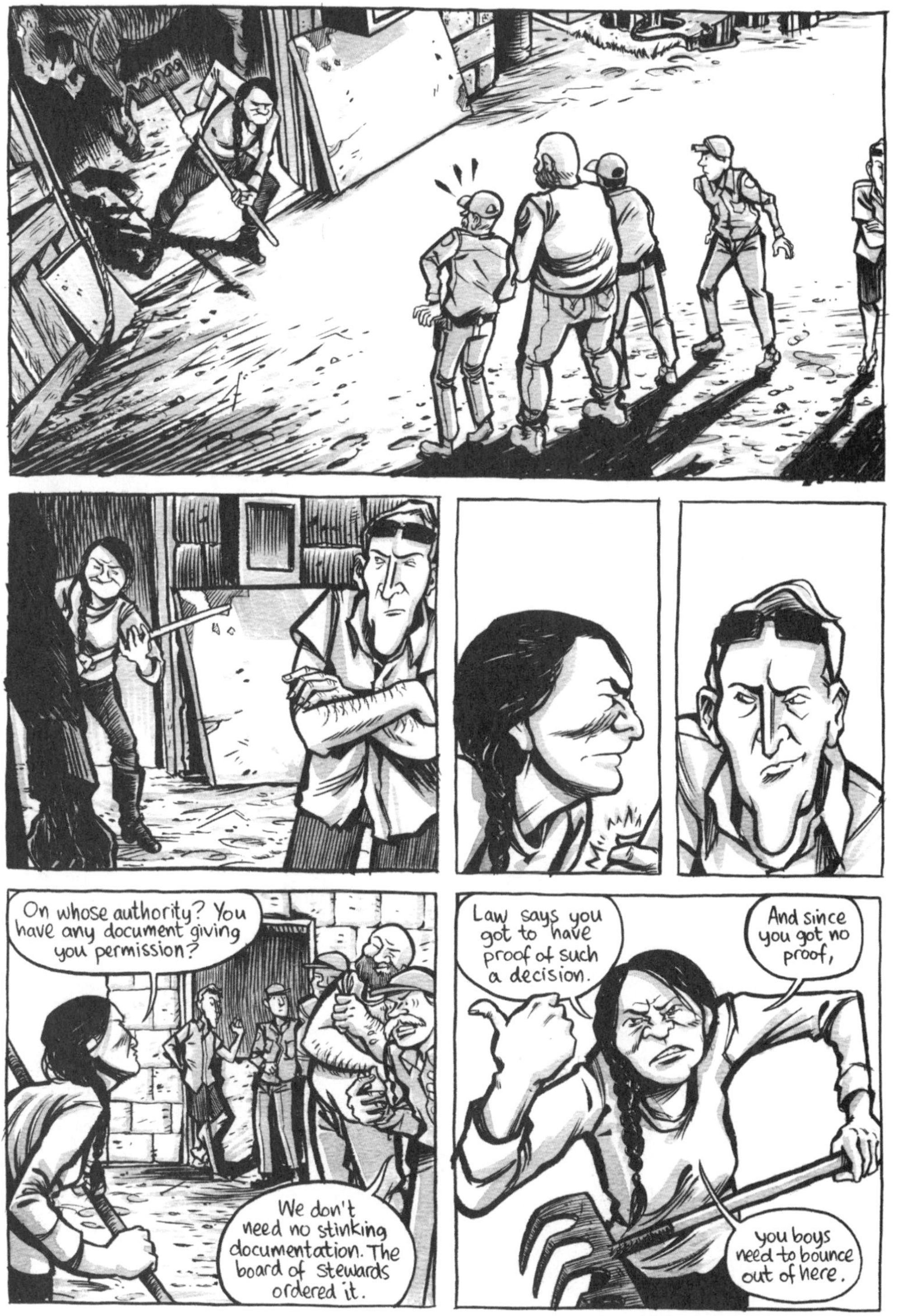
On whose authority? You have any document giving you permission?
We don't need no stinking documentation. The board of stewards ordered it.
Law says you got to have proof of such a decision.
And since you got no proof,
you boys need to bounce out of here.

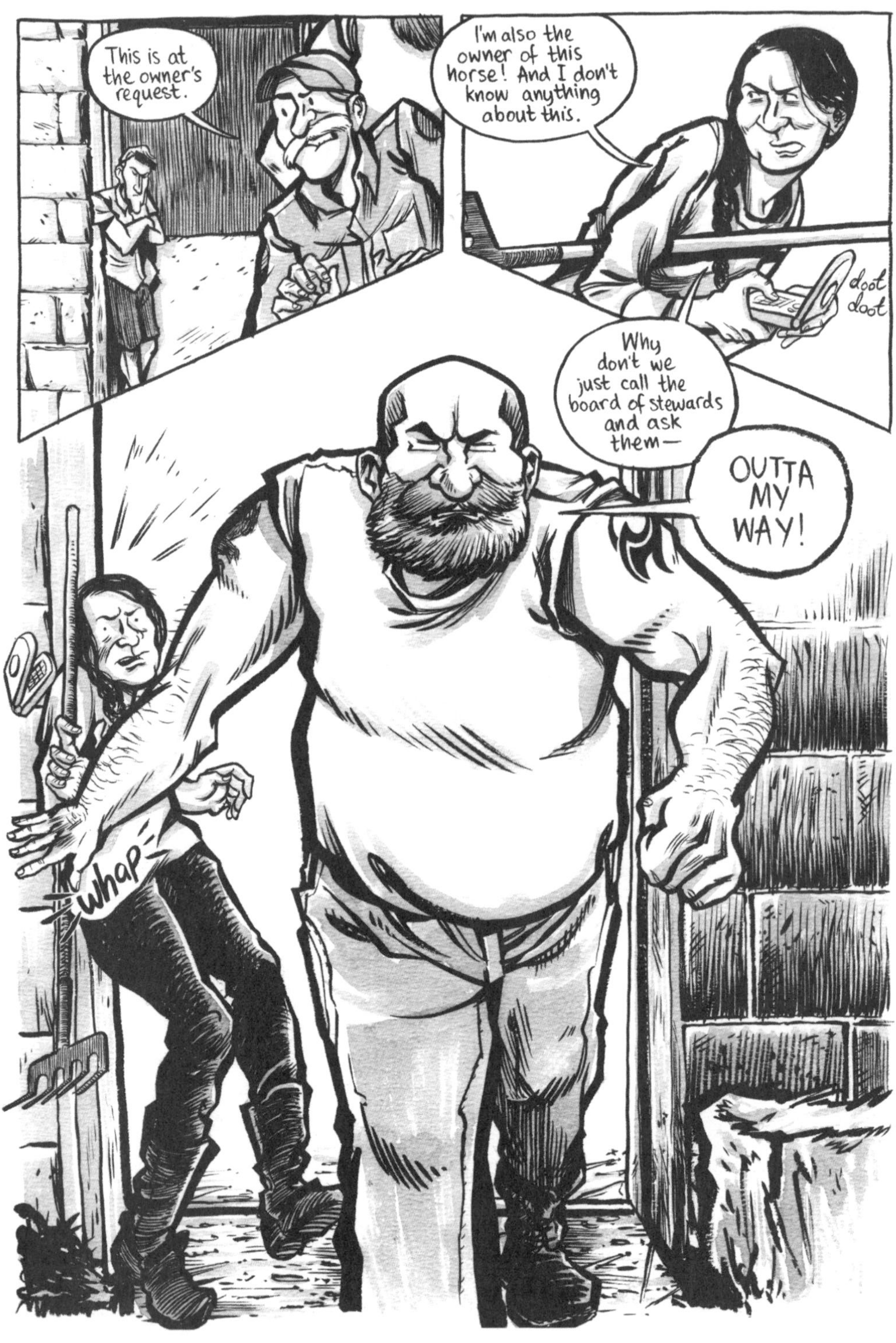

This is at the owner's request.
I'm also the owner of this horse! And I don't know anything about this.
doot doot
Why don't we just call the board of stewards and ask them—
OUTTA MY WAY!
whap

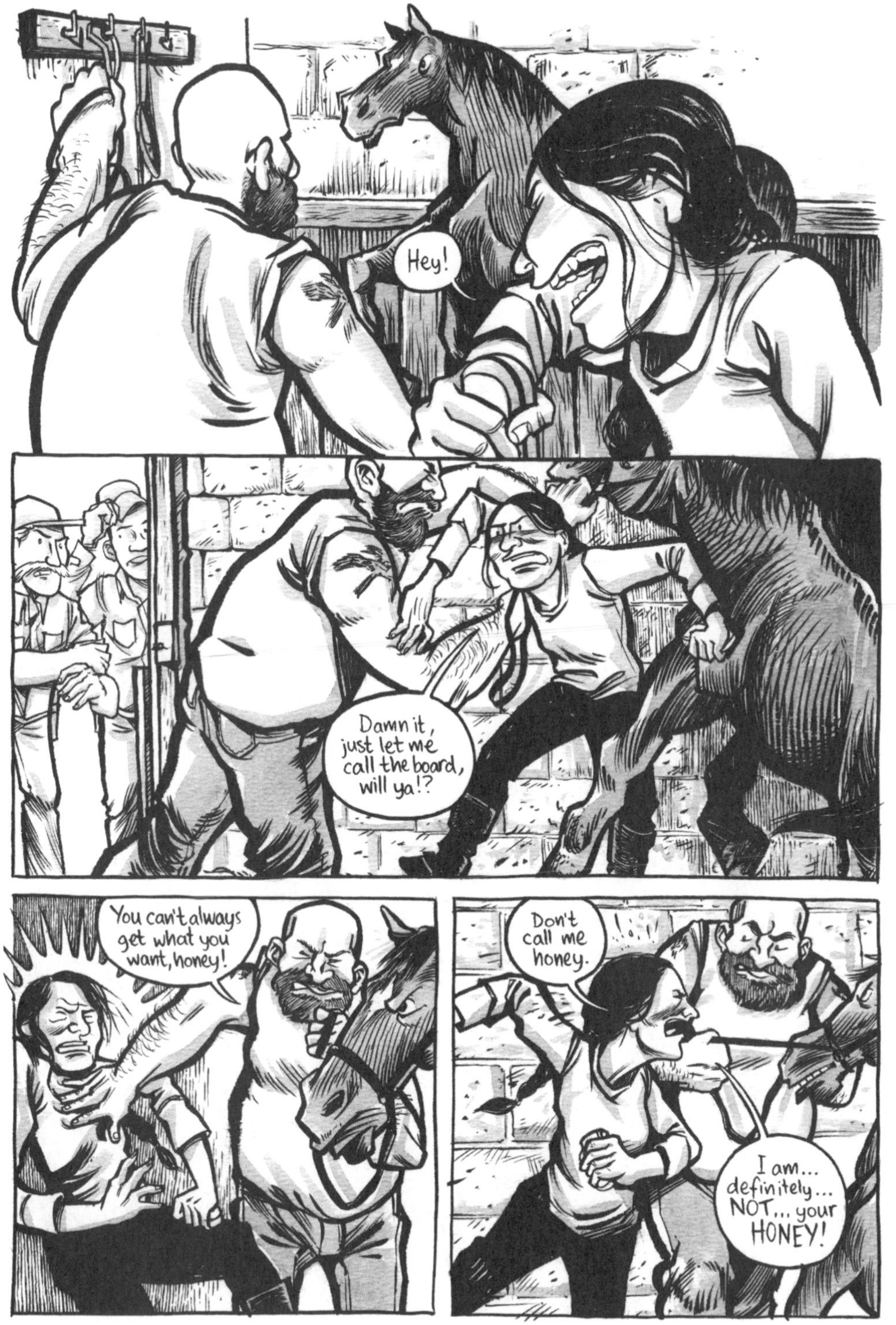
Hey!
Damn it, just let me call the board, will ya!?
You can't always get what you want, honey!
Don't call me honey.
!..!
I am... definitely... NOT... your HONEY!

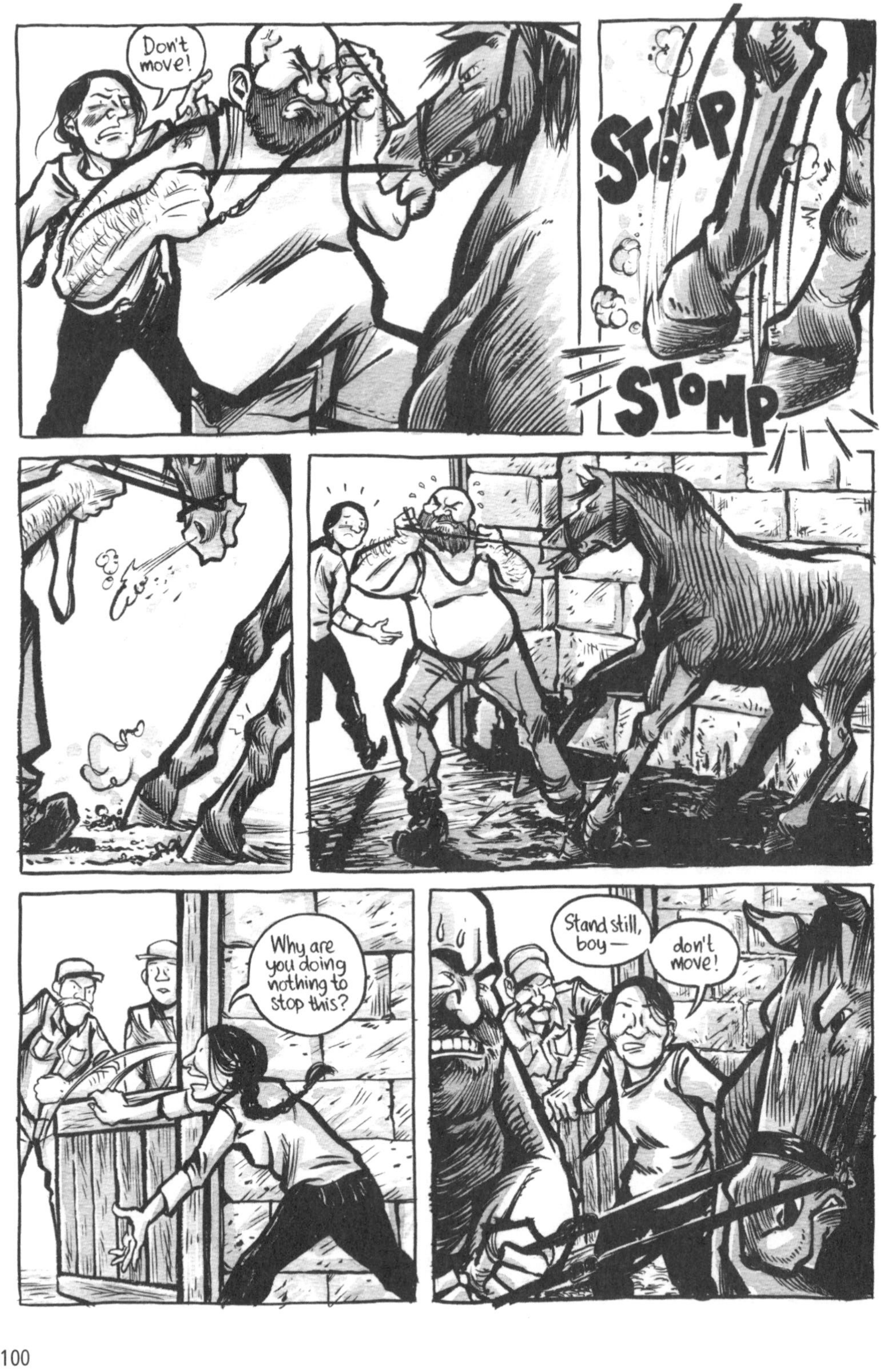
Don't move!
STOMP
STOMP
Why are you doing nothing to stop this?
Stand still, boy—
don't move!

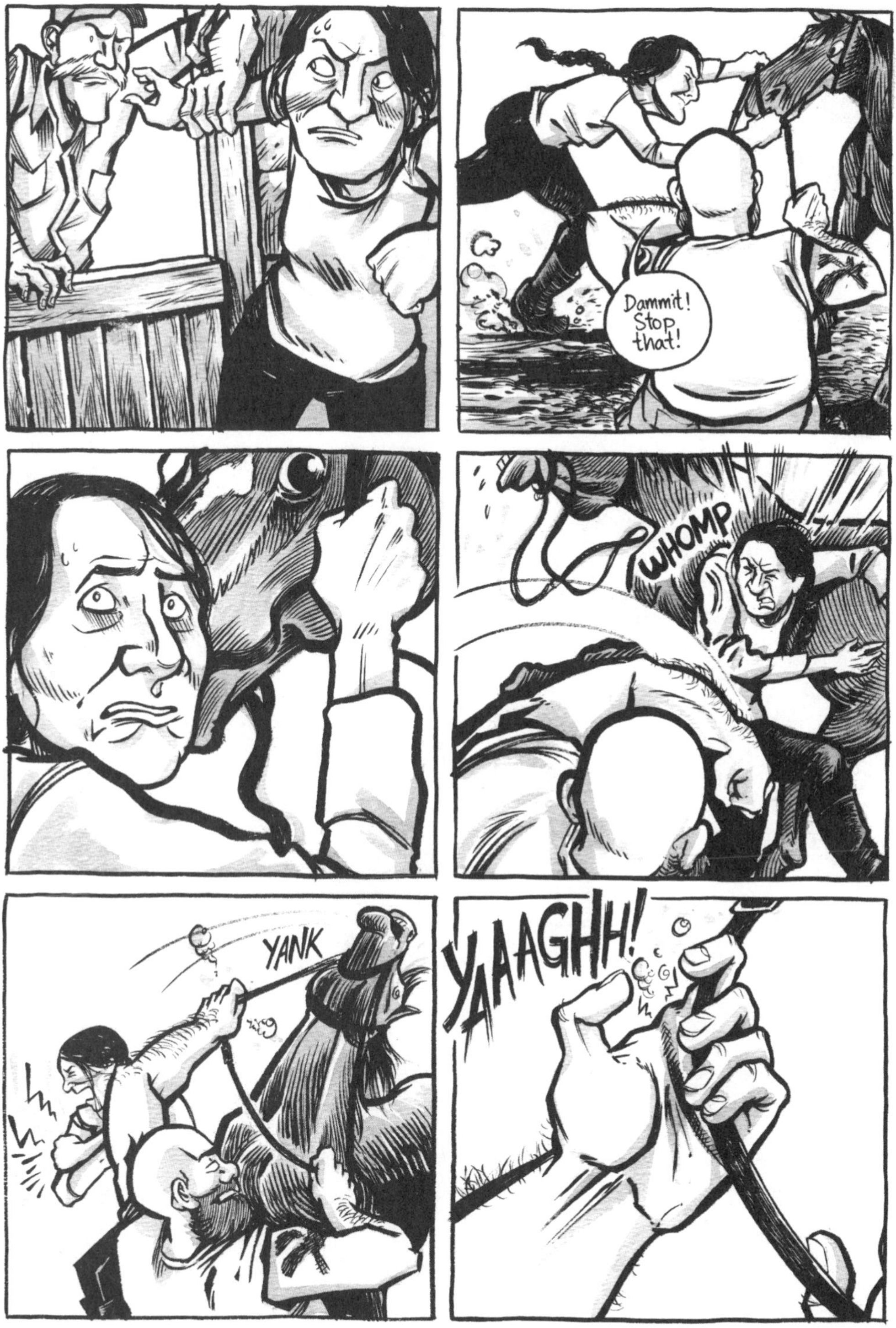

Dammit! Stop that!
WHOMP
YANK
YAAGHH!

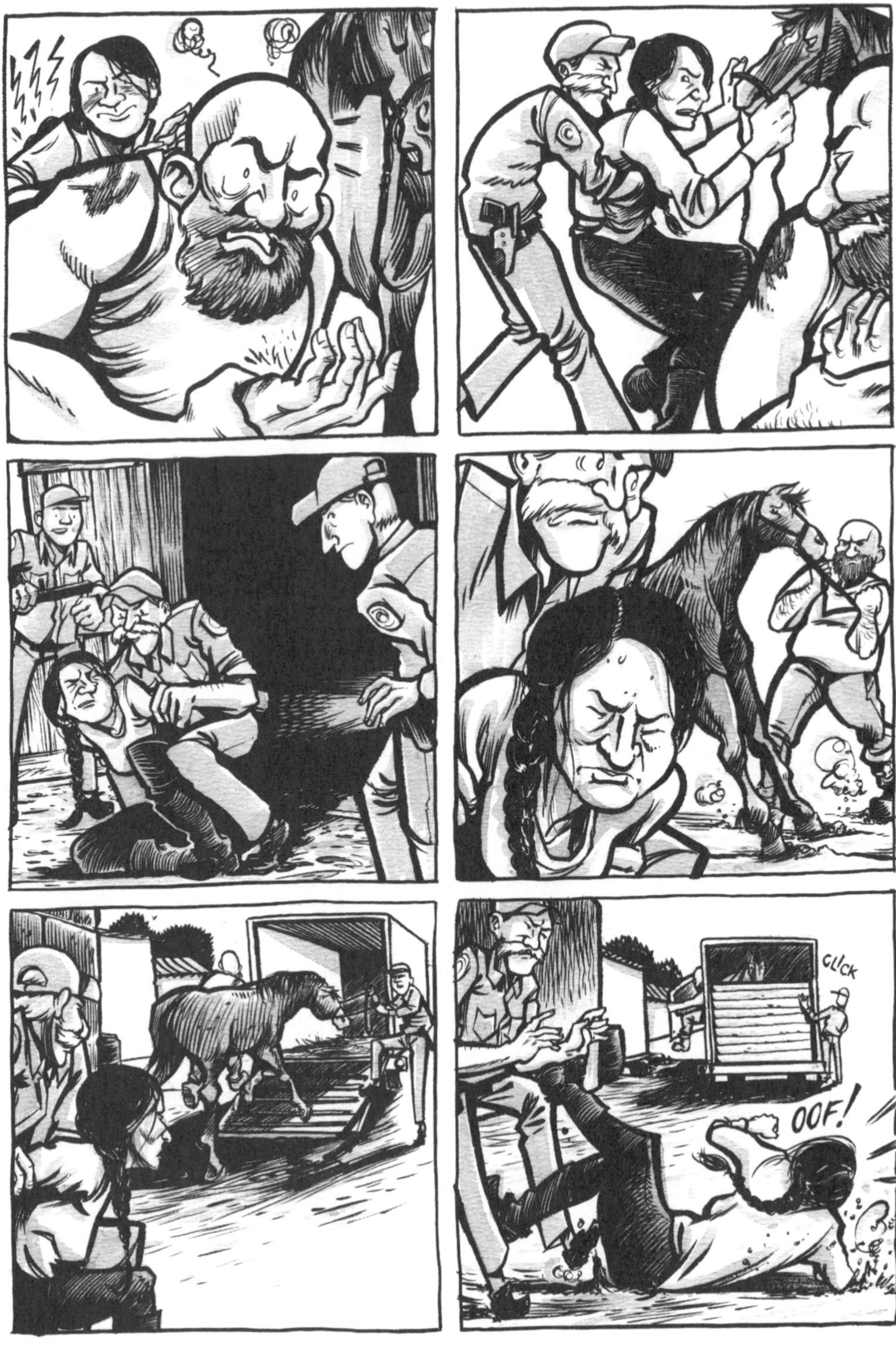
CLICK
OOF!

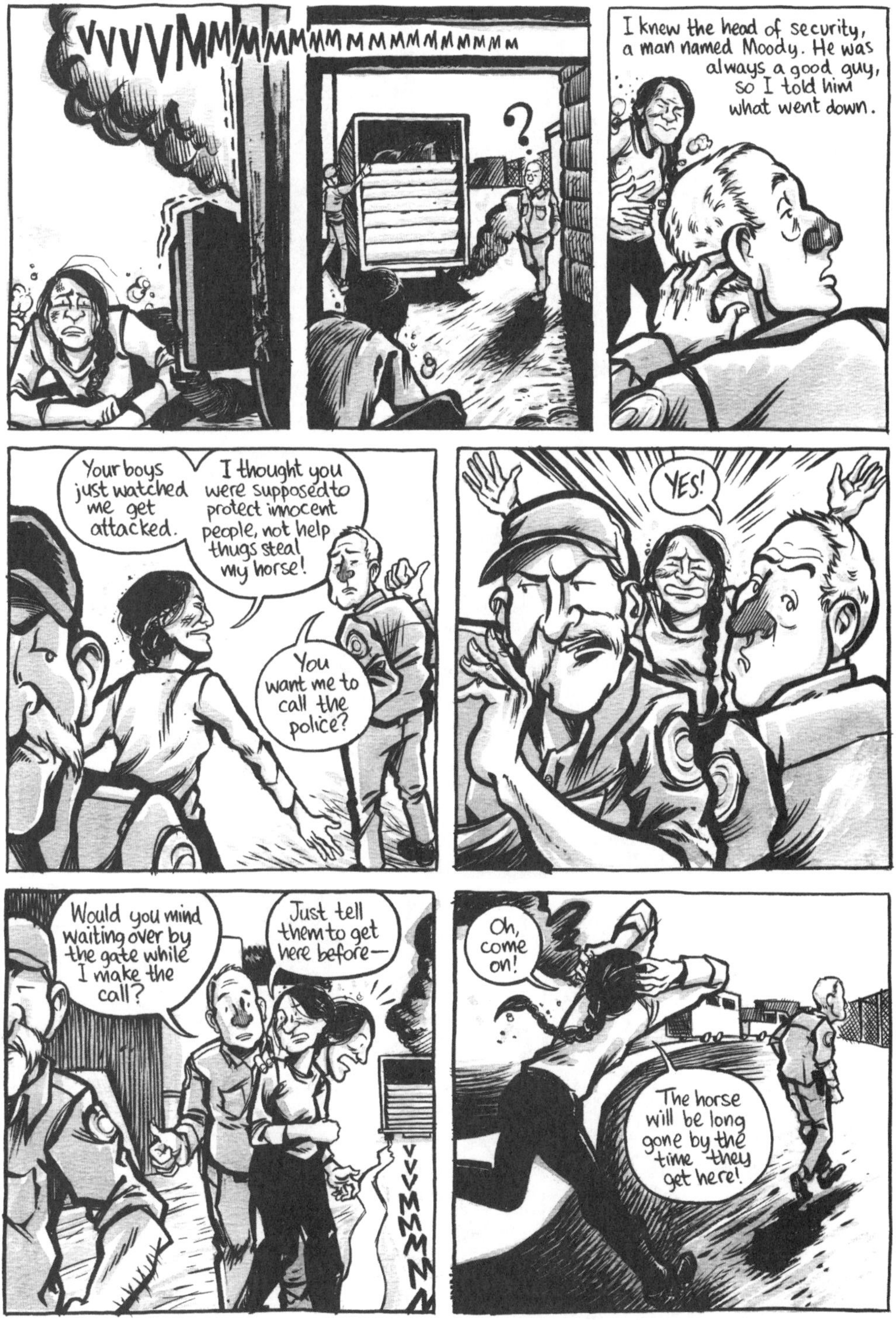
VVVVMMMMMMMMMMMMMMMMMMM
?
I knew the head of security, a man named Moody. He was always a good guy, so I told him what went down.
Your boys just watched me get attacked.
I thought you were supposed to protect innocent people, not help thugs steal my horse!
You want me to call the police?
YES!
Would you mind waiting over by the gate while I make the call?
Just tell them to get here before—
VVVMMMMM
Oh, come on!
The horse will be long gone by the time they get here!

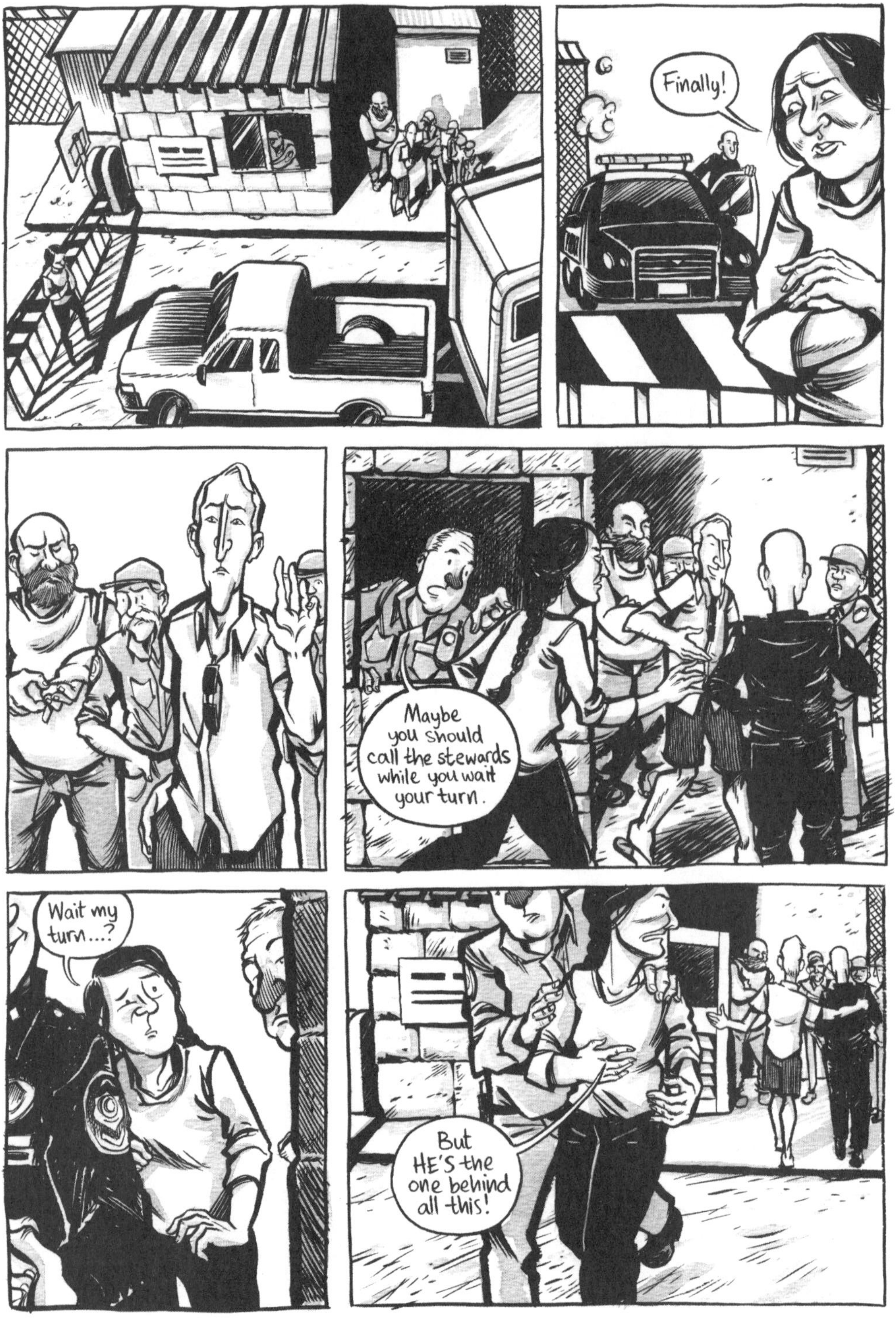
Finally!
Maybe you should call the stewards while you wait your turn.
Wait my turn...?
But HE'S the one behind all this!

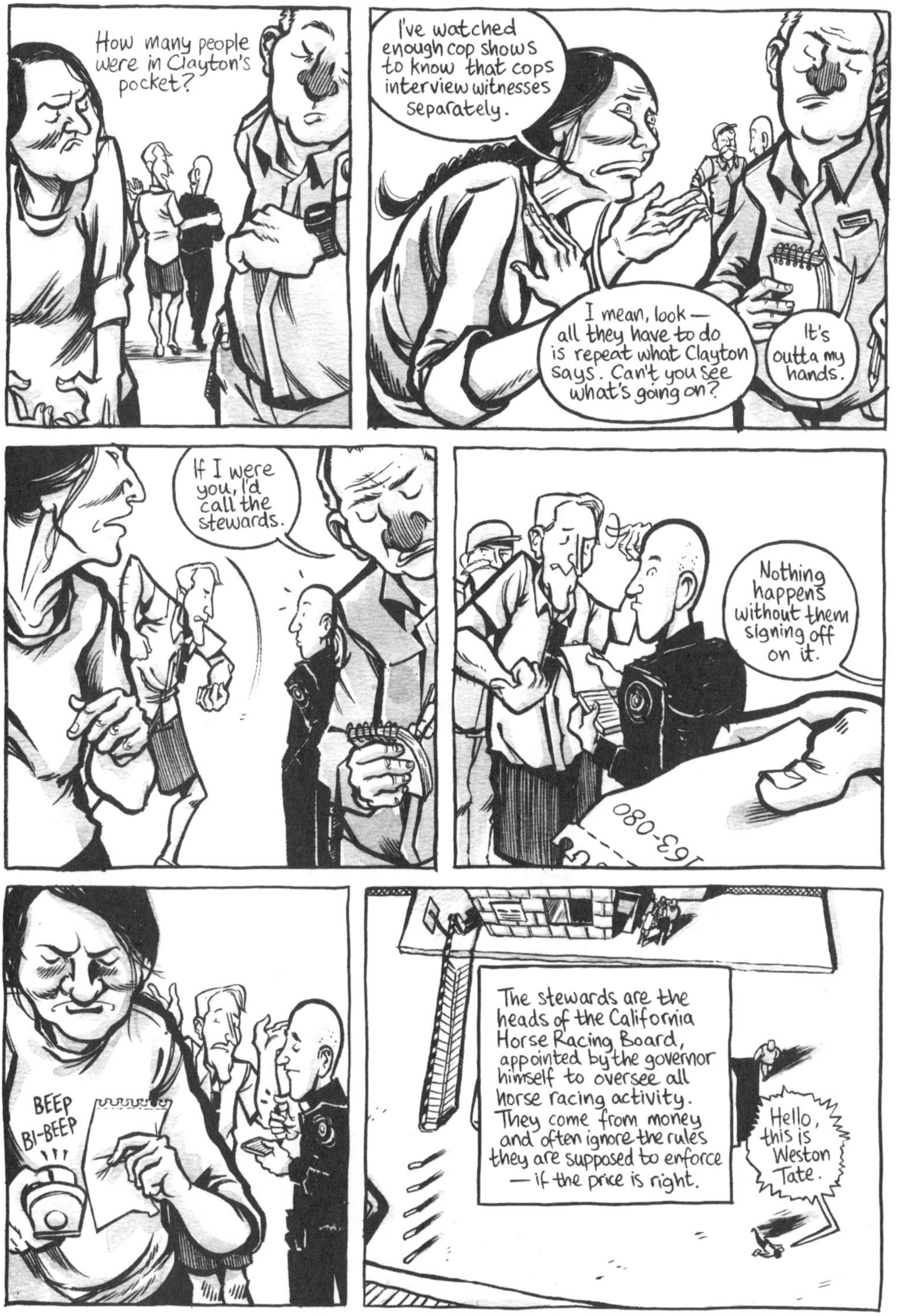
How many people were in Clayton's pocket?
I've watched enough cop shows to know that cops interview witnesses separately.
I mean, look — all they have to do is repeat what Clayton says. Can't you see what's going on?
It's outta my hands.
If I were you, I'd call the stewards.
Nothing happens without them signing off on it.
163-080
BEEP BI-BEEP
The stewards are the heads of the California Horse Racing Board, appointed by the governor himself to oversee all horse racing activity. They come from money and often ignore the rules they are supposed to enforce — if the price is right.
Hello, this is Weston Tate.

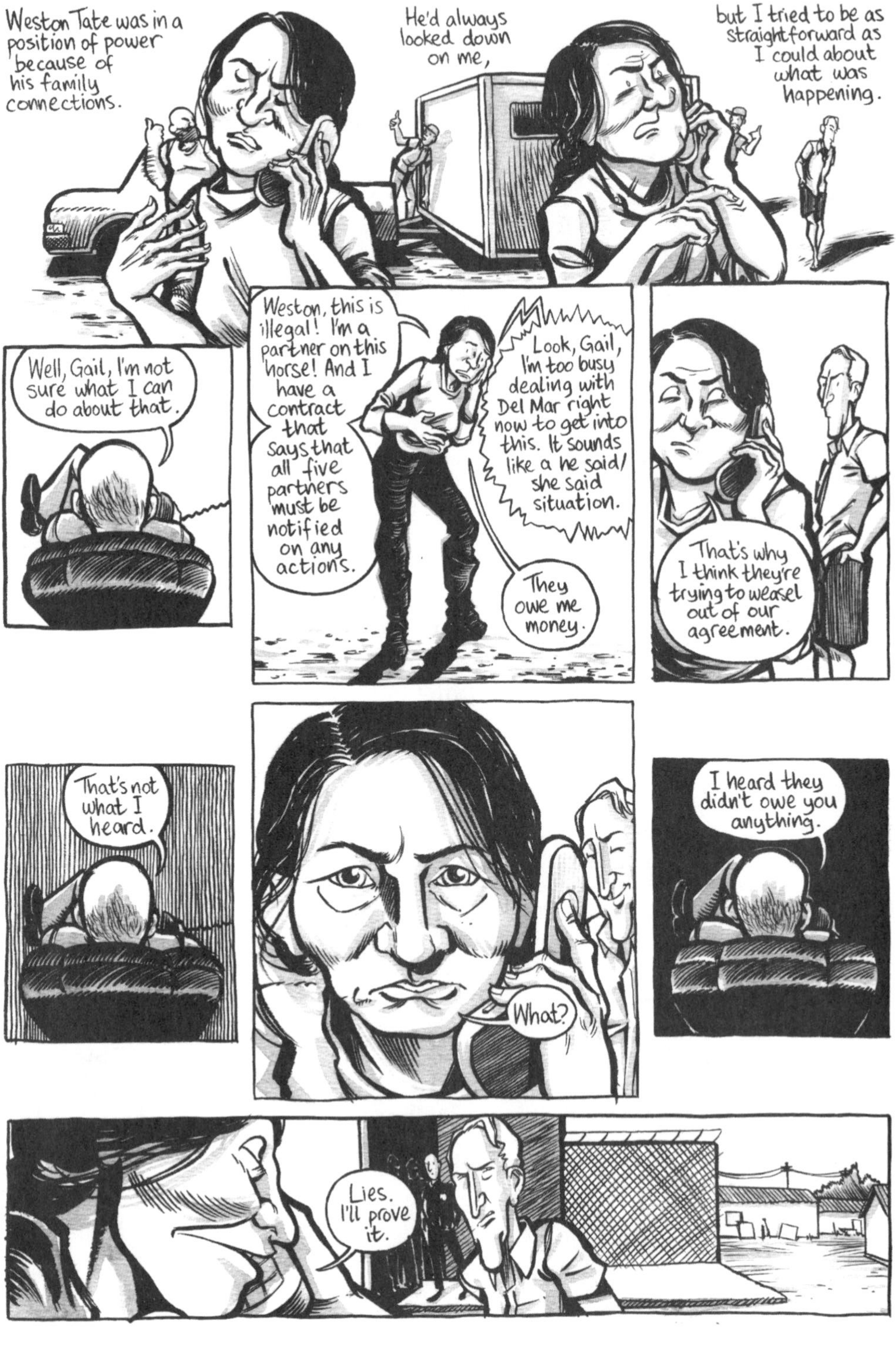
Weston Tate was in a position of power because of his family connections.
He'd always looked down on me,
but I tried to be as straightforward as I could about what was happening.
Well, Gail, I'm not sure what I can do about that.
Weston, this is illegal! I'm a partner on this horse! And I have a contract that says that all five partners must be notified on any actions.
Look, Gail, I'm too busy dealing with Del Mar right now to get into this. It sounds like a he said/she said situation.
They owe me money.
That's why I think they're trying to weasel out of our agreement.
That's not what I heard.
What?
I heard they didn't owe you anything.
Lies. I'll prove it.

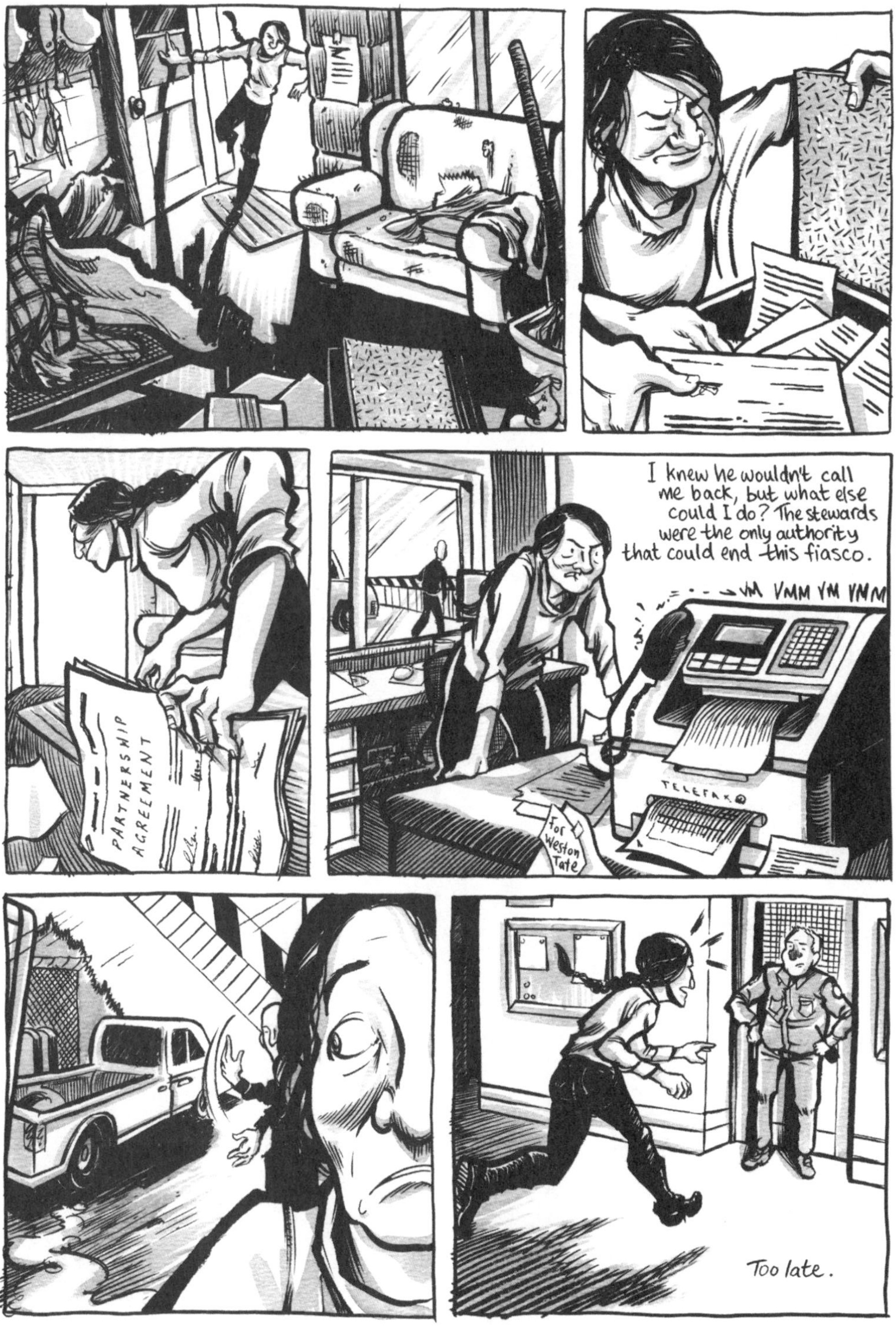

PARTNERSHIP AGREEMENT
I knew he wouldn't call me back, but what else could I do? The stewards were the only authority that could end this fiasco.
VM VMM VM VMM
TELEFAX
For Weston Tate
Too late.

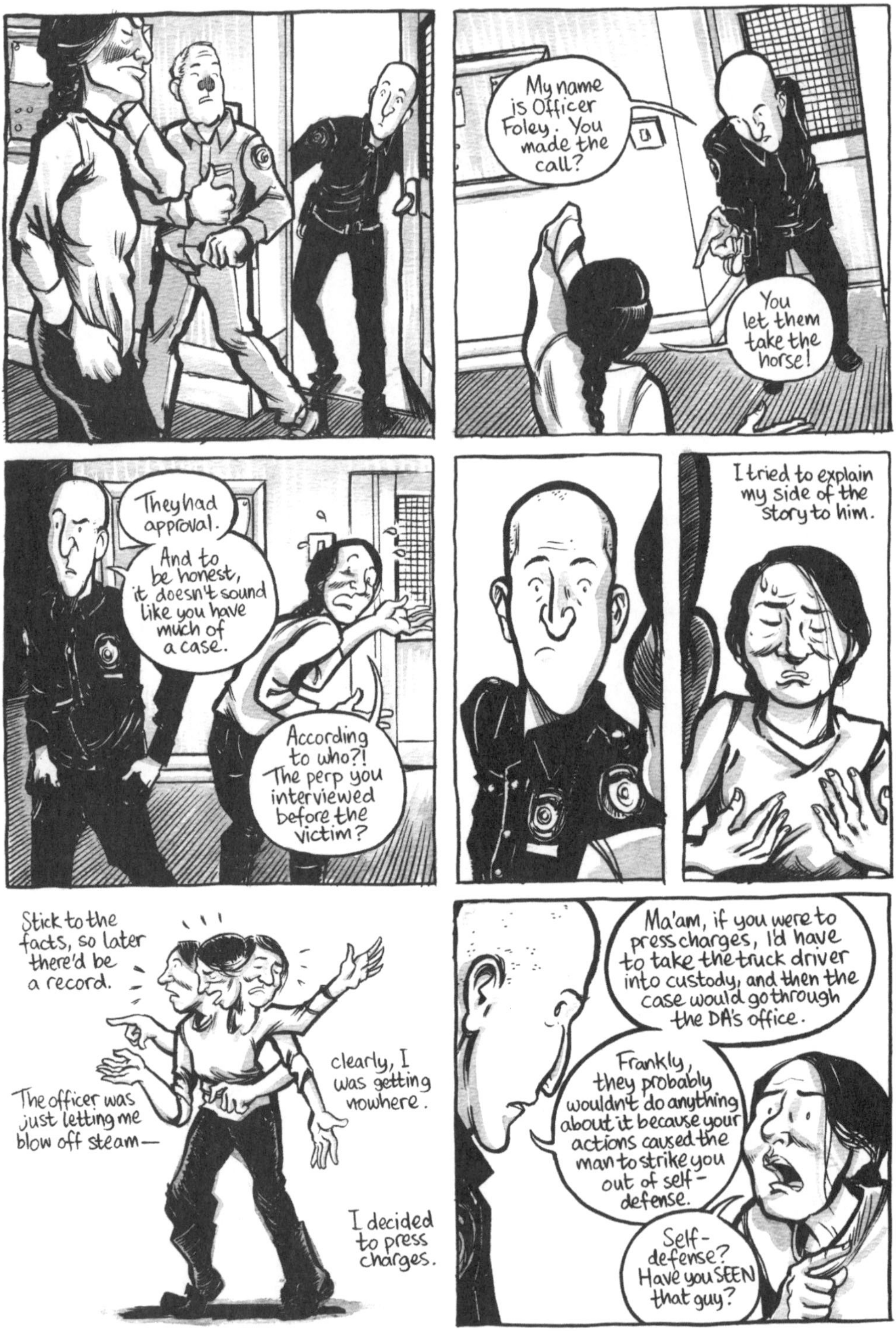
My name is Officer Foley. You made the call?
You let them take the horse!
They had approval.
And to be honest, it doesn't sound like you have much of a case.
According to who?! The perp you interviewed before the victim?
I tried to explain my side of the story to him.
Stick to the facts, so later there'd be a record.
The officer was just letting me blow off steam—
clearly, I was getting nowhere.
I decided to press charges.
Ma'am, if you were to press charges, I'd have to take the truck driver into custody, and then the case would go through the DA's office.
Frankly, they probably wouldn't do anything about it because your actions caused the man to strike you out of self-defense.
Self-defense? Have you SEEN that guy?

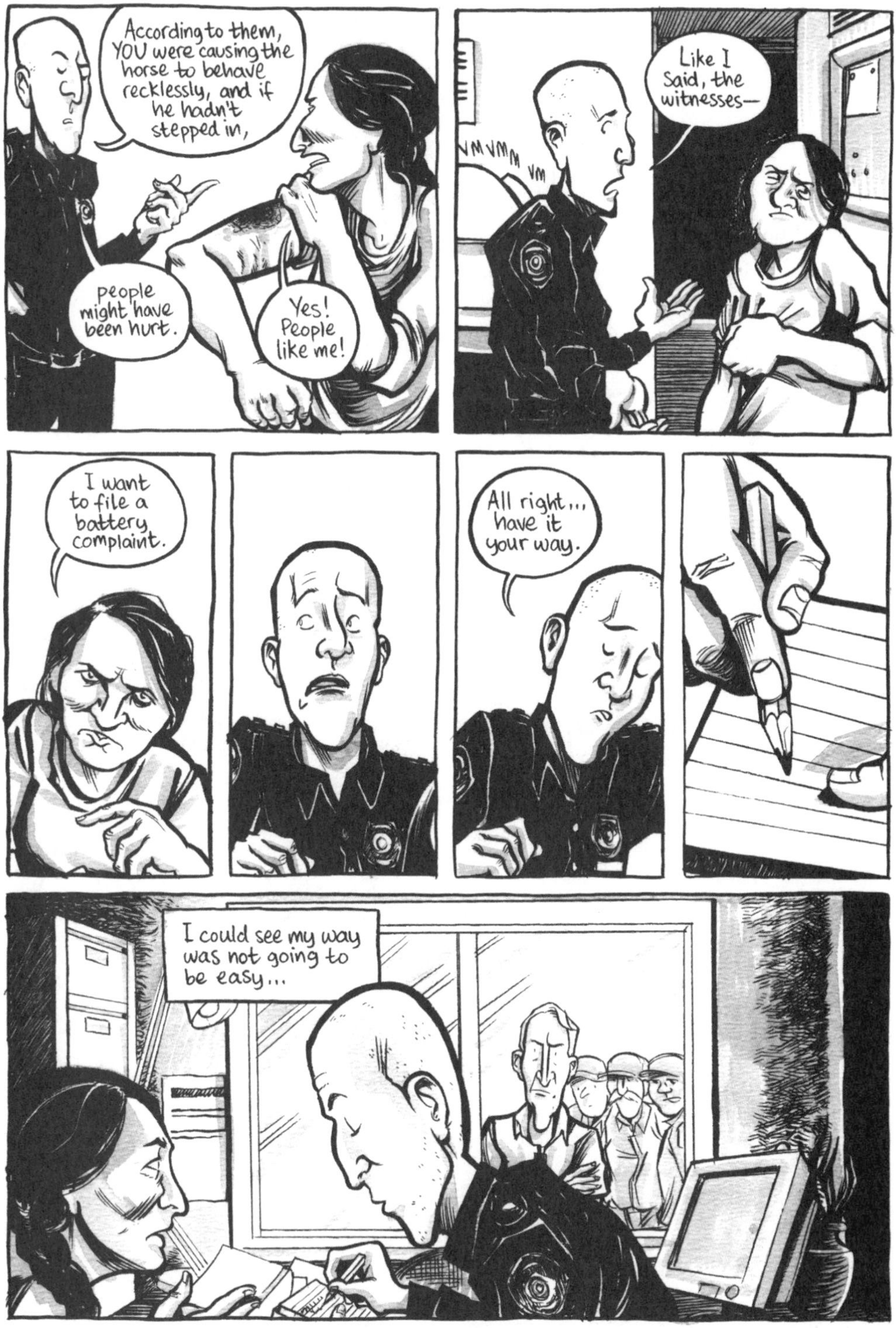
According to them, YOU were causing the horse to behave recklessly, and if he hadn't stepped in,
people might have been hurt.
Yes! People like me!
VMVMM VM
Like I said, the witnesses—
I want to file a battery complaint.
All right... have it your way.
I could see my way was not going to be easy...

I called and wrote many letters complaining to the stewards that Clayton was in breach of contract, that I had been wronged. But I never heard back.

BBZZZZZZZZZZZZ

ZZT—

I was depressed as hell.

I could still stay in the tack room

because I got work exercising horses for another owner.

But it wasn't the same.

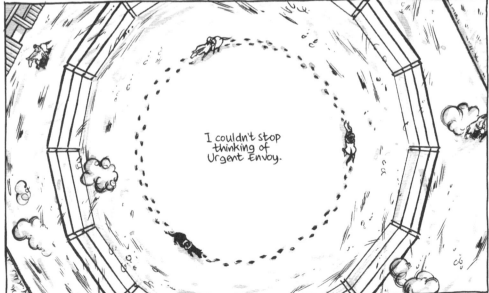

I couldn't stop thinking of Urgent Envoy.

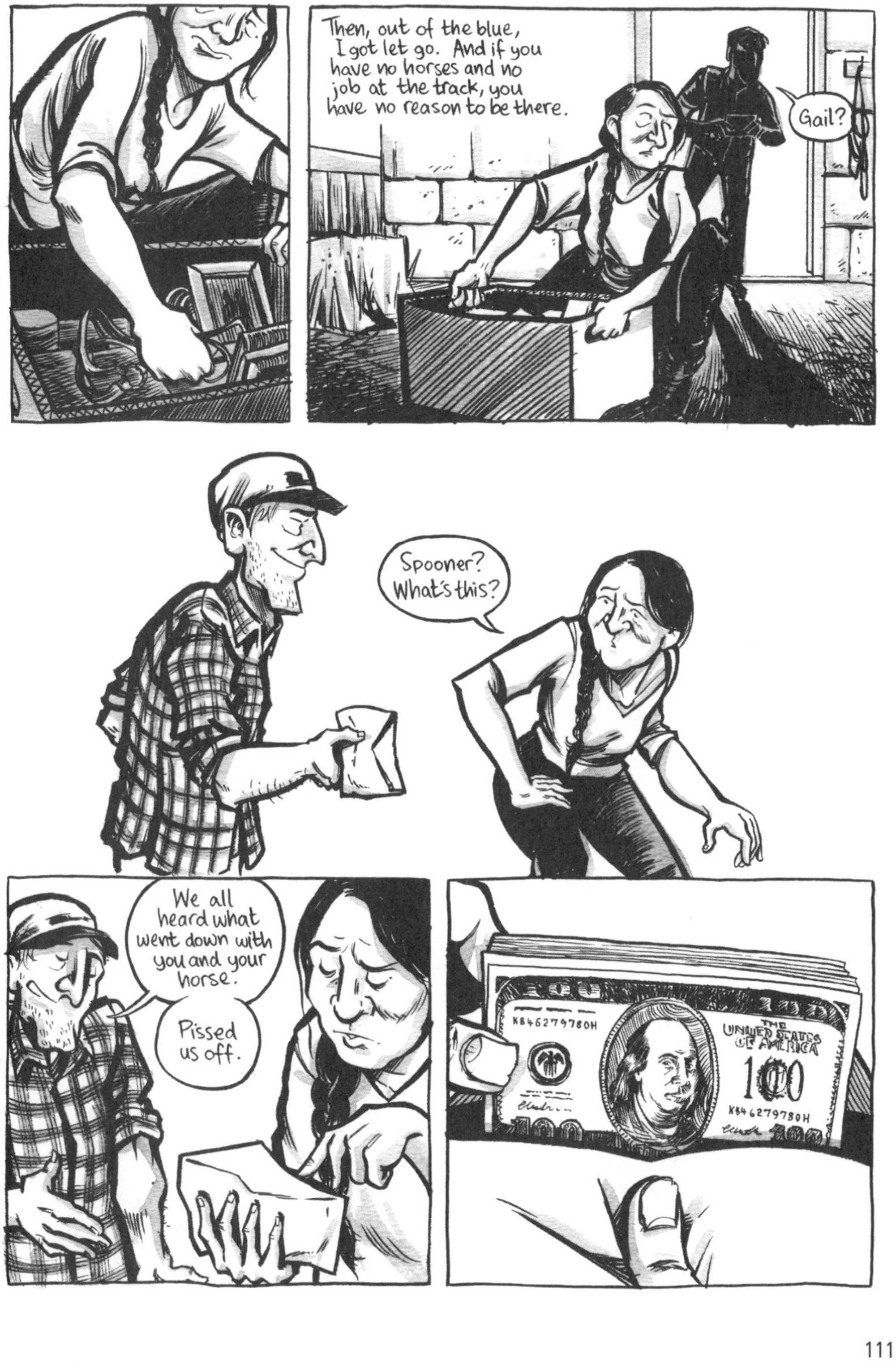
Then, out of the blue, I got let go. And if you have no horses and no job at the track, you have no reason to be there.
Gail?
Spooner? What's this?
We all heard what went down with you and your horse.
Pissed us off.

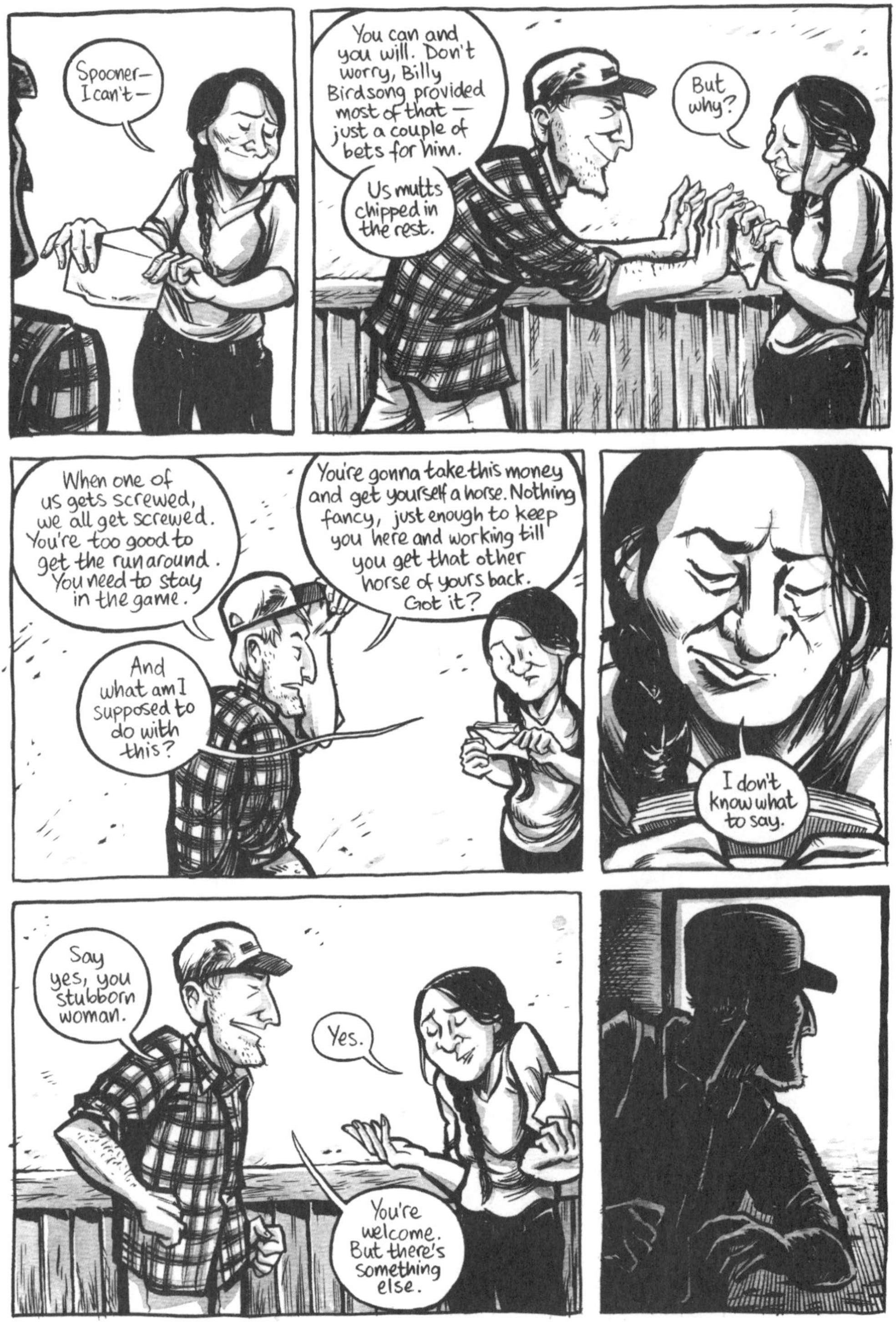
Spooner— I can't—
You can and you will. Don't worry, Billy Birdsong provided most of that— just a couple of bets for him.
Us mutts chipped in the rest.
But why?
When one of us gets screwed, we all get screwed. You're too good to get the runaround. You need to stay in the game.
And what am I supposed to do with this?
You're gonna take this money and get yourself a horse. Nothing fancy, just enough to keep you here and working till you get that other horse of yours back. Got it?
I don't know what to say.
Say yes, you stubborn woman.
Yes.
You're welcome. But there's something else.

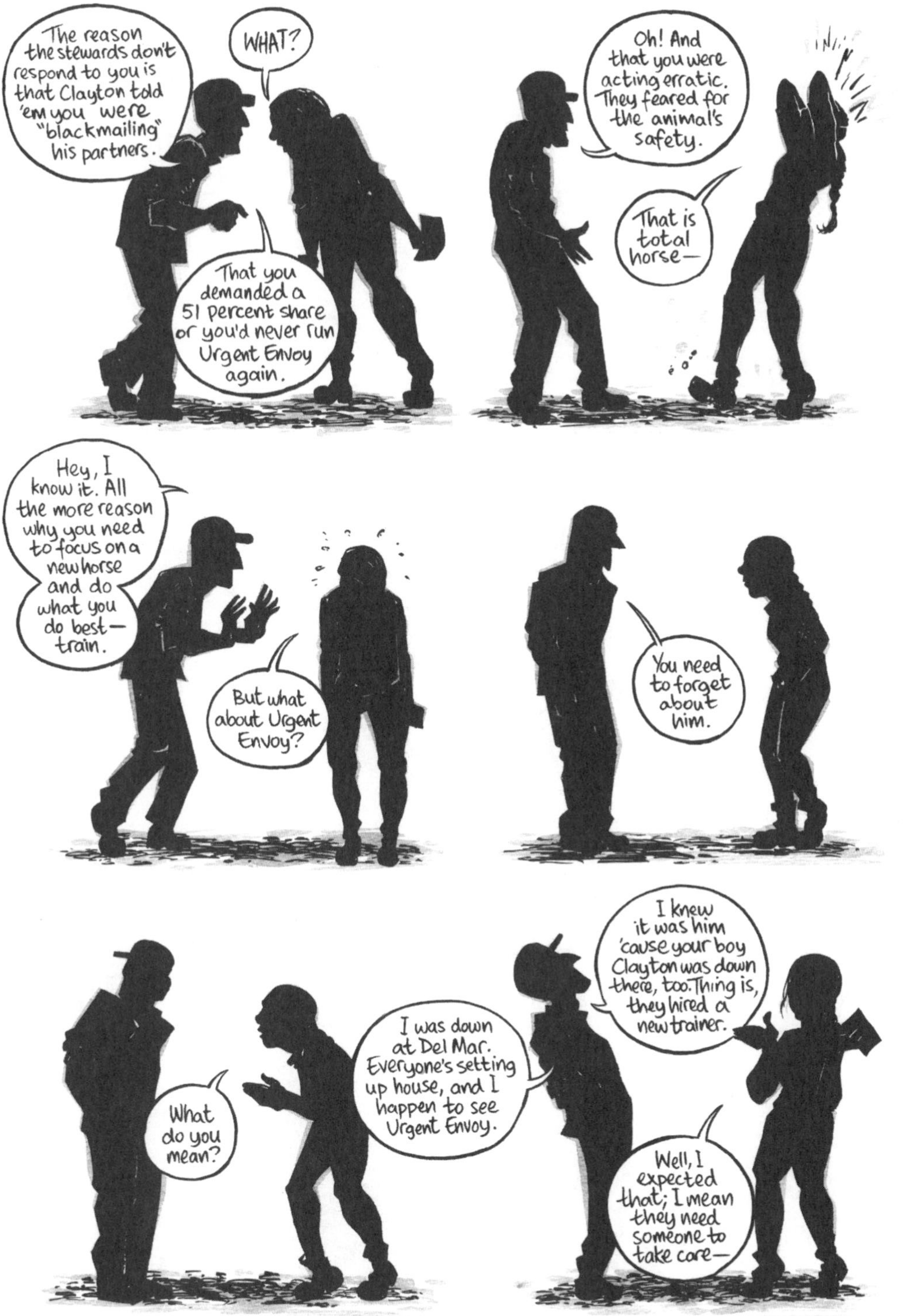
The reason the stewards don't respond to you is that Clayton told 'em you were "blackmailing" his partners.
WHAT?
That you demanded a 51 percent share or you'd never run Urgent Envoy again.
Oh! And that you were acting erratic. They feared for the animal's safety.
That is total horse—
Hey, I know it. All the more reason why you need to focus on a new horse and do what you do best—train.
But what about Urgent Envoy?
You need to forget about him.
What do you mean?
I was down at Del Mar. Everyone's setting up house, and I happen to see Urgent Envoy.
I knew it was him 'cause your boy Clayton was down there, too. Thing is, they hired a new trainer.
Well, I expected that; I mean they need someone to take care—

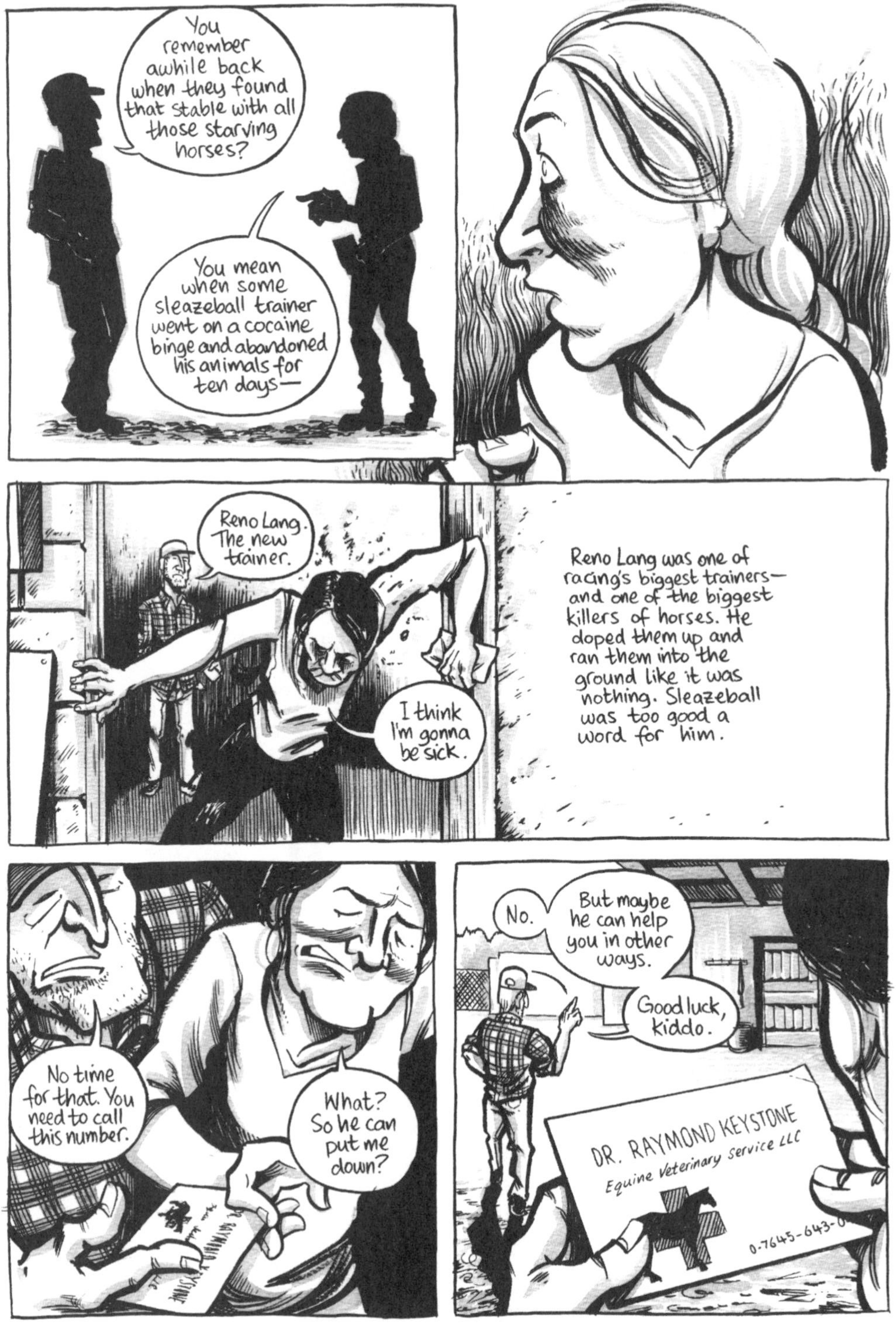
You remember awhile back when they found that stable with all those starving horses?
You mean when some sleazeball trainer went on a cocaine binge and abandoned his animals for ten days—
Reno Lang. The new trainer.
I think I'm gonna be sick.
Reno Lang was one of racing's biggest trainers— and one of the biggest killers of horses. He doped them up and ran them into the ground like it was nothing. Sleazeball was too good a word for him.
No time for that. You need to call this number.
What? So he can put me down?
No.
But maybe he can help you in other ways.
Good luck, kiddo.
DR. RAYMOND KEYSTONE
Equine Veterinary Service LLC
0-7645-643-0

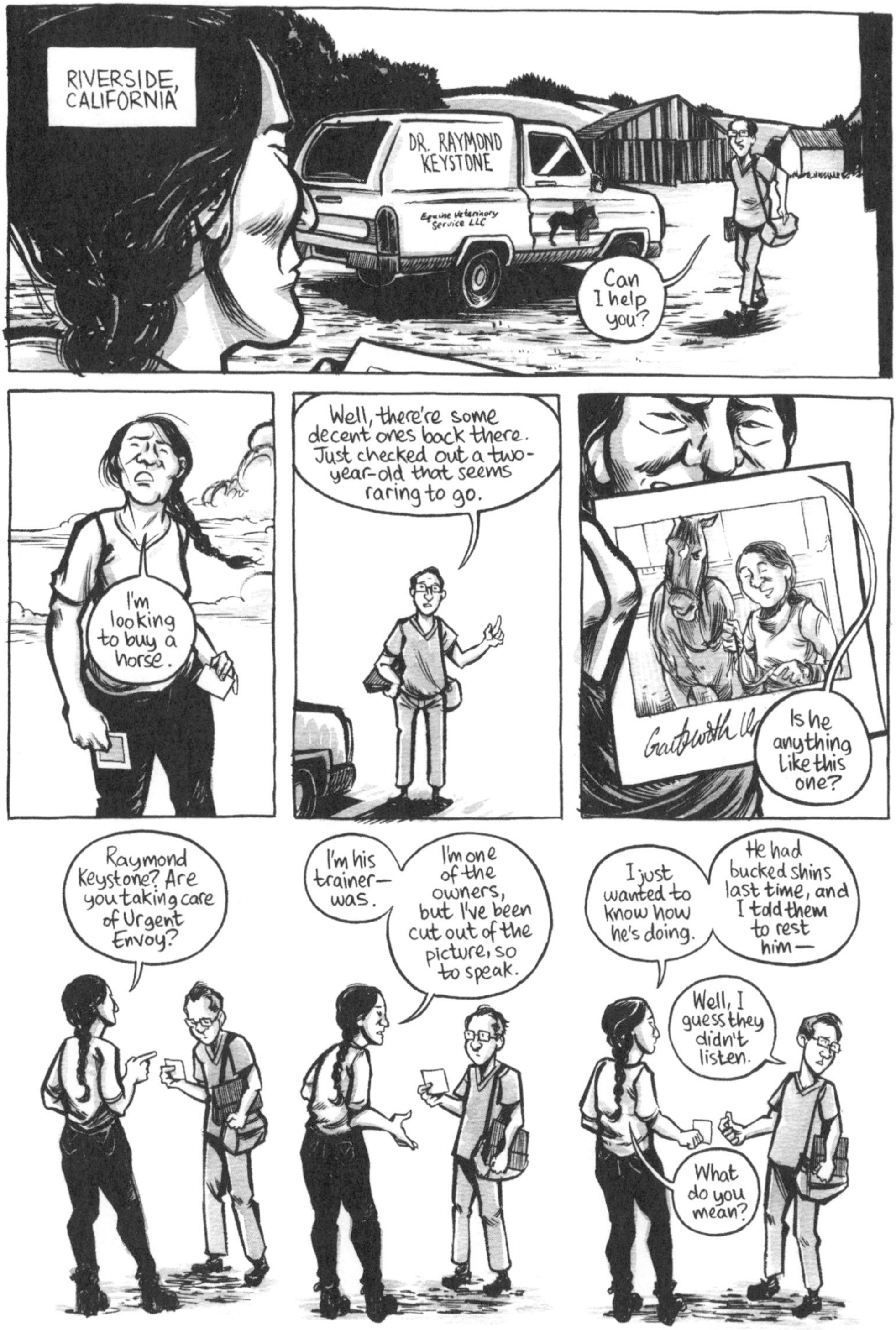
RIVERSIDE, CALIFORNIA
DR. RAYMOND KEYSTONE
Equine Veterinary Service LLC
Can I help you?
I'm looking to buy a horse.
Well, there're some decent ones back there. Just checked out a two-year-old that seems raring to go.
Is he anything like this one?
Raymond Keystone? Are you taking care of Urgent Envoy?
I'm his trainer—was.
I'm one of the owners, but I've been cut out of the picture, so to speak.
I just wanted to know how he's doing.
He had bucked shins last time, and I told them to rest him—
Well, I guess they didn't listen.
What do you mean?

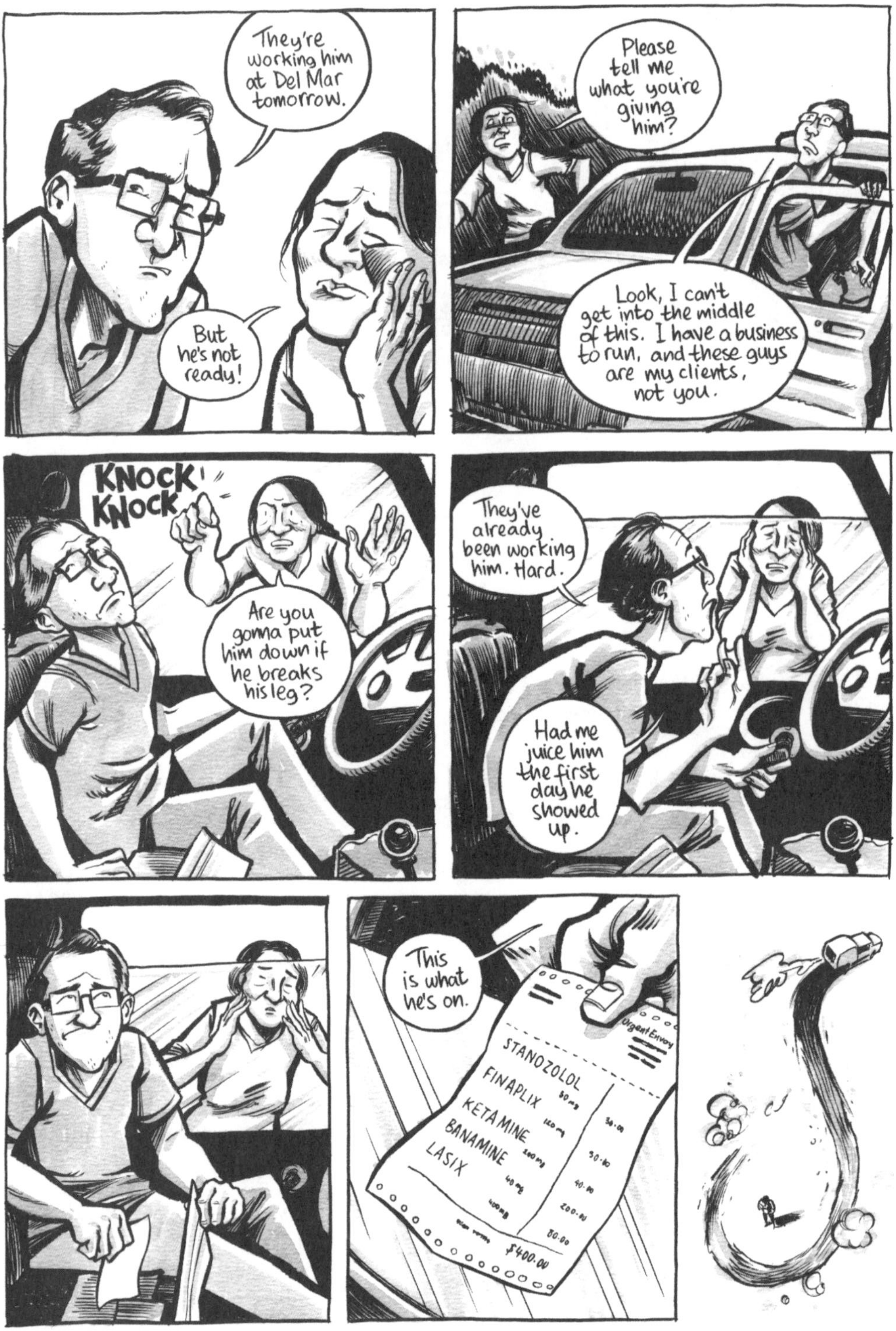
They're working him at Del Mar tomorrow.
But he's not ready!
Please tell me what you're giving him?
Look, I can't get into the middle of this. I have a business to run, and these guys are my clients, not you.
KNOCK KNOCK
Are you gonna put him down if he breaks his leg?
They've already been working him. Hard.
Had me juice him the first day he showed up.
This is what he's on.
Urgent Envoy
STANOZOLOL
FINAPLIX
KETAMINE
BANAMINE
LASIX
30.00
30.00
40.00
200.00
80.00
$400.00

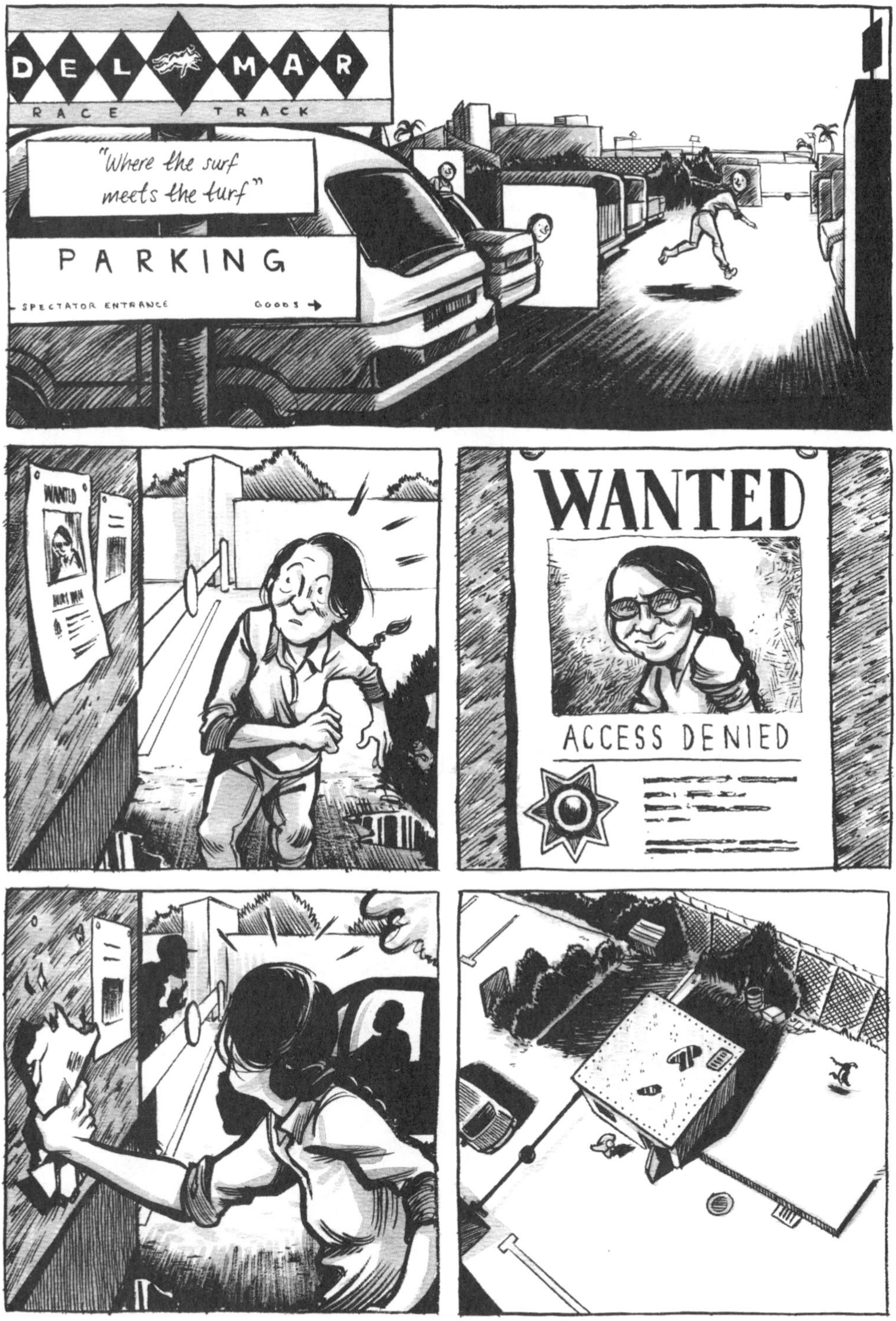
DEL MAR
RACE TRACK
"Where the surf meets the turf"
PARKING
SPECTATOR ENTRANCE
GOODS
WANTED
ACCESS DENIED

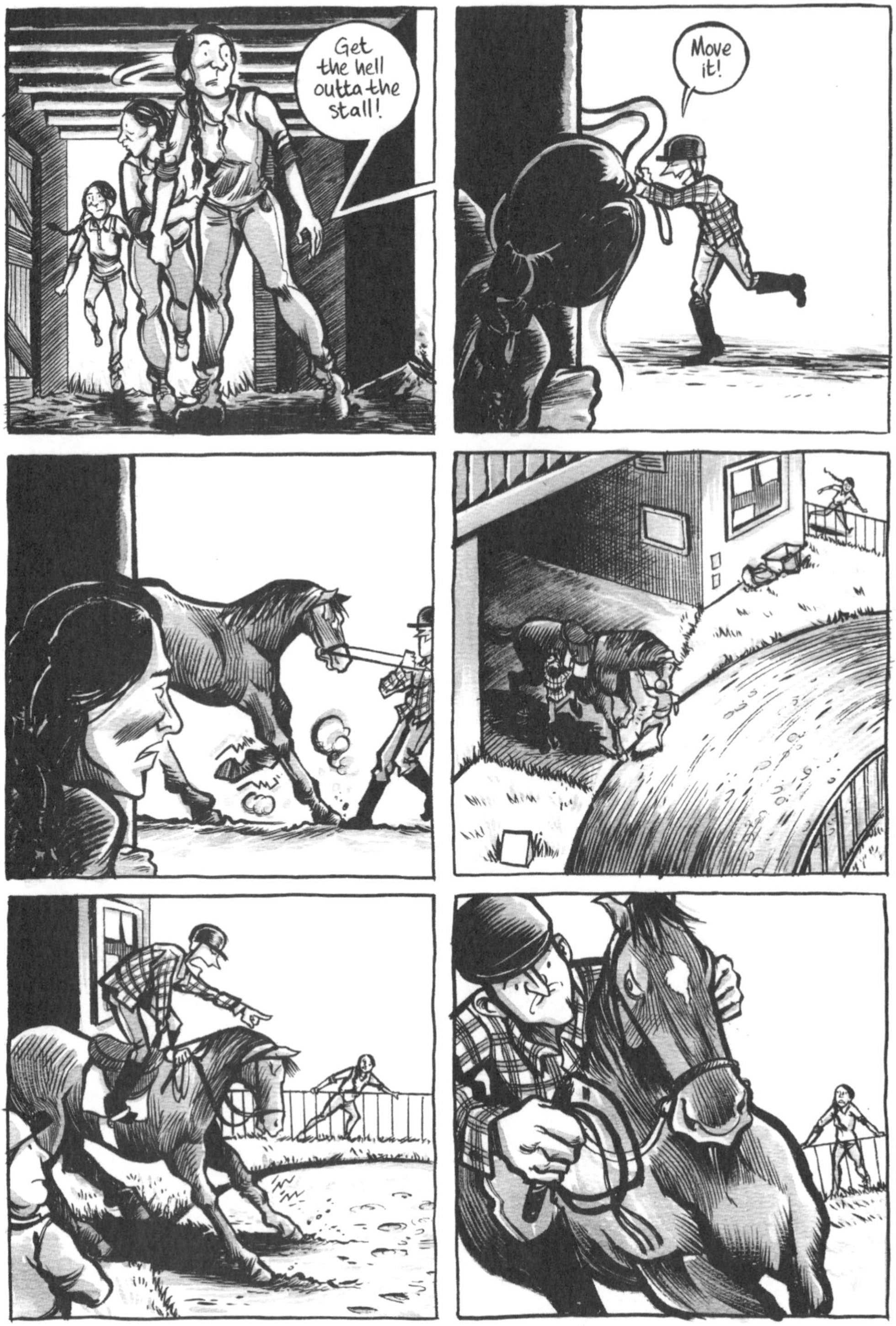
Get the hell outta the stall!
Move it!

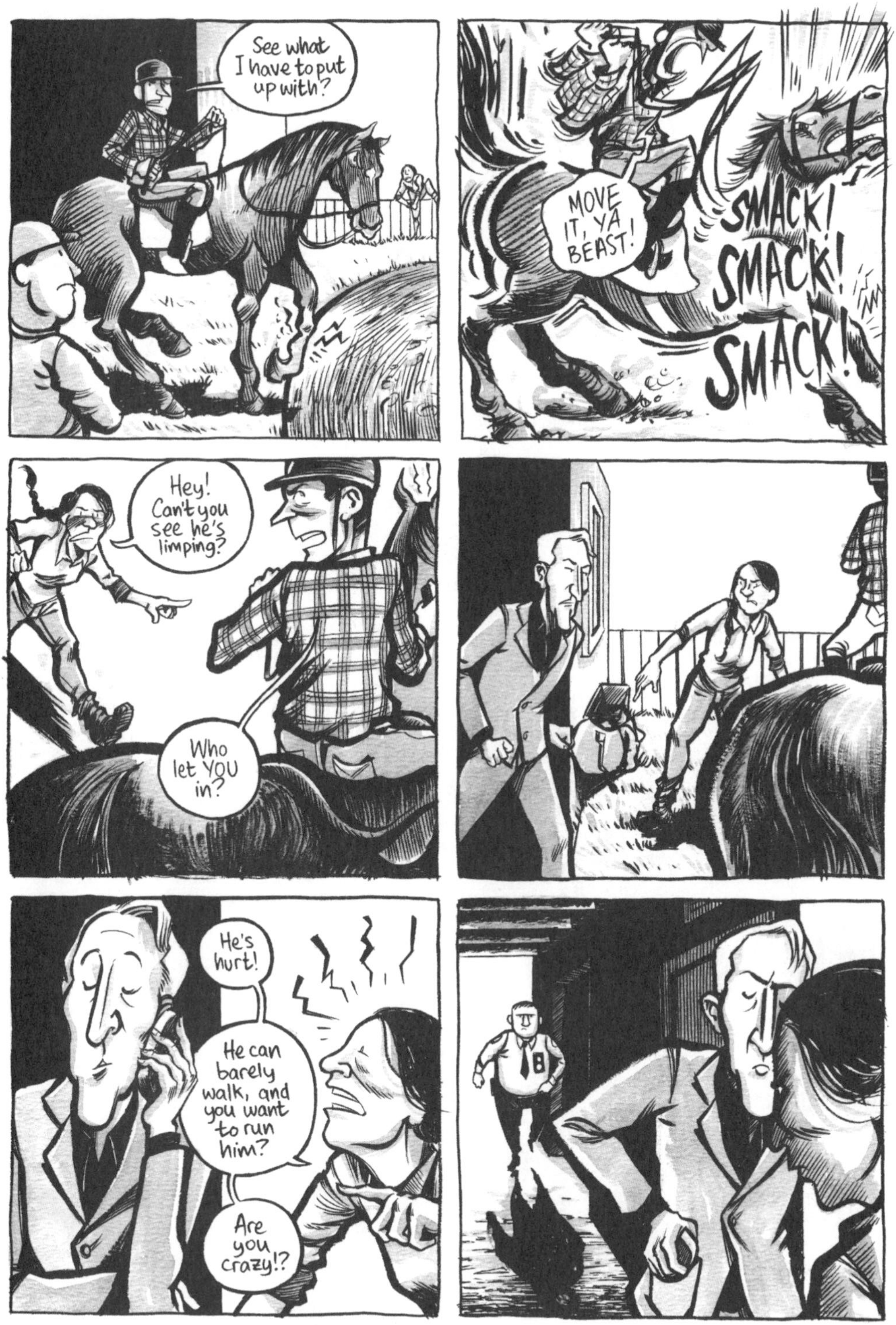
See what I have to put up with?
MOVE IT, YA BEAST!
SMACK! SMACK! SMACK!
Hey! Can't you see he's limping?
Who let YOU in?
He's hurt!
He can barely walk, and you want to run him?
Are you crazy!?

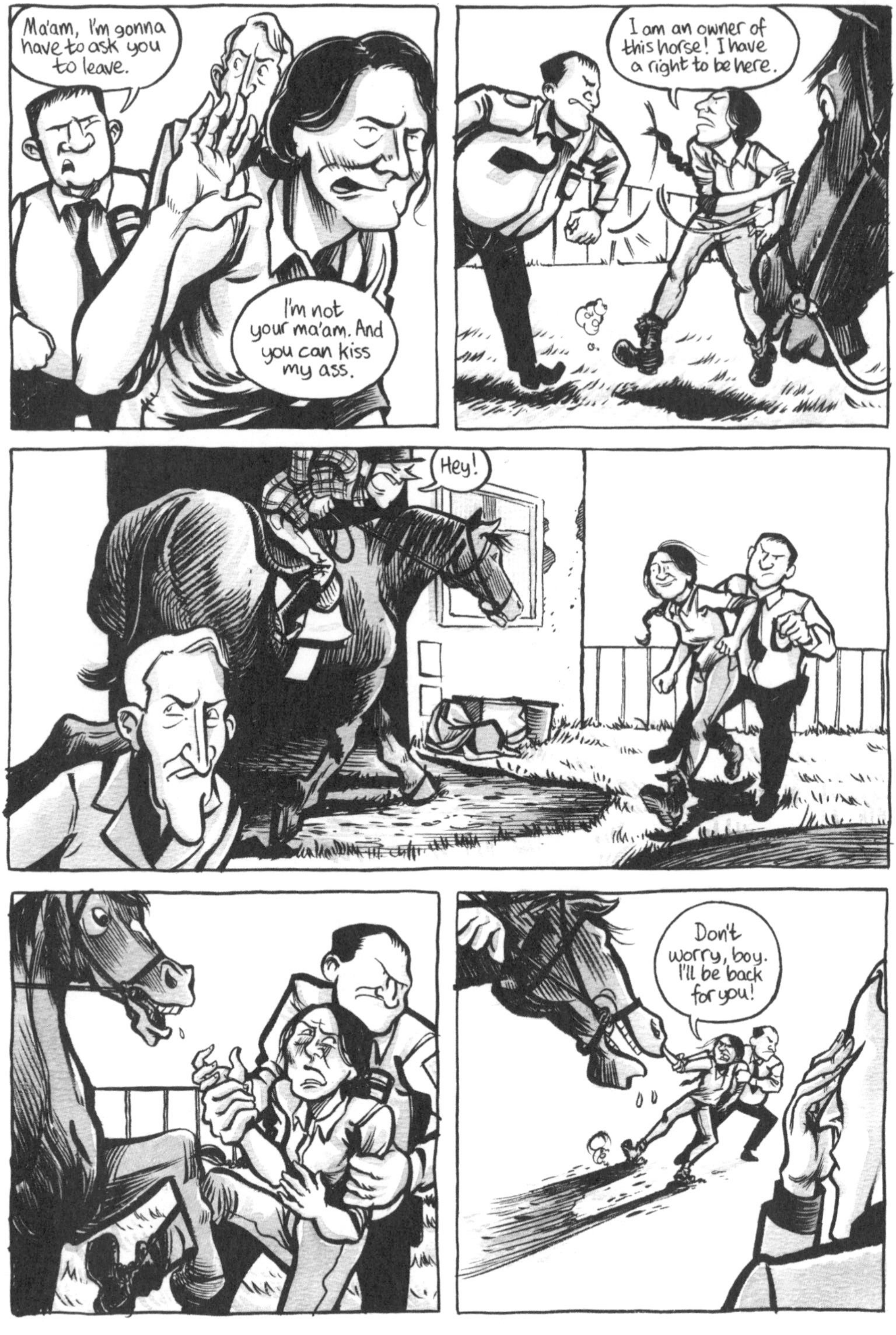
Ma'am, I'm gonna have to ask you to leave.
I'm not your ma'am. And you can kiss my ass.
I am an owner of this horse! I have a right to be here.
Hey!
Don't worry, boy. I'll be back for you!

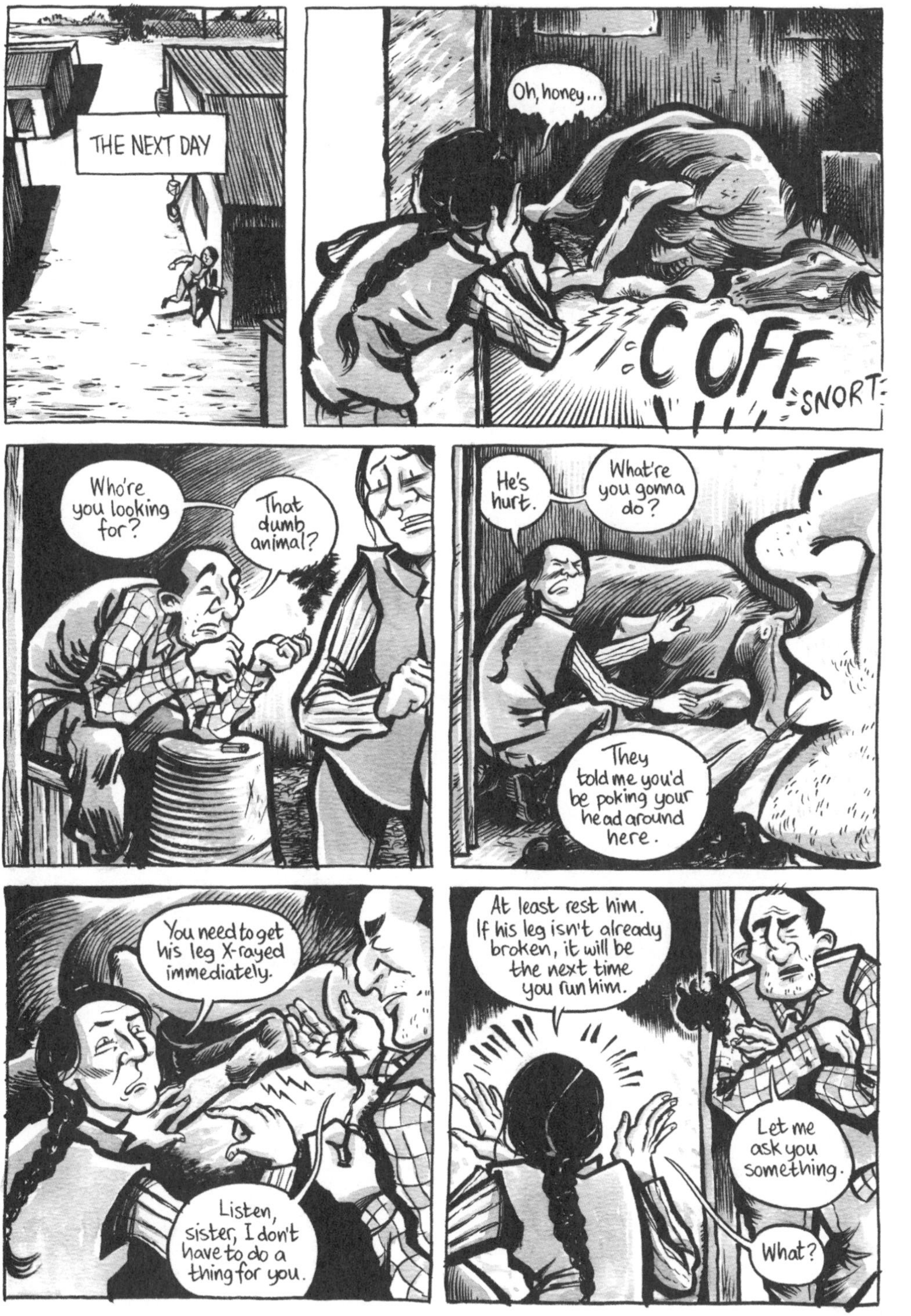
THE NEXT DAY
Oh, honey...
COFF
SNORT
Who're you looking for?
That dumb animal?
He's hurt.
What're you gonna do?
They told me you'd be poking your head around here.
You need to get his leg X-rayed immediately.
Listen, sister, I don't have to do a thing for you.
At least rest him. If his leg isn't already broken, it will be the next time you run him.
Let me ask you something.
What?

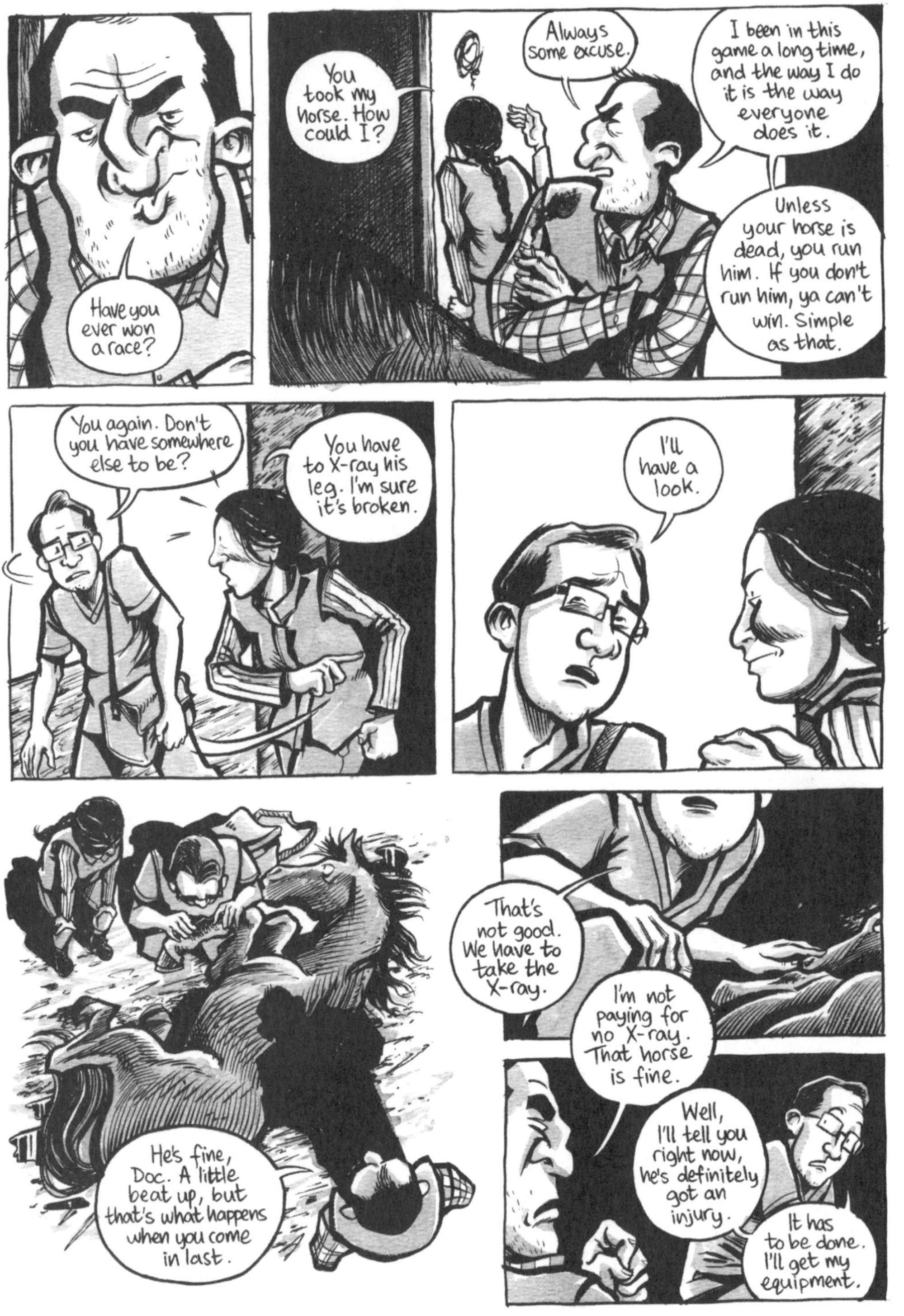
Have you ever won a race?
You took my horse. How could I?
Always some excuse.
I been in this game a long time, and the way I do it is the way everyone does it.
Unless your horse is dead, you run him. If you don't run him, ya can't win. Simple as that.
You again. Don't you have somewhere else to be?
You have to X-ray his leg. I'm sure it's broken.
I'll have a look.
He's fine, Doc. A little beat up, but that's what happens when you come in last.
That's not good. We have to take the X-ray.
I'm not paying for no X-ray. That horse is fine.
Well, I'll tell you right now, he's definitely got an injury.
It has to be done. I'll get my equipment.

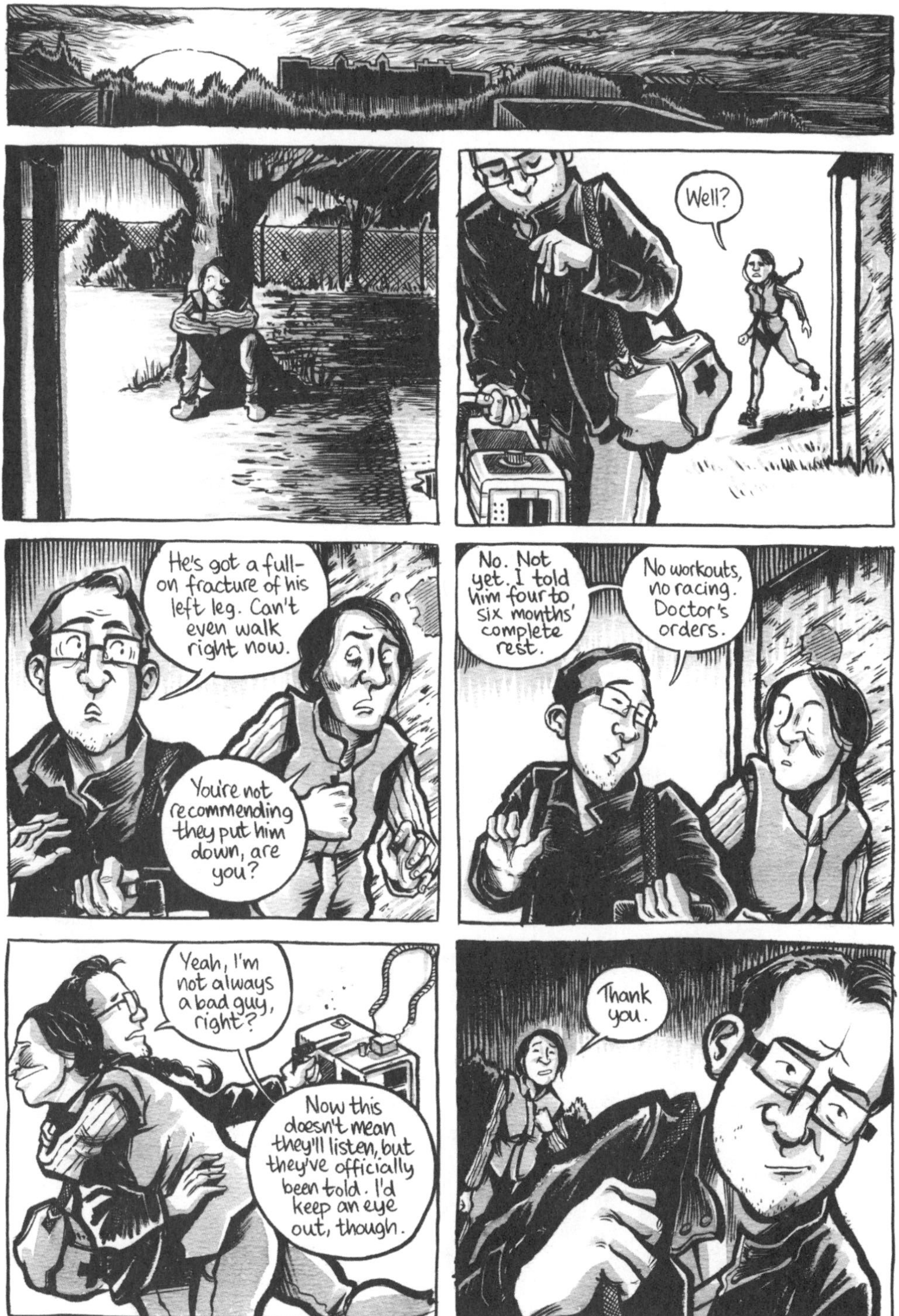
Well?
He's got a full-on fracture of his left leg. Can't even walk right now.
You're not recommending they put him down, are you?
No. Not yet. I told him four to six months' complete rest.
No workouts, no racing. Doctor's orders.
Yeah, I'm not always a bad guy, right?
Now this doesn't mean they'll listen, but they've officially been told. I'd keep an eye out, though.
Thank you.

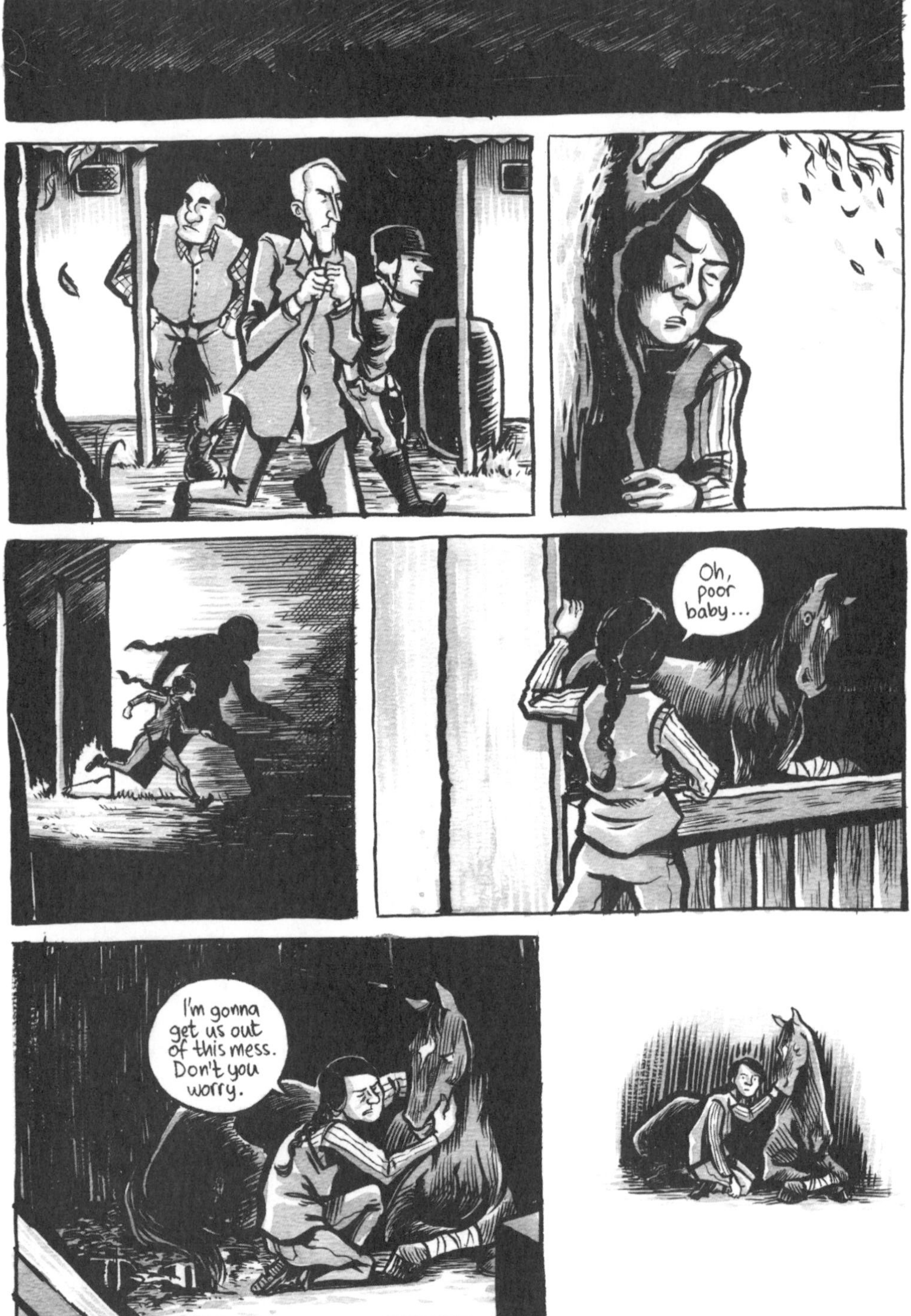
Oh, poor baby...
I'm gonna get us out of this mess. Don't you worry.

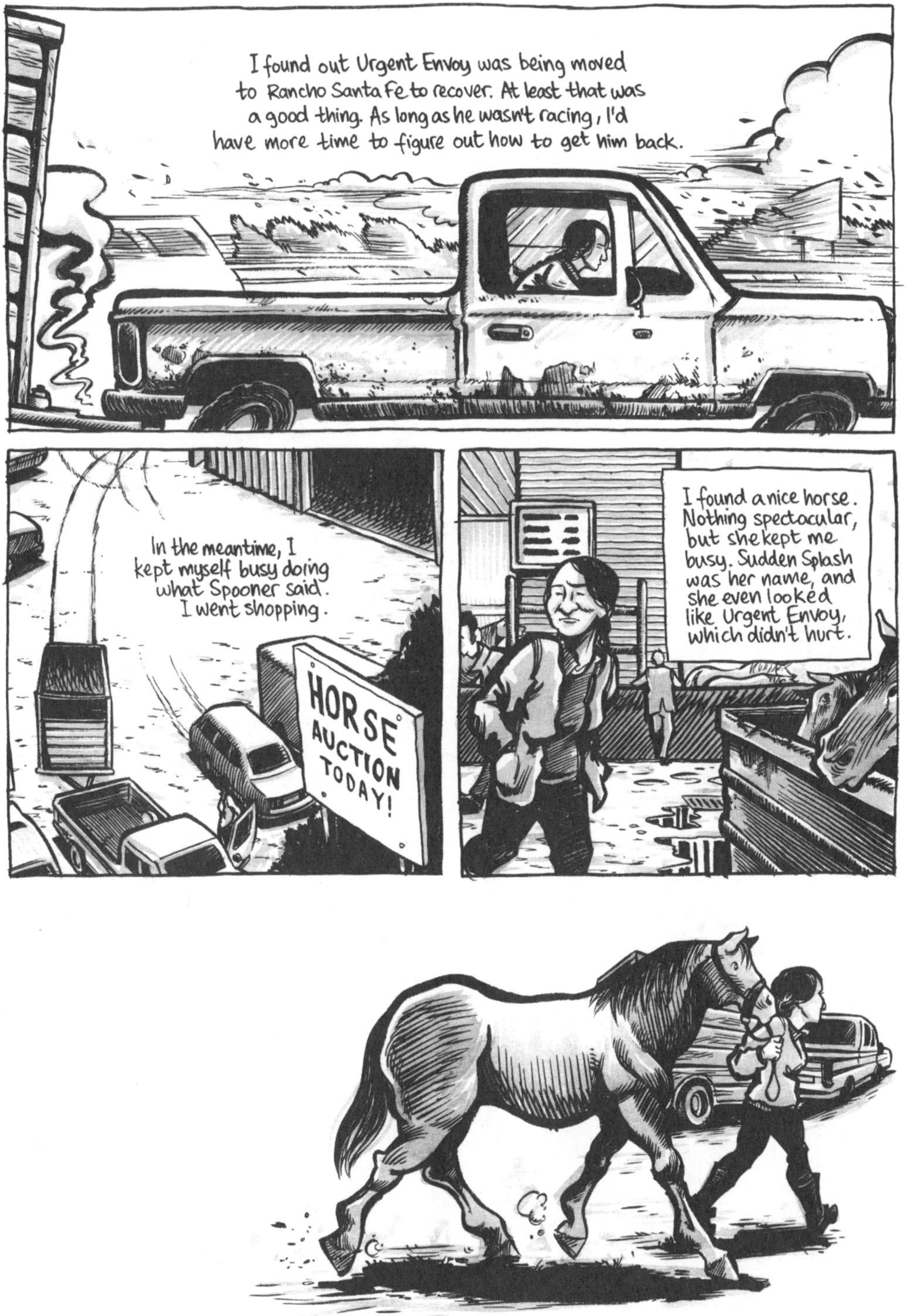
I found out Urgent Envoy was being moved to Rancho Santa Fe to recover. At least that was a good thing. As long as he wasn't racing, I'd have more time to figure out how to get him back.
In the meantime, I kept myself busy doing what Spooner said. I went shopping.
HORSE AUCTION TODAY!
I found a nice horse. Nothing spectacular, but she kept me busy. Sudden Splash was her name, and she even looked like Urgent Envoy, which didn't hurt.

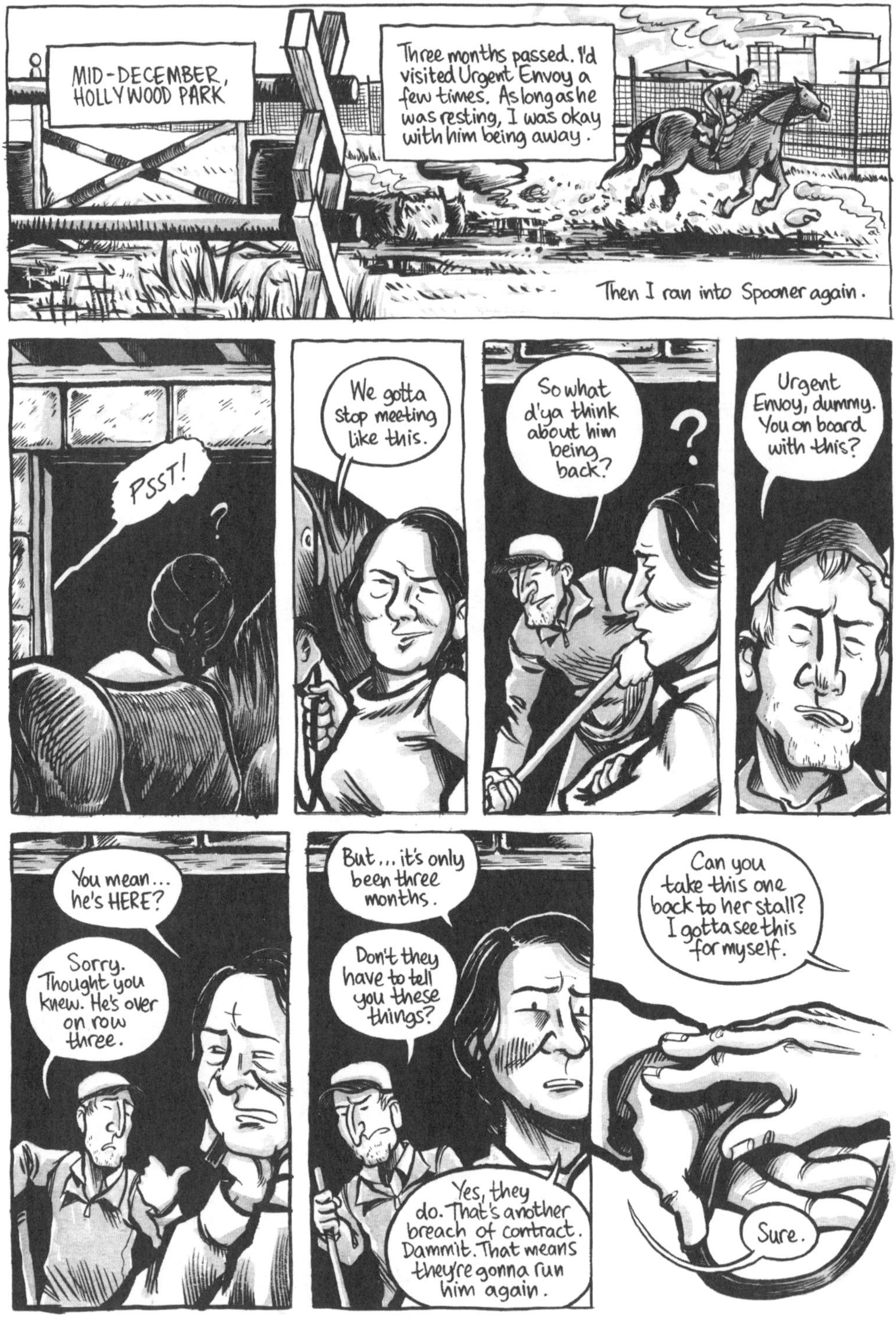
MID-DECEMBER, HOLLYWOOD PARK
Three months passed. I'd visited Urgent Envoy a few times. As long as he was resting, I was okay with him being away.
Then I ran into Spooner again.
PSST!
?
We gotta stop meeting like this.
So what d'ya think about him being back?
?
Urgent Envoy, dummy. You on board with this?
You mean... he's HERE?
Sorry. Thought you knew. He's over on row three.
But... it's only been three months.
Don't they have to tell you these things?
Yes, they do. That's another breach of contract. Dammit. That means they're gonna run him again.
Can you take this one back to her stall? I gotta see this for myself.
Sure.

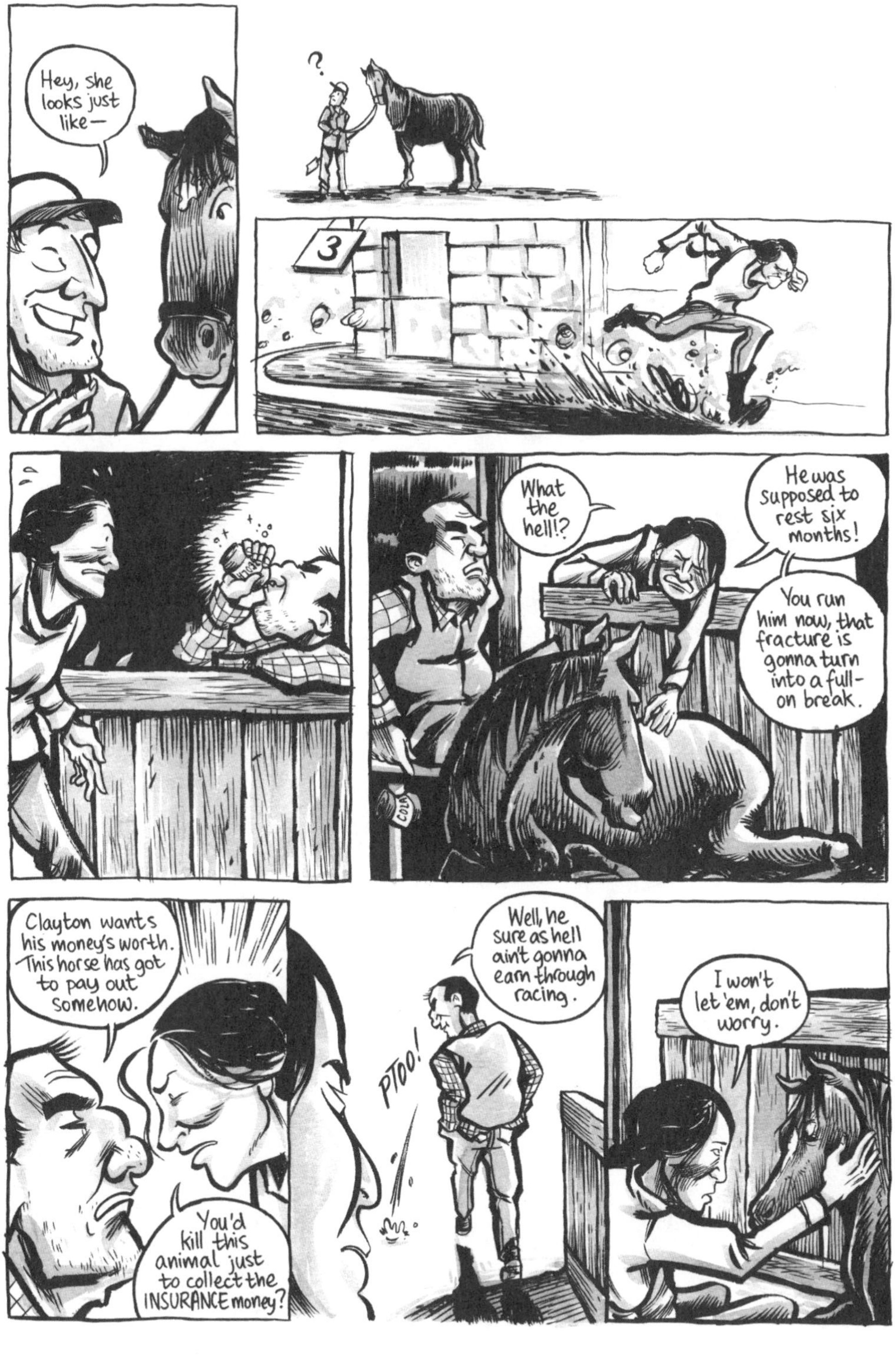
Hey, she looks just like—
?
3
What the hell!?
He was supposed to rest six months!
You run him now, that fracture is gonna turn into a full-on break.
Clayton wants his money's worth. This horse has got to pay out somehow.
You'd kill this animal just to collect the INSURANCE money?
PTOO!
Well, he sure as hell ain't gonna earn through racing.
I won't let 'em, don't worry.

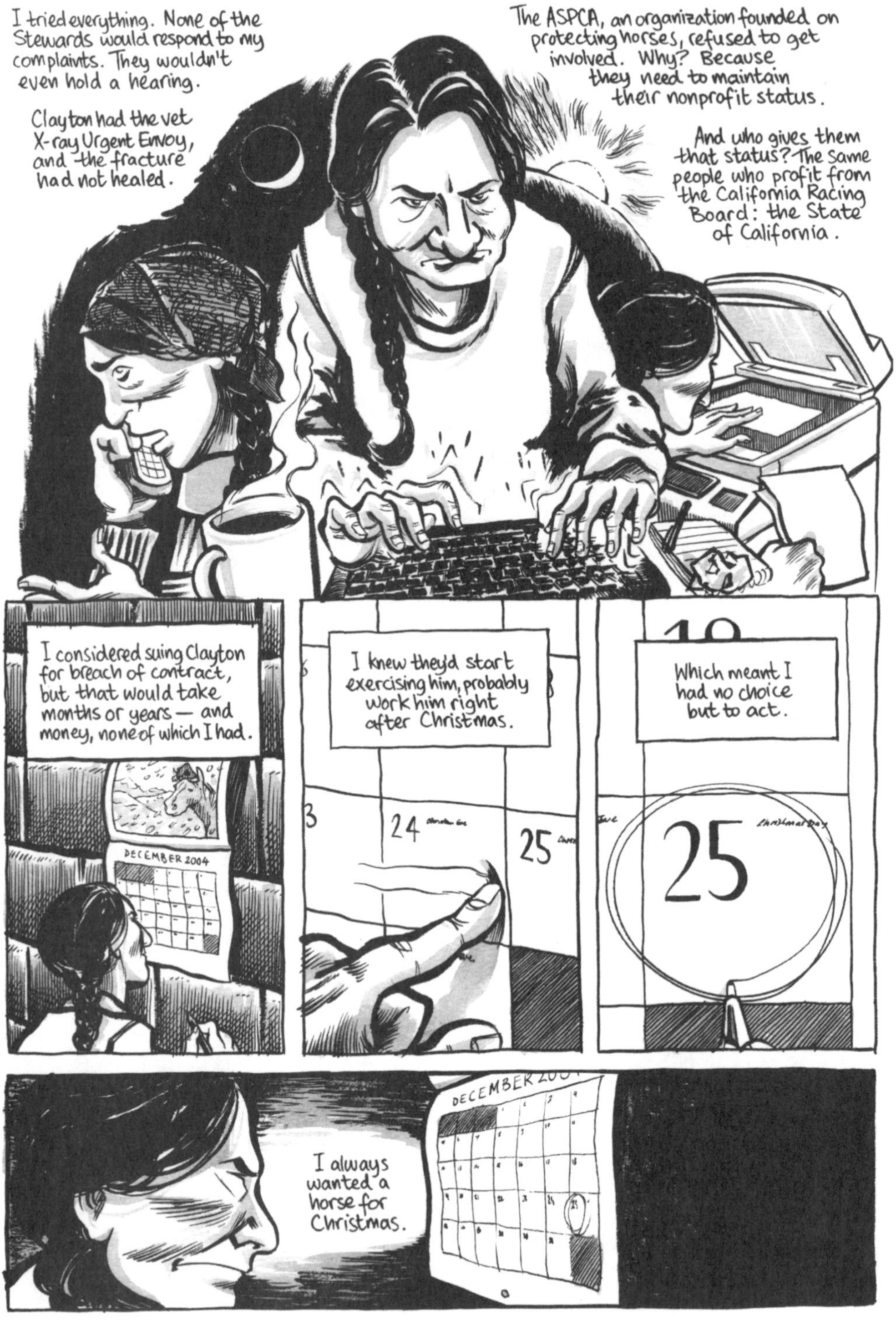
I tried everything. None of the Stewards would respond to my complaints. They wouldn't even hold a hearing.
Clayton had the vet X-ray Urgent Envoy, and the fracture had not healed.
The ASPCA, an organization founded on protecting horses, refused to get involved. Why? Because they need to maintain their nonprofit status.
And who gives them that status? The same people who profit from the California Racing Board: the State of California.
I considered suing Clayton for breach of contract, but that would take months or years — and money, none of which I had.
DECEMBER 2004
I knew they'd start exercising him, probably work him right after Christmas.
24
25
Which meant I had no choice but to act.
25
I always wanted a horse for Christmas.
DECEMBER

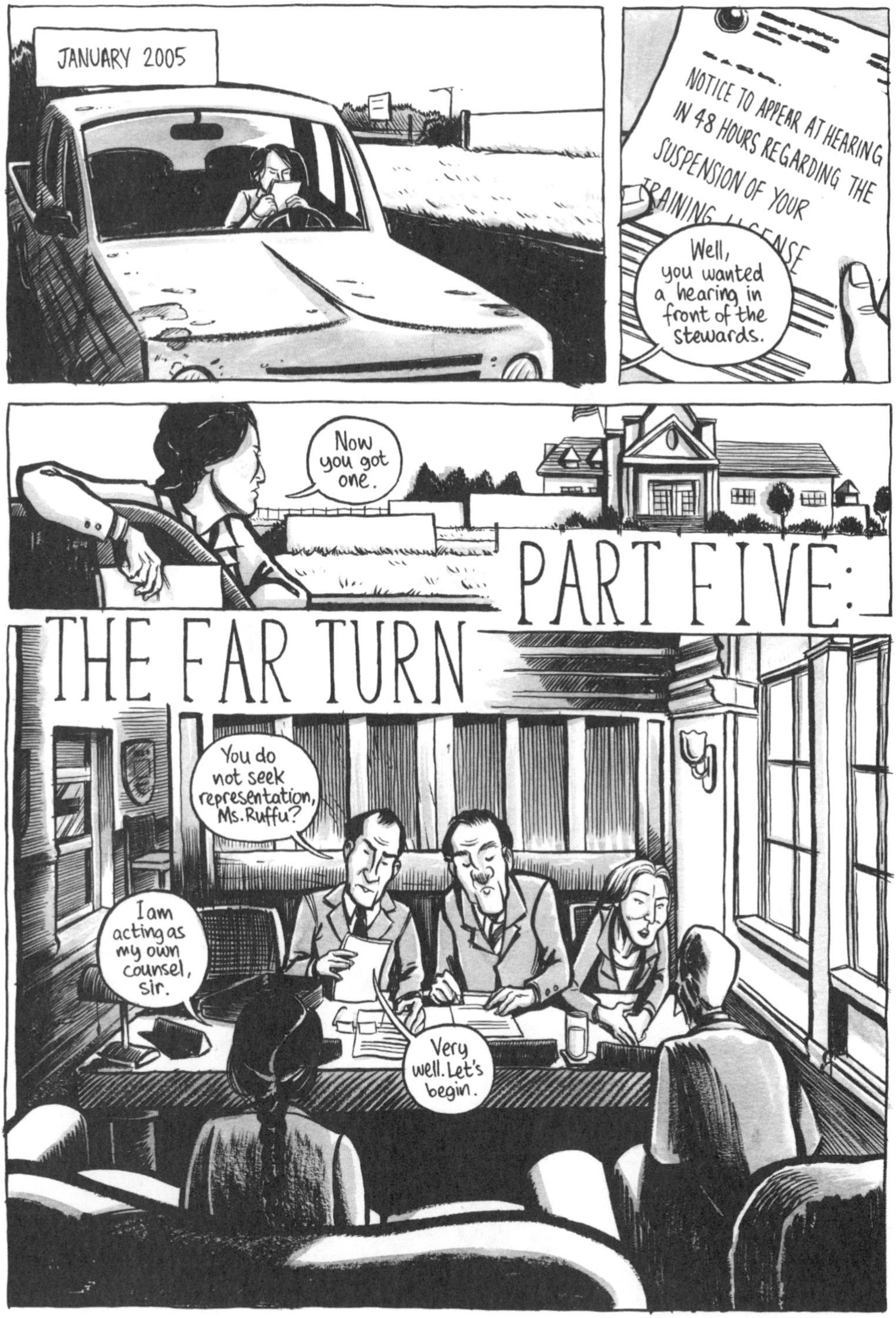
JANUARY 2005
NOTICE TO APPEAR AT HEARING IN 48 HOURS REGARDING THE SUSPENSION OF YOUR
Well, you wanted a hearing in front of the stewards.
Now you got one.
PART FIVE:
THE FAR TURN
You do not seek representation, Ms. Ruffu?
I am acting as my own counsel, sir.
Very well. Let's begin.

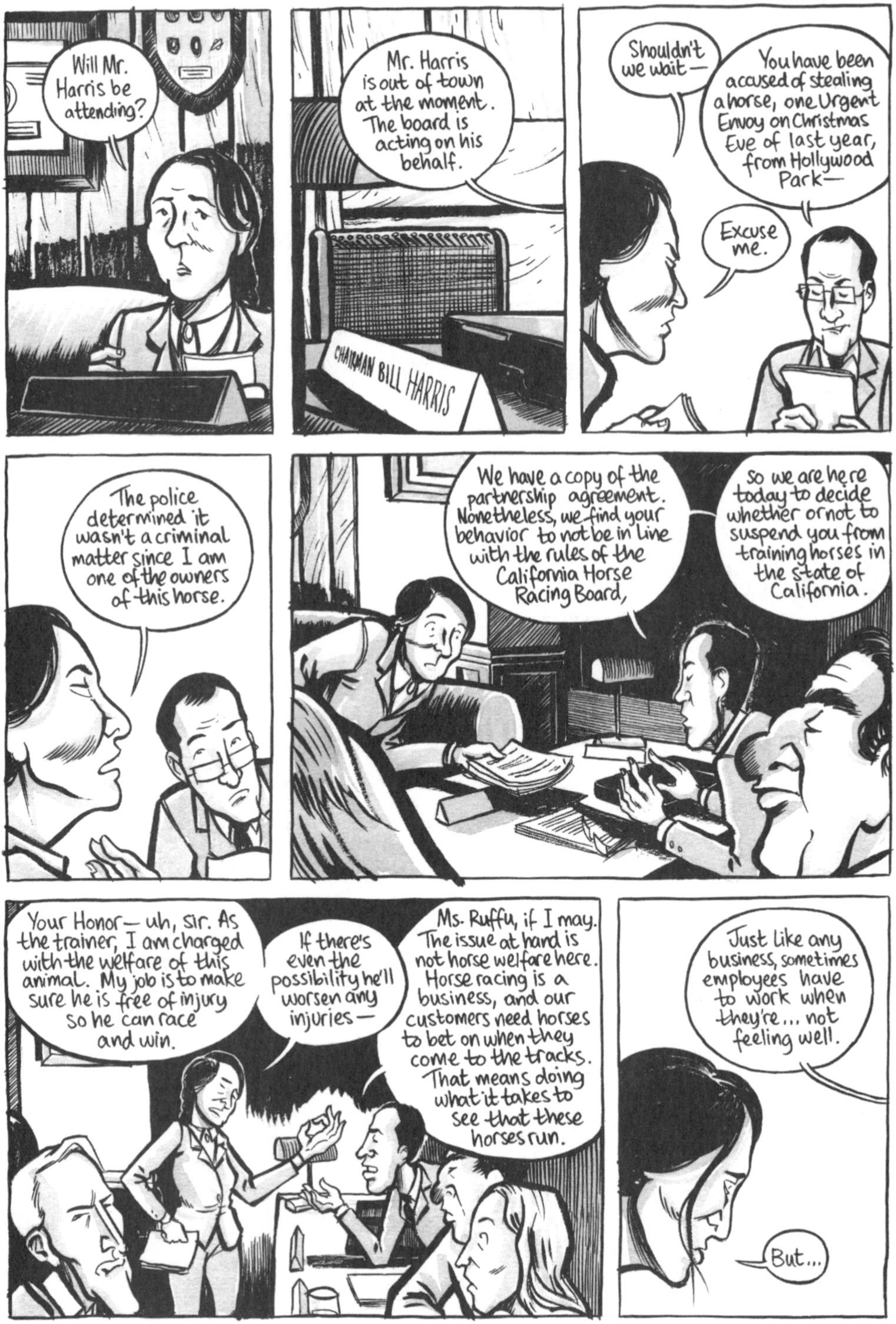

Will Mr. Harris be attending?
Mr. Harris is out of town at the moment. The board is acting on his behalf.
CHAIRMAN BILL HARRIS
Shouldn't we wait—
You have been accused of stealing a horse, one Urgent Envoy on Christmas Eve of last year, from Hollywood Park—
Excuse me.
The police determined it wasn't a criminal matter since I am one of the owners of this horse.
We have a copy of the partnership agreement. Nonetheless, we find your behavior to not be in line with the rules of the California Horse Racing Board,
so we are here today to decide whether or not to suspend you from training horses in the state of California.
Your Honor— uh, sir. As the trainer, I am charged with the welfare of this animal. My job is to make sure he is free of injury so he can race and win.
If there's even the possibility he'll worsen any injuries—
Ms. Ruffu, if I may. The issue at hand is not horse welfare here. Horse racing is a business, and our customers need horses to bet on when they come to the tracks. That means doing what it takes to see that these horses run.
Just like any business, sometimes employees have to work when they're... not feeling well.
But...

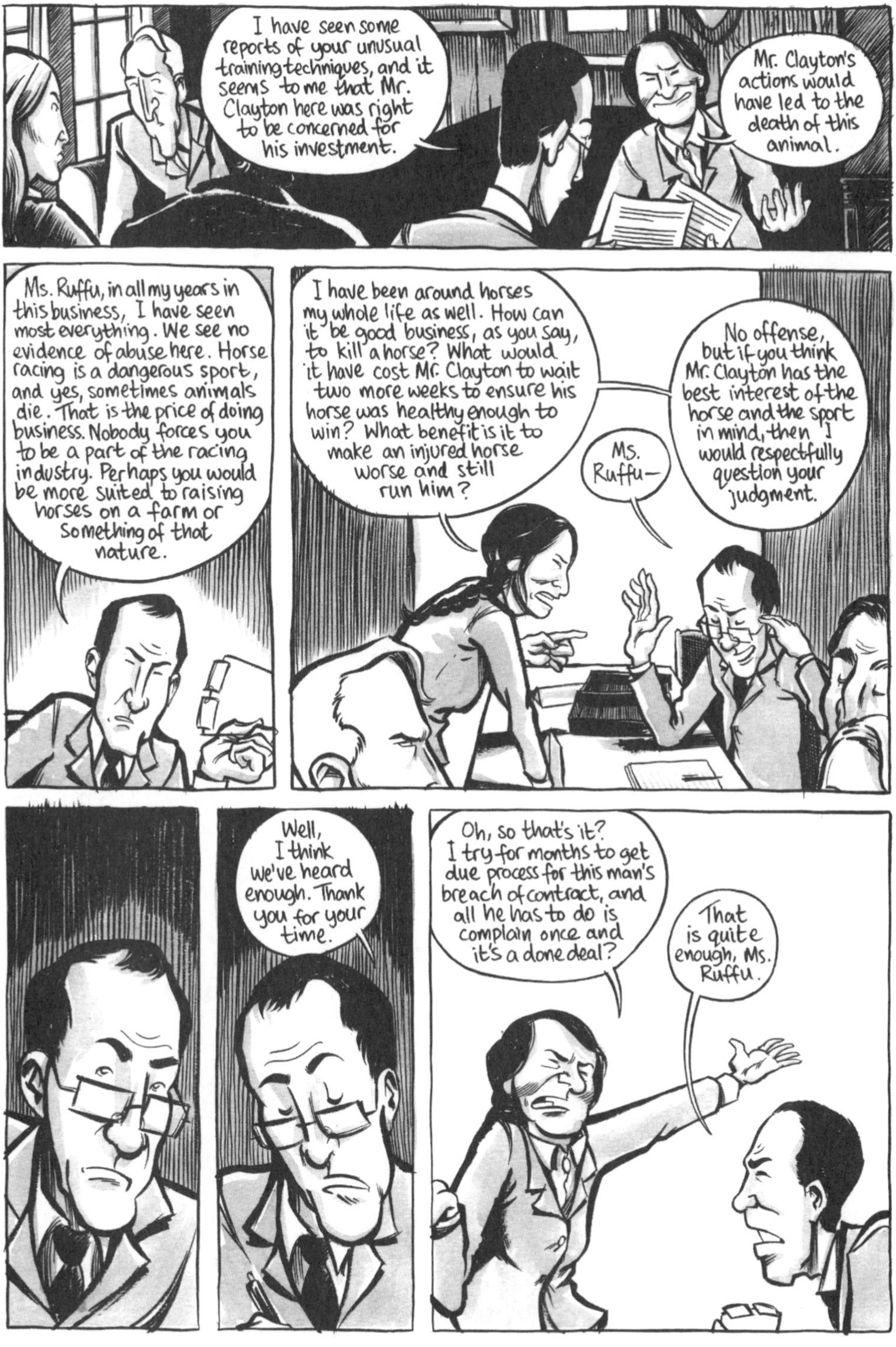

I have seen some reports of your unusual training techniques, and it seems to me that Mr. Clayton here was right to be concerned for his investment.
Mr. Clayton's actions would have led to the death of this animal.
Ms. Ruffu, in all my years in this business, I have seen most everything. We see no evidence of abuse here. Horse racing is a dangerous sport, and yes, sometimes animals die. That is the price of doing business. Nobody forces you to be a part of the racing industry. Perhaps you would be more suited to raising horses on a farm or something of that nature.
I have been around horses my whole life as well. How can it be good business, as you say, to kill a horse? What would it have cost Mr. Clayton to wait two more weeks to ensure his horse was healthy enough to win? What benefit is it to make an injured horse worse and still run him?
No offense, but if you think Mr. Clayton has the best interest of the horse and the sport in mind, then I would respectfully question your judgment.
Ms. Ruffu—
Well, I think we've heard enough. Thank you for your time.
Oh, so that's it? I try for months to get due process for this man's breach of contract, and all he has to do is complain once and it's a done deal?
That is quite enough, Ms. Ruffu.

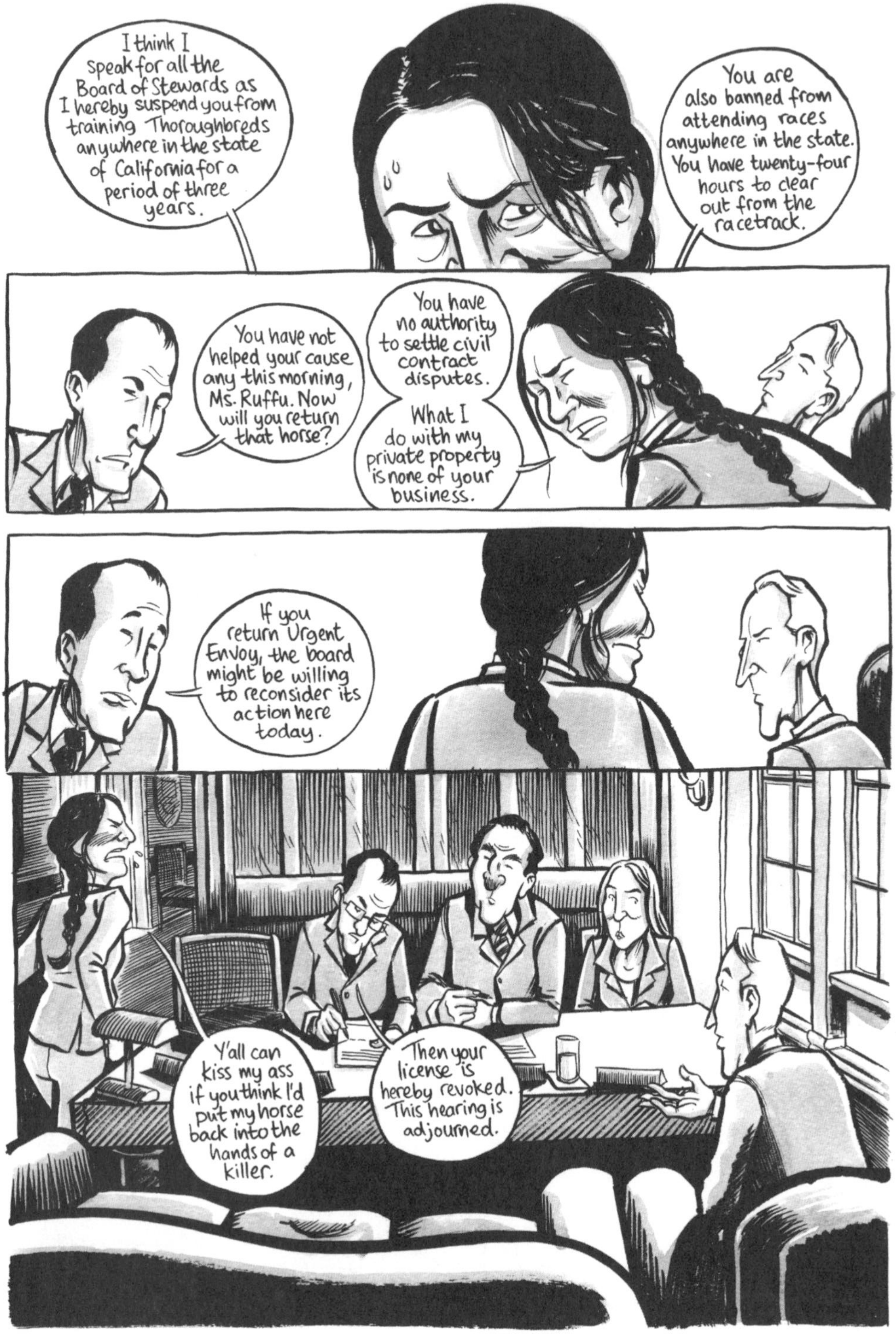

I think I speak for all the Board of Stewards as I hereby suspend you from training Thoroughbreds anywhere in the state of California for a period of three years.
You are also banned from attending races anywhere in the state. You have twenty-four hours to clear out from the racetrack.
You have not helped your cause any this morning, Ms. Ruffu. Now will you return that horse?
You have no authority to settle civil contract disputes.
What I do with my private property is none of your business.
If you return Urgent Envoy, the board might be willing to reconsider its action here today.
Y'all can kiss my ass if you think I'd put my horse back into the hands of a killer.
Then your license is hereby revoked. This hearing is adjourned.

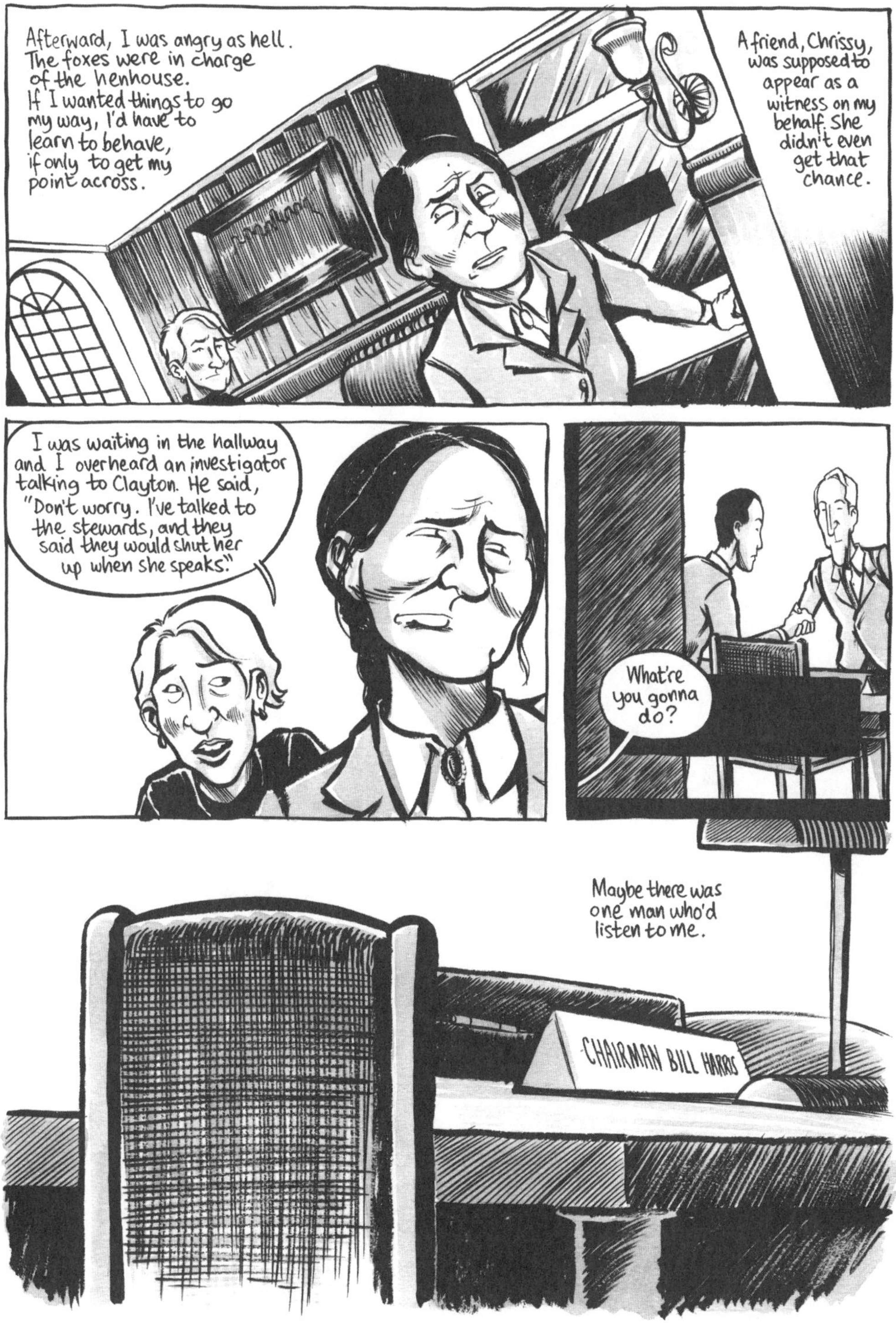
Afterward, I was angry as hell. The foxes were in charge of the henhouse. If I wanted things to go my way, I'd have to learn to behave, if only to get my point across.
A friend, Chrissy, was supposed to appear as a witness on my behalf. She didn't even get that chance.
I was waiting in the hallway and I overheard an investigator talking to Clayton. He said, "Don't worry. I've talked to the stewards, and they said they would shut her up when she speaks."
What're you gonna do?
Maybe there was one man who'd listen to me.
CHAIRMAN BILL HARRIS

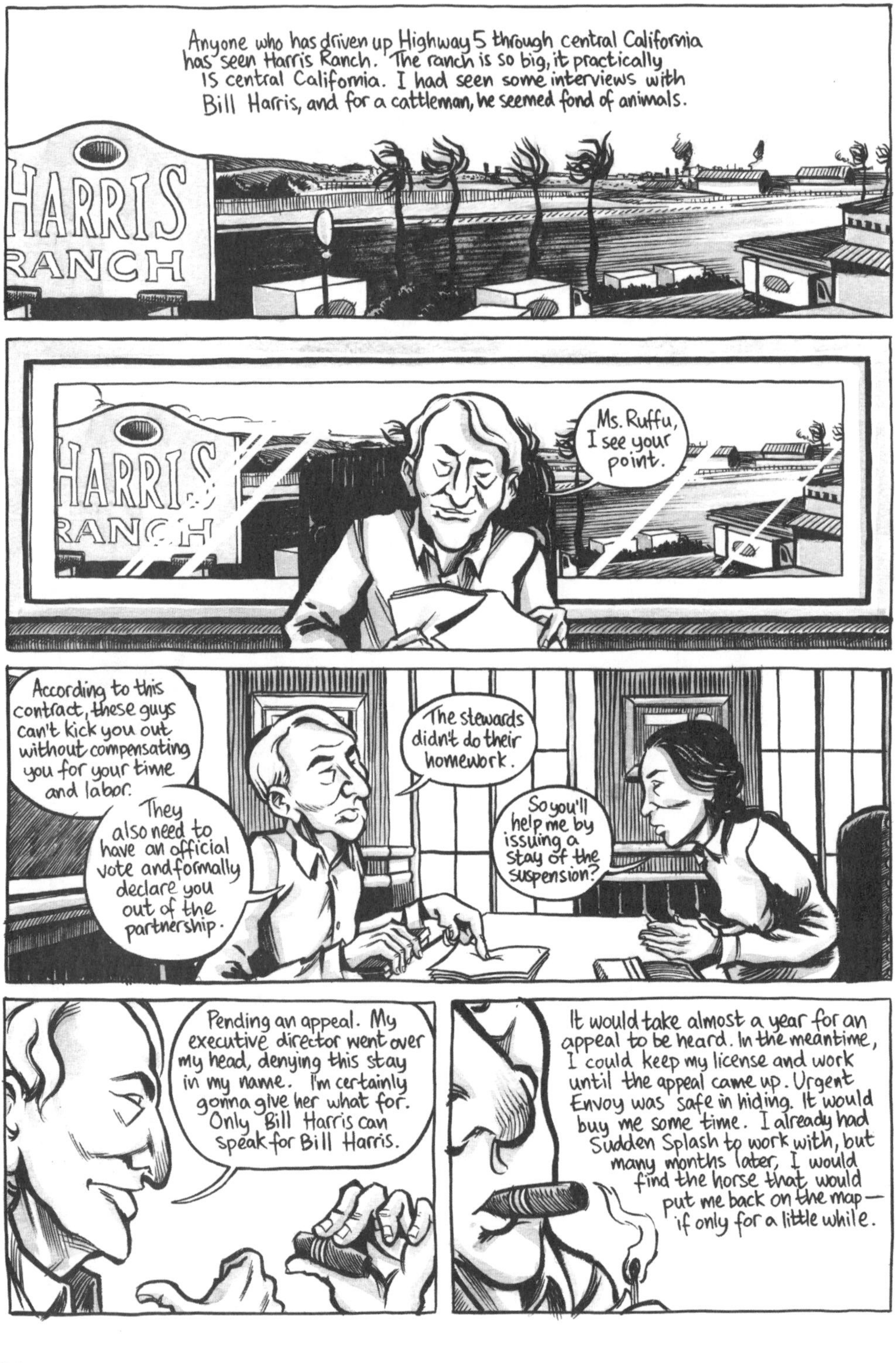
Anyone who has driven up Highway 5 through central California has seen Harris Ranch. The ranch is so big, it practically IS central California. I had seen some interviews with Bill Harris, and for a cattleman, he seemed fond of animals.
HARRIS RANCH
Ms. Ruffu, I see your point.
According to this contract, these guys can't kick you out without compensating you for your time and labor.
They also need to have an official vote and formally declare you out of the partnership.
The stewards didn't do their homework.
So you'll help me by issuing a stay of the suspension?
Pending an appeal. My executive director went over my head, denying this stay in my name. I'm certainly gonna give her what for. Only Bill Harris can speak for Bill Harris.
It would take almost a year for an appeal to be heard. In the meantime, I could keep my license and work until the appeal came up. Urgent Envoy was safe in hiding. It would buy me some time. I already had Sudden Splash to work with, but many months later, I would find the horse that would put me back on the map— if only for a little while.

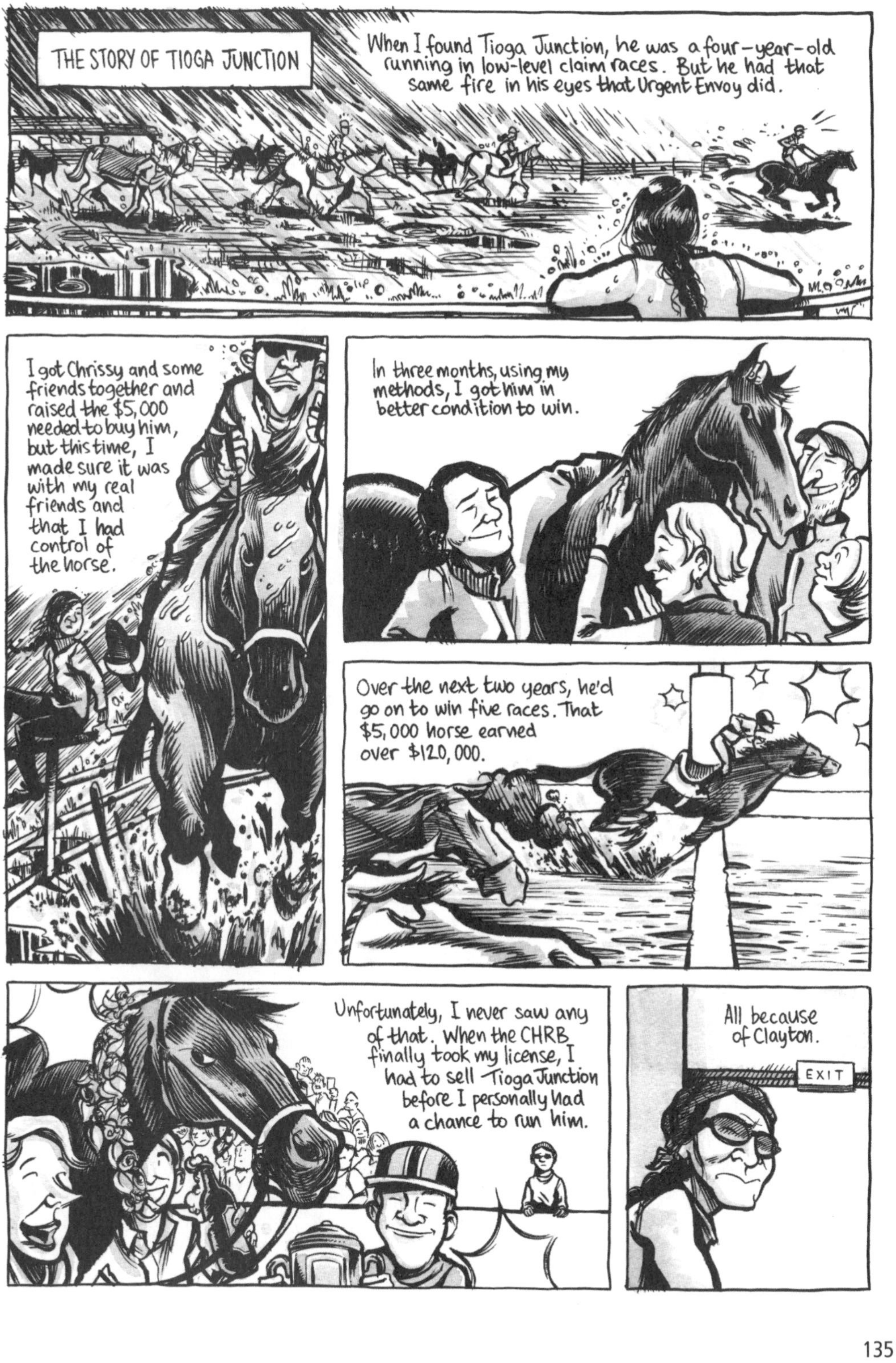
THE STORY OF TIOGA JUNCTION
When I found Tioga Junction, he was a four-year-old running in low-level claim races. But he had that same fire in his eyes that Urgent Envoy did.
I got Chrissy and some friends together and raised the $5,000 needed to buy him, but this time, I made sure it was with my real friends and that I had control of the horse.
In three months, using my methods, I got him in better condition to win.
Over the next two years, he'd go on to win five races. That $5,000 horse earned over $120,000.
Unfortunately, I never saw any of that. When the CHRB finally took my license, I had to sell Tioga Junction before I personally had a chance to run him.
EXIT
All because of Clayton.

I found out later that Clayton had hired his own private investigator, Buford Haines, to dig up dirt. Luckily, I was living a boring life.

KA-CHK!

Clayton was not one to let up. He wanted that horse back, and he wasn't above treating me like a criminal.

Hollywood Park

WANTED

REWARD!

THOROUGHBRED HORSE NAMED URGENT ENVOY KIDNAPPED BY GAIL RUFFU ON CHRISTMAS DAY 2004. REWARD FOR INFORMATION LEADING TO HIS WHEREABOUTS.

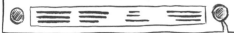

Where on Earth does he get these photos? He's been following me!

SCRUNCH

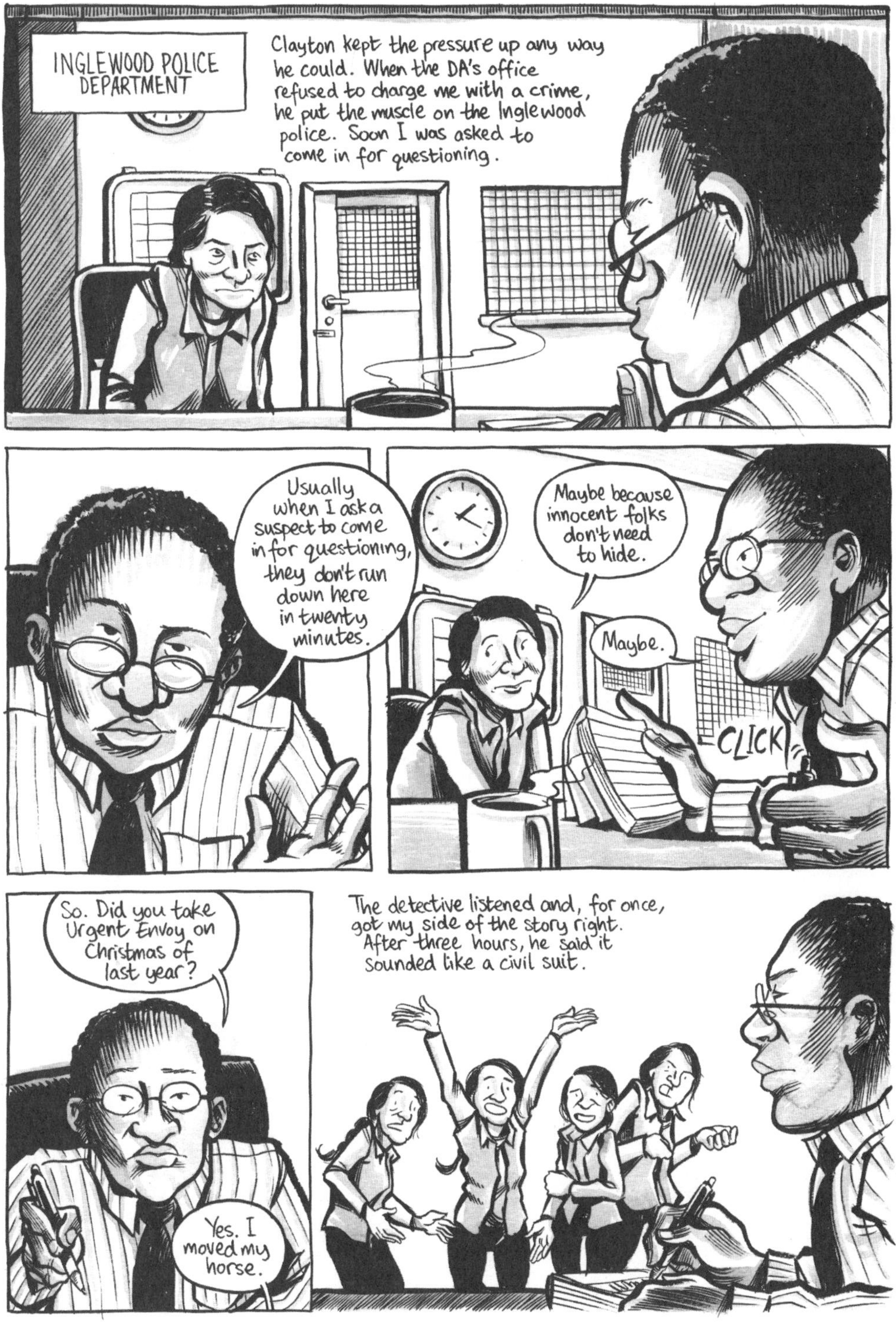
INGLEWOOD POLICE DEPARTMENT
Clayton kept the pressure up any way he could. When the DA's office refused to charge me with a crime, he put the muscle on the Inglewood police. Soon I was asked to come in for questioning.
Usually when I ask a suspect to come in for questioning, they don't run down here in twenty minutes.
Maybe because innocent folks don't need to hide.
Maybe.
CLICK
So. Did you take Urgent Envoy on Christmas of last year?
Yes. I moved my horse.
The detective listened and, for once, got my side of the story right. After three hours, he said it sounded like a civil suit.

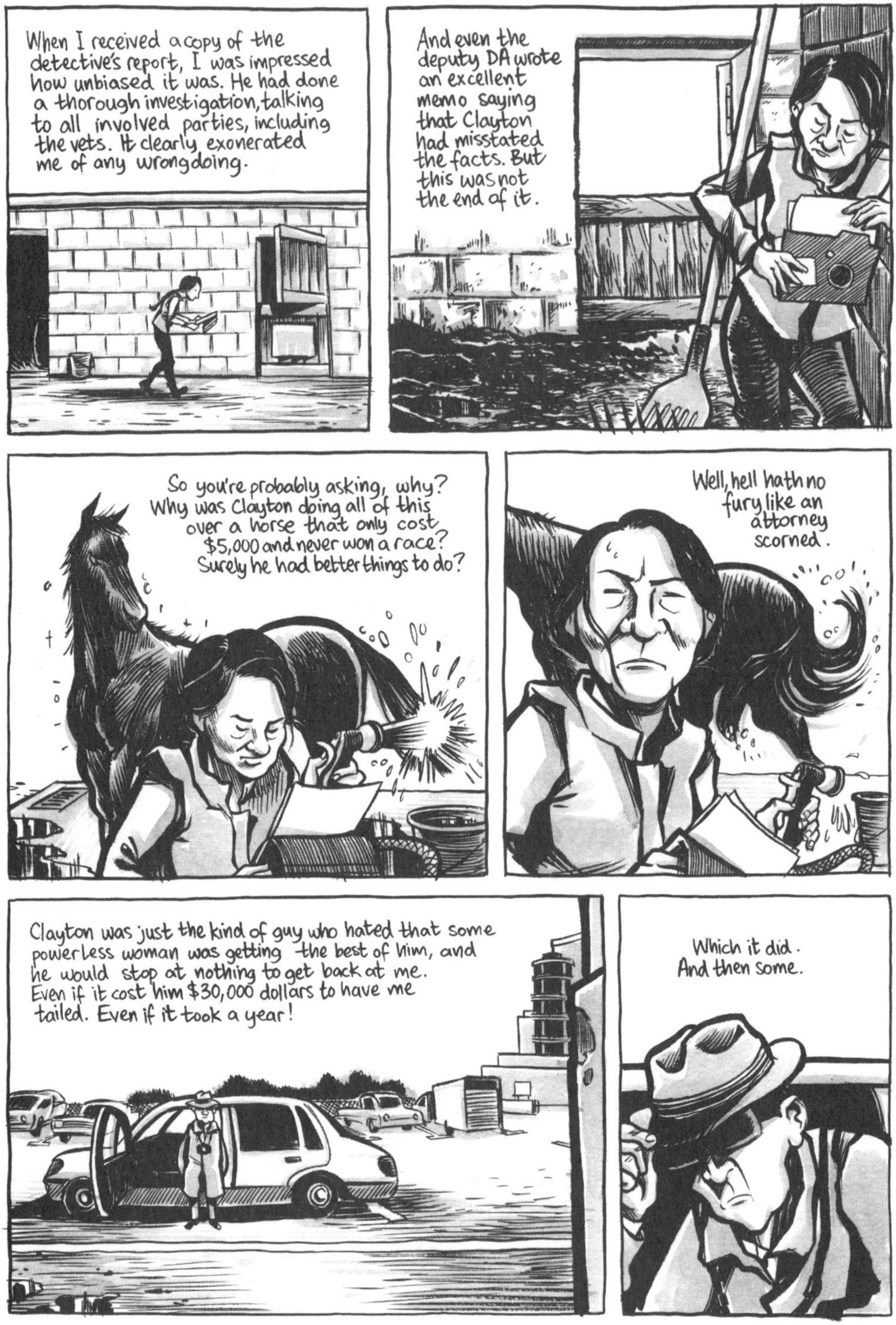
When I received a copy of the detective's report, I was impressed how unbiased it was. He had done a thorough investigation, talking to all involved parties, including the vets. It clearly exonerated me of any wrongdoing.
And even the deputy DA wrote an excellent memo saying that Clayton had misstated the facts. But this was not the end of it.
So you're probably asking, why? Why was Clayton doing all of this over a horse that only cost $5,000 and never won a race? Surely he had better things to do?
Well, hell hath no fury like an attorney scorned.
Clayton was just the kind of guy who hated that some powerless woman was getting the best of him, and he would stop at nothing to get back at me. Even if it cost him $30,000 dollars to have me tailed. Even if it took a year!
Which it did. And then some.

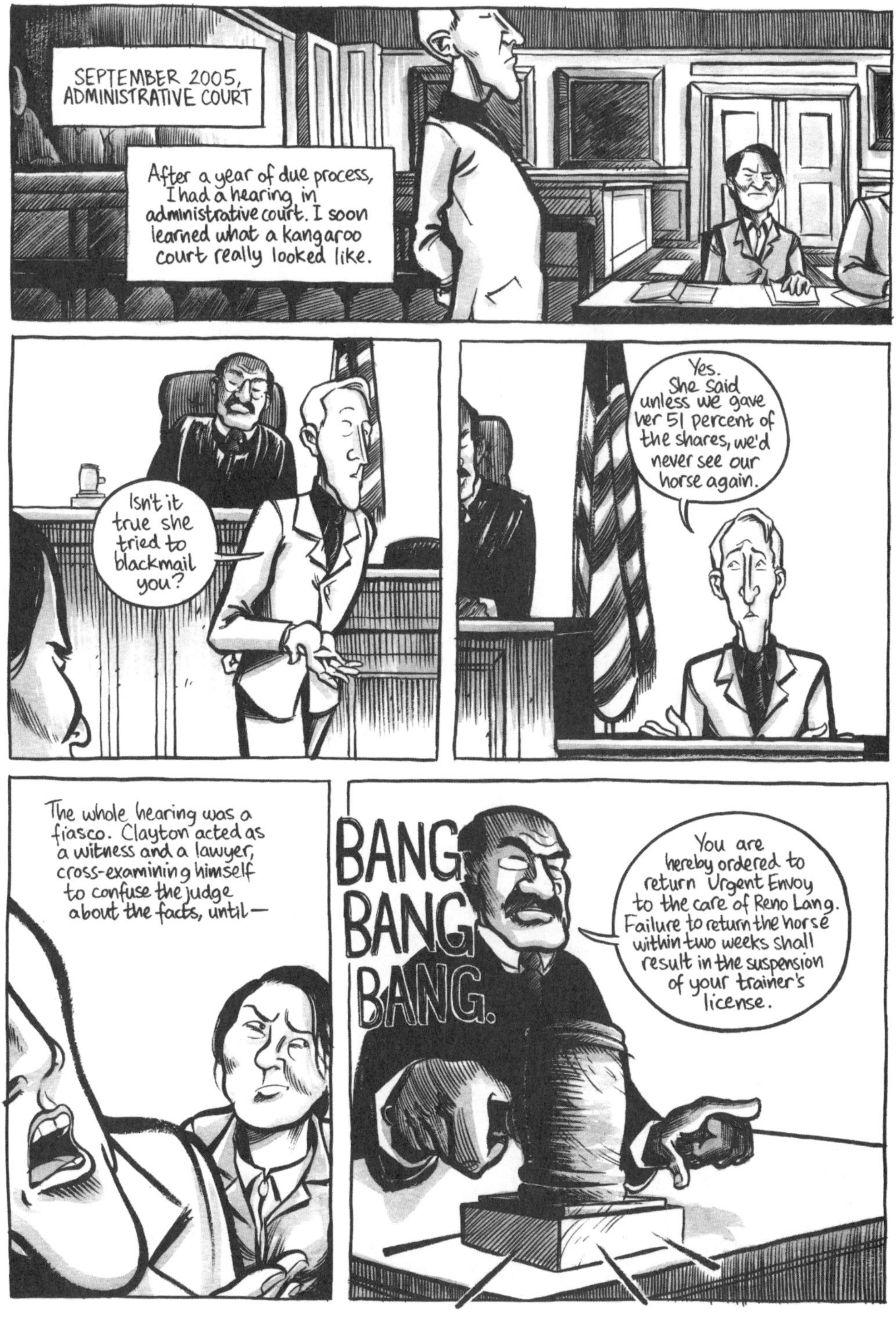
SEPTEMBER 2005, ADMINISTRATIVE COURT
After a year of due process, I had a hearing in administrative court. I soon learned what a kangaroo court really looked like.
Isn't it true she tried to blackmail you?
Yes. She said unless we gave her 51 percent of the shares, we'd never see our horse again.
The whole hearing was a fiasco. Clayton acted as a witness and a lawyer, cross-examining himself to confuse the judge about the facts, until—
BANG BANG BANG.
You are hereby ordered to return Urgent Envoy to the care of Reno Lang. Failure to return the horse within two weeks shall result in the suspension of your trainer's license.

BANG.

I don't care if you put me in the electric chair;

that horse will never be abused by those clowns again!

Your partners acted in accordance with your syndicate agreement.

My decision is final.

Good day.

Based on that decision, the CHRB suspended my license for real.

APPLICATION FOR LICENSE TO TRAIN HORSES IN THE STATE OF CALIFORNIA

SUSPENDED

PLEASE FILL OUT IN BLUE INK

NAME GAIL RUFFU

That's when things got tough.

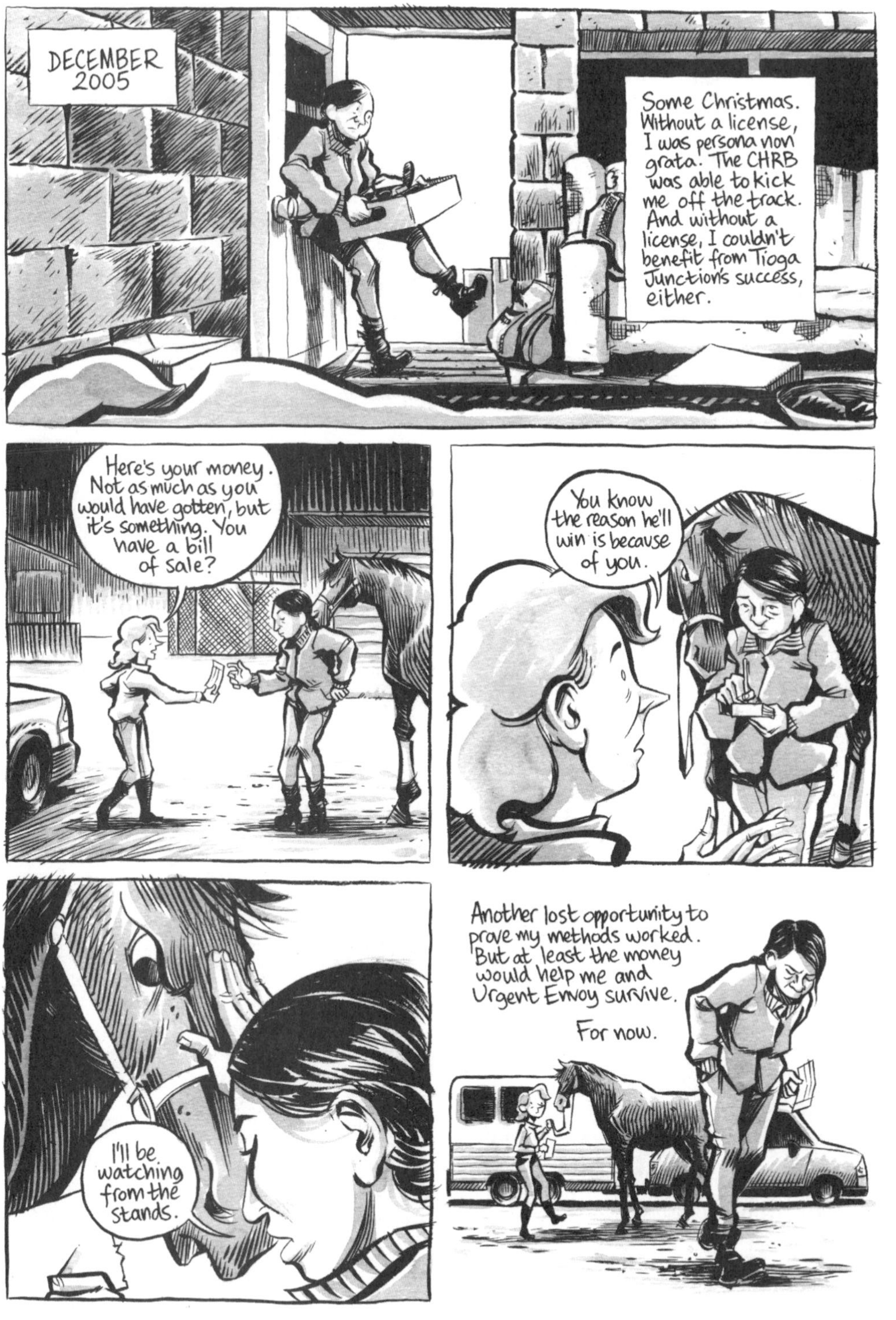
DECEMBER 2005
Some Christmas. Without a license, I was persona non grata. The CHRB was able to kick me off the track. And without a license, I couldn't benefit from Tioga Junction's success, either.
Here's your money. Not as much as you would have gotten, but it's something. You have a bill of sale?
You know the reason he'll win is because of you.
I'll be watching from the stands.
Another lost opportunity to prove my methods worked. But at least the money would help me and Urgent Envoy survive.
For now.

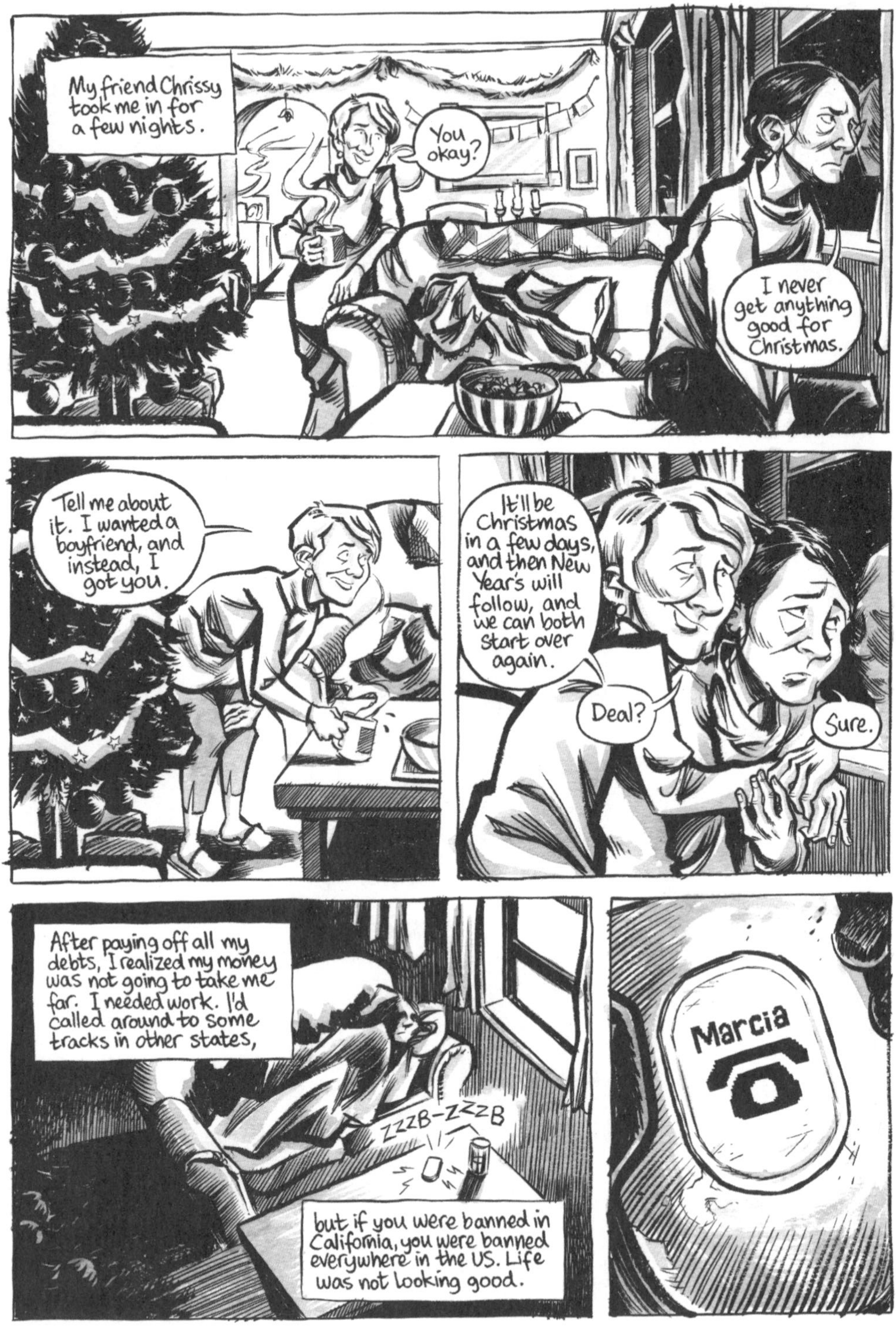
My friend Chrissy took me in for a few nights.
You okay?
I never get anything good for Christmas.
Tell me about it. I wanted a boyfriend, and instead, I got you.
It'll be Christmas in a few days, and then New Year's will follow, and we can both start over again.
Deal?
Sure.
After paying off all my debts, I realized my money was not going to take me far. I needed work. I'd called around to some tracks in other states,
ZZZB-ZZZB
but if you were banned in California, you were banned everywhere in the US. Life was not looking good.
Marcia

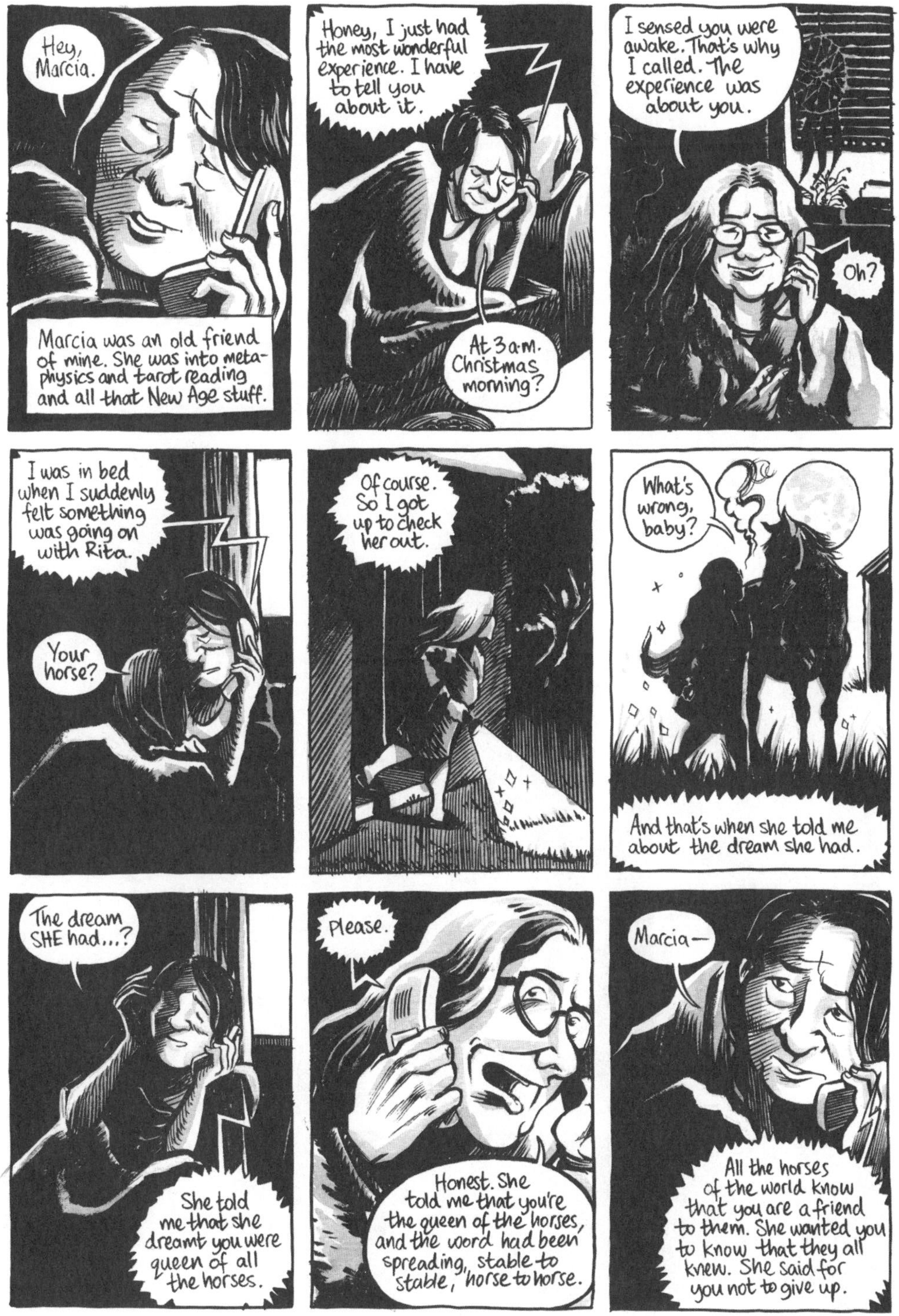
Hey, Marcia.
Marcia was an old friend of mine. She was into metaphysics and tarot reading and all that New Age stuff.
Honey, I just had the most wonderful experience. I have to tell you about it.
At 3 a.m. Christmas morning?
I sensed you were awake. That's why I called. The experience was about you.
Oh?
I was in bed when I suddenly felt something was going on with Rita.
Your horse?
Of course. So I got up to check her out.
What's wrong, baby?
And that's when she told me about the dream she had.
The dream SHE had...?
She told me that she dreamt you were queen of all the horses.
Please.
Honest. She told me that you're the queen of the horses, and the word had been spreading, stable to stable, horse to horse.
Marcia—
All the horses of the world know that you are a friend to them. She wanted you to know that they all knew. She said for you not to give up.

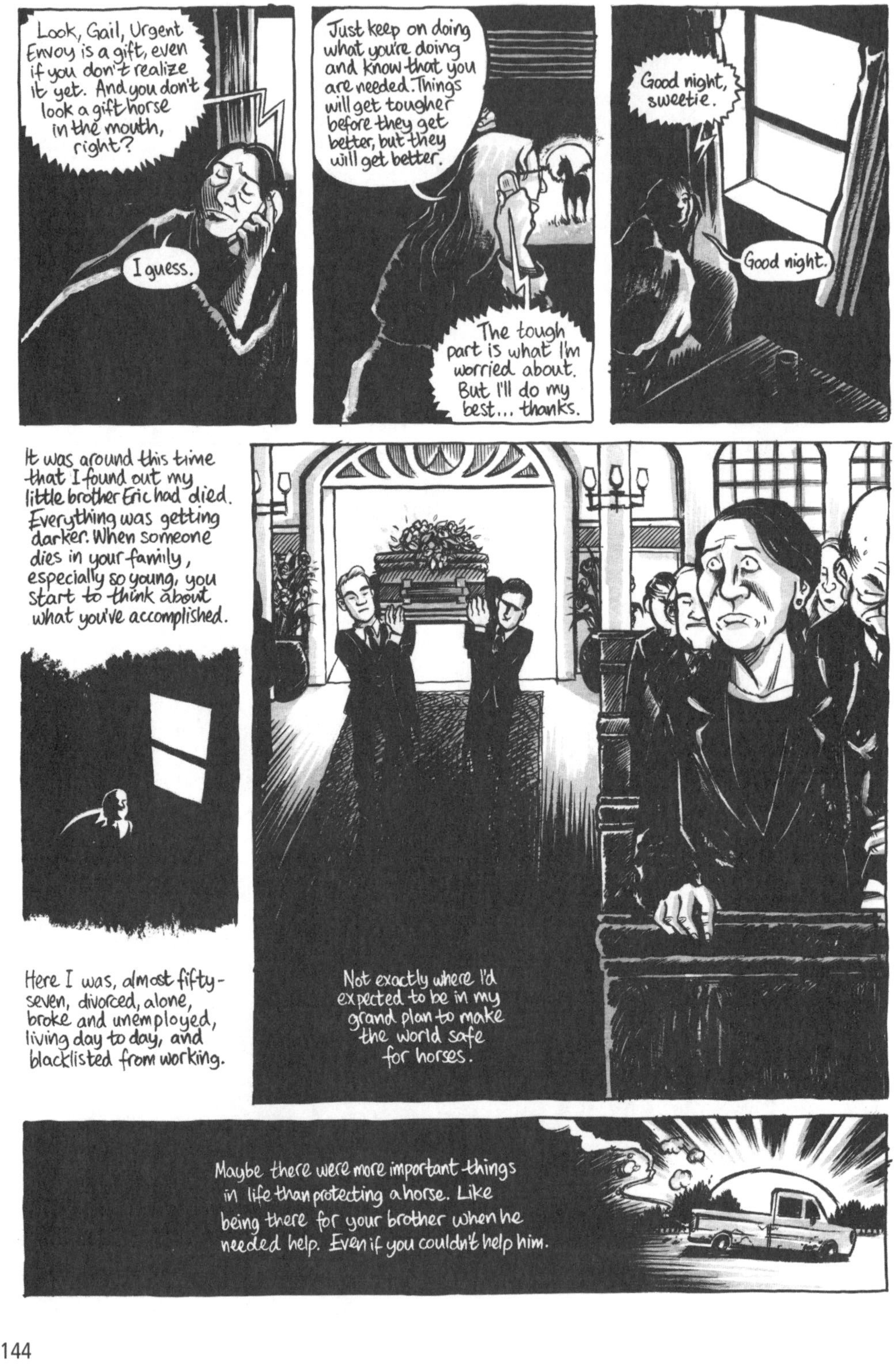
Look, Gail, Urgent Envoy is a gift, even if you don't realize it yet. And you don't look a gift horse in the mouth, right?
I guess.
Just keep on doing what you're doing and know that you are needed. Things will get tougher before they get better, but they will get better.
The tough part is what I'm worried about. But I'll do my best... thanks.
Good night, sweetie.
Good night.
It was around this time that I found out my little brother Eric had died. Everything was getting darker. When someone dies in your family, especially so young, you start to think about what you've accomplished.
Here I was, almost fifty-seven, divorced, alone, broke and unemployed, living day to day, and blacklisted from working.
Not exactly where I'd expected to be in my grand plan to make the world safe for horses.
Maybe there were more important things in life than protecting a horse. Like being there for your brother when he needed help. Even if you couldn't help him.

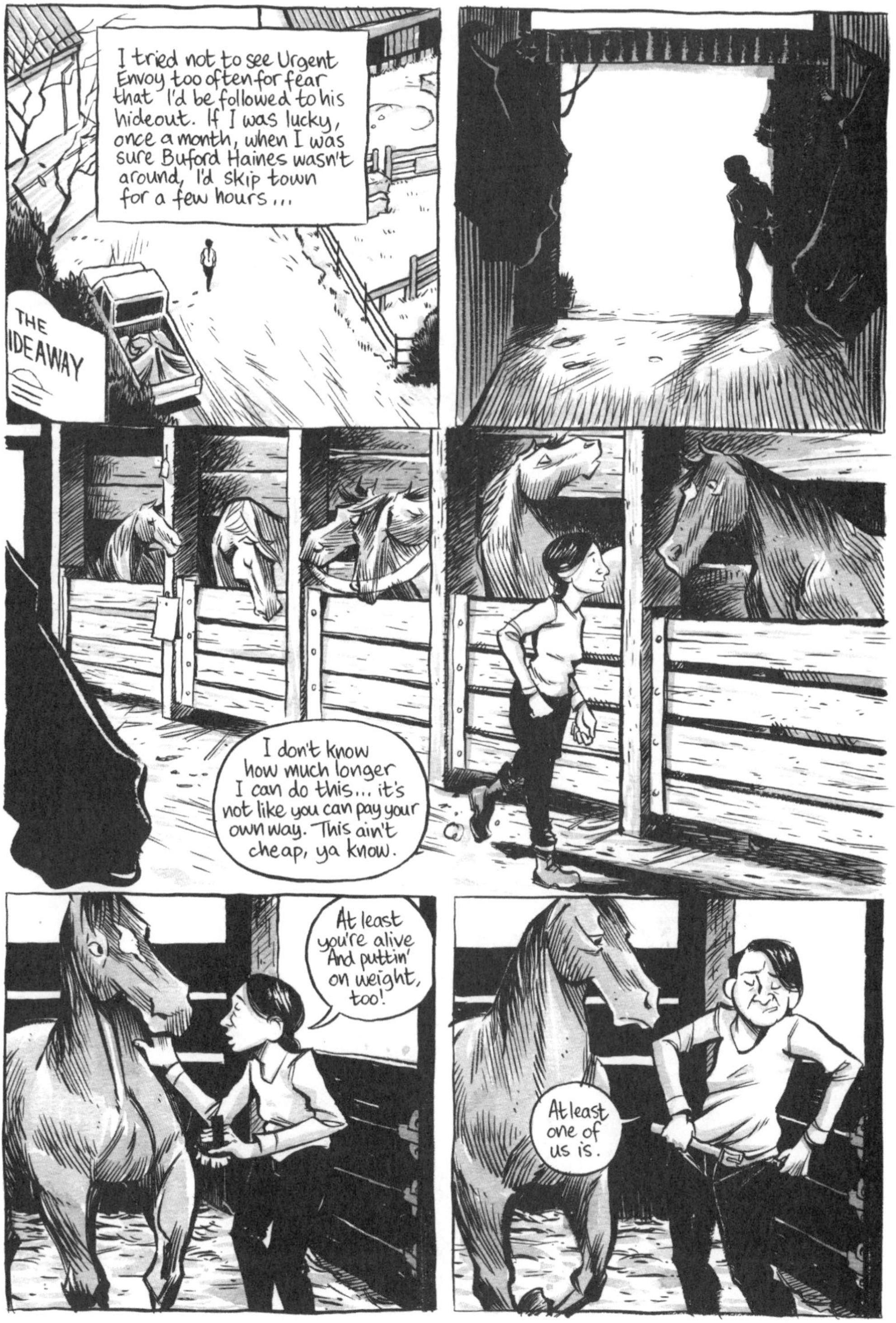
I tried not to see Urgent Envoy too often for fear that I'd be followed to his hideout. If I was lucky, once a month, when I was sure Buford Haines wasn't around, I'd skip town for a few hours...
THE IDEAWAY
I don't know how much longer I can do this... it's not like you can pay your own way. This ain't cheap, ya know.
At least you're alive And puttin' on weight, too!
At least one of us is.

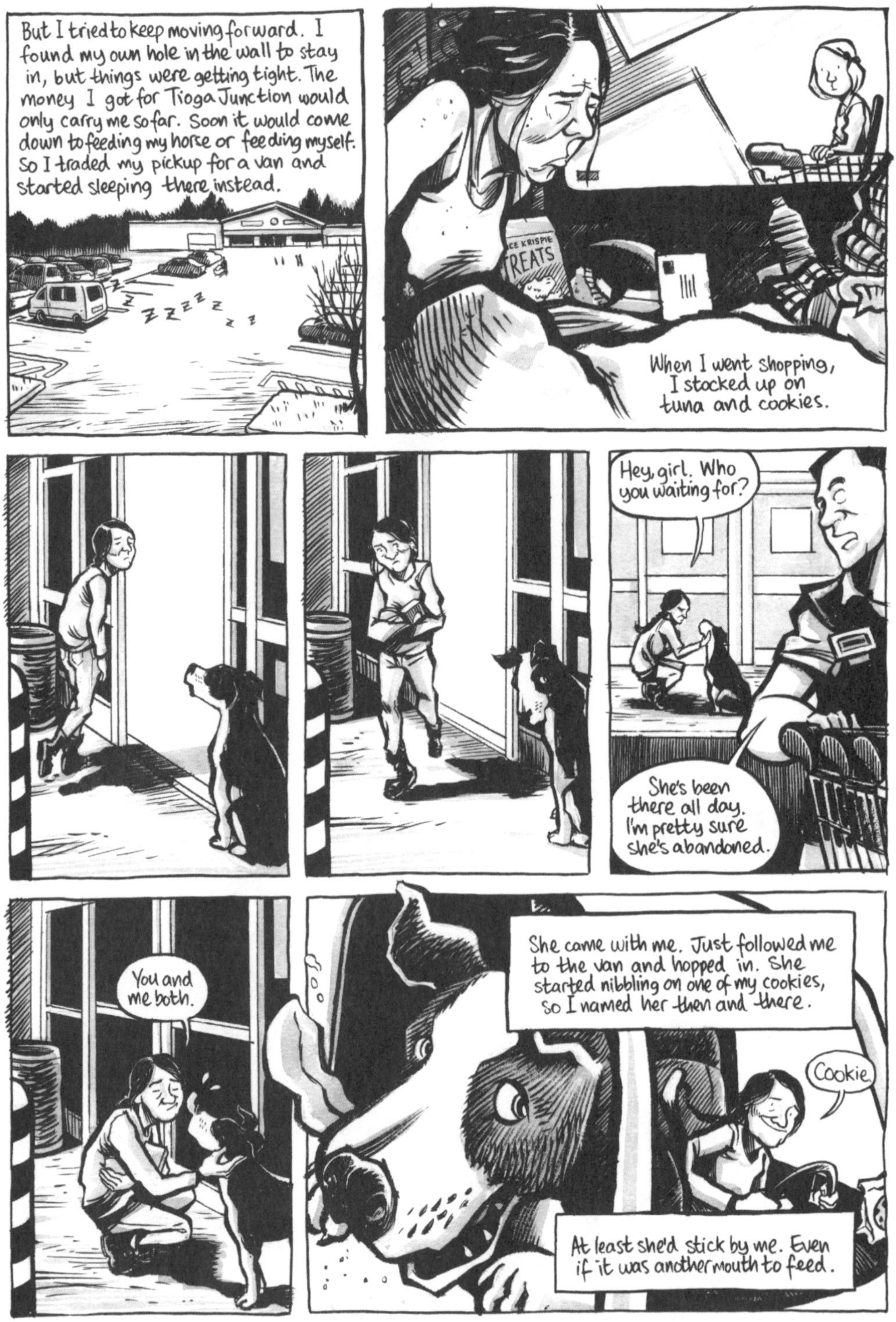
But I tried to keep moving forward. I found my own hole in the wall to stay in, but things were getting tight. The money I got for Tioga Junction would only carry me so far. Soon it would come down to feeding my horse or feeding myself. So I traded my pickup for a van and started sleeping there instead.
ZZZZZZZZ
TREATS
When I went shopping, I stocked up on tuna and cookies.
Hey, girl. Who you waiting for?
She's been there all day. I'm pretty sure she's abandoned.
You and me both.
She came with me. Just followed me to the van and hopped in. She started nibbling on one of my cookies, so I named her then and there.
Cookie.
At least she'd stick by me. Even if it was another mouth to feed.

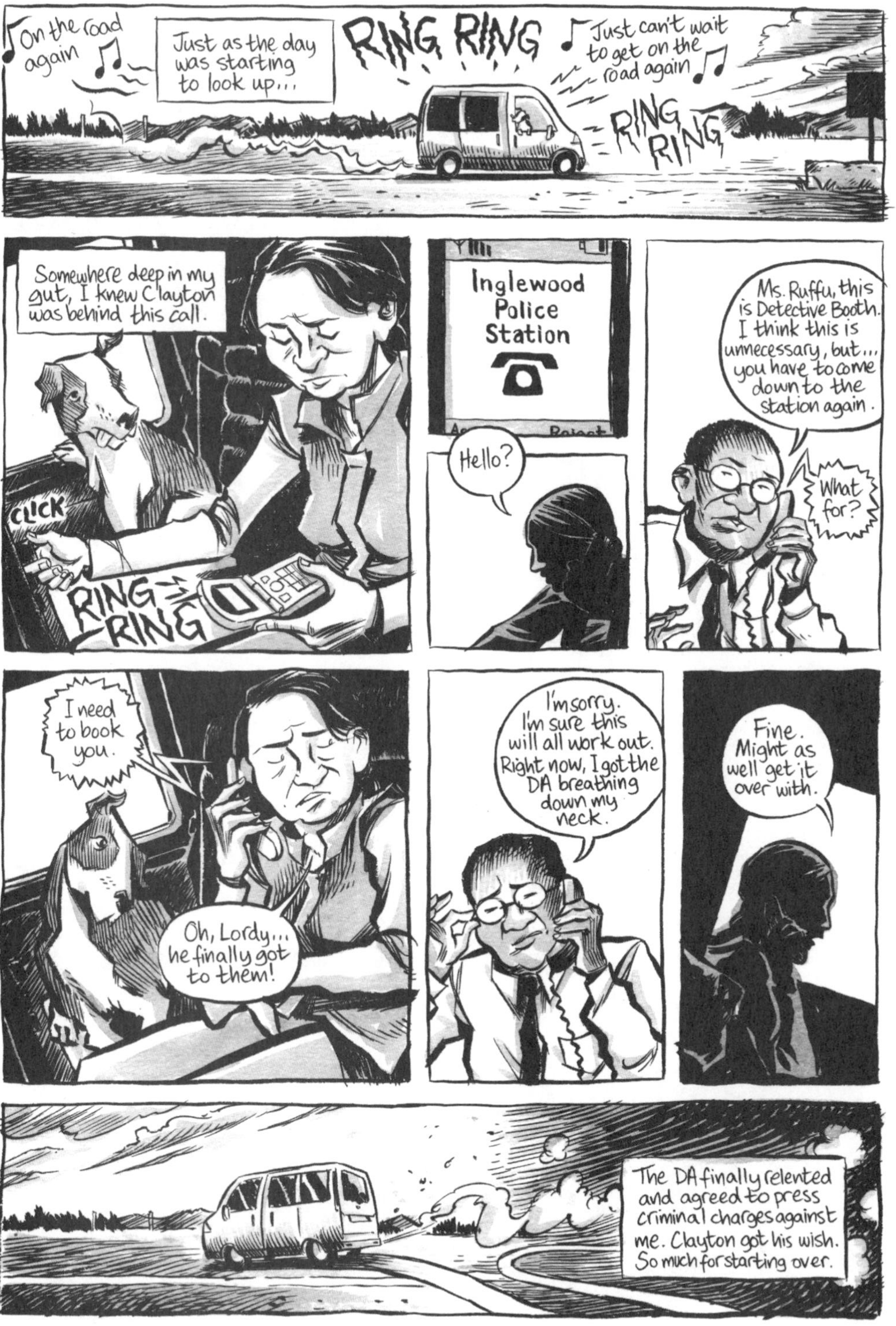
On the road again
Just as the day was starting to look up...
RING RING
Just can't wait to get on the road again
RING RING
Somewhere deep in my gut, I knew Clayton was behind this call.
CLICK
RING RING
Inglewood Police Station
Hello?
Ms. Ruffu, this is Detective Booth. I think this is unnecessary, but... you have to come down to the station again.
What for?
I need to book you.
Oh, Lordy... he finally got to them!
I'm sorry. I'm sure this will all work out. Right now, I got the DA breathing down my neck.
Fine. Might as well get it over with.
The DA finally relented and agreed to press criminal charges against me. Clayton got his wish. So much for starting over.

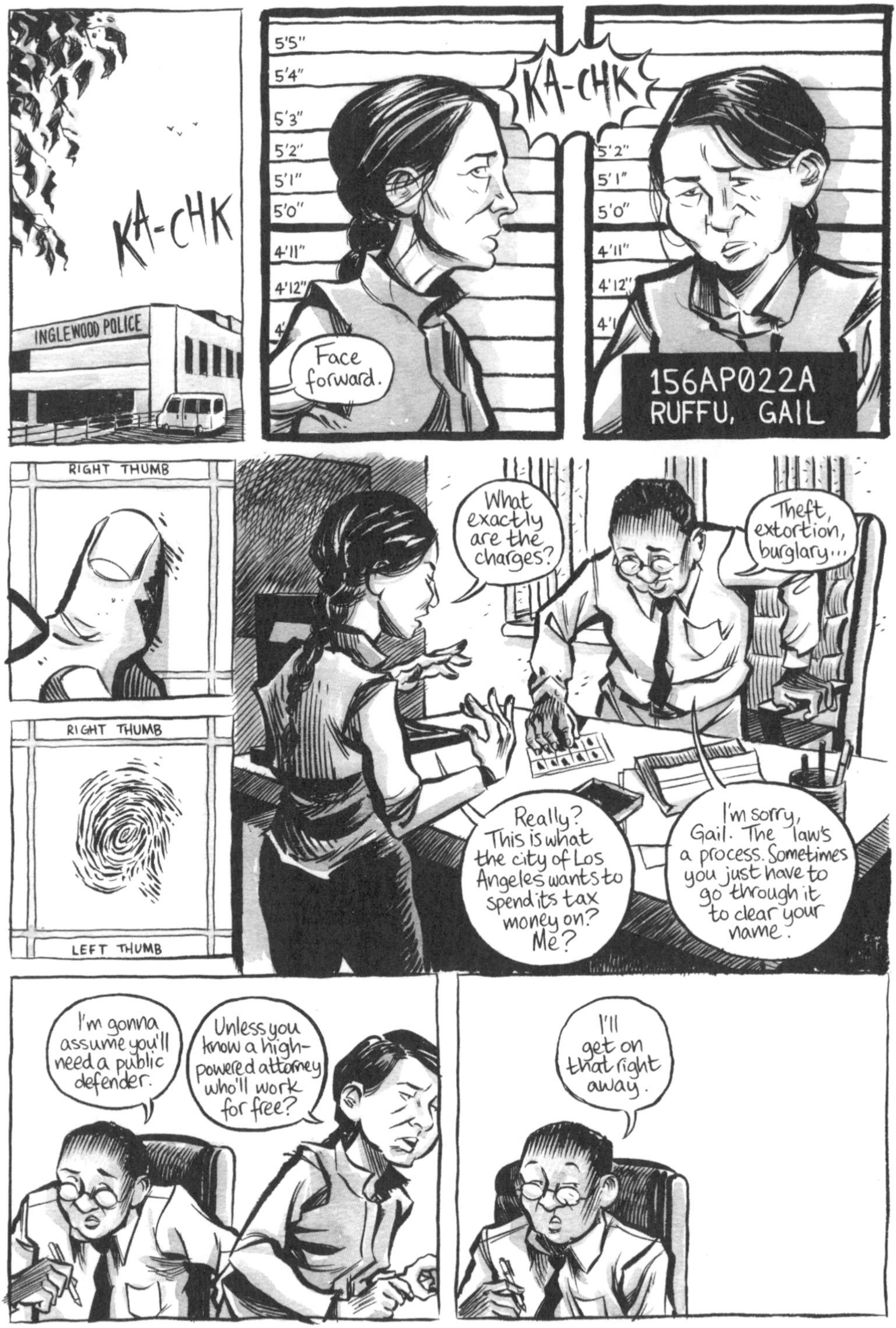
KA-CHK
INGLEWOOD POLICE
5'5"
5'4"
5'3"
5'2"
5'1"
5'0"
4'11"
4'12"
KA-CHK
Face forward.
156AP022A
RUFFU, GAIL
RIGHT THUMB
RIGHT THUMB
LEFT THUMB
What exactly are the charges?
Theft, extortion, burglary...
Really? This is what the city of Los Angeles wants to spend its tax money on? Me?
I'm sorry, Gail. The law's a process. Sometimes you just have to go through it to clear your name.
I'm gonna assume you'll need a public defender.
Unless you know a high-powered attorney who'll work for free?
I'll get on that right away.

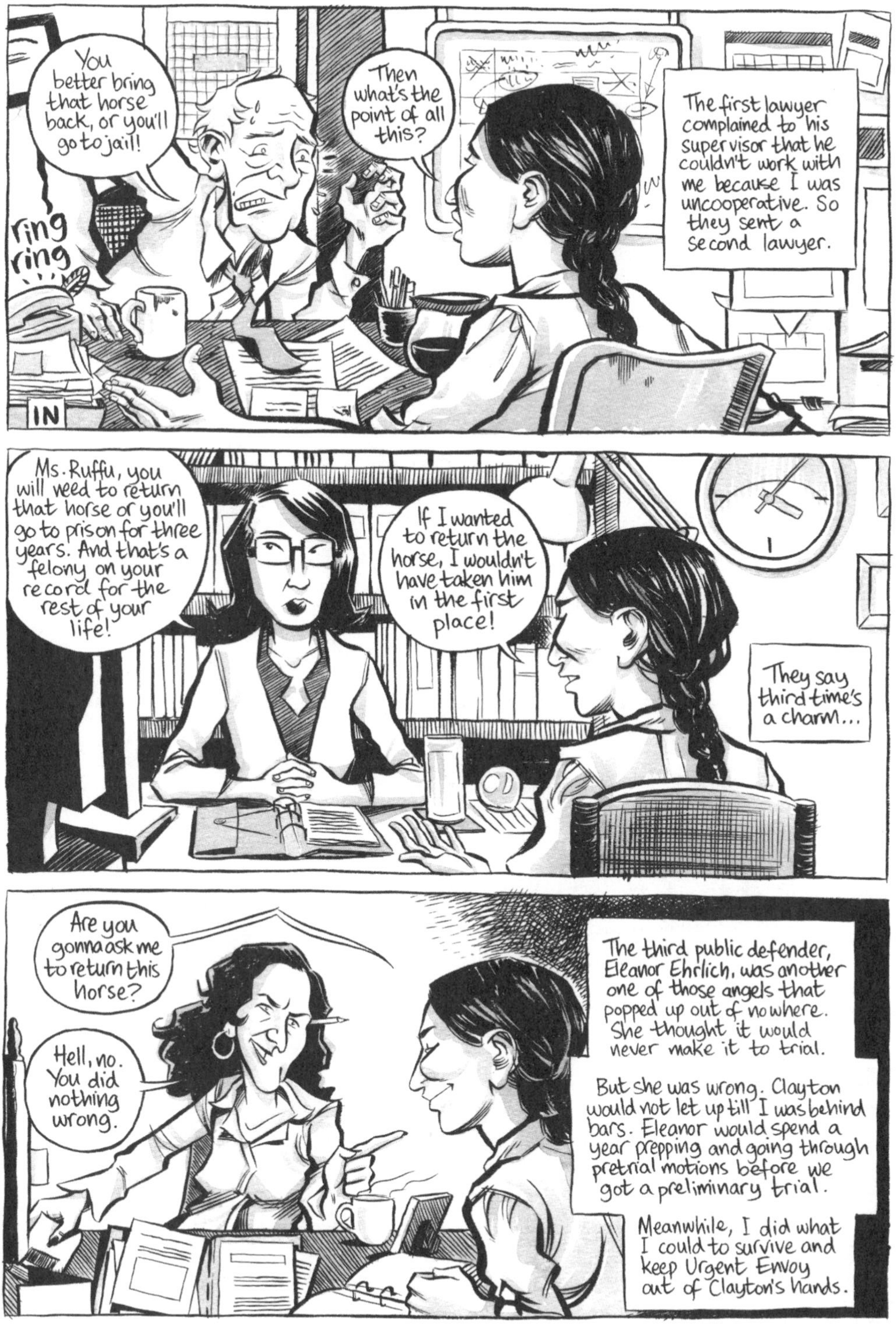
You better bring that horse back, or you'll go to jail!
ring ring
IN
Then what's the point of all this?
The first lawyer complained to his supervisor that he couldn't work with me because I was uncooperative. So they sent a second lawyer.
Ms. Ruffu, you will need to return that horse or you'll go to prison for three years. And that's a felony on your record for the rest of your life!
If I wanted to return the horse, I wouldn't have taken him in the first place!
They say third time's a charm...
Are you gonna ask me to return this horse?
Hell, no. You did nothing wrong.
The third public defender, Eleanor Ehrlich, was another one of those angels that popped up out of nowhere. She thought it would never make it to trial.
But she was wrong. Clayton would not let up till I was behind bars. Eleanor would spend a year prepping and going through pretrial motions before we got a preliminary trial.
Meanwhile, I did what I could to survive and keep Urgent Envoy out of Clayton's hands.

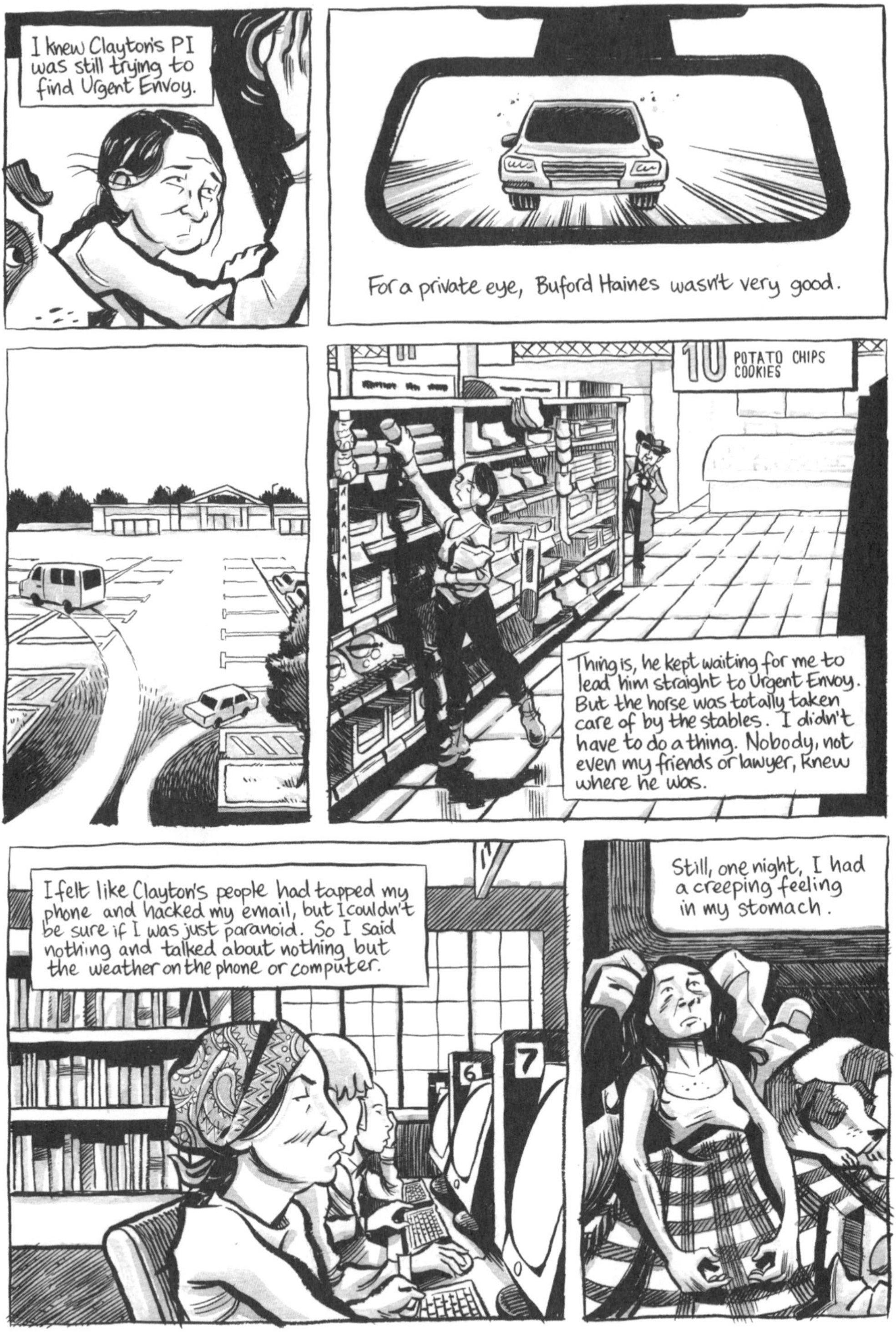

I knew Clayton's PI was still trying to find Urgent Envoy.
For a private eye, Buford Haines wasn't very good.
10
POTATO CHIPS
COOKIES
Thing is, he kept waiting for me to lead him straight to Urgent Envoy. But the horse was totally taken care of by the stables. I didn't have to do a thing. Nobody, not even my friends or lawyer, knew where he was.
I felt like Clayton's people had tapped my phone and hacked my email, but I couldn't be sure if I was just paranoid. So I said nothing and talked about nothing but the weather on the phone or computer.
6
7
Still, one night, I had a creeping feeling in my stomach.

I suddenly felt they were close to finding out where I was keeping him.

THE HIDEAWAY

BOARDING STABLES

Hey, boy.

I've missed you.

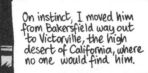

On instinct, I moved him from Bakersfield way out to Victorville, the high desert of California, where no one would find him.

I was starting to really feel like an outlaw now.

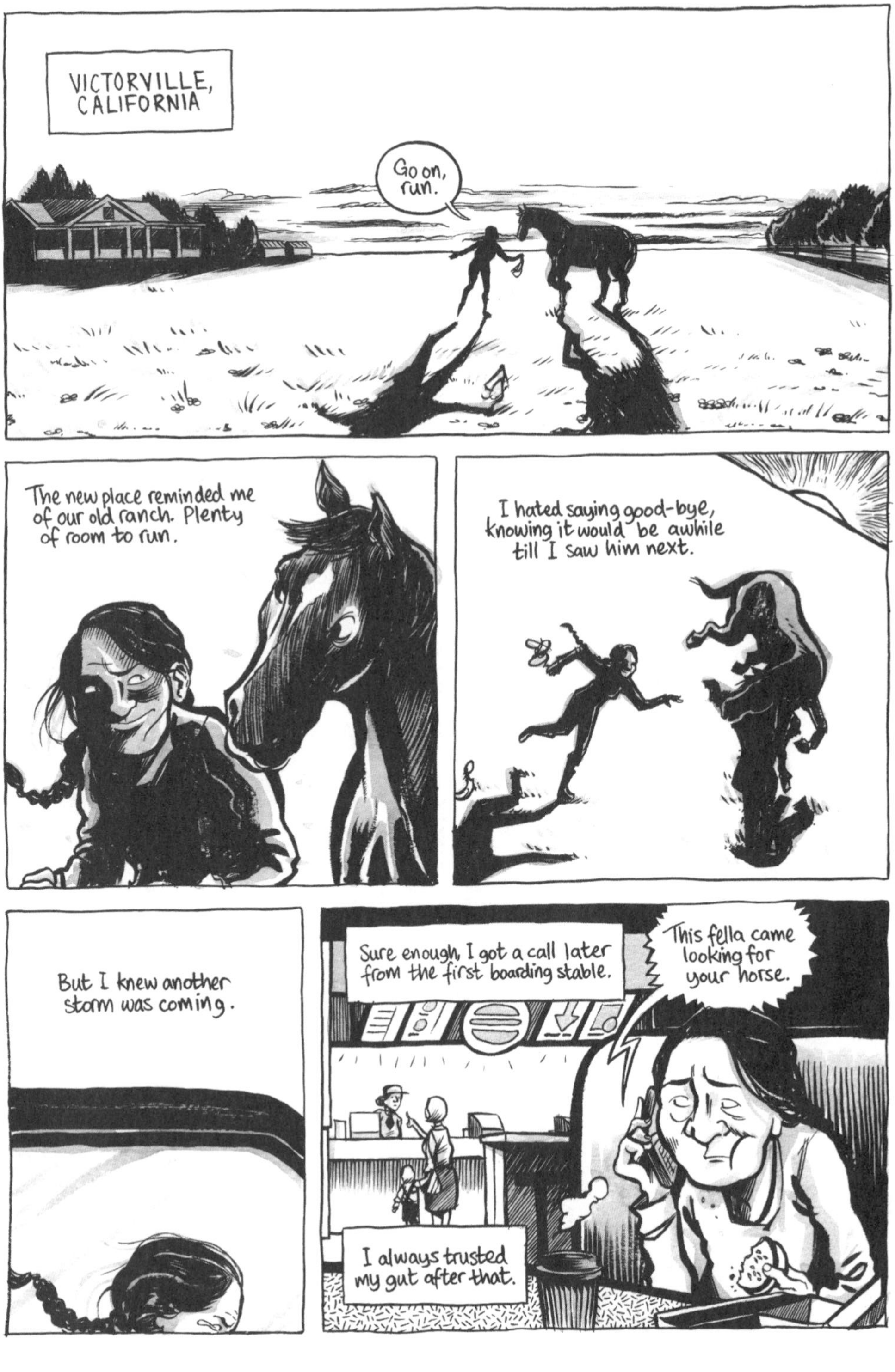
VICTORVILLE, CALIFORNIA
Go on, run.
The new place reminded me of our old ranch. Plenty of room to run.
I hated saying good-bye, knowing it would be awhile till I saw him next.
But I knew another storm was coming.
Sure enough, I got a call later from the first boarding stable.
This fella came looking for your horse.
I always trusted my gut after that.

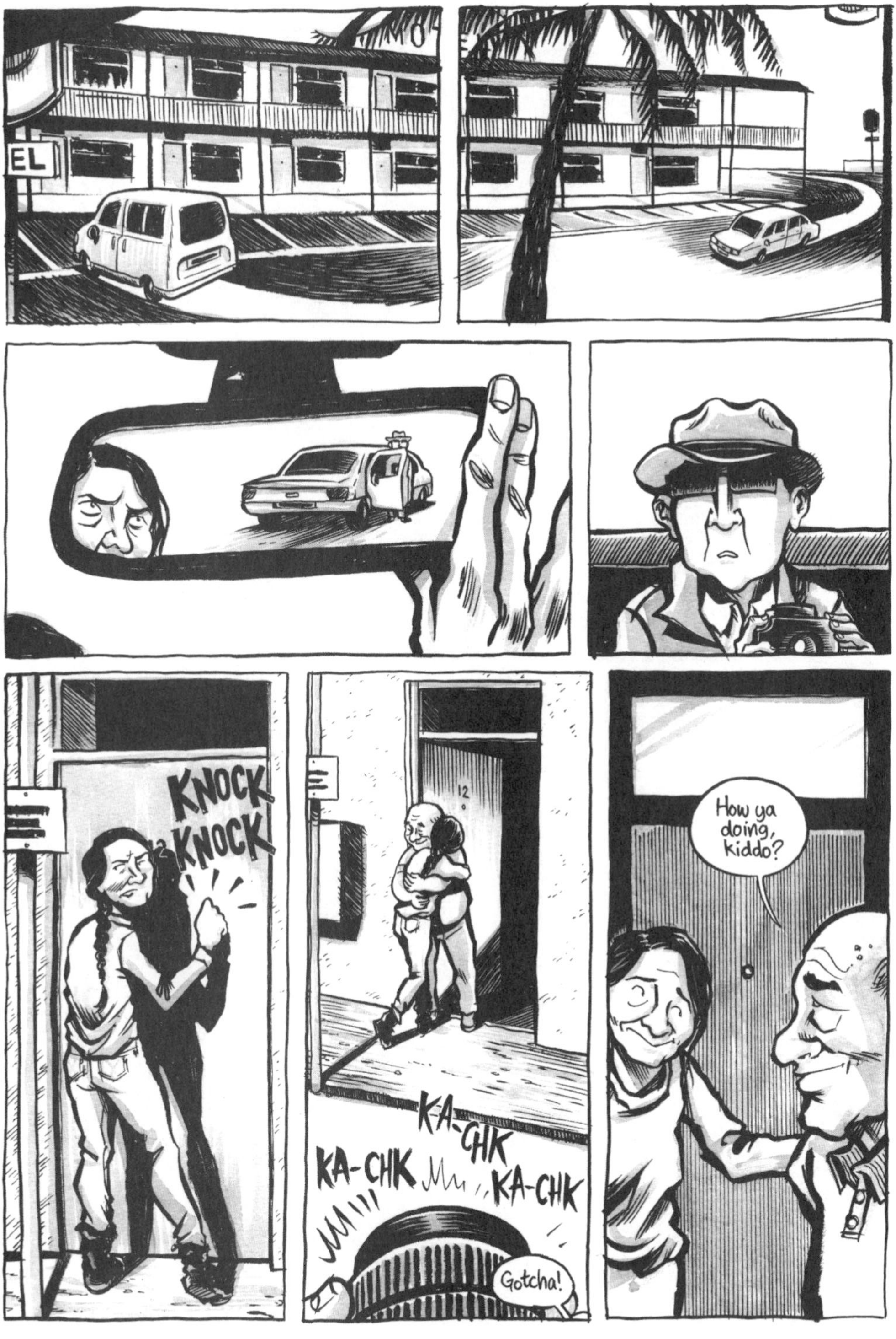
EL
KNOCK
KNOCK
12
KA-CHK
KA-CHK
KA-CHK
Gotcha!
How ya doing, kiddo?

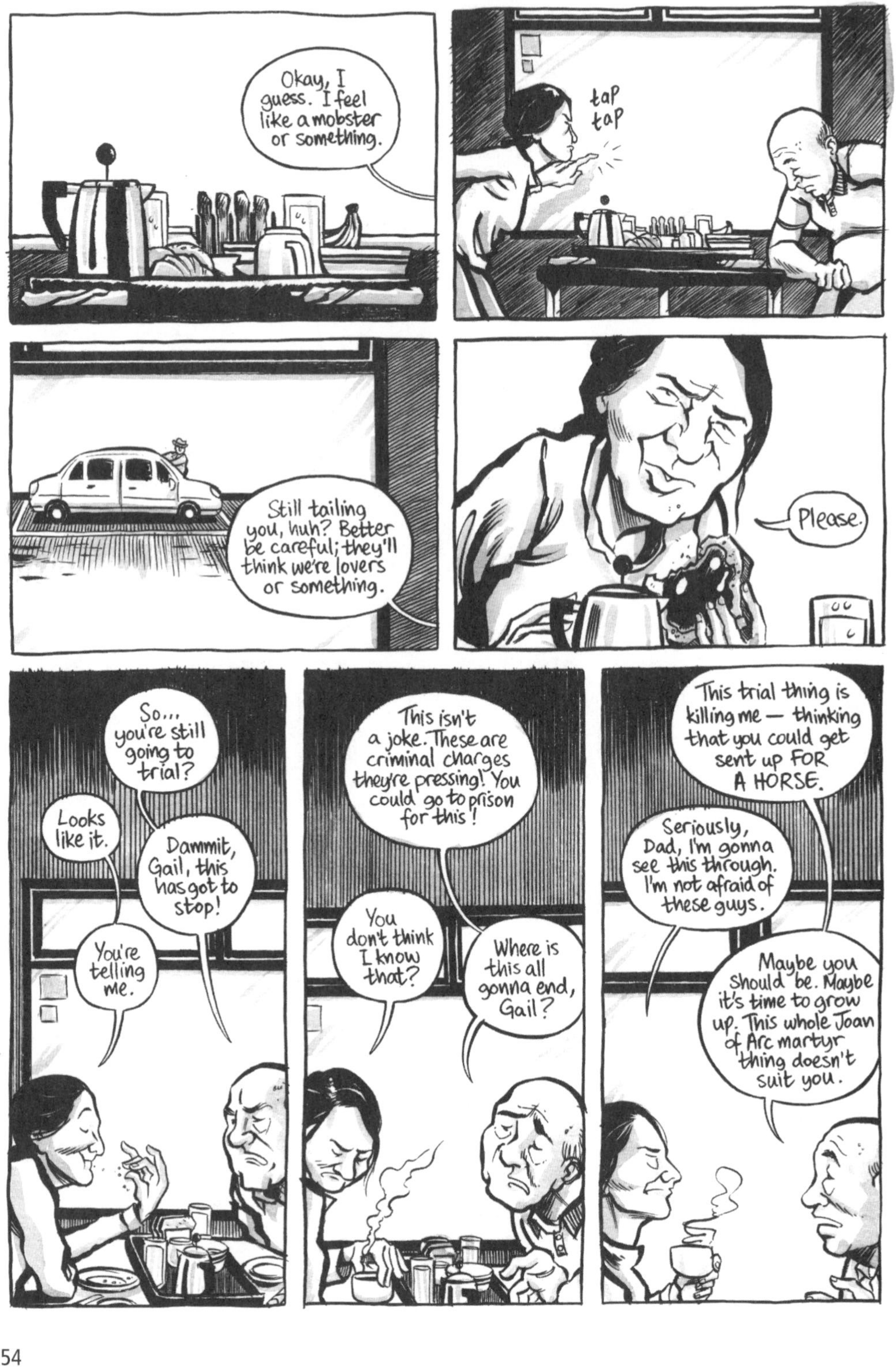
Okay, I guess. I feel like a mobster or something.
tap tap
Still tailing you, huh? Better be careful; they'll think we're lovers or something.
Please.
So... you're still going to trial?
Looks like it.
Dammit, Gail, this has got to stop!
You're telling me.
This isn't a joke. These are criminal charges they're pressing! You could go to prison for this!
You don't think I know that?
Where is this all gonna end, Gail?
This trial thing is killing me — thinking that you could get sent up FOR A HORSE.
Seriously, Dad, I'm gonna see this through. I'm not afraid of these guys.
Maybe you should be. Maybe it's time to grow up. This whole Joan of Arc martyr thing doesn't suit you.

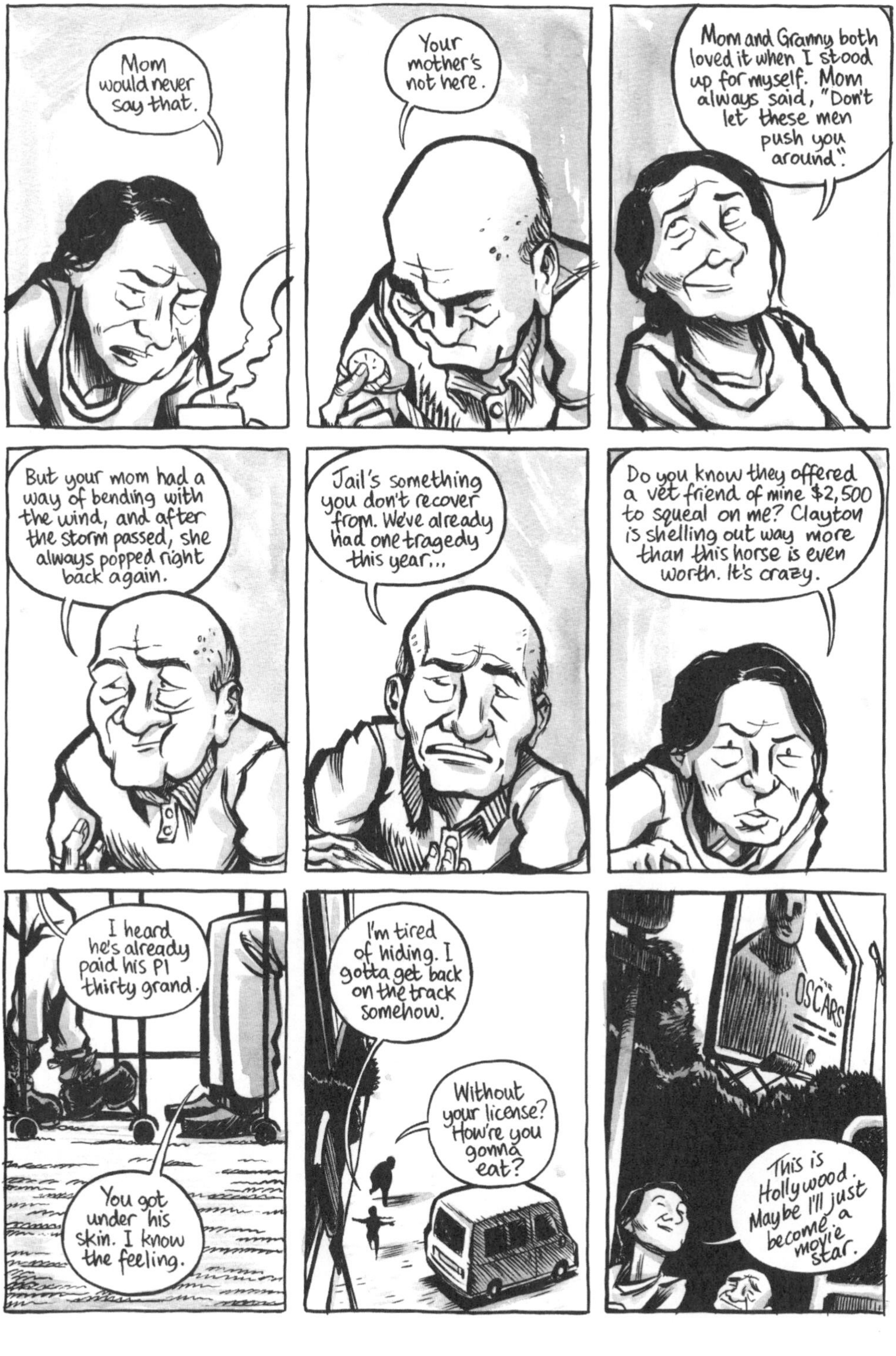
Mom would never say that.
Your mother's not here.
Mom and Granny both loved it when I stood up for myself. Mom always said, "Don't let these men push you around".
But your mom had a way of bending with the wind, and after the storm passed, she always popped right back again.
Jail's something you don't recover from. We've already had one tragedy this year...
Do you know they offered a vet friend of mine $2,500 to squeal on me? Clayton is shelling out way more than this horse is even worth. It's crazy.
I heard he's already paid his PI thirty grand.
You got under his skin. I know the feeling.
I'm tired of hiding. I gotta get back on the track somehow.
Without your license? How're you gonna eat?
OSCARS
This is Hollywood. Maybe I'll just become a movie star.

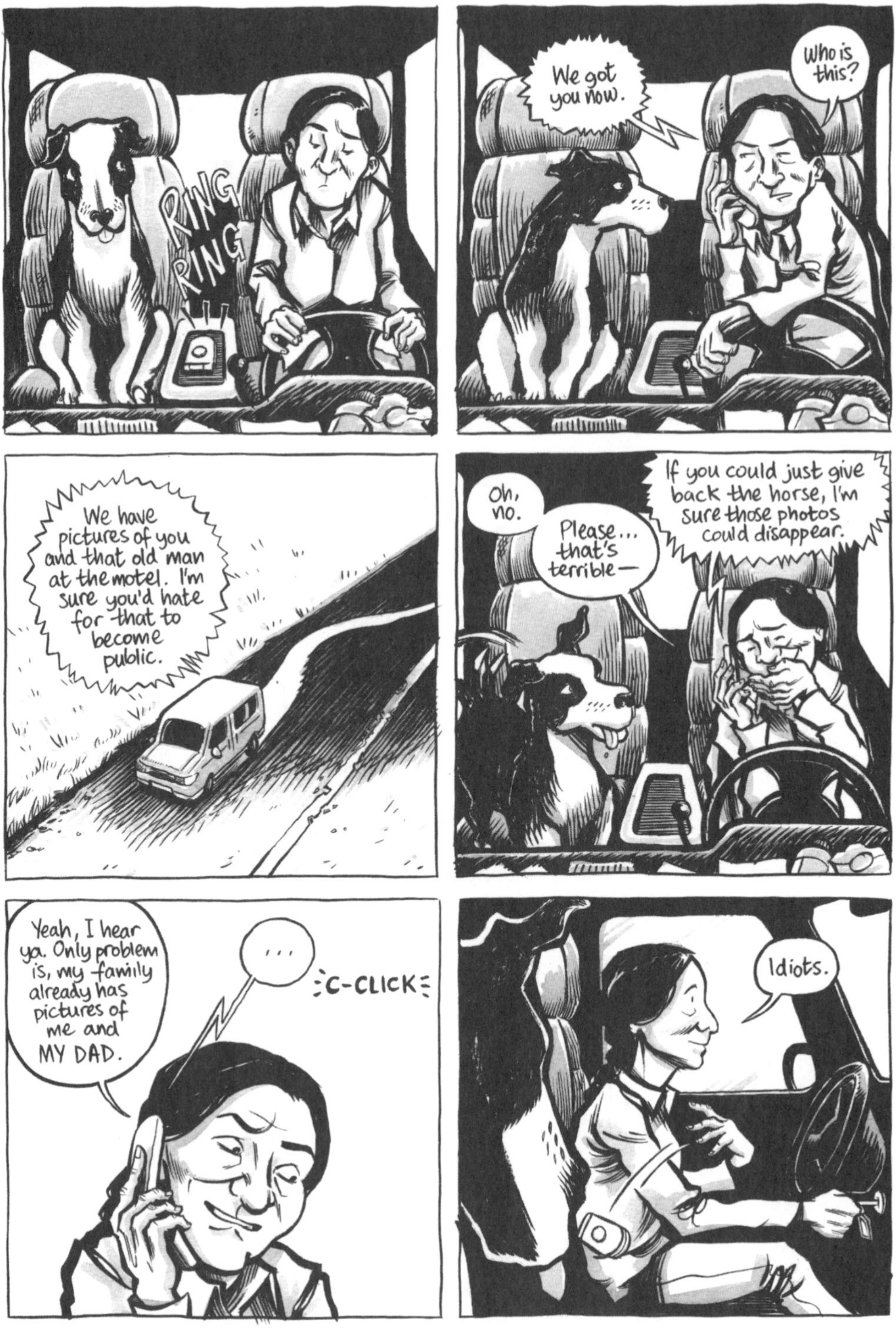
RING RING
We got you now.
Who is this?
We have pictures of you and that old man at the motel. I'm sure you'd hate for that to become public.
Oh, no.
Please... that's terrible—
If you could just give back the horse, I'm sure those photos could disappear.
Yeah, I hear ya. Only problem is, my family already has pictures of me and MY DAD.
...
C-CLICK
Idiots.

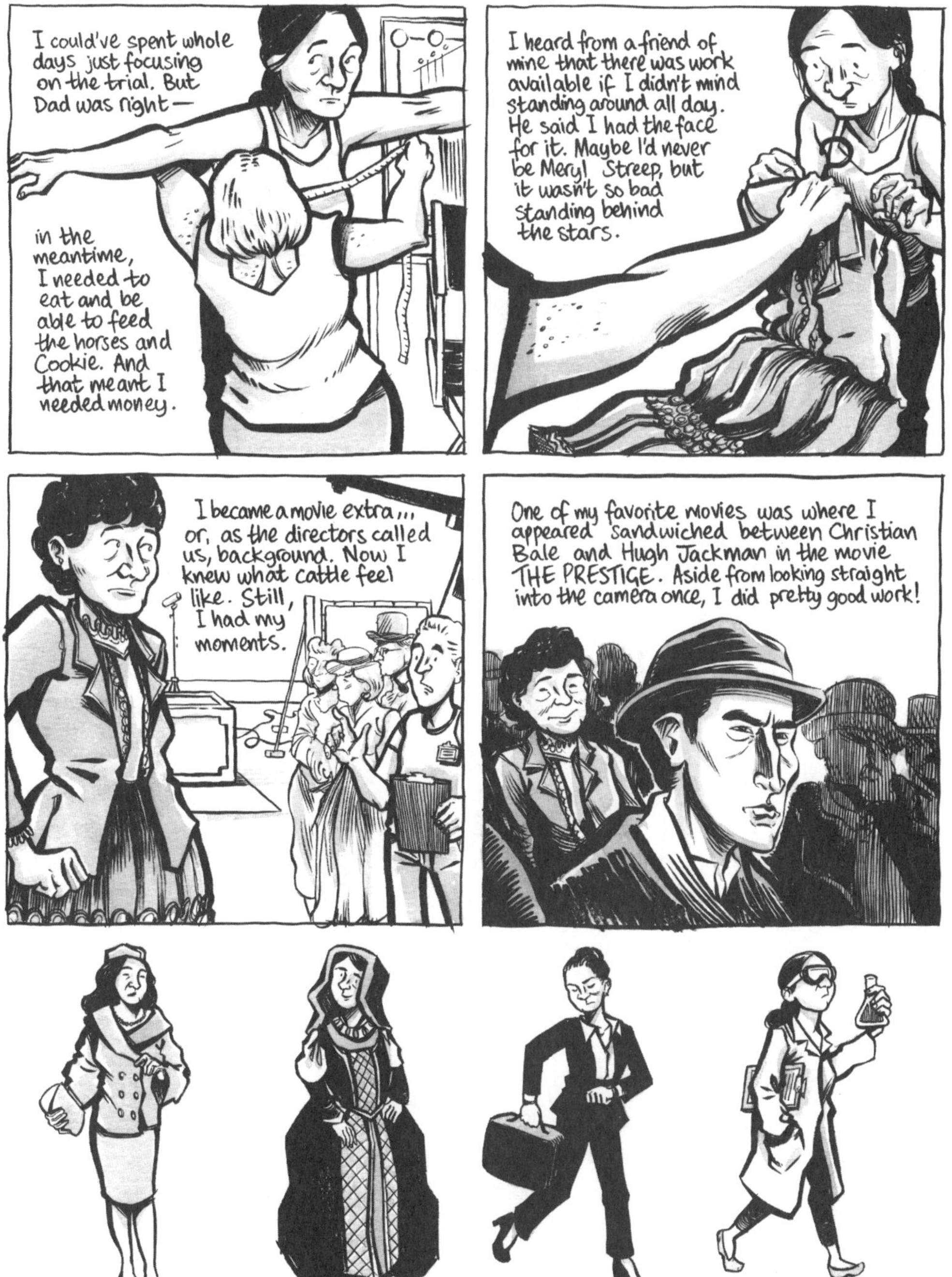
I could've spent whole days just focusing on the trial. But Dad was right—
in the meantime, I needed to eat and be able to feed the horses and Cookie. And that meant I needed money.
I heard from a friend of mine that there was work available if I didn't mind standing around all day. He said I had the face for it. Maybe I'd never be Meryl Streep, but it wasn't so bad standing behind the stars.
I became a movie extra... or, as the directors called us, background. Now I knew what cattle feel like. Still, I had my moments.
One of my favorite movies was where I appeared sandwiched between Christian Bale and Hugh Jackman in the movie THE PRESTIGE. Aside from looking straight into the camera once, I did pretty good work!

I did about forty background "acting" gigs. I had a character's face, they told me. But after a while, I started getting itchy. I missed being around horses.

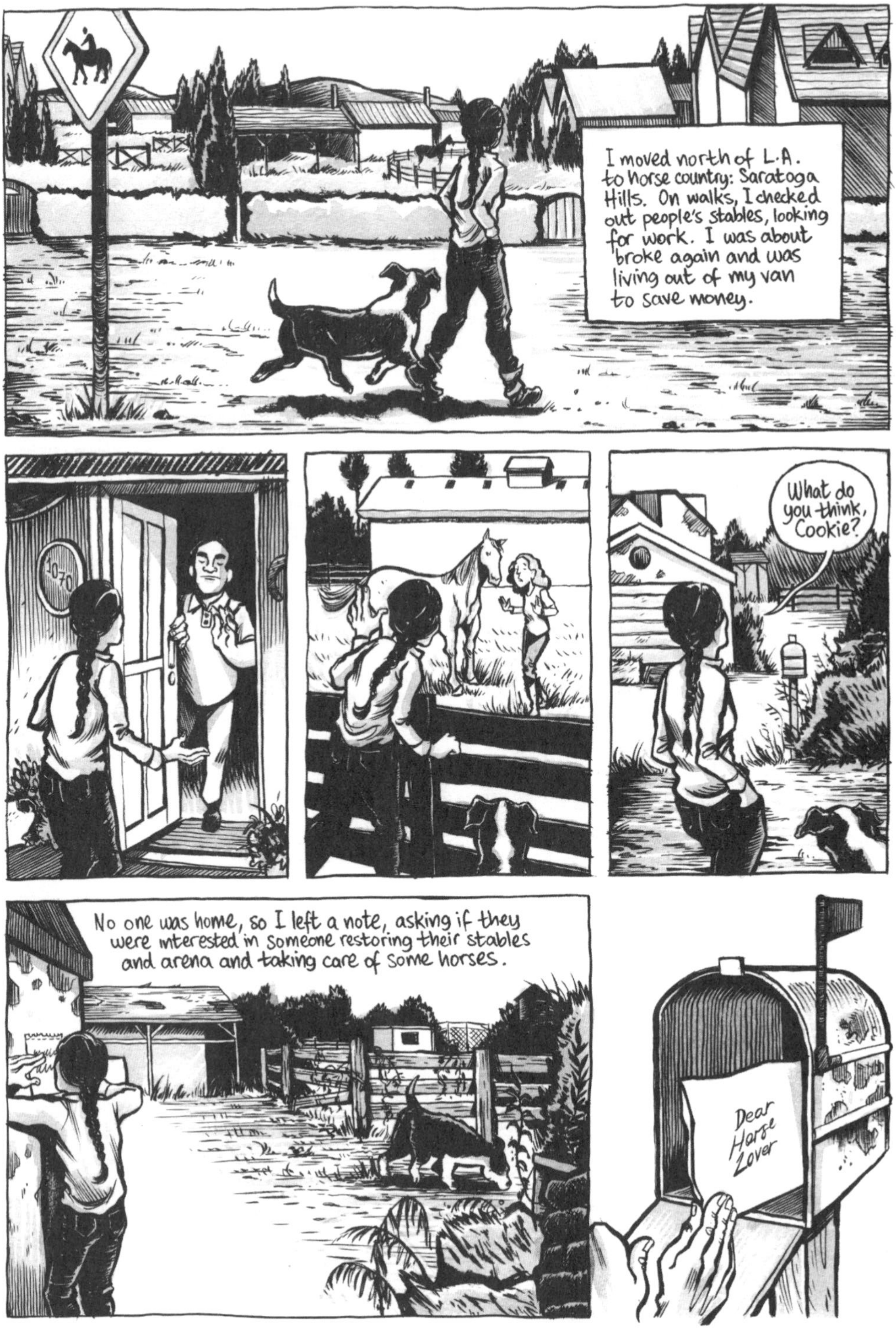

I moved north of L.A. to horse country: Saratoga Hills. On walks, I checked out people's stables, looking for work. I was about broke again and was living out of my van to save money.
1070
What do you think, Cookie?
No one was home, so I left a note, asking if they were interested in someone restoring their stables and arena and taking care of some horses.
Dear Horse Lover

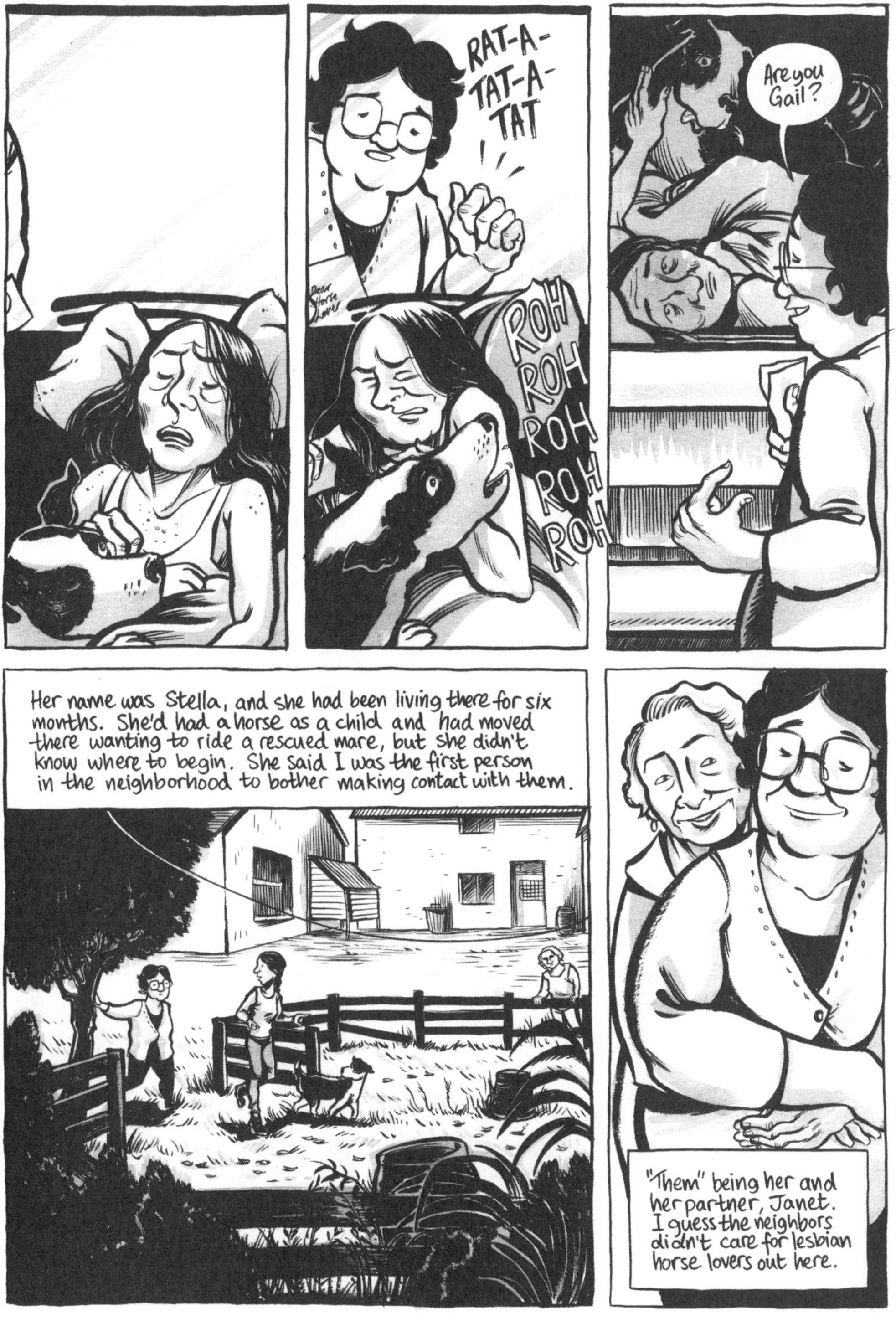
RAT-A-TAT-A-TAT
Dear Horse Lovers
ROH ROH ROH ROH ROH
Are you Gail?
Her name was Stella, and she had been living there for six months. She'd had a horse as a child and had moved there wanting to ride a rescued mare, but she didn't know where to begin. She said I was the first person in the neighborhood to bother making contact with them.
"Them" being her and her partner, Janet. I guess the neighbors didn't care for lesbian horse lovers out here.

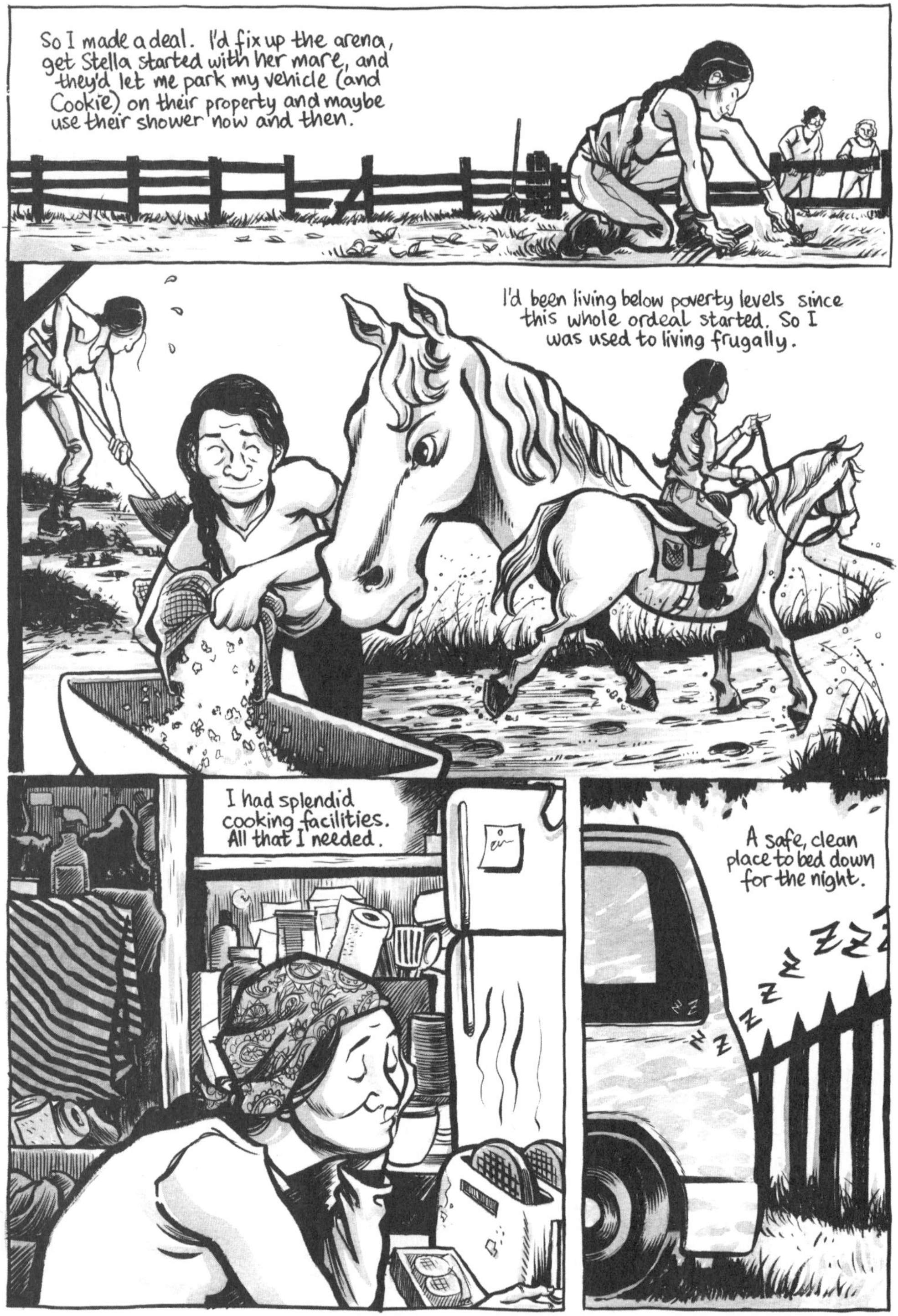
So I made a deal. I'd fix up the arena, get Stella started with her mare, and they'd let me park my vehicle (and Cookie) on their property and maybe use their shower now and then.
I'd been living below poverty levels since this whole ordeal started. So I was used to living frugally.
I had splendid cooking facilities. All that I needed.
A safe, clean place to bed down for the night.
ZZZ
Z
Z
Z
Z Z

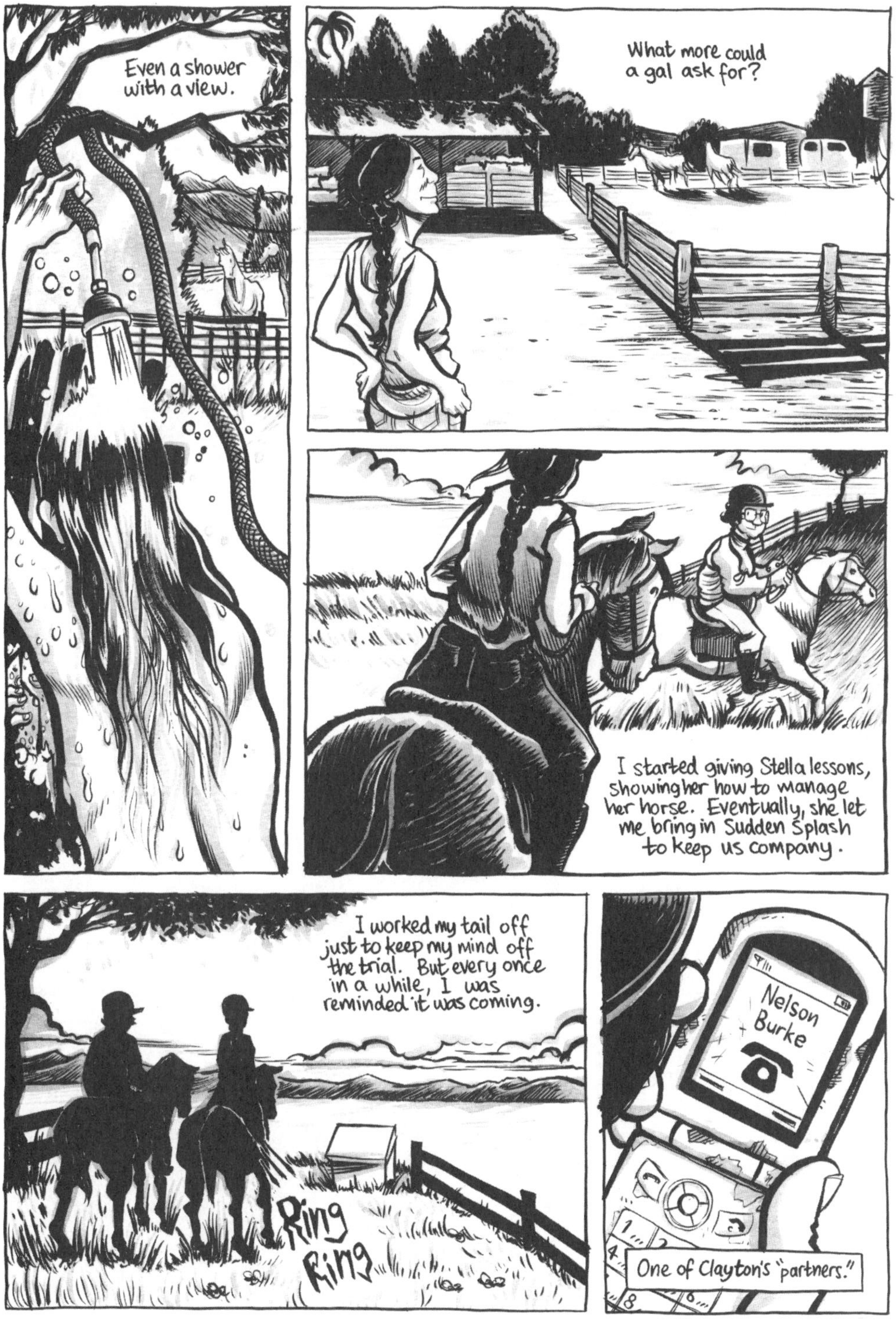
Even a shower with a view.
What more could a gal ask for?
I started giving Stella lessons, showing her how to manage her horse. Eventually, she let me bring in Sudden Splash to keep us company.
I worked my tail off just to keep my mind off the trial. But every once in a while, I was reminded it was coming.
Ring
Ring
Nelson Burke
One of Clayton's "partners."

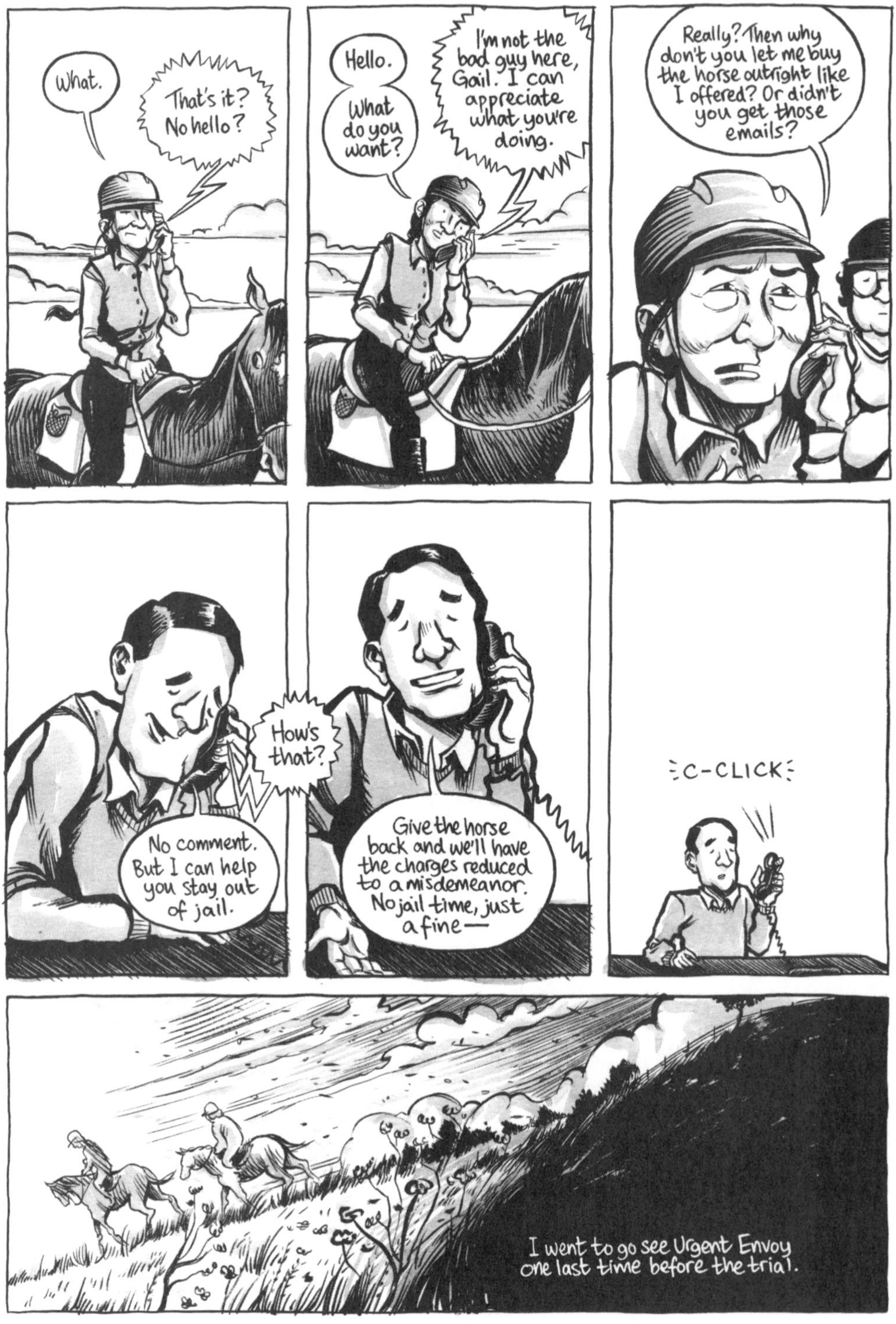
What.
That's it? No hello?
Hello.
What do you want?
I'm not the bad guy here, Gail. I can appreciate what you're doing.
Really? Then why don't you let me buy the horse outright like I offered? Or didn't you get those emails?
How's that?
No comment. But I can help you stay out of jail.
Give the horse back and we'll have the charges reduced to a misdemeanor. No jail time, just a fine—
C-CLICK
I went to go see Urgent Envoy one last time before the trial.

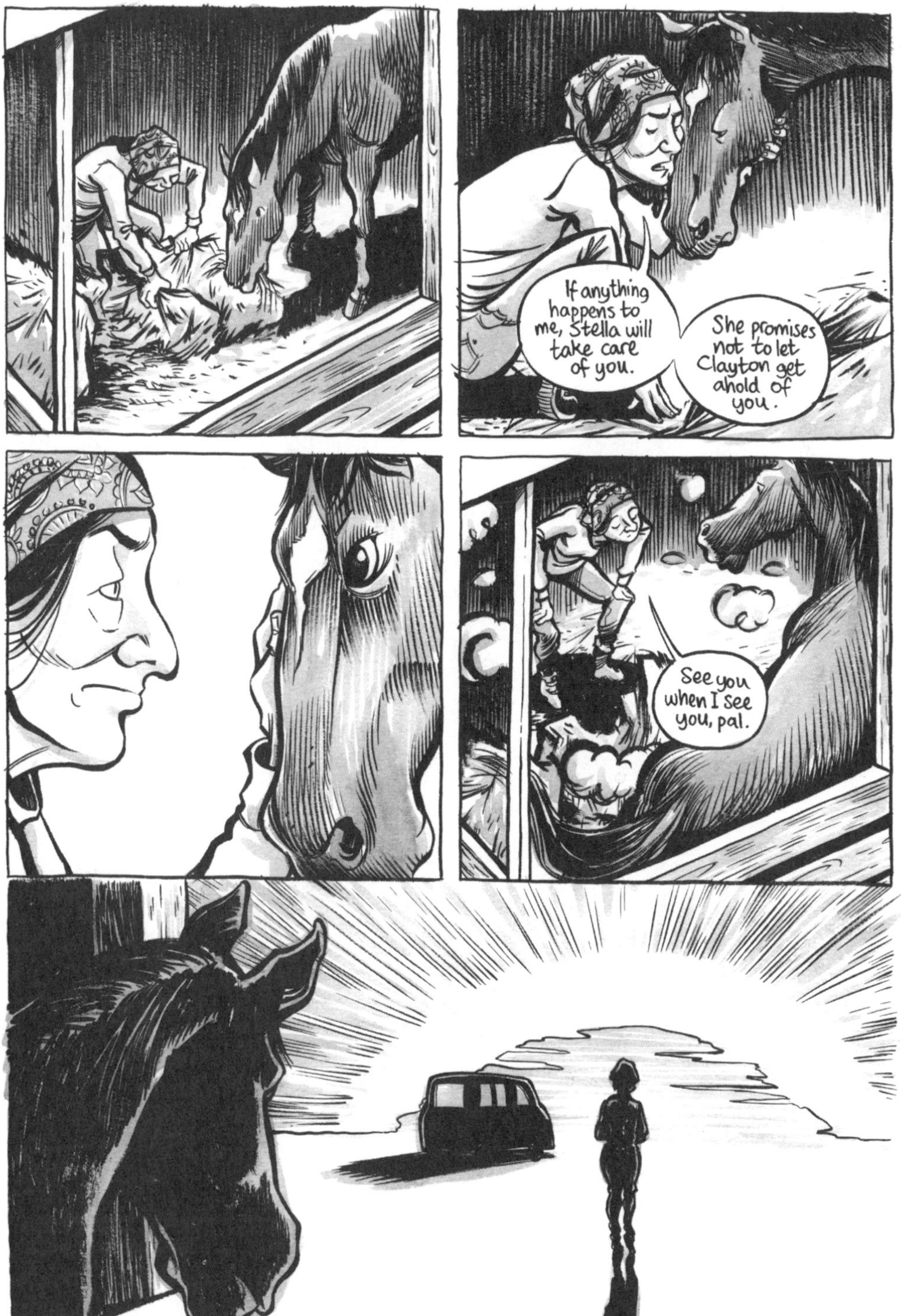
If anything happens to me, Stella will take care of you.
She promises not to let Clayton get ahold of you.
See you when I see you, pal.

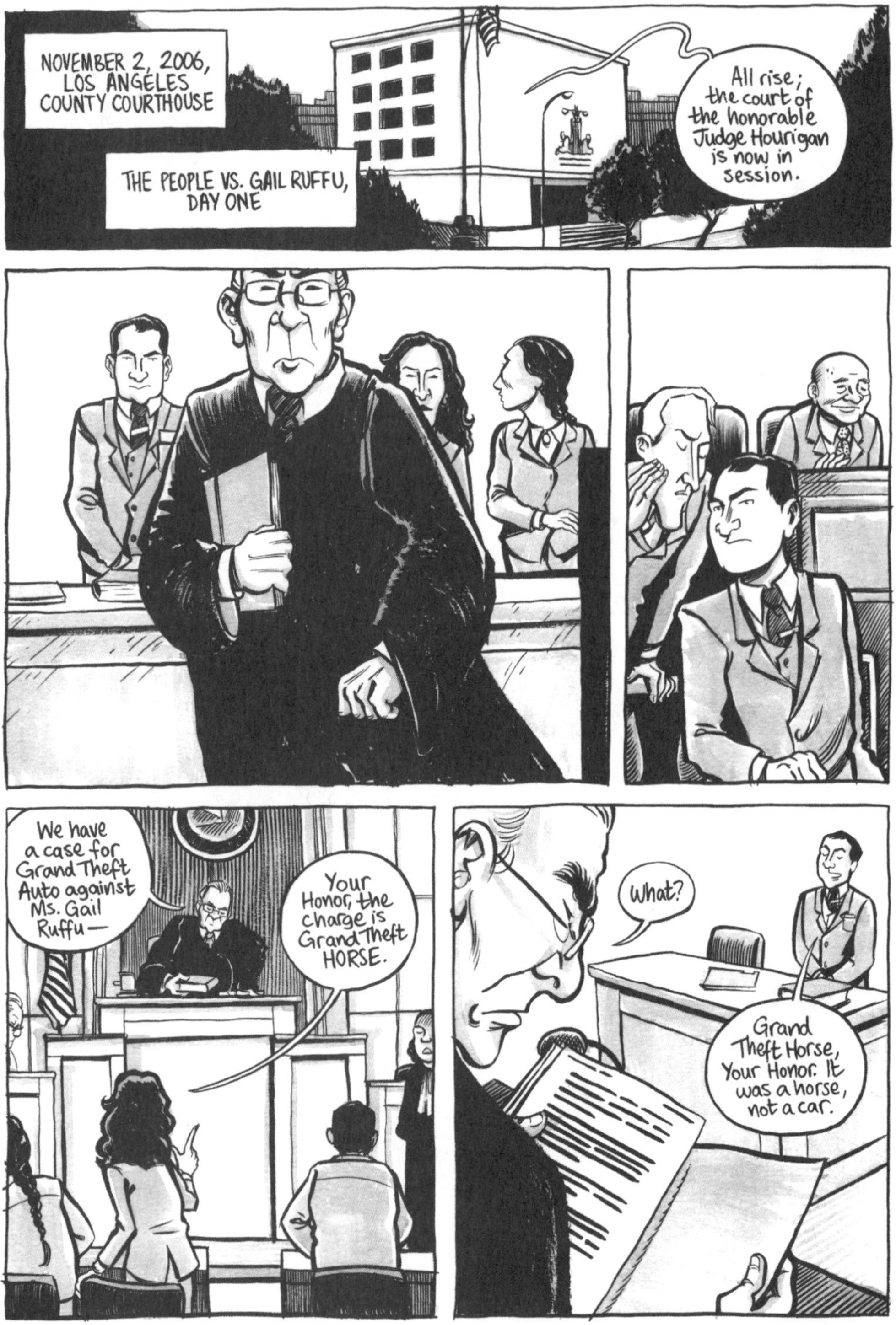

NOVEMBER 2, 2006, LOS ANGELES COUNTY COURTHOUSE
THE PEOPLE VS. GAIL RUFFU, DAY ONE
All rise; the court of the honorable Judge Hourigan is now in session.
We have a case for Grand Theft Auto against Ms. Gail Ruffu—
Your Honor, the charge is Grand Theft HORSE.
What?
Grand Theft Horse, Your Honor. It was a horse, not a car.

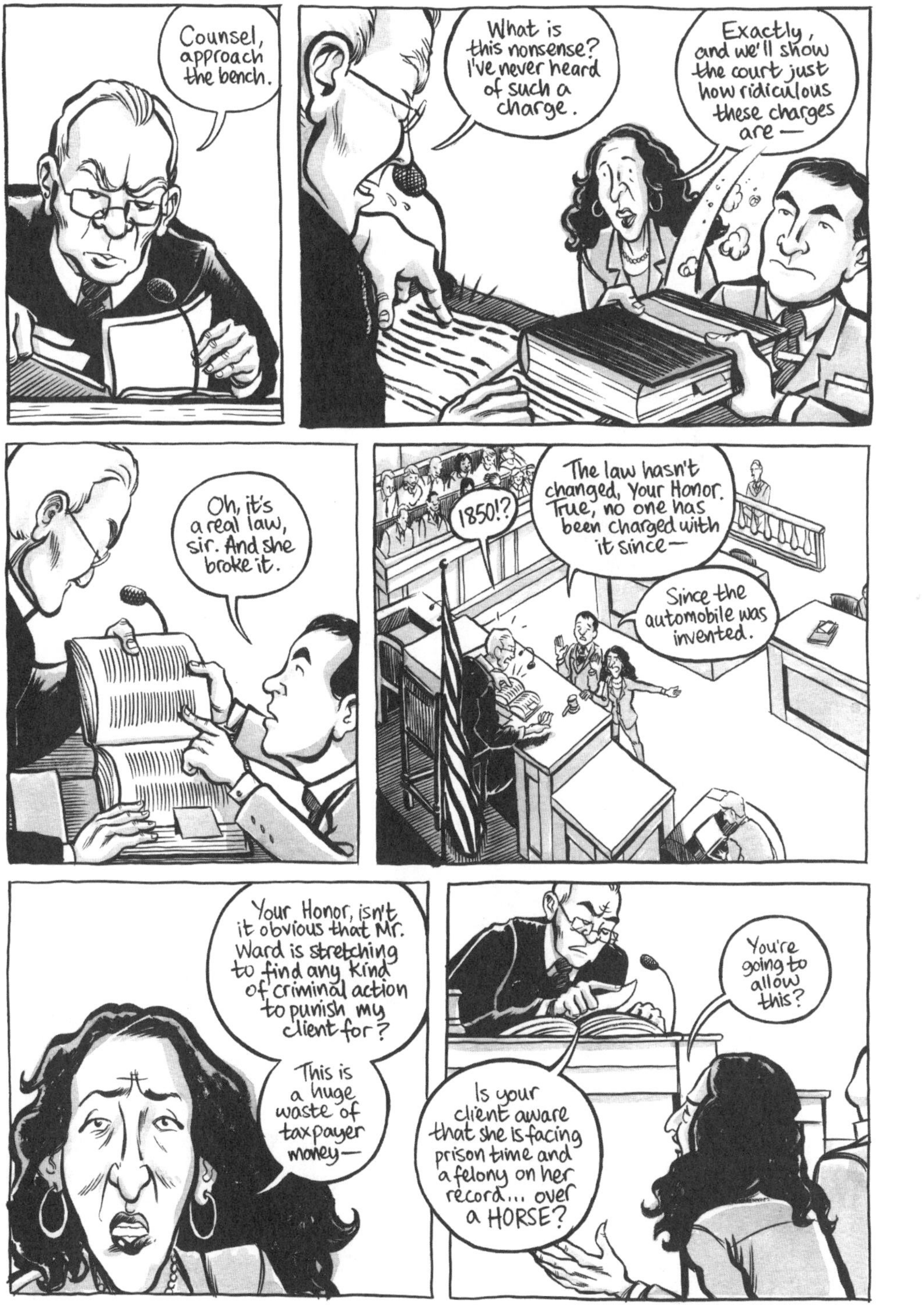
Counsel, approach the bench.
What is this nonsense? I've never heard of such a charge.
Exactly, and we'll show the court just how ridiculous these charges are—
Oh, it's a real law, sir. And she broke it.
1850!?
The law hasn't changed, Your Honor. True, no one has been charged with it since—
Since the automobile was invented.
Your Honor, isn't it obvious that Mr. Ward is stretching to find any kind of criminal action to punish my client for?
This is a huge waste of taxpayer money—
You're going to allow this?
Is your client aware that she is facing prison time and a felony on her record... over a HORSE?

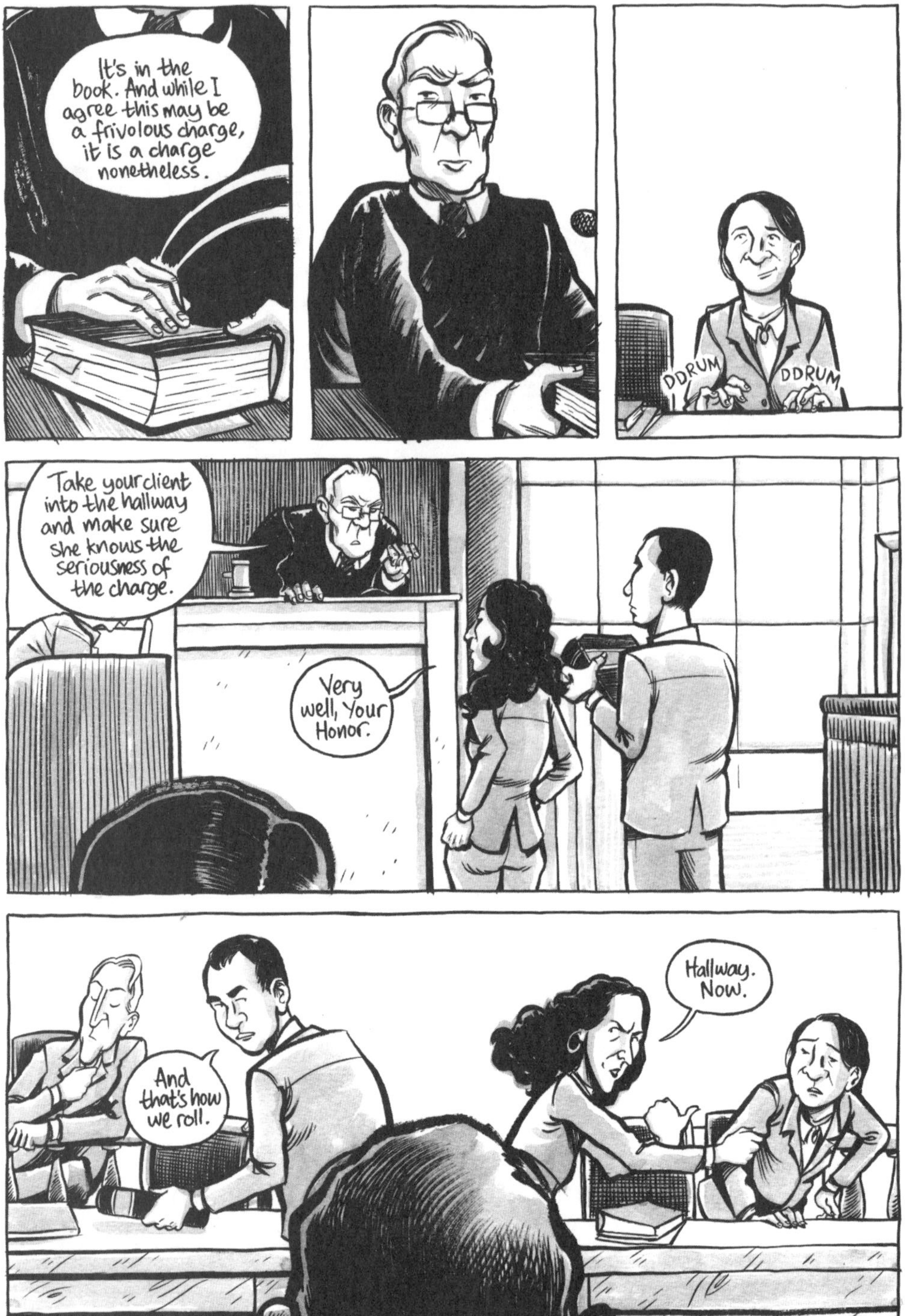
It's in the book. And while I agree this may be a frivolous charge, it is a charge nonetheless.
DDRUM
DDRUM
Take your client into the hallway and make sure she knows the seriousness of the charge.
Very well, Your Honor.
And that's how we roll.
Hallway. Now.

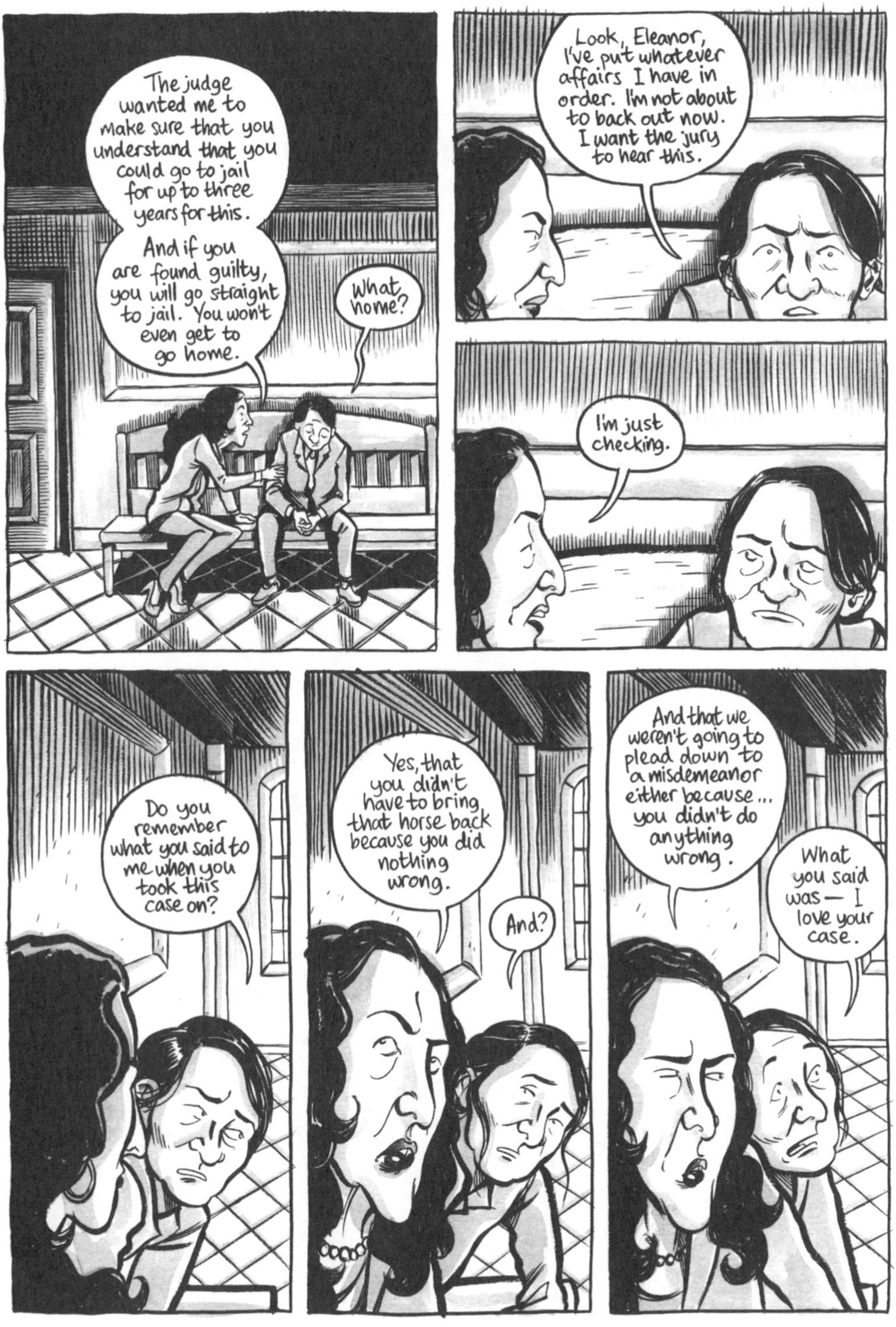
The judge wanted me to make sure that you understand that you could go to jail for up to three years for this.
And if you are found guilty, you will go straight to jail. You won't even get to go home.
What home?
Look, Eleanor, I've put whatever affairs I have in order. I'm not about to back out now. I want the jury to hear this.
I'm just checking.
Do you remember what you said to me when you took this case on?
Yes, that you didn't have to bring that horse back because you did nothing wrong.
And?
And that we weren't going to plead down to a misdemeanor either because... you didn't do anything wrong.
What you said was— I love your case.

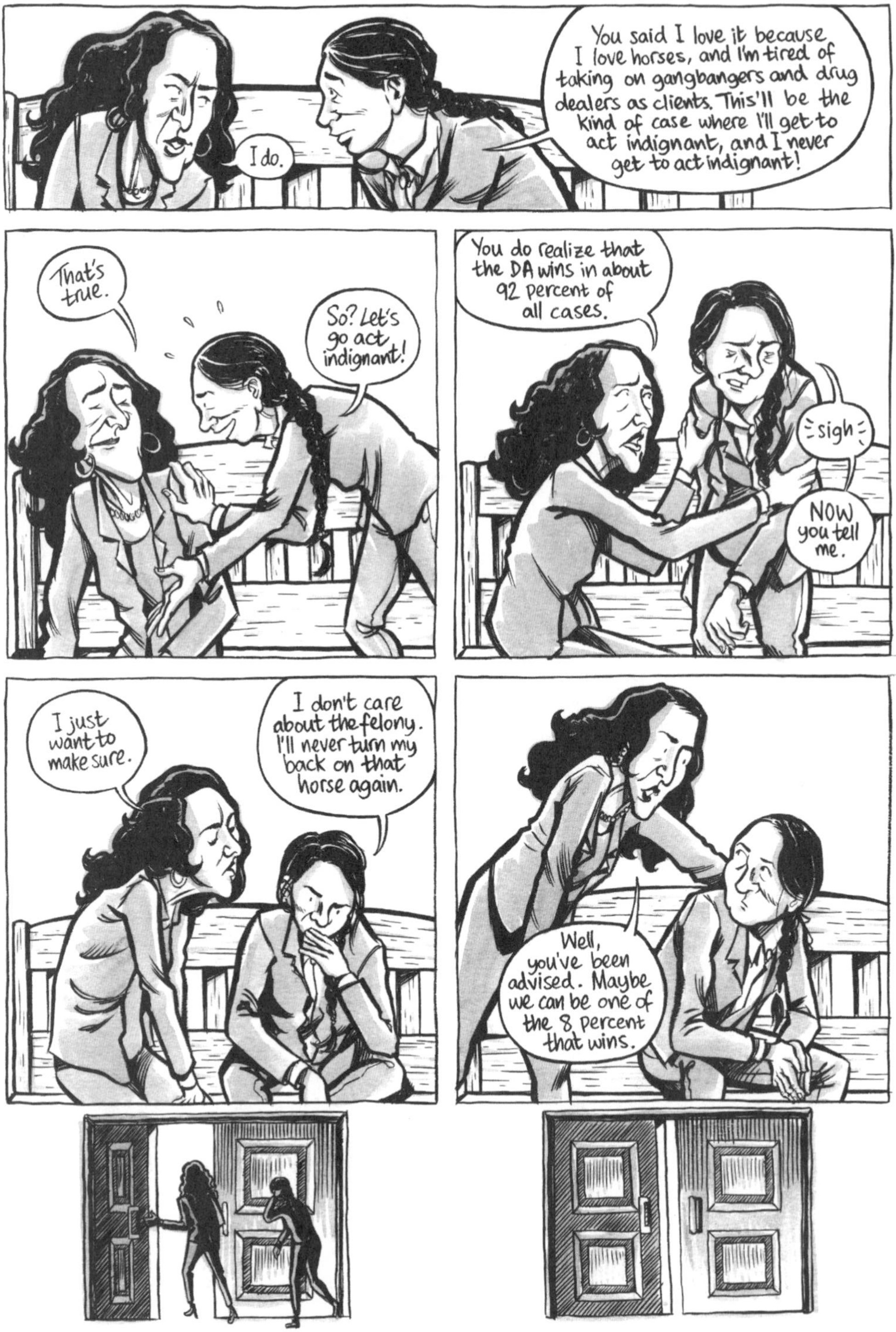
I do.
You said I love it because I love horses, and I'm tired of taking on gangbangers and drug dealers as clients. This'll be the kind of case where I'll get to act indignant, and I never get to act indignant!
That's true.
So? Let's go act indignant!
You do realize that the DA wins in about 92 percent of all cases.
sigh
NOW you tell me.
I just want to make sure.
I don't care about the felony. I'll never turn my back on that horse again.
Well, you've been advised. Maybe we can be one of the 8 percent that wins.

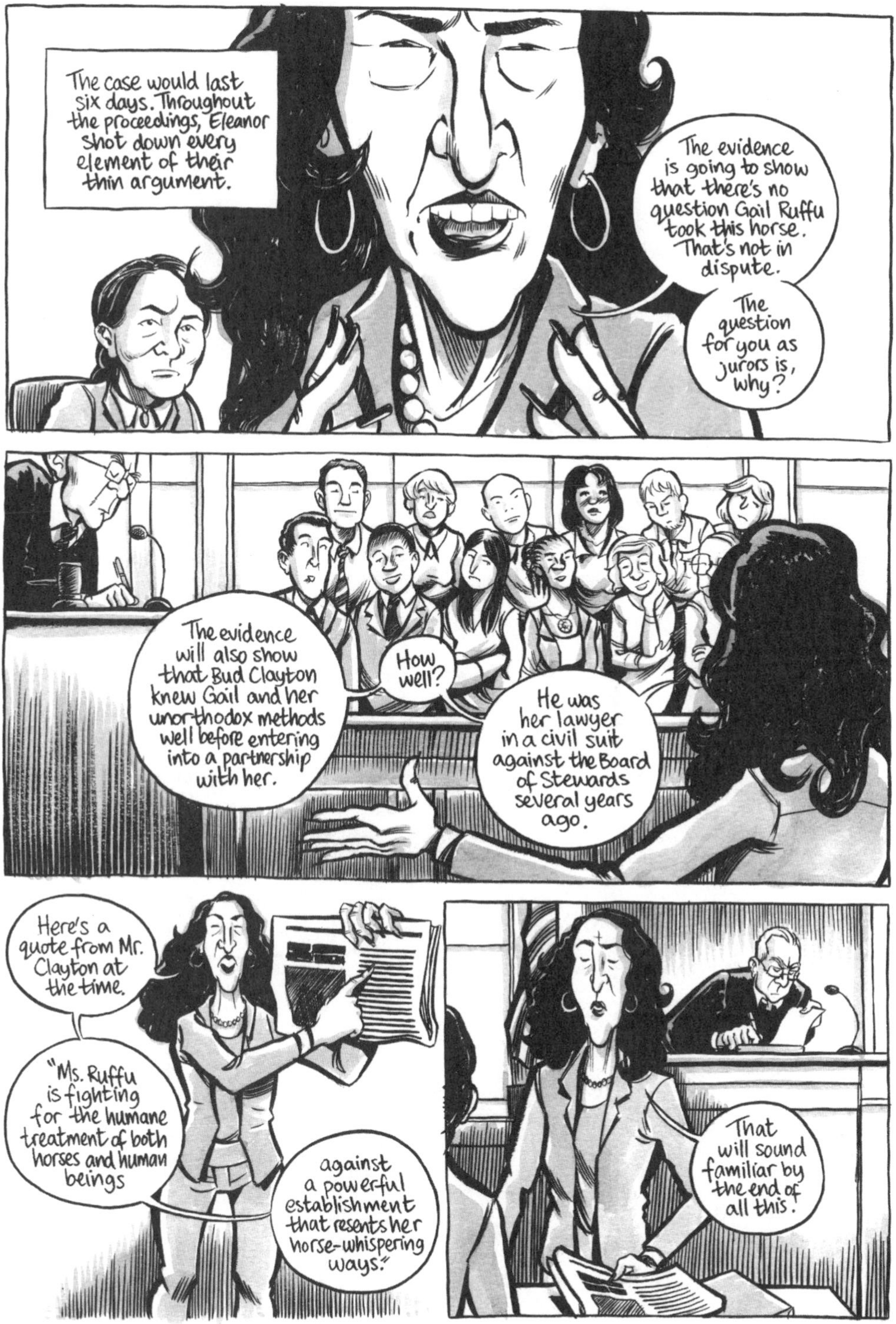
The case would last six days. Throughout the proceedings, Eleanor shot down every element of their thin argument.
The evidence is going to show that there's no question Gail Ruffu took this horse. That's not in dispute.
The question for you as jurors is, why?
The evidence will also show that Bud Clayton knew Gail and her unorthodox methods well before entering into a partnership with her.
How well?
He was her lawyer in a civil suit against the Board of Stewards several years ago.
Here's a quote from Mr. Clayton at the time.
"Ms. Ruffu is fighting for the humane treatment of both horses and human beings
against a powerful establishment that resents her horse-whispering ways."
That will sound familiar by the end of all this.

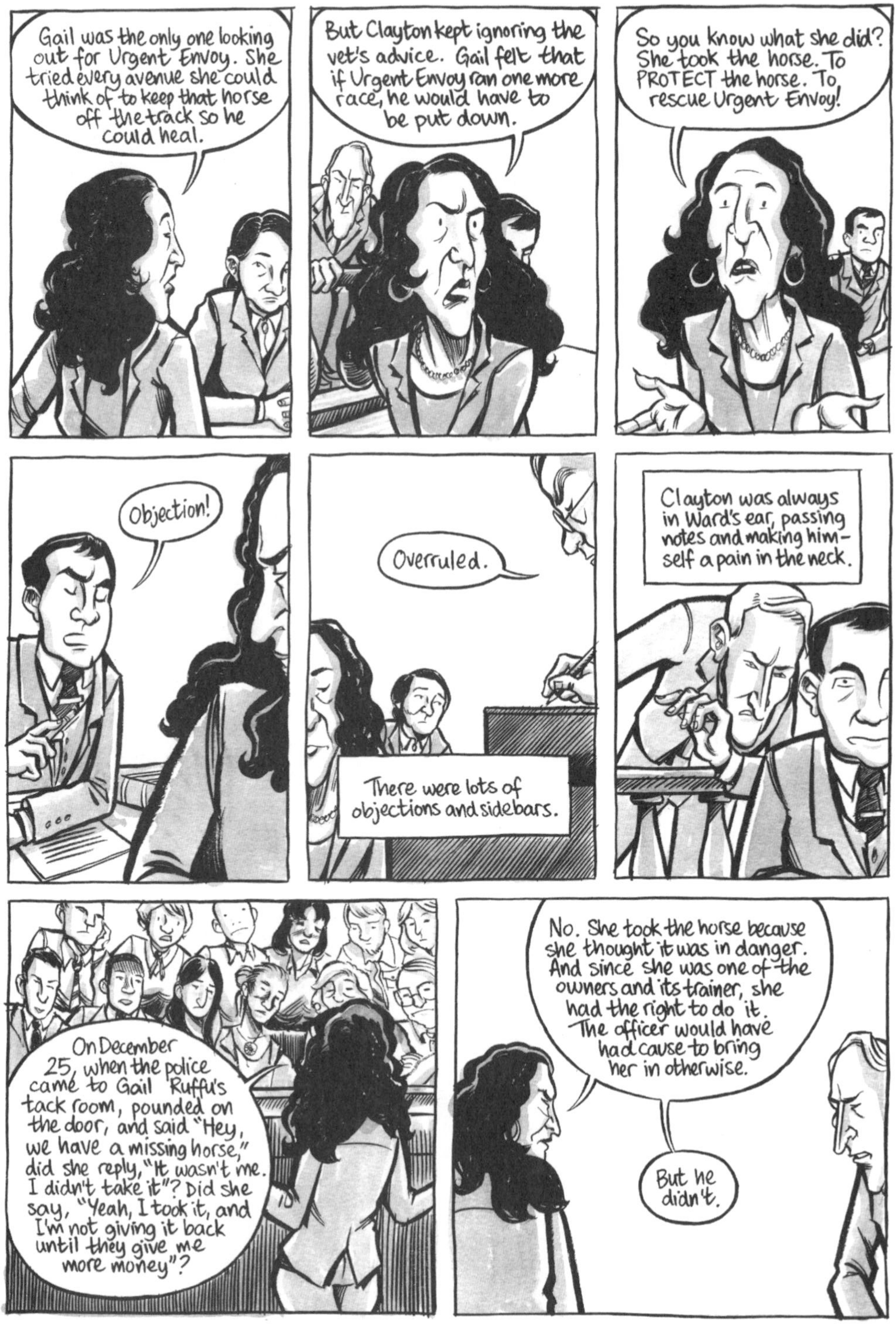
Gail was the only one looking out for Urgent Envoy. She tried every avenue she could think of to keep that horse off the track so he could heal.
But Clayton kept ignoring the vet's advice. Gail felt that if Urgent Envoy ran one more race, he would have to be put down.
So you know what she did? She took the horse. To PROTECT the horse. To rescue Urgent Envoy!
Objection!
Overruled.
There were lots of objections and sidebars.
Clayton was always in Ward's ear, passing notes and making him-self a pain in the neck.
On December 25, when the police came to Gail Ruffu's tack room, pounded on the door, and said "Hey, we have a missing horse," did she reply, "It wasn't me. I didn't take it"? Did she say, "Yeah, I took it, and I'm not giving it back until they give me more money"?
No. She took the horse because she thought it was in danger. And since she was one of the owners and its trainer, she had the right to do it. The officer would have had cause to bring her in otherwise.
But he didn't.

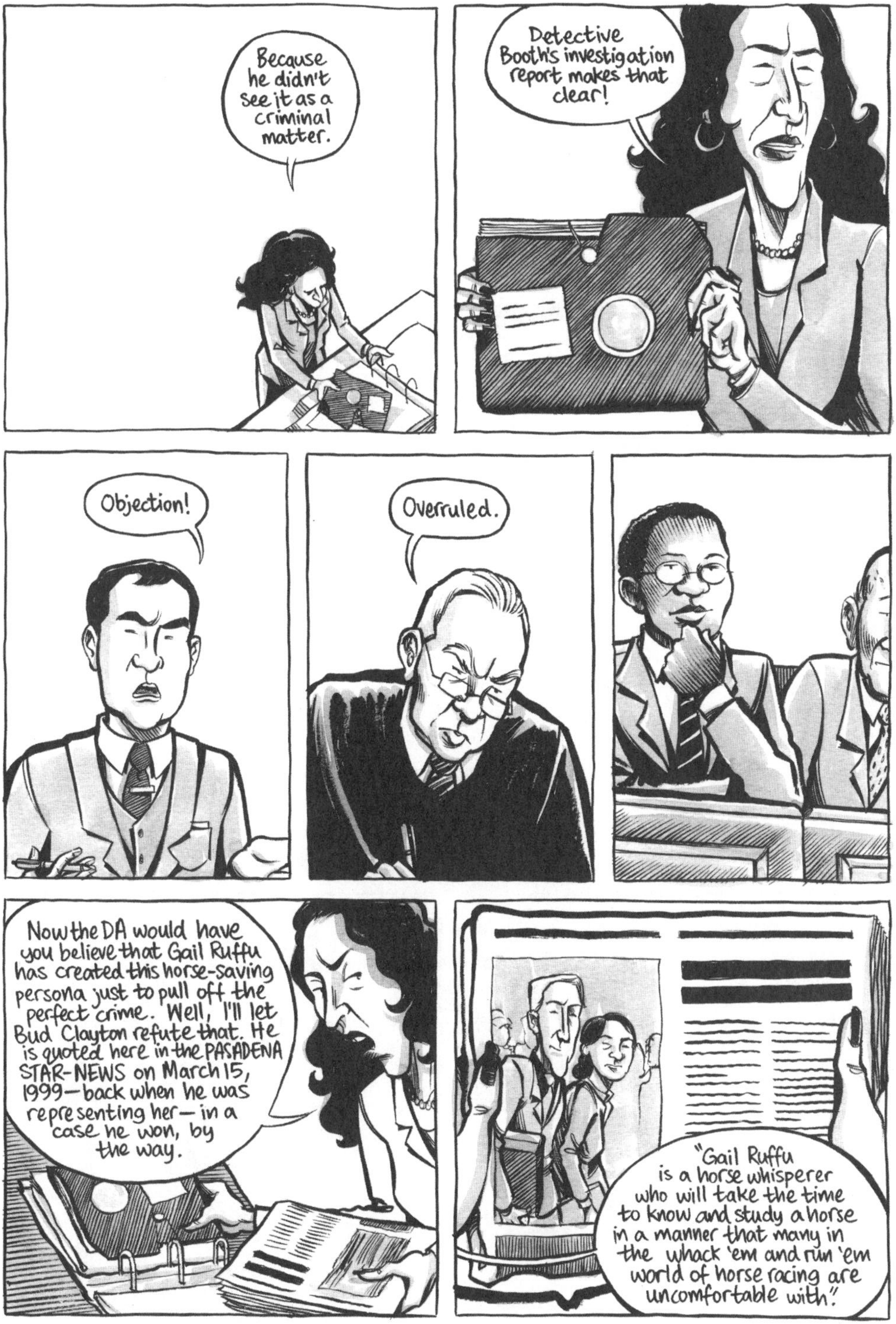
Because he didn't see it as a criminal matter.
Detective Booth's investigation report makes that clear!
Objection!
Overruled.
Now the DA would have you believe that Gail Ruffu has created this horse-saving persona just to pull off the perfect crime. Well, I'll let Bud Clayton refute that. He is quoted here in the PASADENA STAR-NEWS on March 15, 1999—back when he was representing her—in a case he won, by the way.
"Gail Ruffu is a horse whisperer who will take the time to know and study a horse in a manner that many in the whack 'em and run 'em world of horse racing are uncomfortable with."

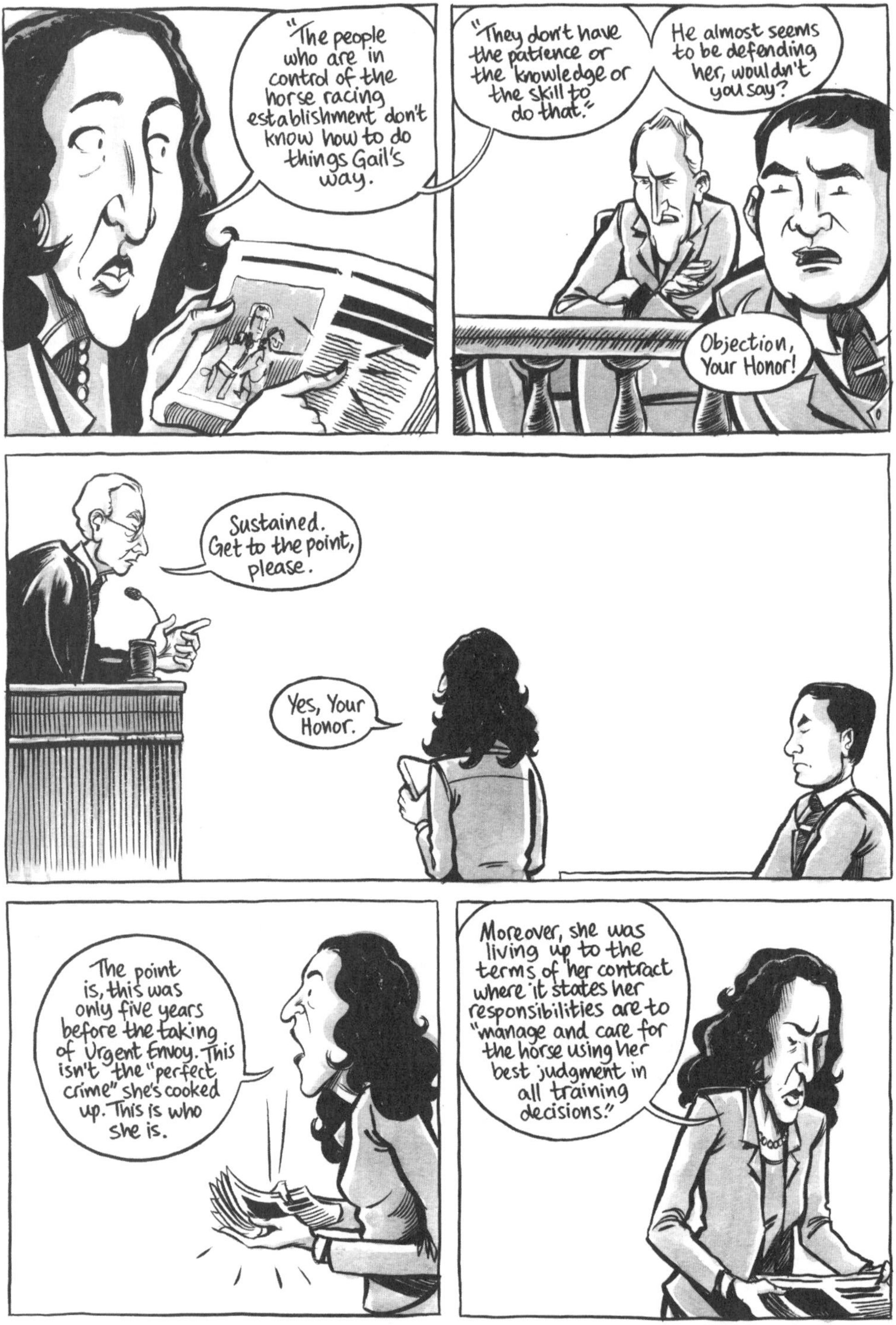
"The people who are in control of the horse racing establishment don't know how to do things Gail's way.
They don't have the patience or the knowledge or the skill to do that."
He almost seems to be defending her, wouldn't you say?
Objection, Your Honor!
Sustained. Get to the point, please.
Yes, Your Honor.
The point is, this was only five years before the taking of Urgent Envoy. This isn't the "perfect crime" she's cooked up. This is who she is.
Moreover, she was living up to the terms of her contract where it states her responsibilities are to "manage and care for the horse using her best judgment in all training decisions."

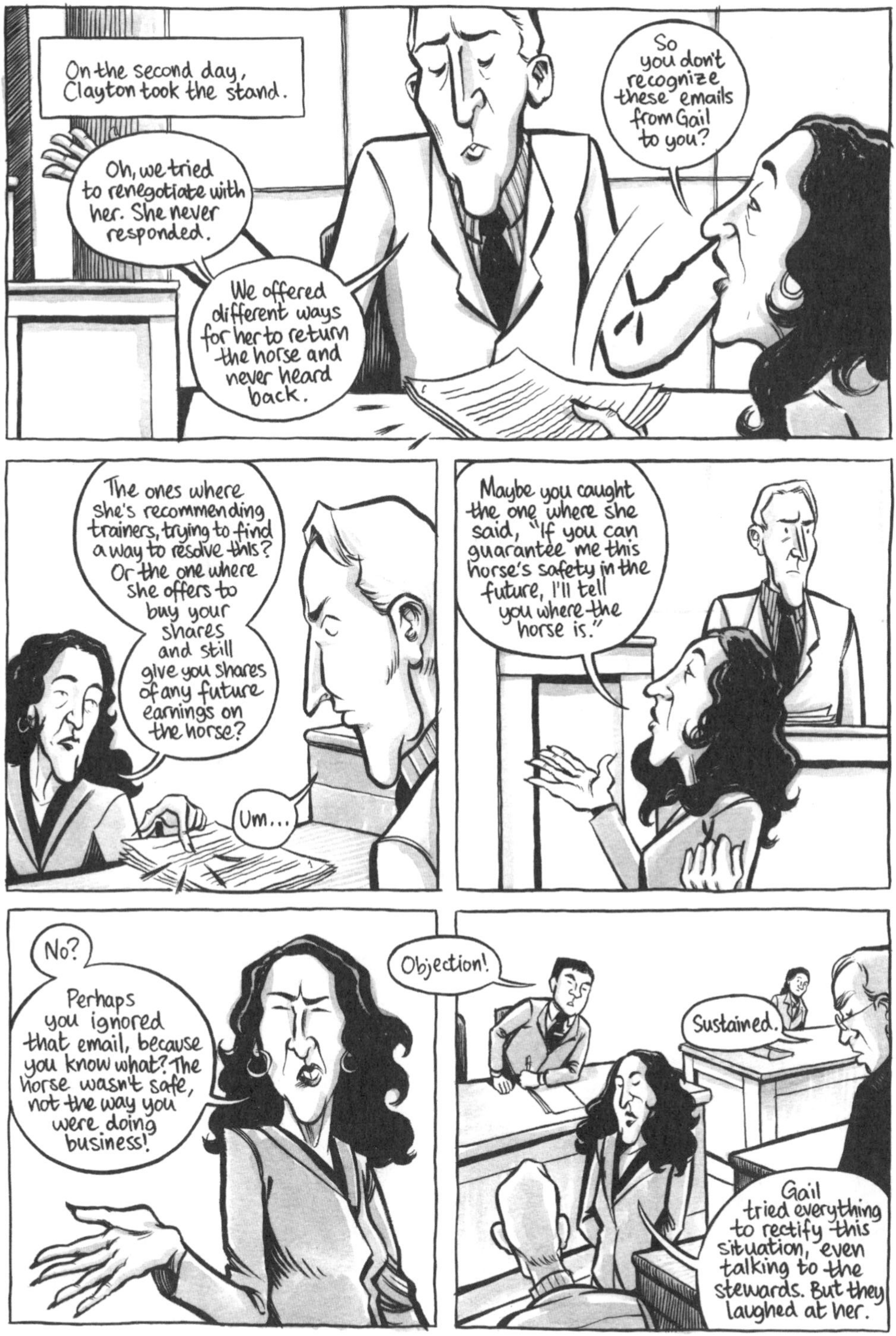
On the second day, Clayton took the stand.
So you don't recognize these emails from Gail to you?
Oh, we tried to renegotiate with her. She never responded.
We offered different ways for her to return the horse and never heard back.
The ones where she's recommending trainers, trying to find a way to resolve this? Or the one where she offers to buy your shares and still give you shares of any future earnings on the horse?
Um...
Maybe you caught the one where she said, "If you can guarantee me this horse's safety in the future, I'll tell you where the horse is."
No?
Perhaps you ignored that email, because you know what? The horse wasn't safe, not the way you were doing business!
Objection!
Sustained.
Gail tried everything to rectify this situation, even talking to the stewards. But they laughed at her.

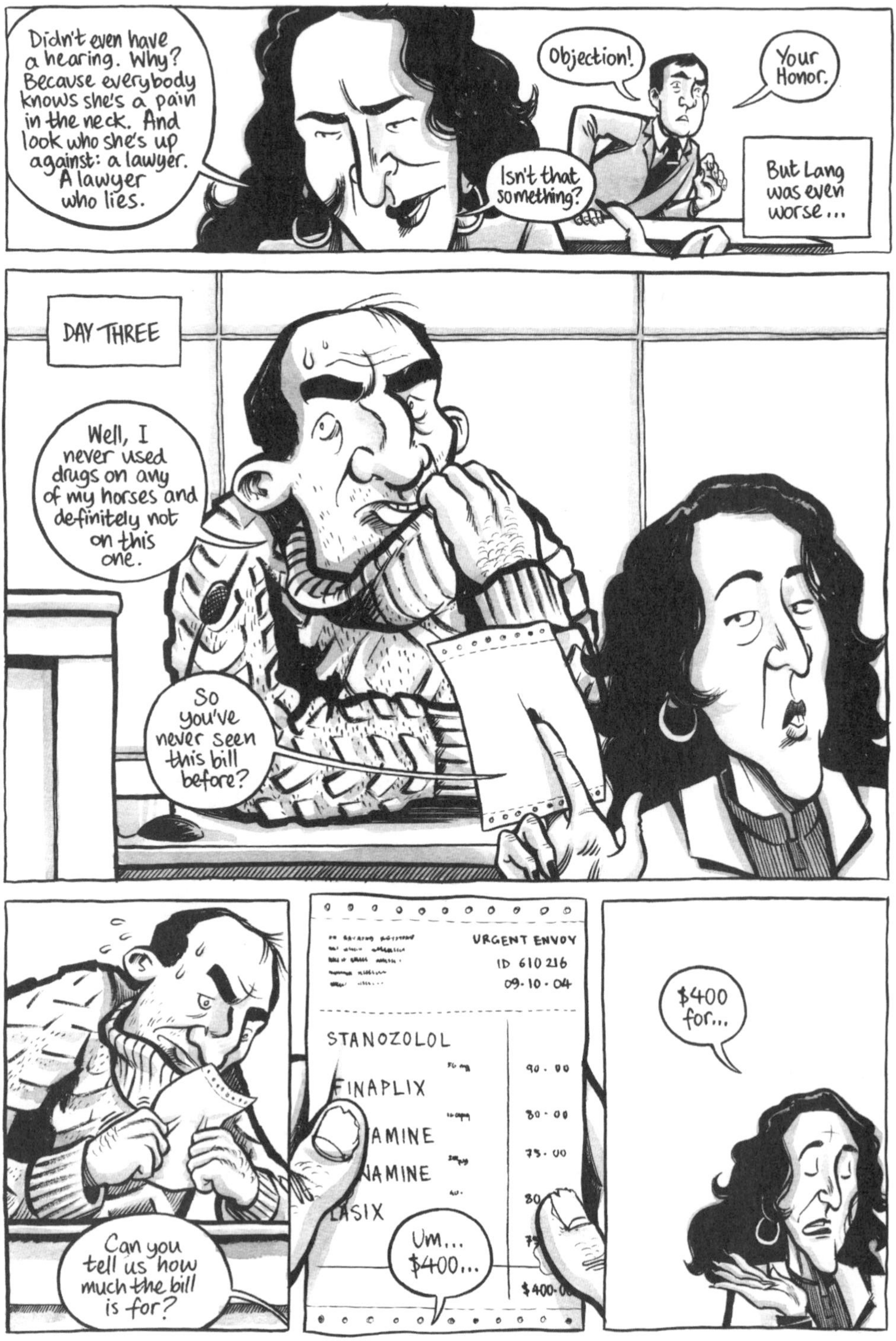

Didn't even have a hearing. Why? Because everybody knows she's a pain in the neck. And look who she's up against: a lawyer. A lawyer who lies.
Isn't that something?
Objection!
Your Honor.
But Lang was even worse...
DAY THREE
Well, I never used drugs on any of my horses and definitely not on this one.
So you've never seen this bill before?
URGENT ENVOY
ID 610216
09.10.04
STANOZOLOL
FINAPLIX
LASIX
90.00
80.00
75.00
Can you tell us how much the bill is for?
Um... $400...
$400 for...

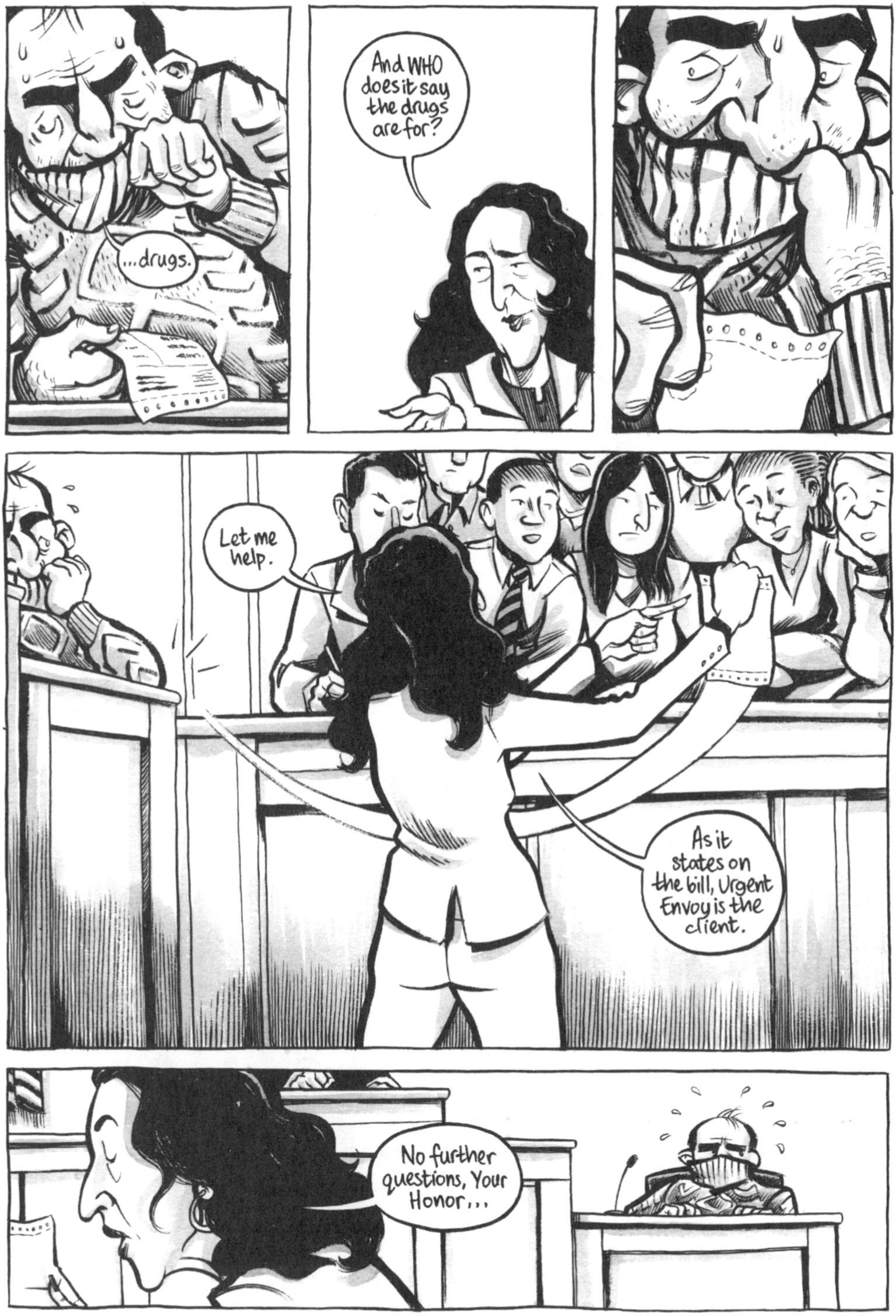
...drugs.
And WHO does it say the drugs are for?
Let me help.
As it states on the bill, Urgent Envoy is the client.
No further questions, Your Honor...

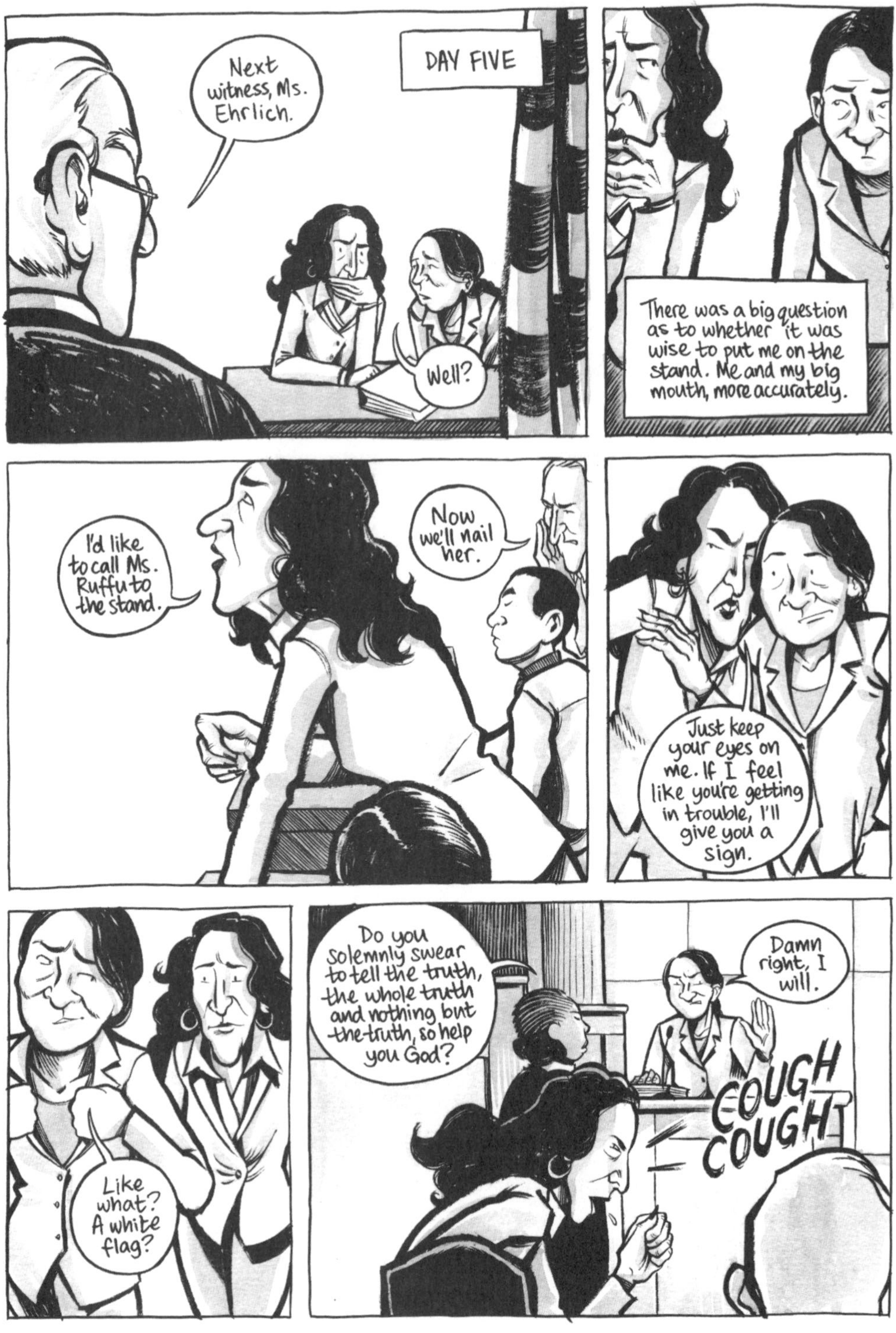

DAY FIVE
Next witness, Ms. Ehrlich.
Well?
There was a big question as to whether it was wise to put me on the stand. Me and my big mouth, more accurately.
I'd like to call Ms. Ruffu to the stand.
Now we'll nail her.
Just keep your eyes on me. If I feel like you're getting in trouble, I'll give you a sign.
Like what? A white flag?
Do you solemnly swear to tell the truth, the whole truth and nothing but the truth, so help you God?
Damn right, I will.
COUGH
COUGH

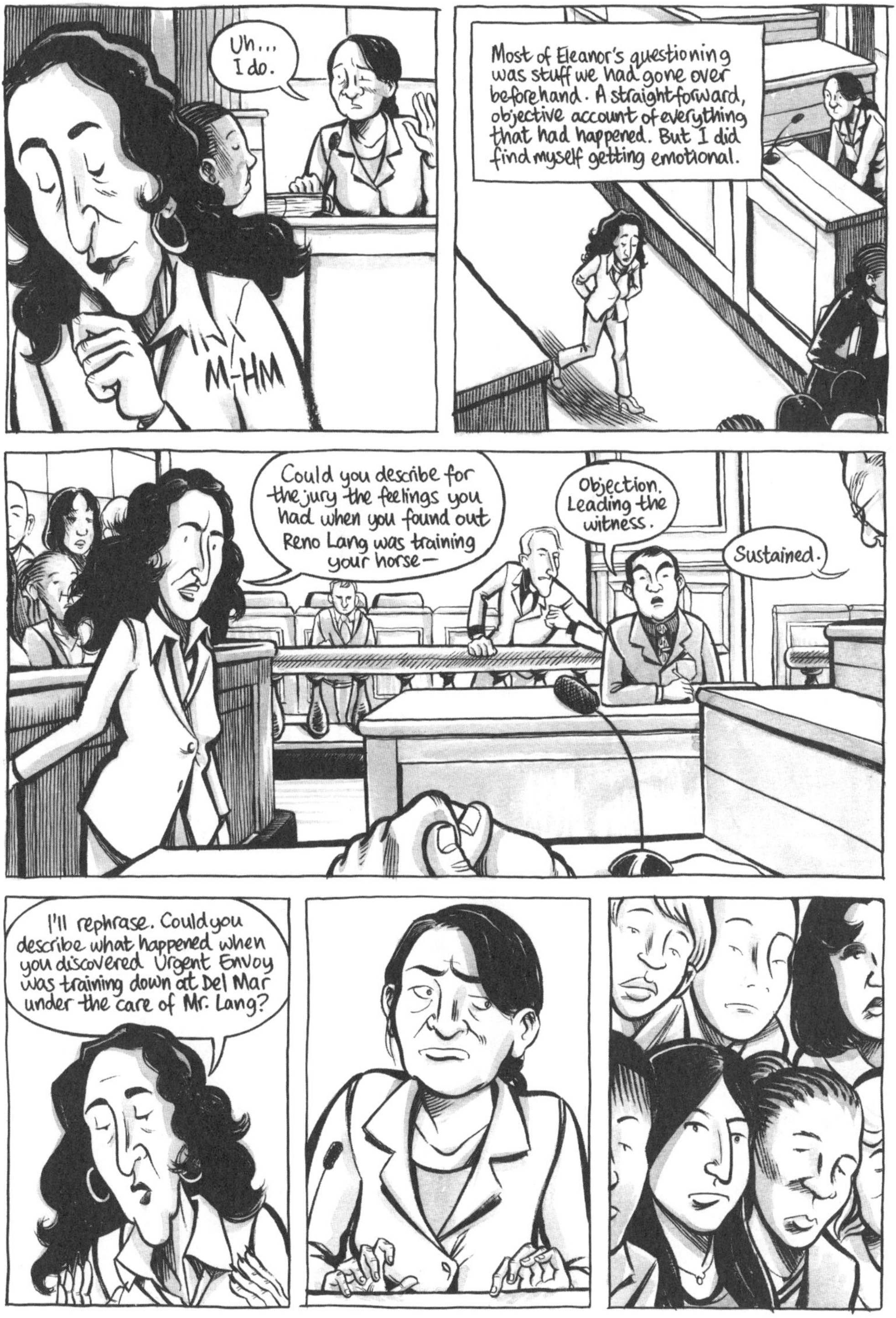
Uh... I do.
M-HM
Most of Eleanor's questioning was stuff we had gone over beforehand. A straightforward, objective account of everything that had happened. But I did find myself getting emotional.
Could you describe for the jury the feelings you had when you found out Reno Lang was training your horse—
Objection. Leading the witness.
Sustained.
I'll rephrase. Could you describe what happened when you discovered Urgent Envoy was training down at Del Mar under the care of Mr. Lang?

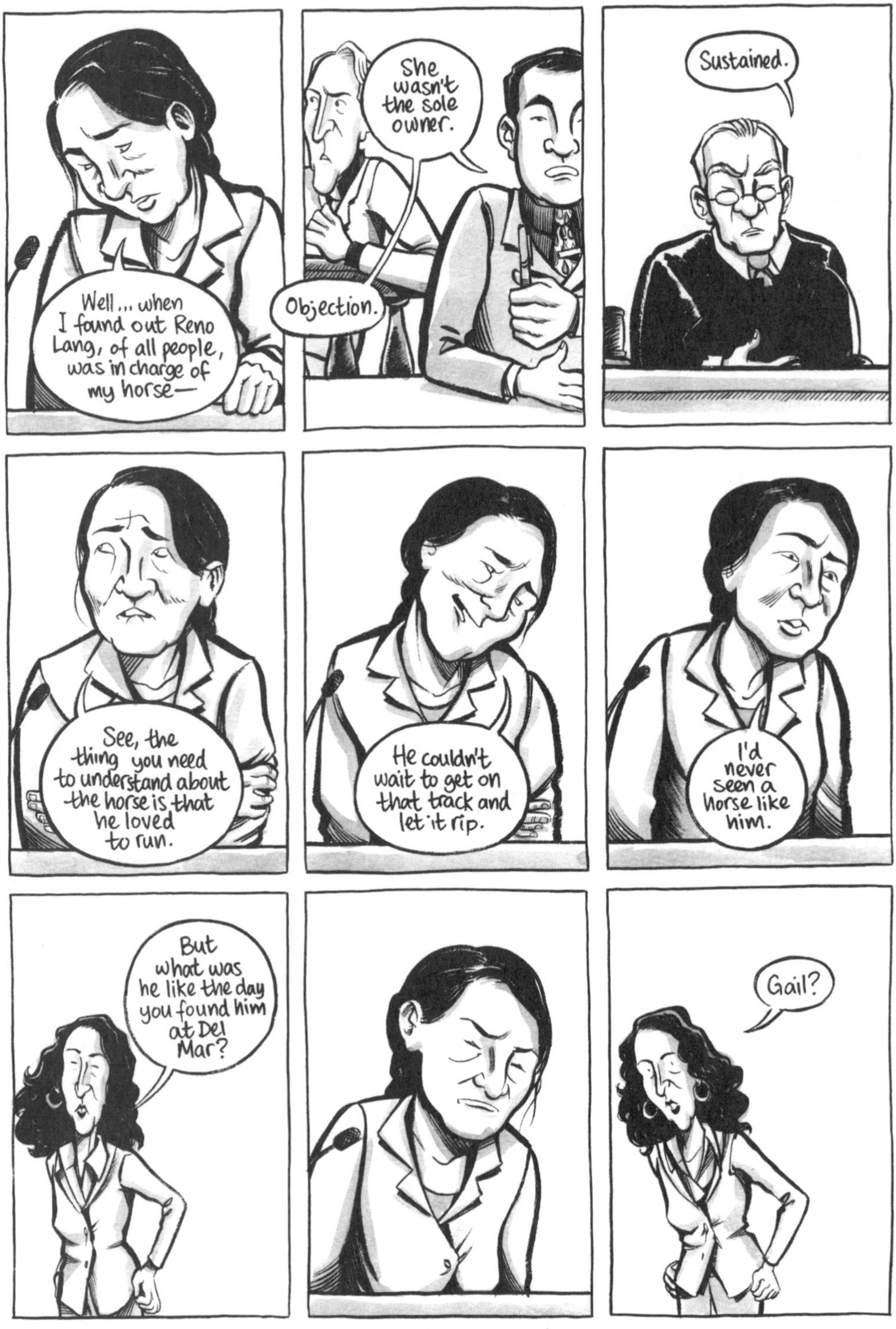

Well... when I found out Reno Lang, of all people, was in charge of my horse—
Objection.
She wasn't the sole owner.
Sustained.
See, the thing you need to understand about the horse is that he loved to run.
He couldn't wait to get on that track and let it rip.
I'd never seen a horse like him.
But what was he like the day you found him at Del Mar?
Gail?

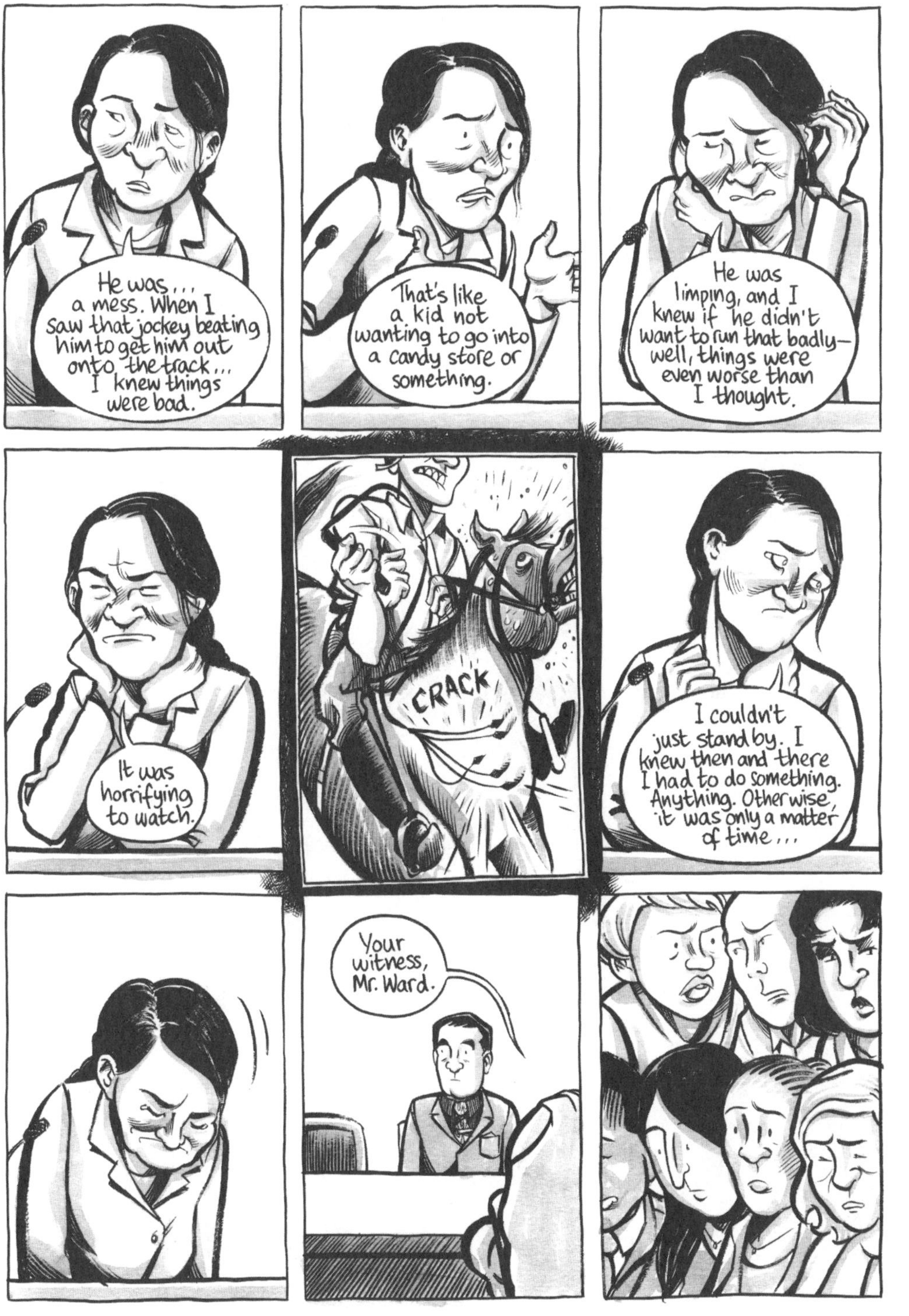
He was... a mess. When I saw that jockey beating him to get him out onto the track... I knew things were bad.
That's like a kid not wanting to go into a candy store or something.
He was limping, and I knew if he didn't want to run that badly— well, things were even worse than I thought.
It was horrifying to watch.
CRACK
I couldn't just stand by. I knew then and there I had to do something. Anything. Otherwise, it was only a matter of time...
Your witness, Mr. Ward.

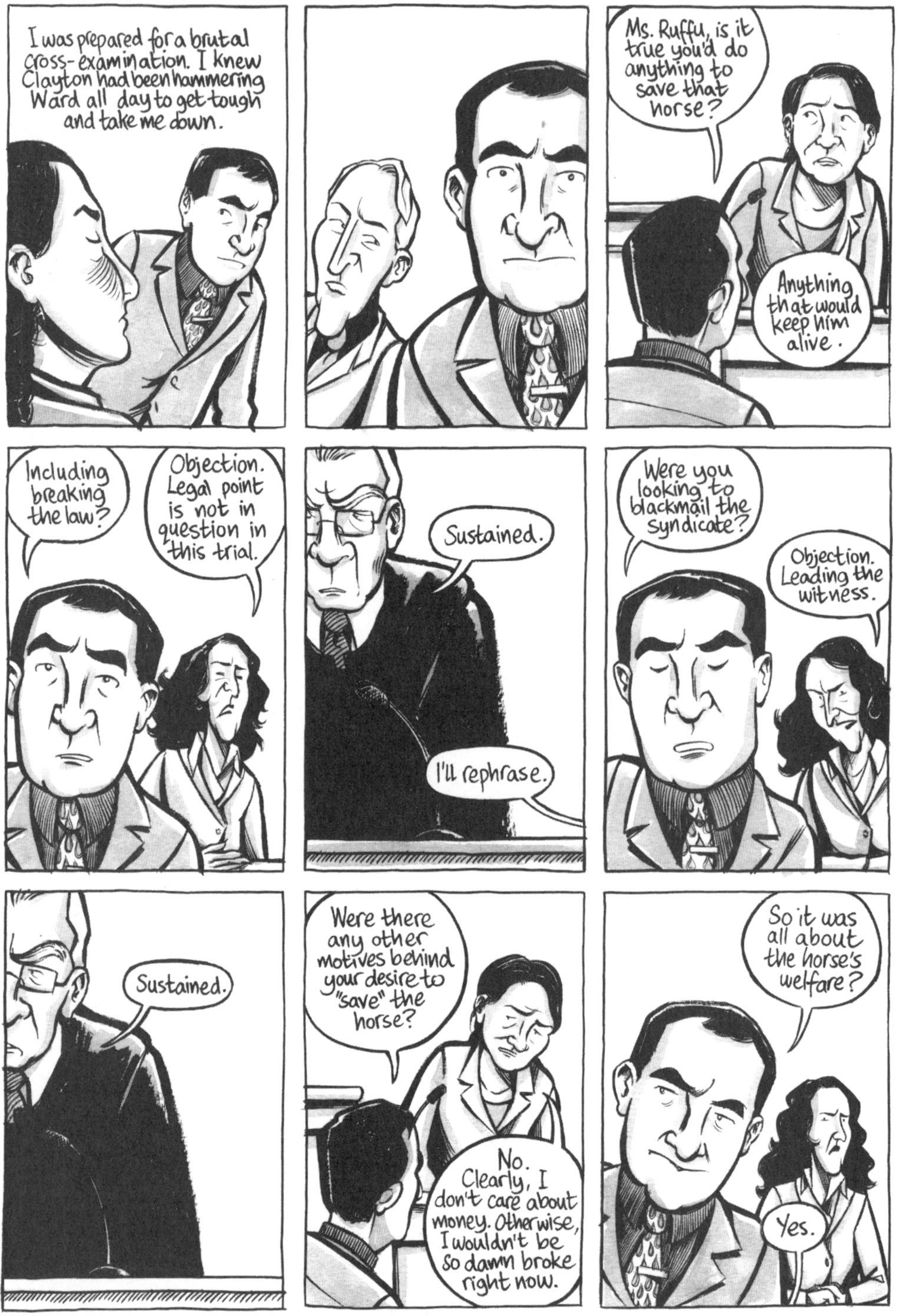
I was prepared for a brutal cross-examination. I knew Clayton had been hammering Ward all day to get tough and take me down.
Ms. Ruffu, is it true you'd do anything to save that horse?
Anything that would keep him alive.
Including breaking the law?
Objection. Legal point is not in question in this trial.
Sustained.
I'll rephrase.
Were you looking to blackmail the syndicate?
Objection. Leading the witness.
Sustained.
Were there any other motives behind your desire to "save" the horse?
No. Clearly, I don't care about money. Otherwise, I wouldn't be so damn broke right now.
So it was all about the horse's welfare?
Yes.

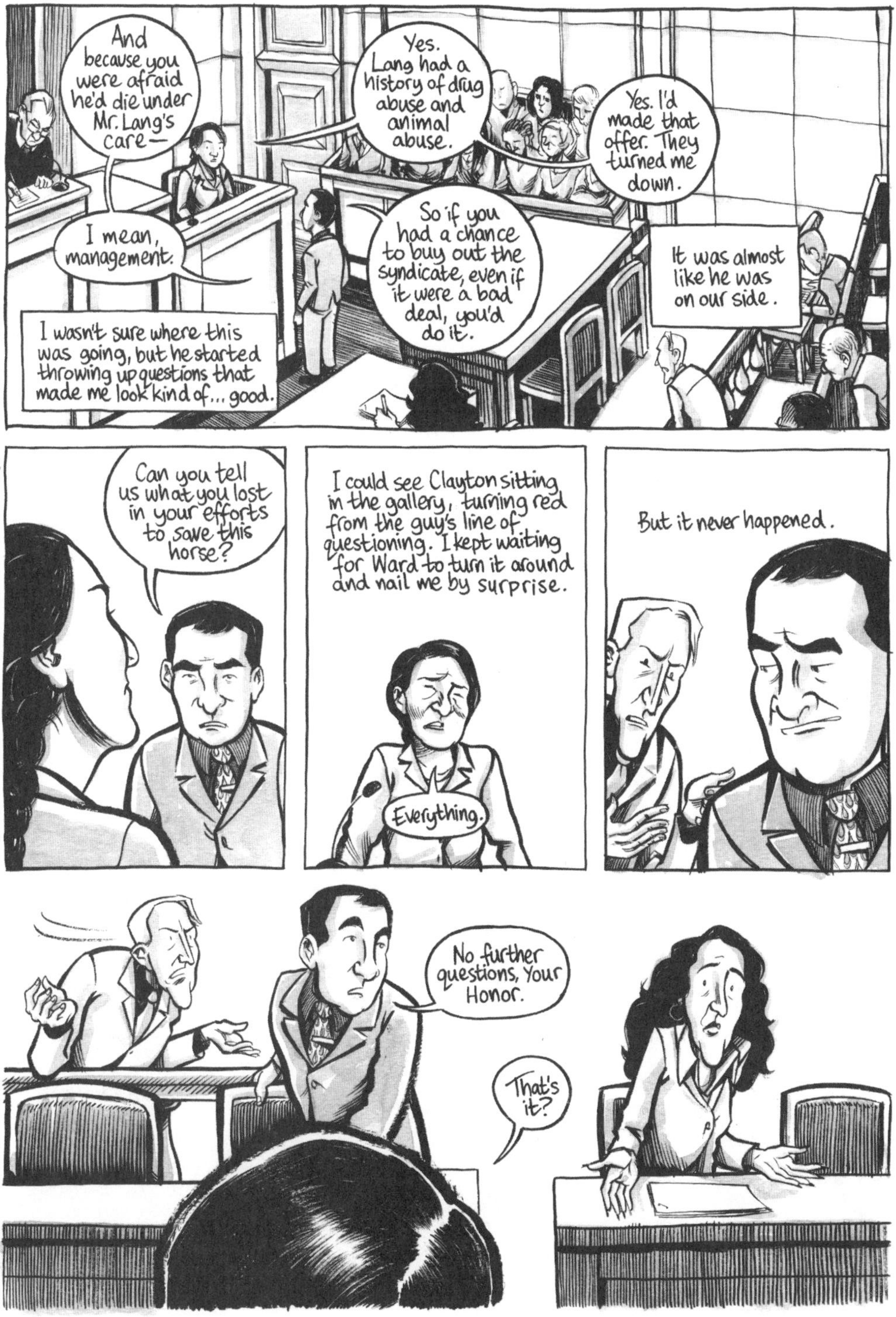

And because you were afraid he'd die under Mr. Lang's care—
I mean, management.
Yes. Lang had a history of drug abuse and animal abuse.
So if you had a chance to buy out the syndicate, even if it were a bad deal, you'd do it.
Yes. I'd made that offer. They turned me down.
I wasn't sure where this was going, but he started throwing up questions that made me look kind of... good.
It was almost like he was on our side.
Can you tell us what you lost in your efforts to save this horse?
I could see Clayton sitting in the gallery, turning red from the guy's line of questioning. I kept waiting for Ward to turn it around and nail me by surprise.
Everything.
But it never happened.
No further questions, Your Honor.
That's it?

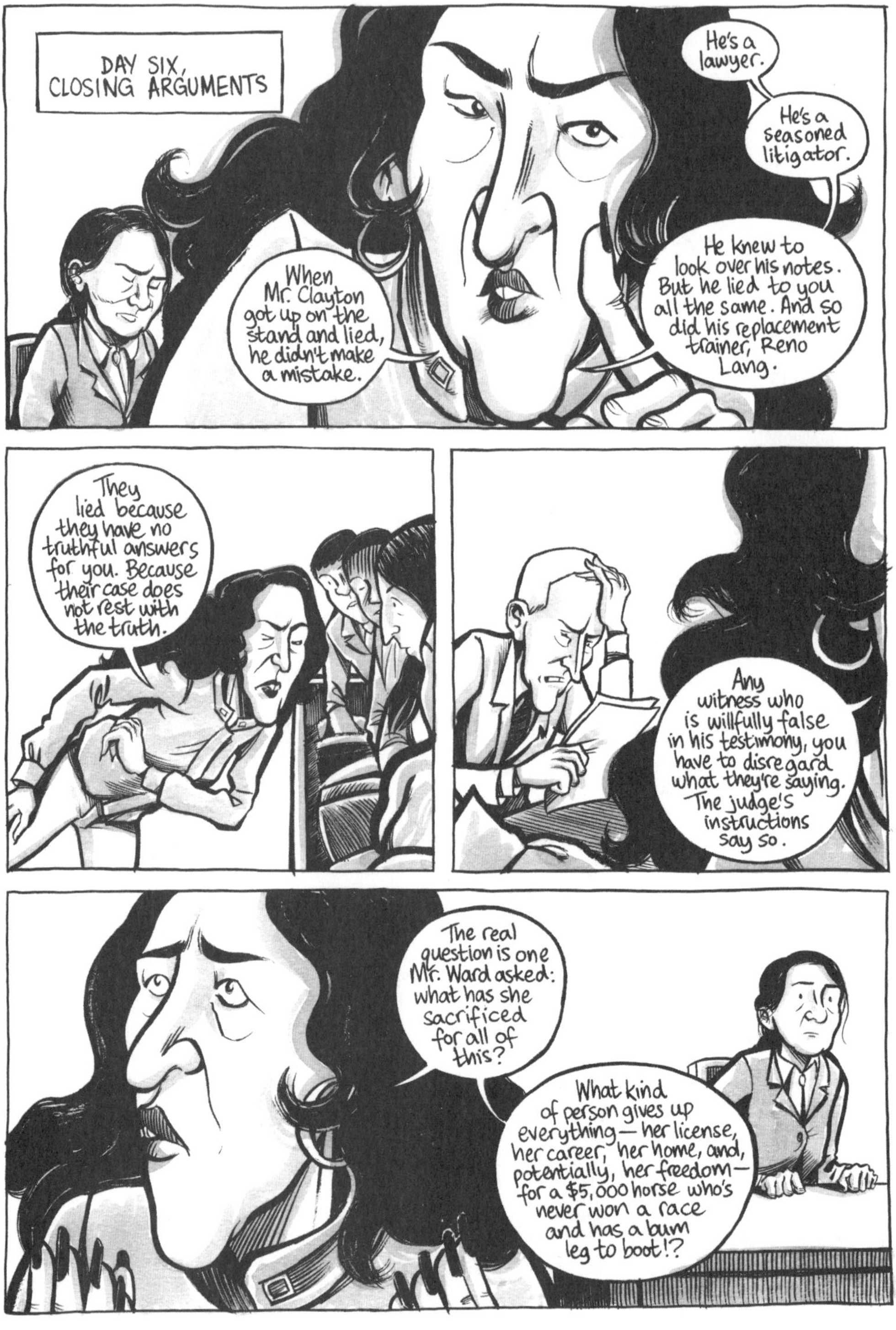
DAY SIX, CLOSING ARGUMENTS
He's a lawyer.
He's a seasoned litigator.
When Mr. Clayton got up on the stand and lied, he didn't make a mistake.
He knew to look over his notes. But he lied to you all the same. And so did his replacement trainer, Reno Lang.
They lied because they have no truthful answers for you. Because their case does not rest with the truth.
Any witness who is willfully false in his testimony, you have to disregard what they're saying. The judge's instructions say so.
The real question is one Mr. Ward asked: what has she sacrificed for all of this?
What kind of person gives up everything— her license, her career, her home, and, potentially, her freedom— for a $5,000 horse who's never won a race and has a bum leg to boot!?

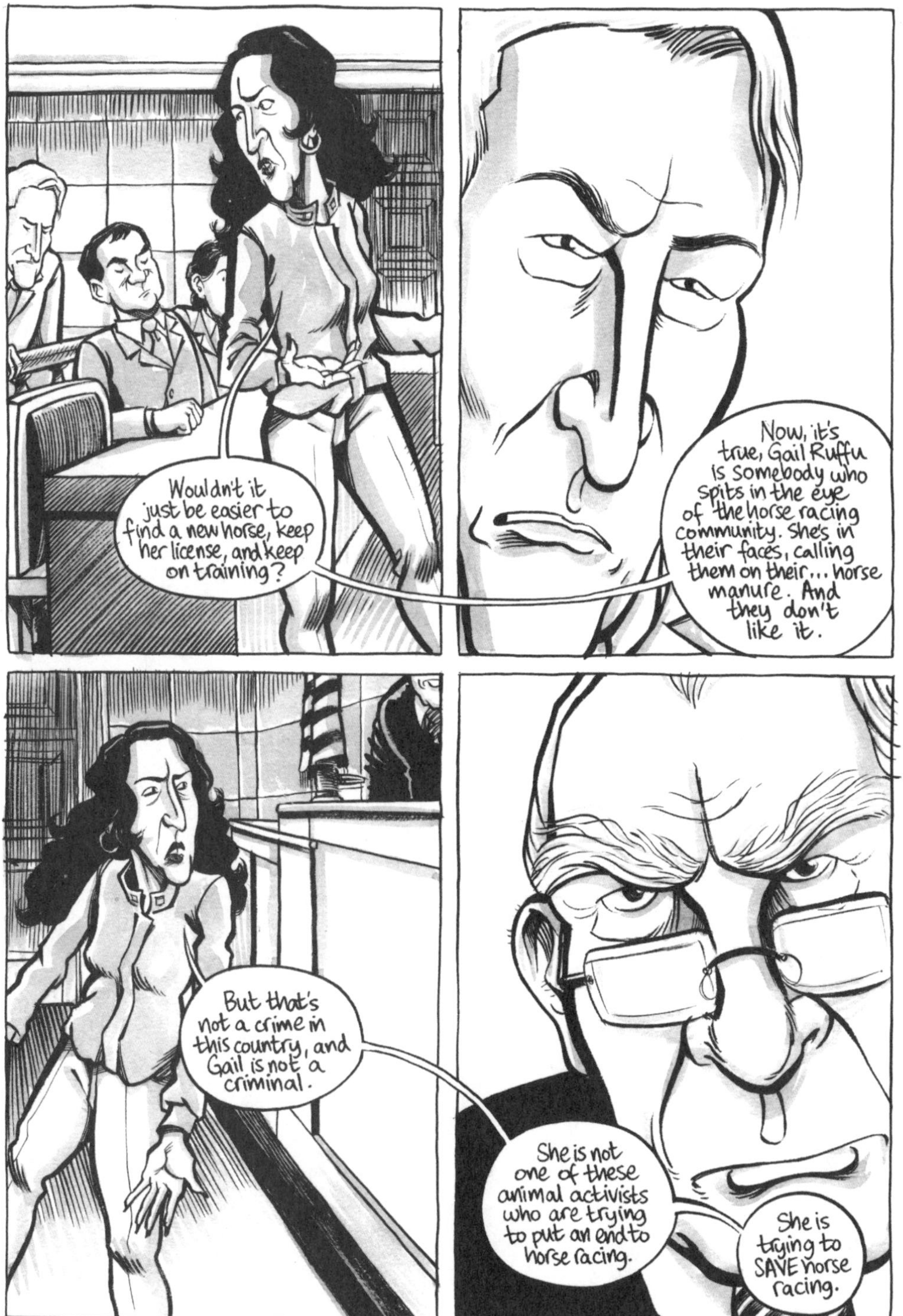
Wouldn't it just be easier to find a new horse, keep her license, and keep on training?
Now, it's true, Gail Ruffu is somebody who spits in the eye of the horse racing community. She's in their faces, calling them on their... horse manure. And they don't like it.
But that's not a crime in this country, and Gail is not a criminal.
She is not one of these animal activists who are trying to put an end to horse racing.
She is trying to SAVE horse racing.

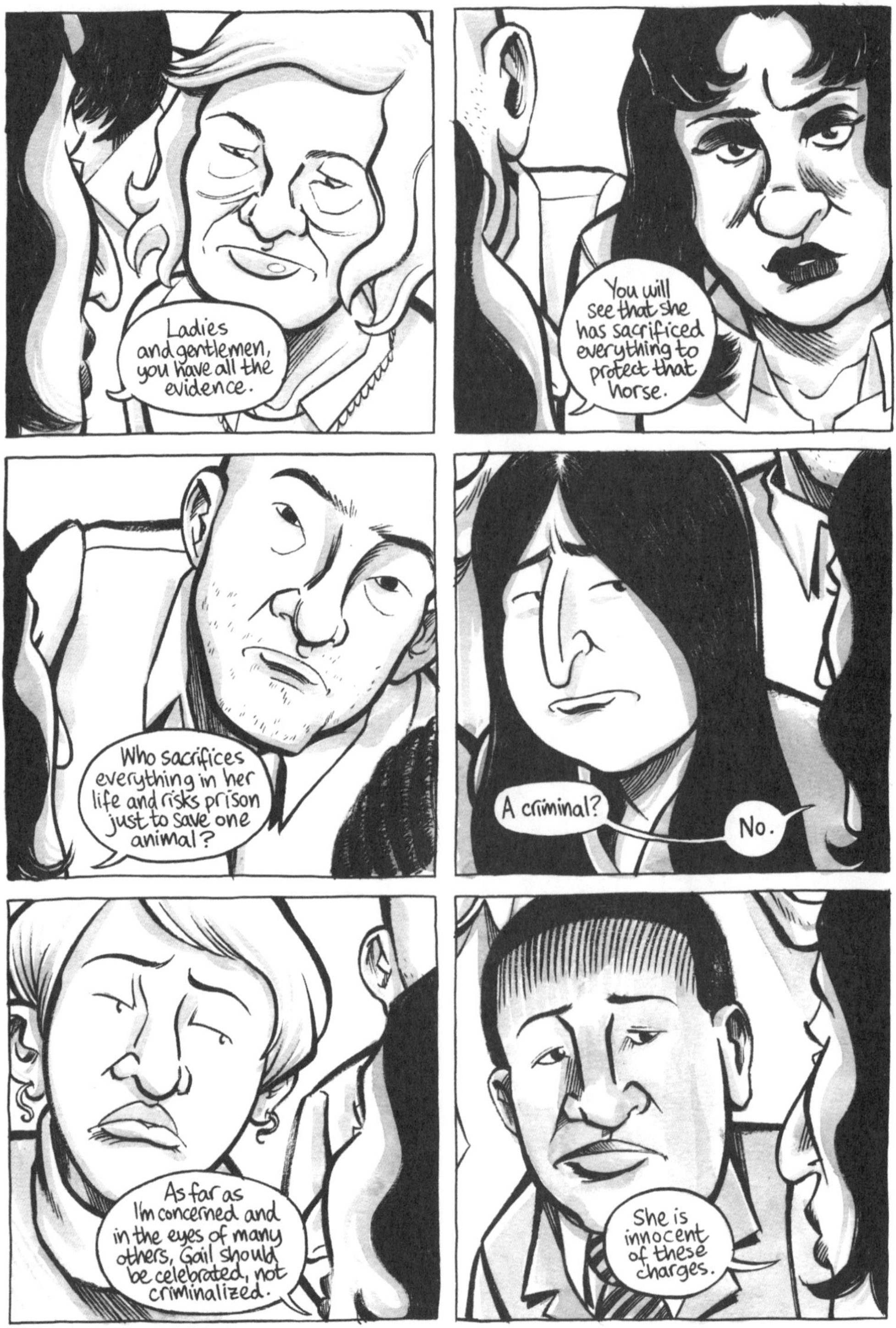
Ladies and gentlemen, you have all the evidence.
You will see that she has sacrificed everything to protect that horse.
Who sacrifices everything in her life and risks prison just to save one animal?
A criminal?
No.
As far as I'm concerned and in the eyes of many others, Gail should be celebrated, not criminalized.
She is innocent of these charges.

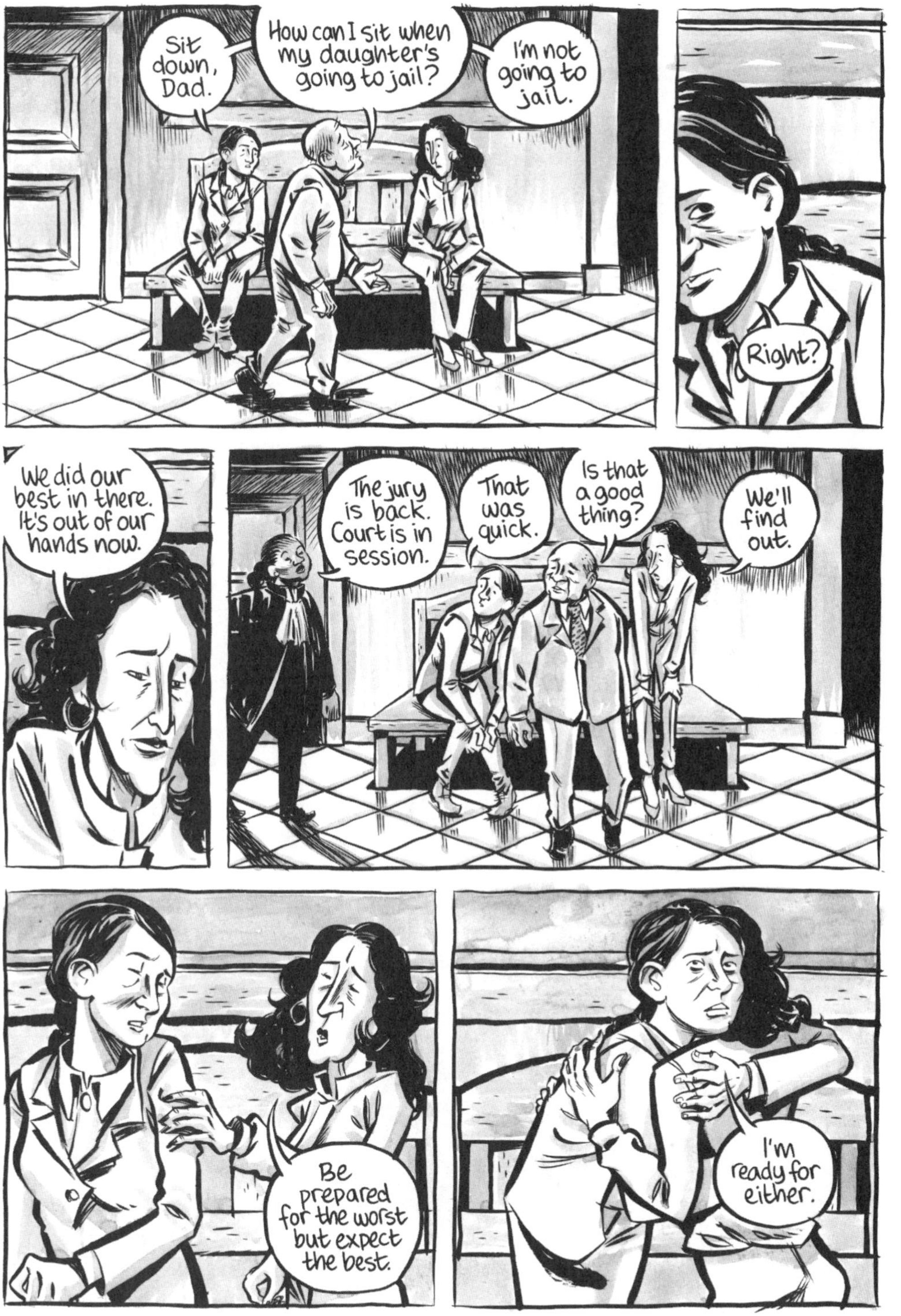
Sit down, Dad.
How can I sit when my daughter's going to jail?
I'm not going to jail.
Right?
We did our best in there. It's out of our hands now.
The jury is back. Court is in session.
That was quick.
Is that a good thing?
We'll find out.
Be prepared for the worst but expect the best.
I'm ready for either.

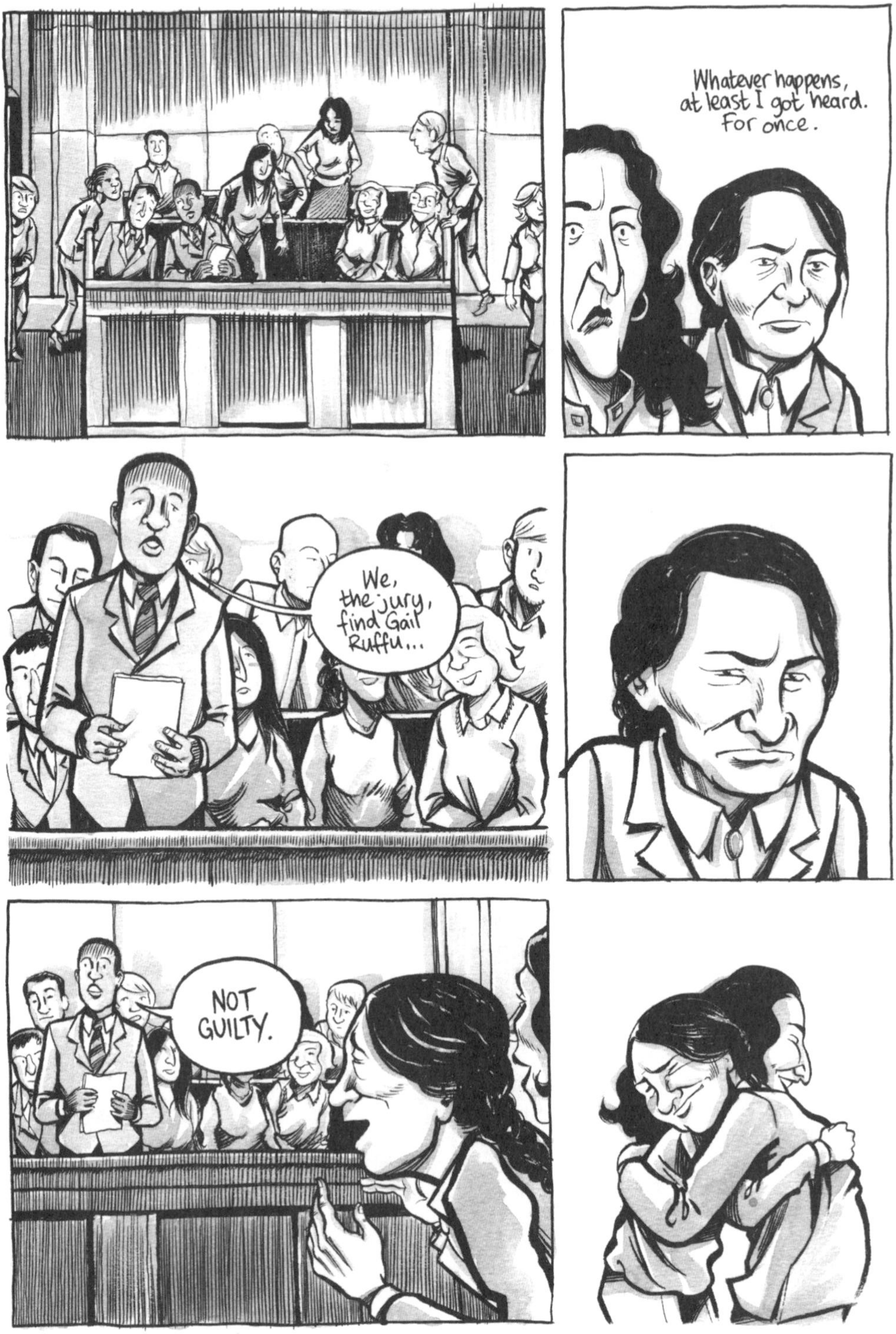
Whatever happens, at least I got heard. For once.
We, the jury, find Gail Ruffu...
NOT GUILTY.

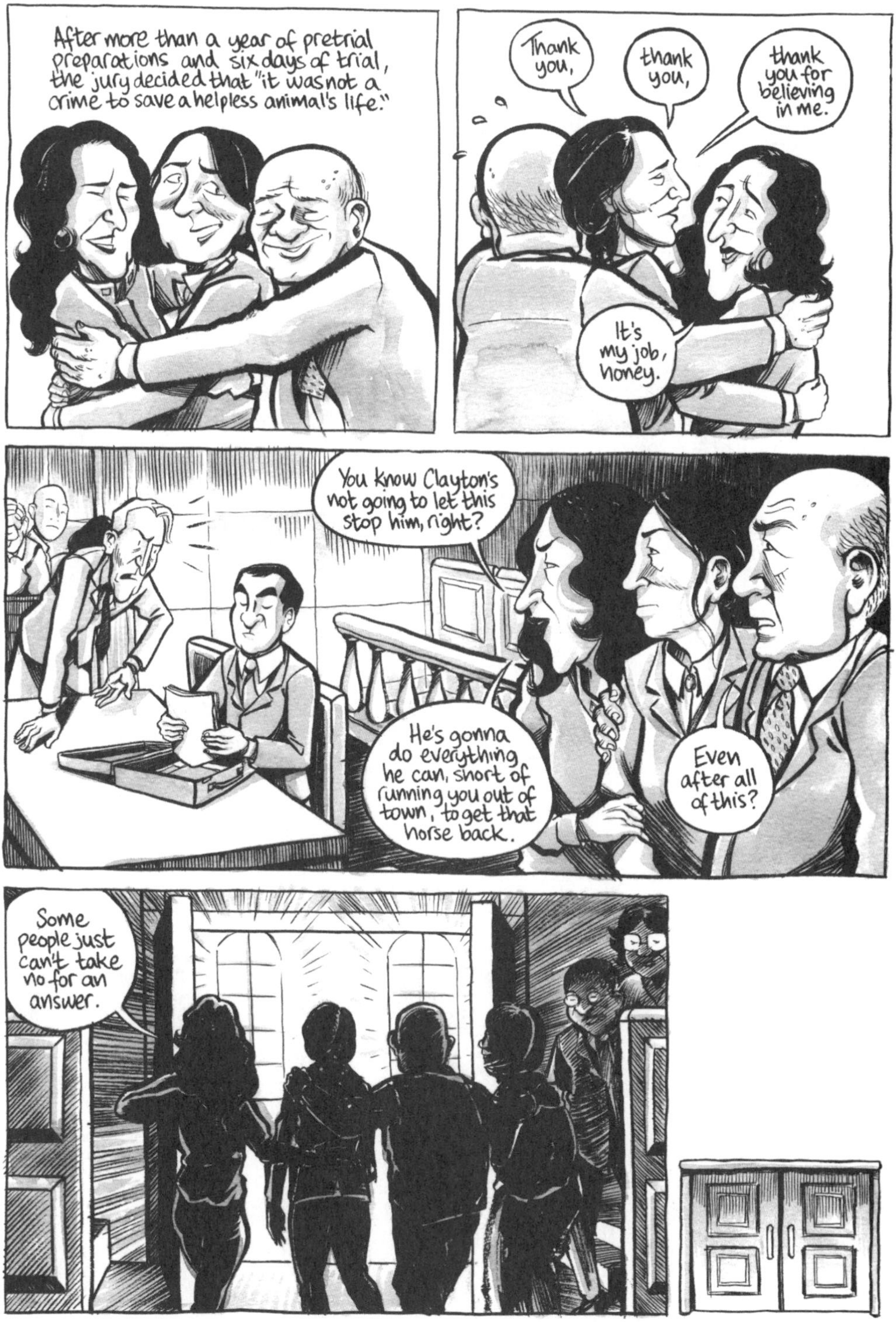
After more than a year of pretrial preparations and six days of trial, the jury decided that "it was not a crime to save a helpless animal's life."
Thank you,
thank you,
thank you for believing in me.
It's my job, honey.
You know Clayton's not going to let this stop him, right?
He's gonna do everything he can, short of running you out of town, to get that horse back.
Even after all of this?
Some people just can't take no for an answer.

PART SIX: THE HOME STRETCH

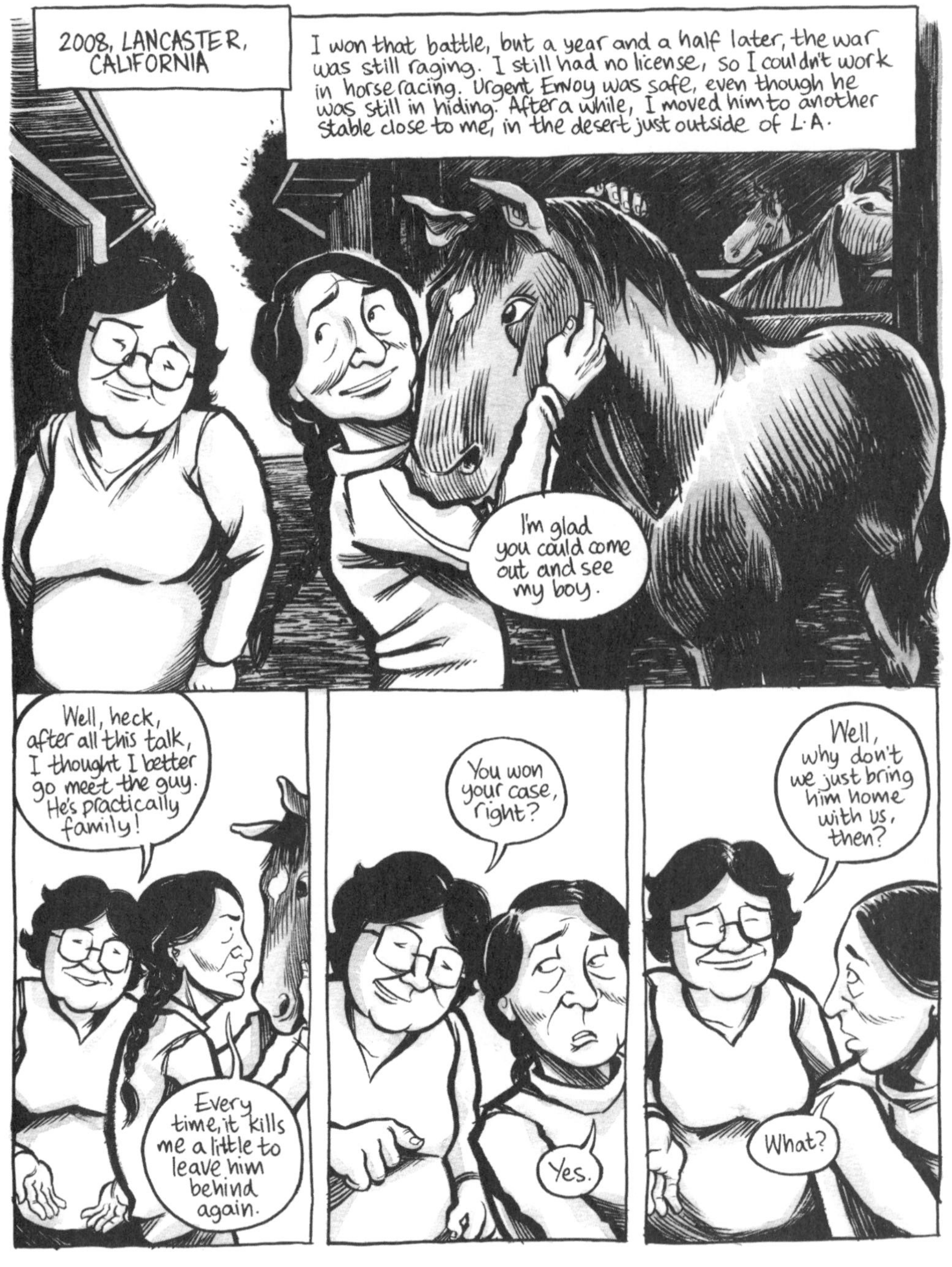

2008, LANCASTER, CALIFORNIA
I won that battle, but a year and a half later, the war was still raging. I still had no license, so I couldn't work in horse racing. Urgent Envoy was safe, even though he was still in hiding. After a while, I moved him to another stable close to me, in the desert just outside of L.A.
I'm glad you could come out and see my boy.
Well, heck, after all this talk, I thought I better go meet the guy. He's practically family!
Every time, it kills me a little to leave him behind again.
You won your case, right?
Yes.
Well, why don't we just bring him home with us, then?
What?

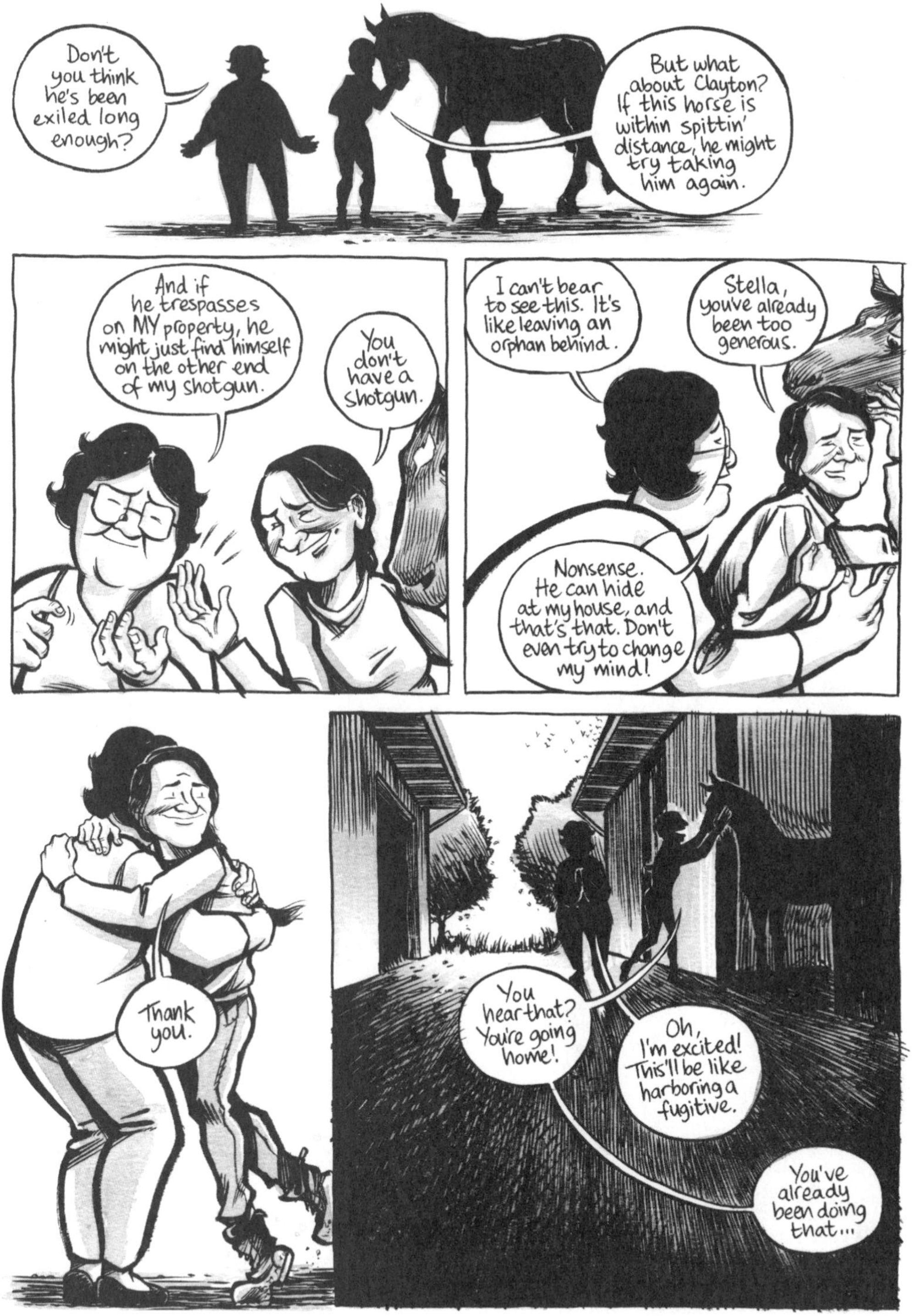
Don't you think he's been exiled long enough?
But what about Clayton? If this horse is within spittin' distance, he might try taking him again.
And if he trespasses on MY property, he might just find himself on the other end of my shotgun.
You don't have a shotgun.
I can't bear to see this. It's like leaving an orphan behind.
Stella, you've already been too generous.
Nonsense. He can hide at my house, and that's that. Don't even try to change my mind!
Thank you.
You hear that? You're going home!
Oh, I'm excited! This'll be like harboring a fugitive.
You've already been doing that...

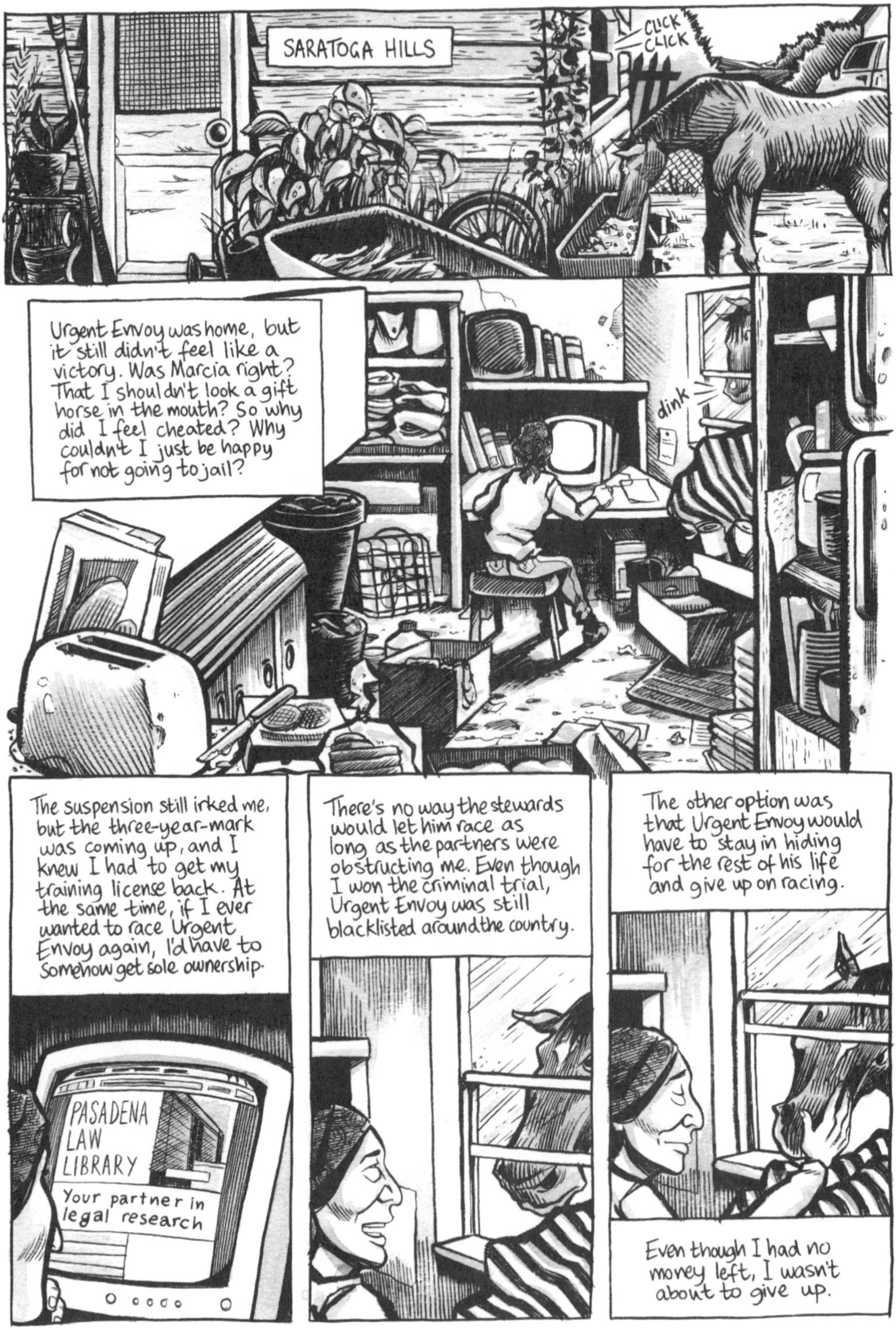
SARATOGA HILLS
CLICK CLICK
Urgent Envoy was home, but it still didn't feel like a victory. Was Marcia right? That I shouldn't look a gift horse in the mouth? So why did I feel cheated? Why couldn't I just be happy for not going to jail?
dink
The suspension still irked me, but the three-year-mark was coming up, and I knew I had to get my training license back. At the same time, if I ever wanted to race Urgent Envoy again, I'd have to somehow get sole ownership.
PASADENA LAW LIBRARY
Your partner in legal research
There's no way the stewards would let him race as long as the partners were obstructing me. Even though I won the criminal trial, Urgent Envoy was still blacklisted around the country.
The other option was that Urgent Envoy would have to stay in hiding for the rest of his life and give up on racing.
Even though I had no money left, I wasn't about to give up.

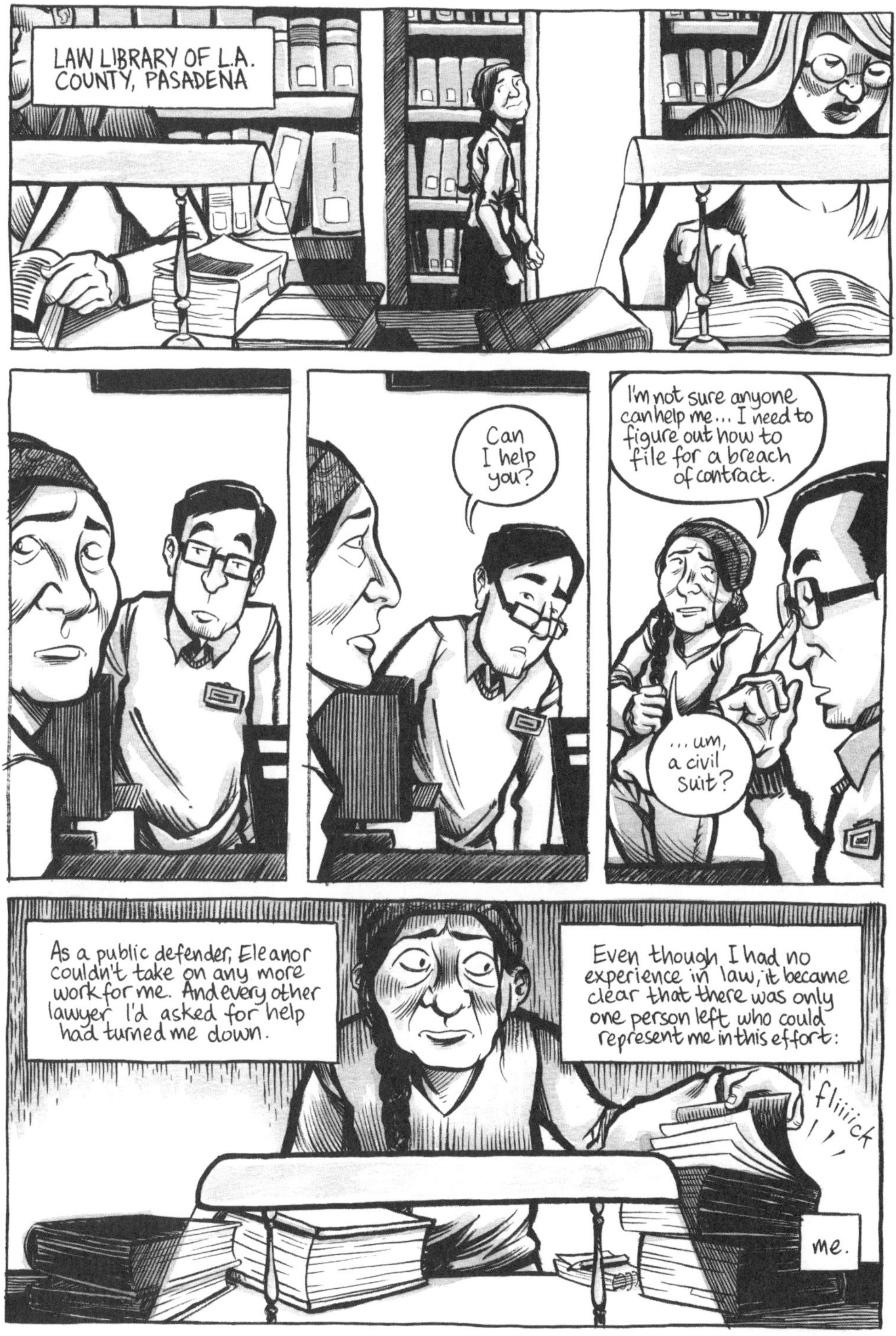

LAW LIBRARY OF L.A. COUNTY, PASADENA
Can I help you?
I'm not sure anyone can help me... I need to figure out how to file for a breach of contract.
...um, a civil suit?
As a public defender, Eleanor couldn't take on any more work for me. And every other lawyer I'd asked for help had turned me down.
Even though I had no experience in law, it became clear that there was only one person left who could represent me in this effort:
fliiiick
me.

Now, where to begin...

an acceptance is an agreement, by express act of implied from conduct, to the ter n offer, including the prescribed manner of acceptance, so that an enforceable cont ormed. In what is known as a battle of the forms, when the process of offer and a ance is not followed, it is still possible to have an enforceable contract, as ment bove with respect to contracts implied in fact. The Uniform Commercial "UCC") dispenses with the mirror image rule in § 2-207. UCC § 2-207 provides definite and seasonable expression of acceptance...operates as" an acceptance, hough it varies the terms of the original offer. Such an expression is typically interp s an acceptance when it purports to accept and agrees on the following terms of the al offer: subject matter, quantity, and price. However, such an expression is not inte d as an acceptance if it is "expressly conditional" on the original offeror's assent aried terms, discussed below. This language is known as the proviso. When the p not used, the terms of the contract are determined by subsection 2. When the p used, but there is no assent by the original offeror to the offeree's varied terms, y arties go ahead and perform (act like they have a contract, hence a contract impl act) the terms of the contract are determined by subsection 3. So, the terms of a co

I learned Spanish when I lived in Spain as a teen, German when I lived in Germany.

But this legal jargon might as well have been in Martian.

No wonder law school costs so much...

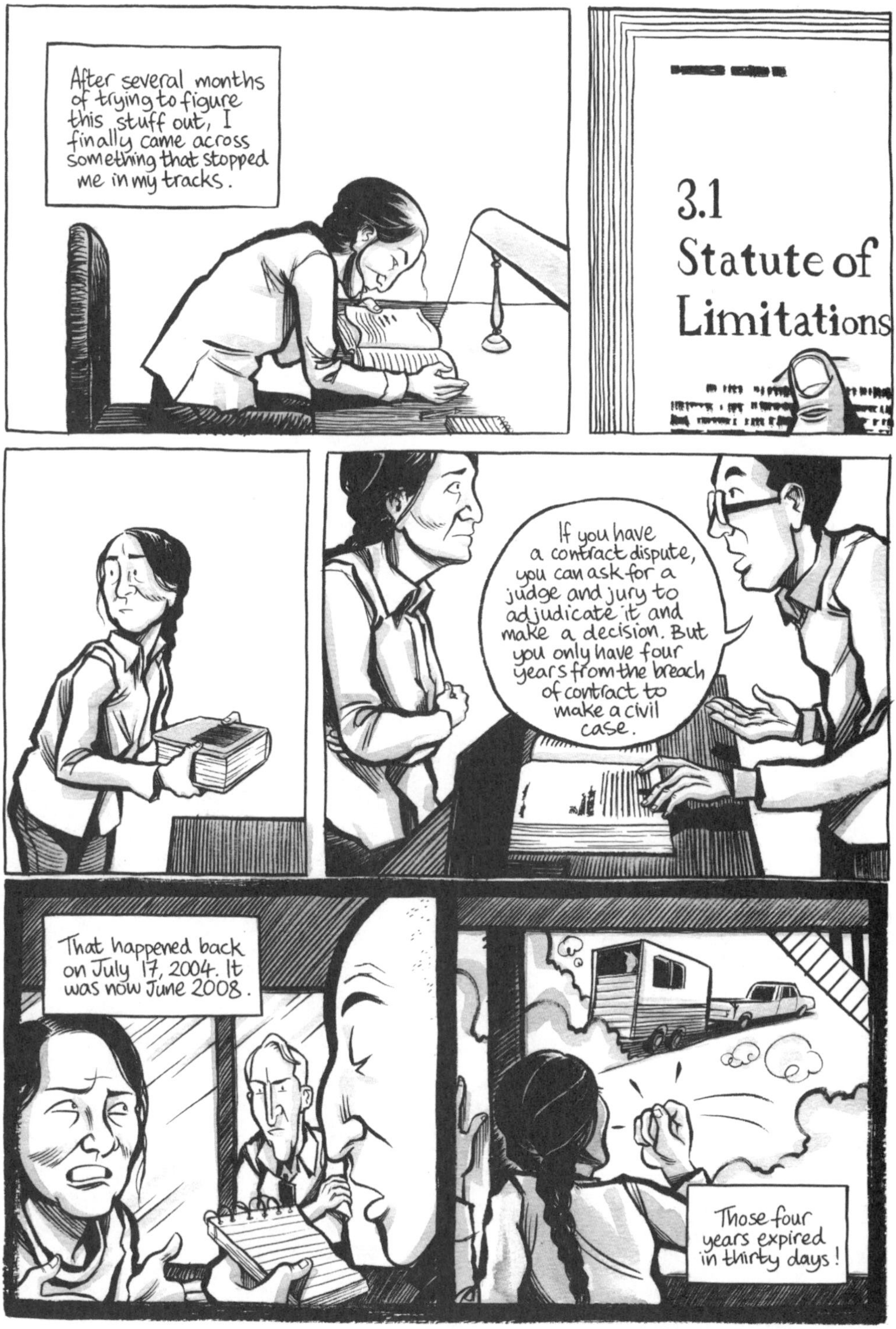
After several months of trying to figure this stuff out, I finally came across something that stopped me in my tracks.
3.1 Statute of Limitations
If you have a contract dispute, you can ask for a judge and jury to adjudicate it and make a decision. But you only have four years from the breach of contract to make a civil case.
That happened back on July 17, 2004. It was now June 2008.
Those four years expired in thirty days!

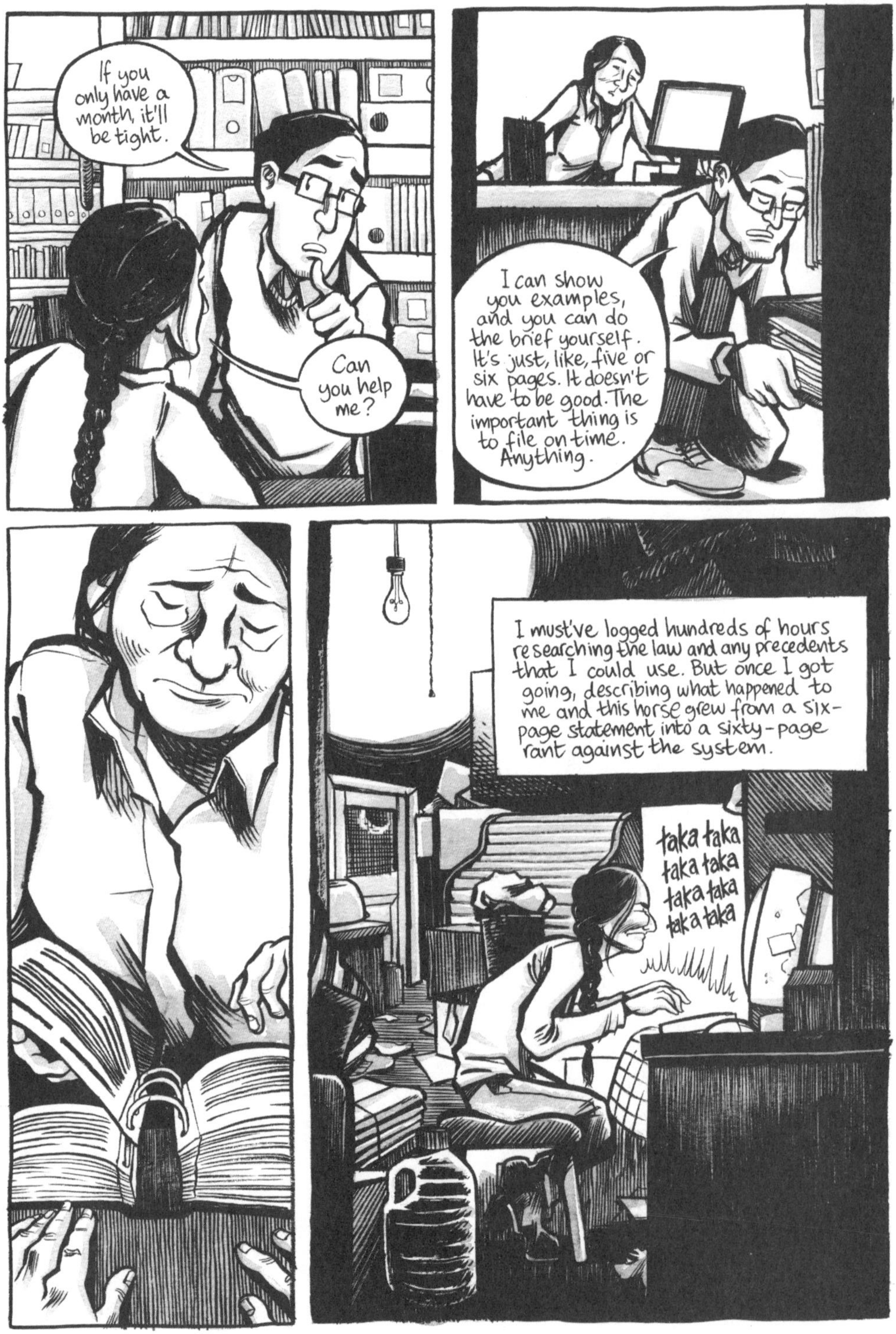
If you only have a month, it'll be tight.
Can you help me?
I can show you examples, and you can do the brief yourself. It's just, like, five or six pages. It doesn't have to be good. The important thing is to file on time. Anything.
I must've logged hundreds of hours researching the law and any precedents that I could use. But once I got going, describing what happened to me and this horse grew from a six-page statement into a sixty-page rant against the system.
taka taka taka taka taka taka taka taka

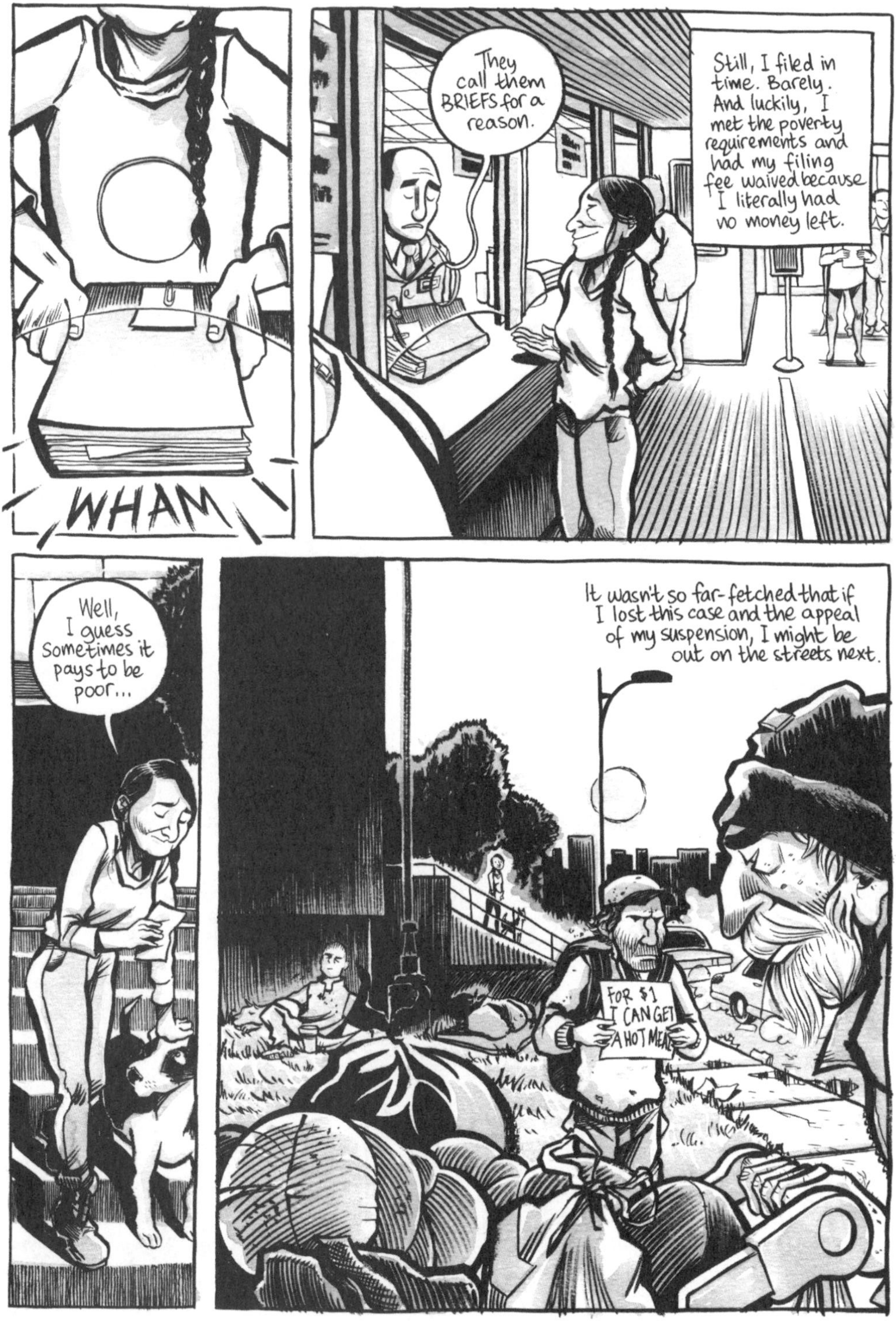
WHAM
They call them BRIEFS for a reason.
Still, I filed in time. Barely. And luckily, I met the poverty requirements and had my filing fee waived because I literally had no money left.
Well, I guess sometimes it pays to be poor...
It wasn't so far-fetched that if I lost this case and the appeal of my suspension, I might be out on the streets next.
FOR $1 I CAN GET A HOT MEAL

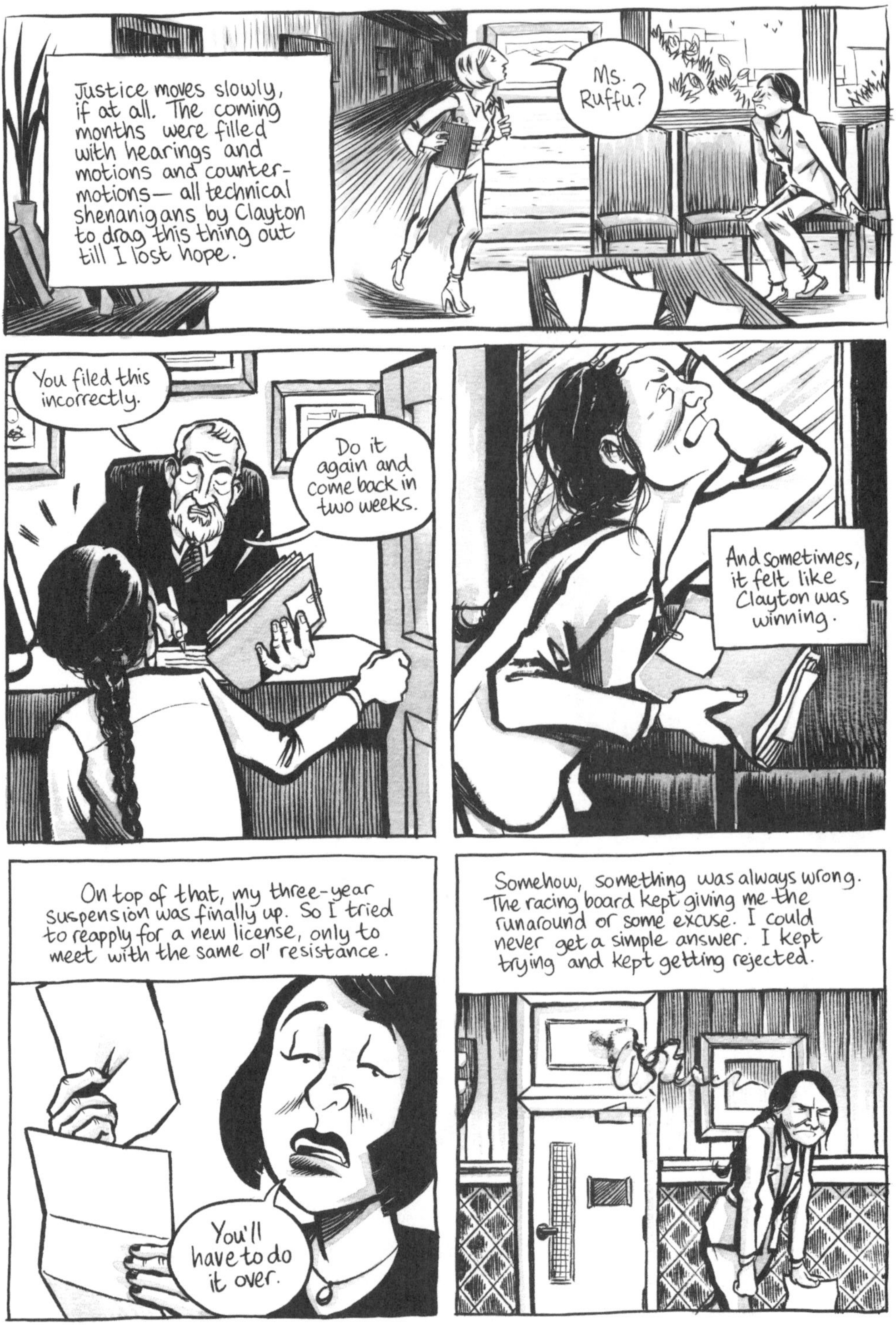
Justice moves slowly, if at all. The coming months were filled with hearings and motions and counter-motions— all technical shenanigans by Clayton to drag this thing out till I lost hope.
Ms. Ruffu?
You filed this incorrectly.
Do it again and come back in two weeks.
And sometimes, it felt like Clayton was winning.
On top of that, my three-year suspension was finally up. So I tried to reapply for a new license, only to meet with the same ol' resistance.
You'll have to do it over.
Somehow, something was always wrong. The racing board kept giving me the runaround or some excuse. I could never get a simple answer. I kept trying and kept getting rejected.

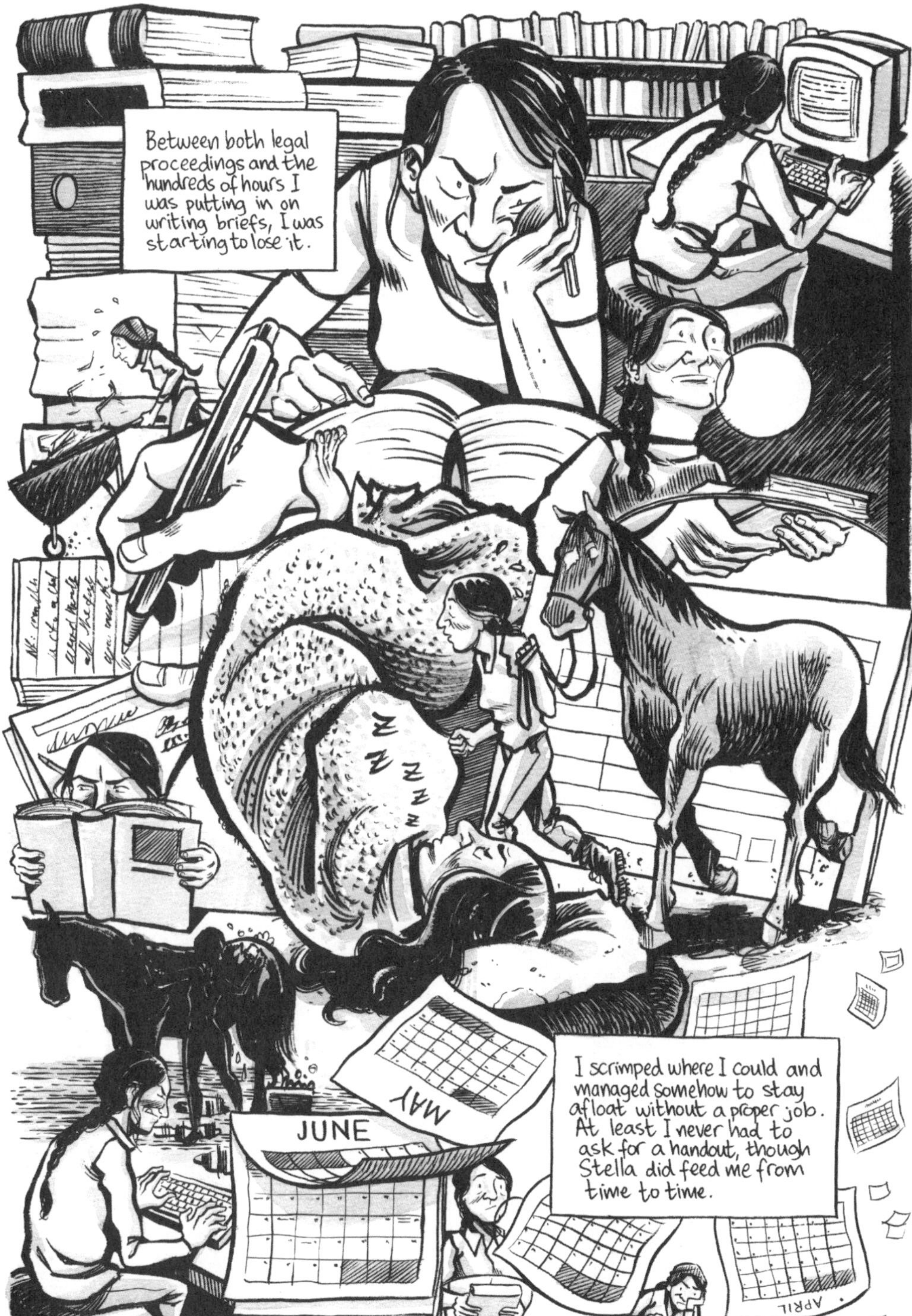
Between both legal proceedings and the hundreds of hours I was putting in on writing briefs, I was starting to lose it.
MAY
JUNE
I scrimped where I could and managed somehow to stay afloat without a proper job. At least I never had to ask for a handout, though Stella did feed me from time to time.
APRIL

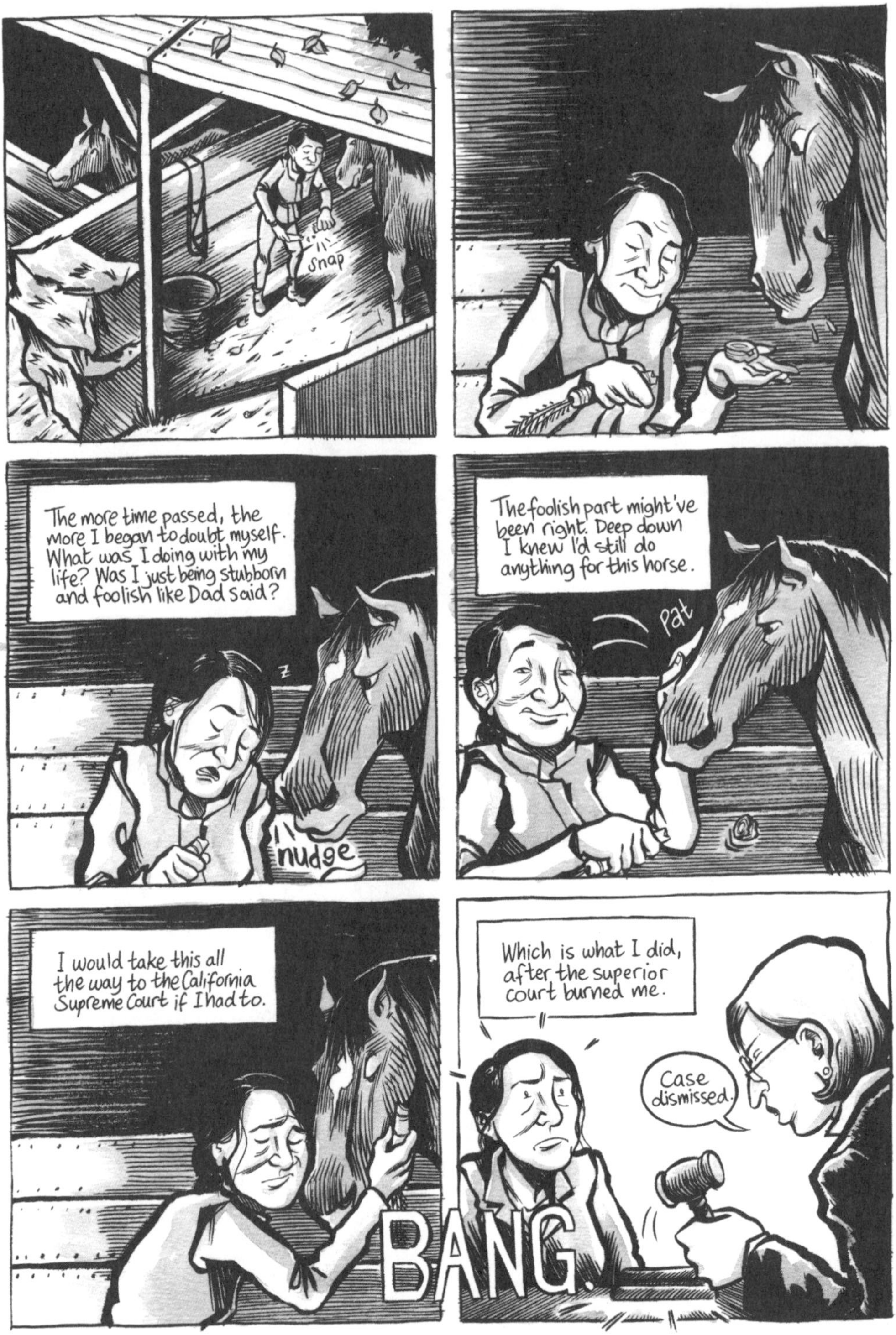

snap
The more time passed, the more I began to doubt myself. What was I doing with my life? Was I just being stubborn and foolish like Dad said?
z
nudge
The foolish part might've been right. Deep down I knew I'd still do anything for this horse.
Pat
I would take this all the way to the California Supreme Court if I had to.
Which is what I did, after the superior court burned me.
Case dismissed.
BANG.

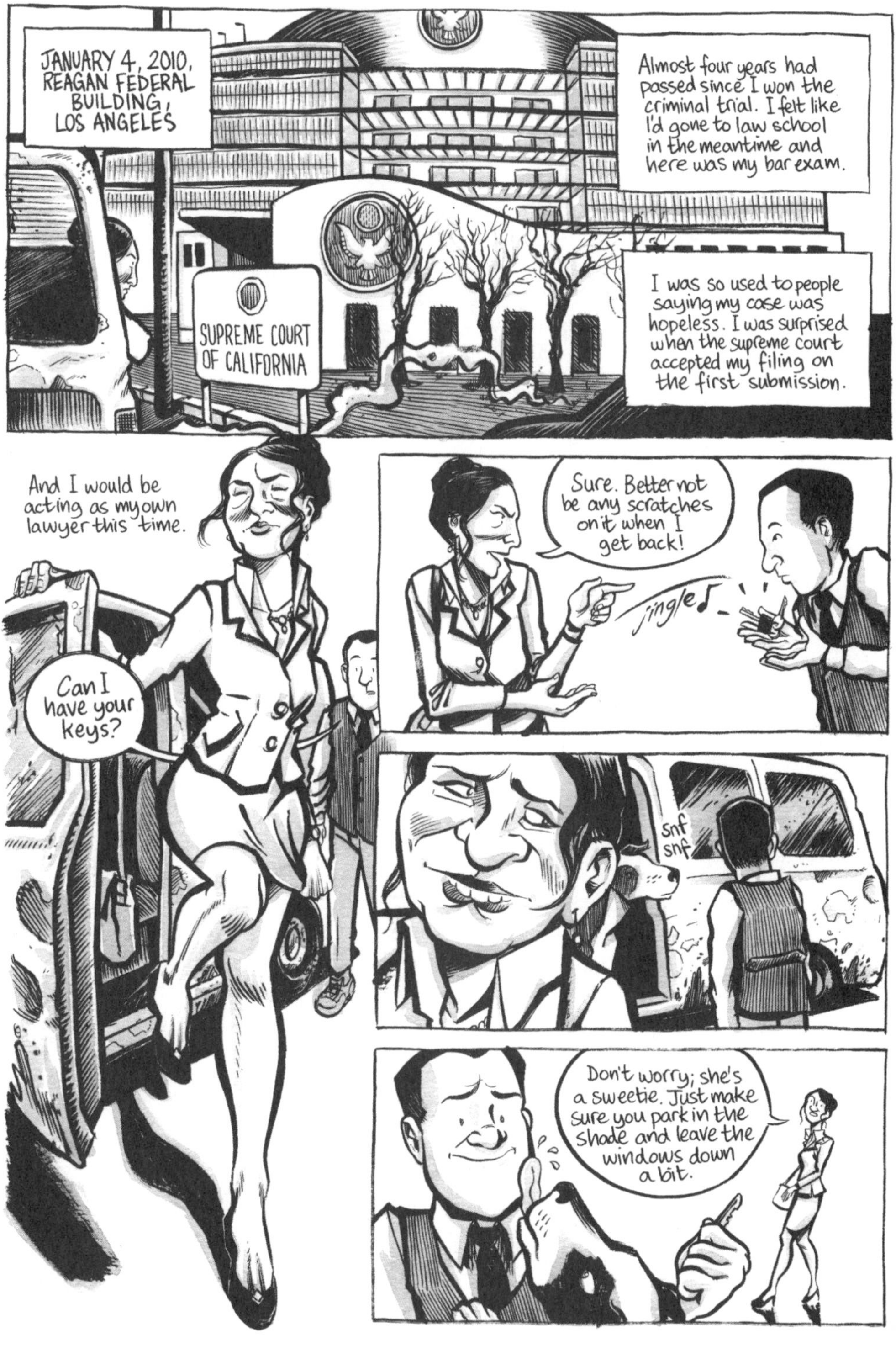
JANUARY 4, 2010, REAGAN FEDERAL BUILDING, LOS ANGELES
Almost four years had passed since I won the criminal trial. I felt like I'd gone to law school in the meantime and here was my bar exam.
SUPREME COURT OF CALIFORNIA
I was so used to people saying my case was hopeless. I was surprised when the supreme court accepted my filing on the first submission.
And I would be acting as my own lawyer this time.
Can I have your keys?
Sure. Better not be any scratches on it when I get back!
jingle
snf
snf
Don't worry; she's a sweetie. Just make sure you park in the shade and leave the windows down a bit.

They don't open till 10.

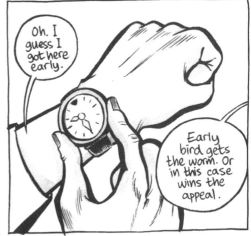

Oh. I guess I got here early.

Early bird gets the worm. Or in this case wins the appeal.

Does everyone dress that way back at your firm?

I'm not an attorney.

Oh. I thought maybe you worked for Erin Brockovitch.

jingle

That was a joke.

The opponent, I assume. He looks familiar.

You see a lot of rattlesnakes in your line of work?

Every day.

I'm Curtis Thompson. Lawyer, though you probably guessed that.

Gail Ruffu. Horse thief.

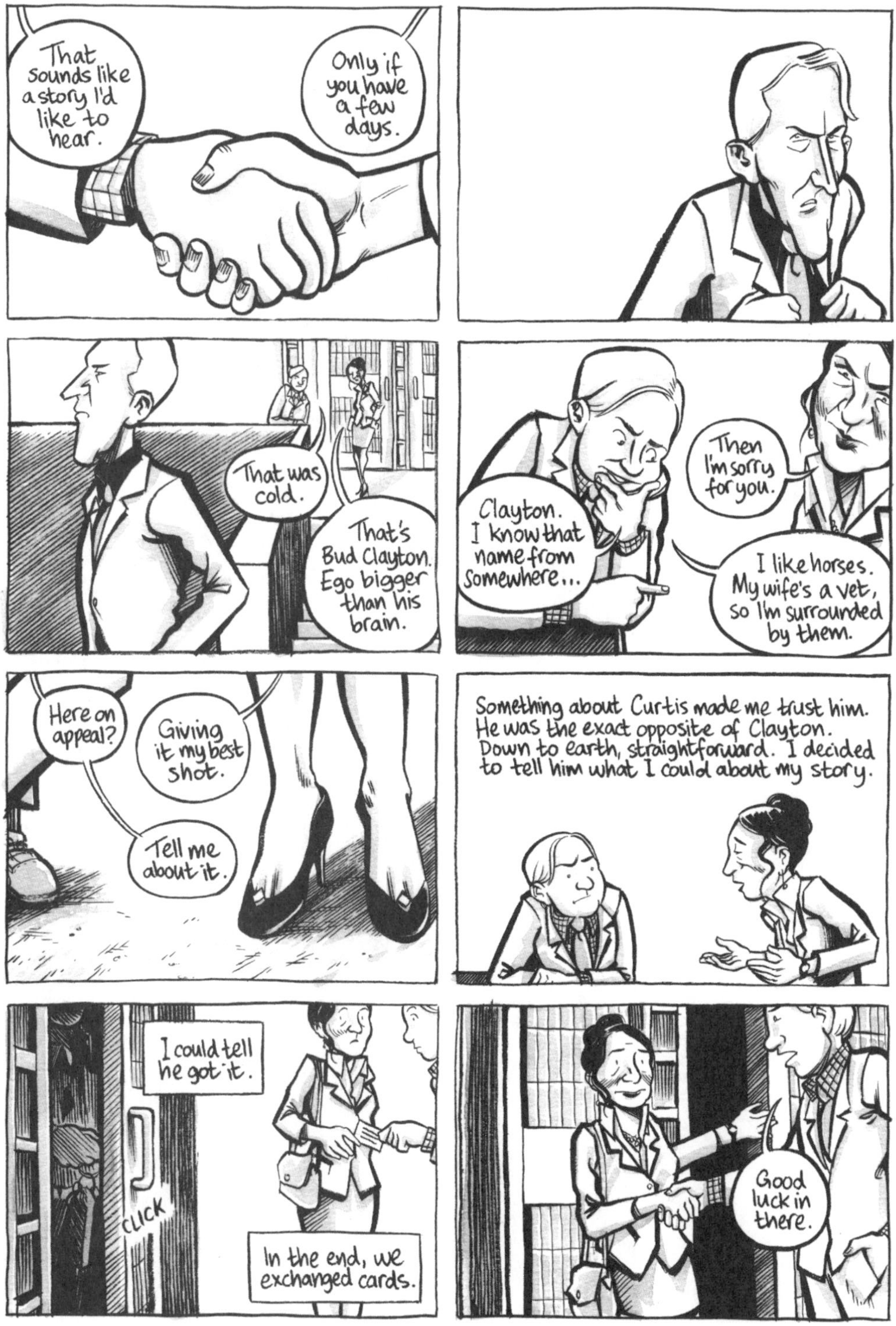
That sounds like a story I'd like to hear.
Only if you have a few days.
That was cold.
That's Bud Clayton. Ego bigger than his brain.
Clayton. I know that name from somewhere...
Then I'm sorry for you.
I like horses. My wife's a vet, so I'm surrounded by them.
Here on appeal?
Giving it my best shot.
Tell me about it.
Something about Curtis made me trust him. He was the exact opposite of Clayton. Down to earth, straightforward. I decided to tell him what I could about my story.
I could tell he got it.
CLICK
In the end, we exchanged cards.
Good luck in there.

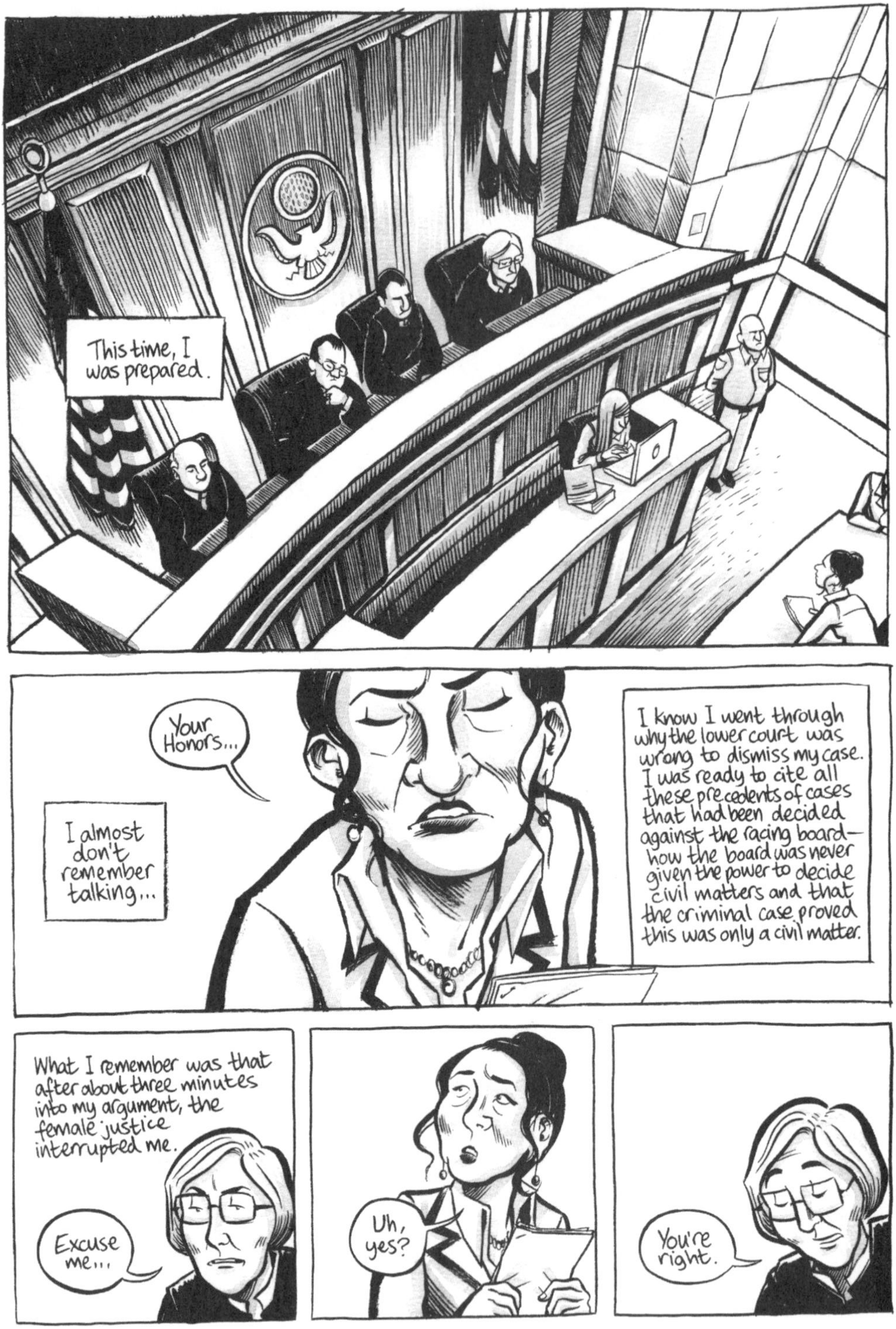
This time, I was prepared.
Your Honors...
I almost don't remember talking...
I know I went through why the lower court was wrong to dismiss my case. I was ready to cite all these precedents of cases that had been decided against the racing board—how the board was never given the power to decide civil matters and that the criminal case proved this was only a civil matter.
What I remember was that after about three minutes into my argument, the female justice interrupted me.
Excuse me...
Uh, yes?
You're right.

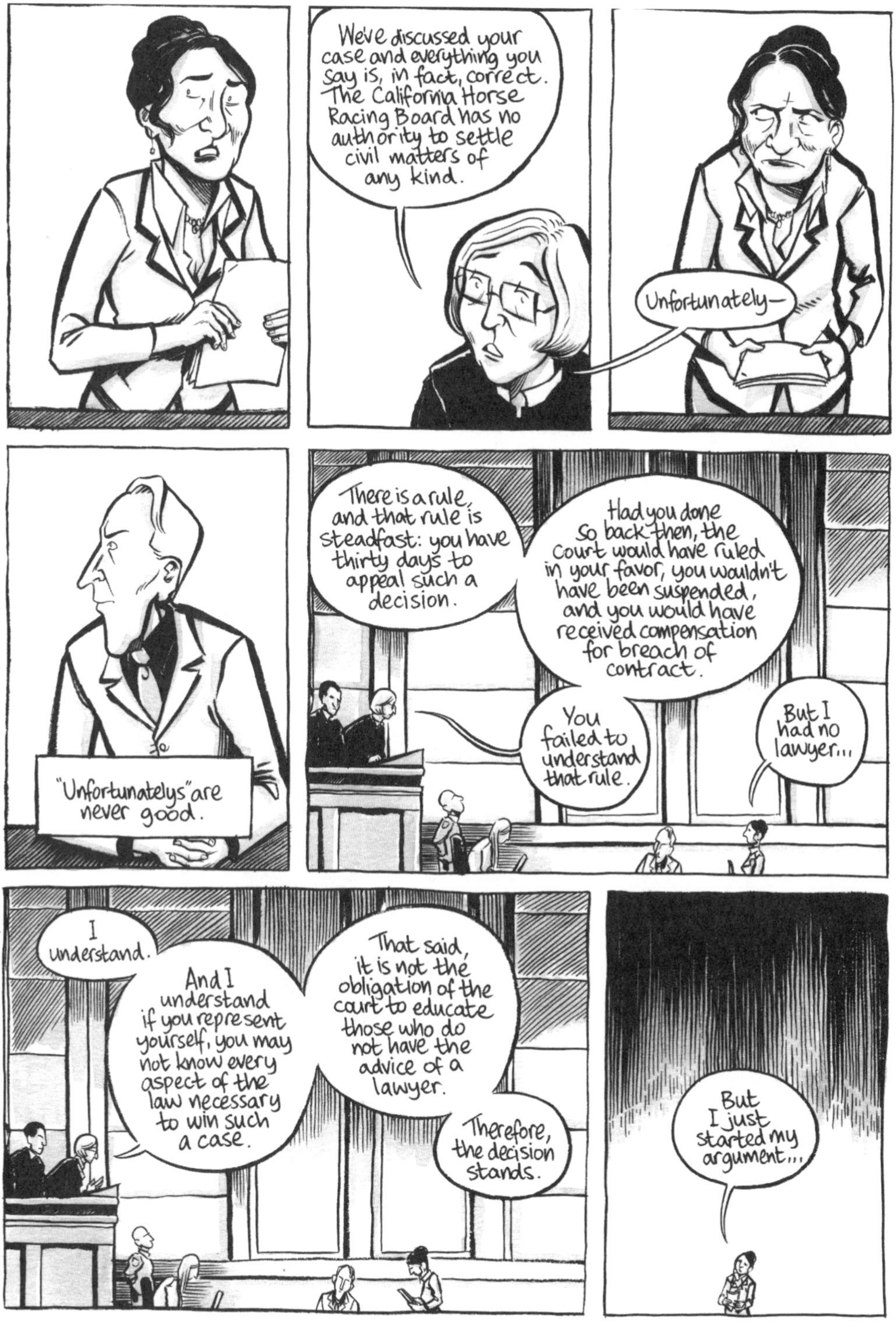
We've discussed your case and everything you say is, in fact, correct. The California Horse Racing Board has no authority to settle civil matters of any kind.
Unfortunately—
"Unfortunatelys" are never good.
There is a rule, and that rule is steadfast: you have thirty days to appeal such a decision.
Had you done so back then, the court would have ruled in your favor, you wouldn't have been suspended, and you would have received compensation for breach of contract.
You failed to understand that rule.
But I had no lawyer...
I understand.
And I understand if you represent yourself, you may not know every aspect of the law necessary to win such a case.
That said, it is not the obligation of the court to educate those who do not have the advice of a lawyer.
Therefore, the decision stands.
But I just started my argument...

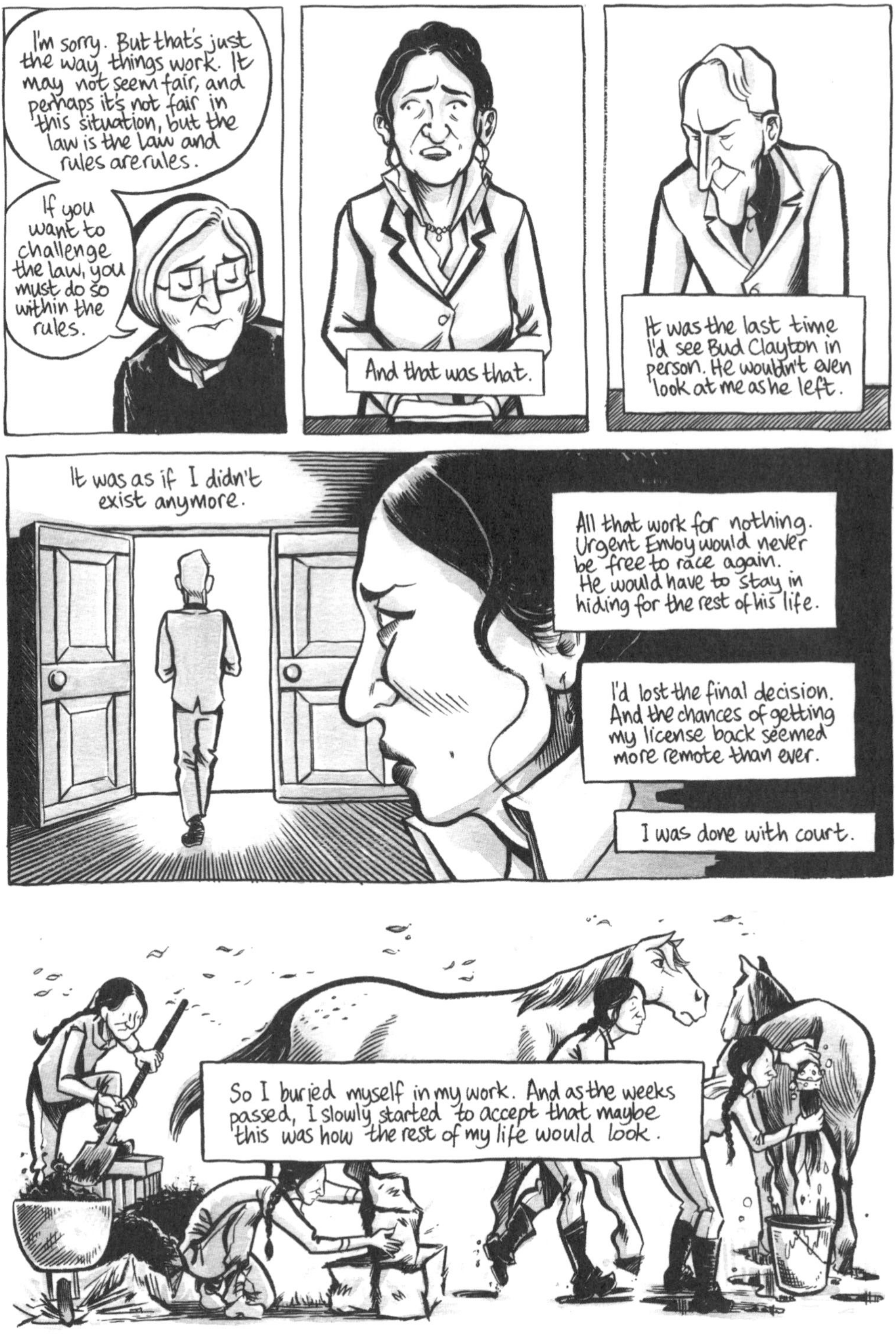
I'm sorry. But that's just the way things work. It may not seem fair, and perhaps it's not fair in this situation, but the law is the law and rules are rules.
If you want to challenge the law, you must do so within the rules.
And that was that.
It was the last time I'd see Bud Clayton in person. He wouldn't even look at me as he left.
It was as if I didn't exist anymore.
All that work for nothing. Urgent Envoy would never be free to race again. He would have to stay in hiding for the rest of his life.
I'd lost the final decision. And the chances of getting my license back seemed more remote than ever.
I was done with court.
So I buried myself in my work. And as the weeks passed, I slowly started to accept that maybe this was how the rest of my life would look.

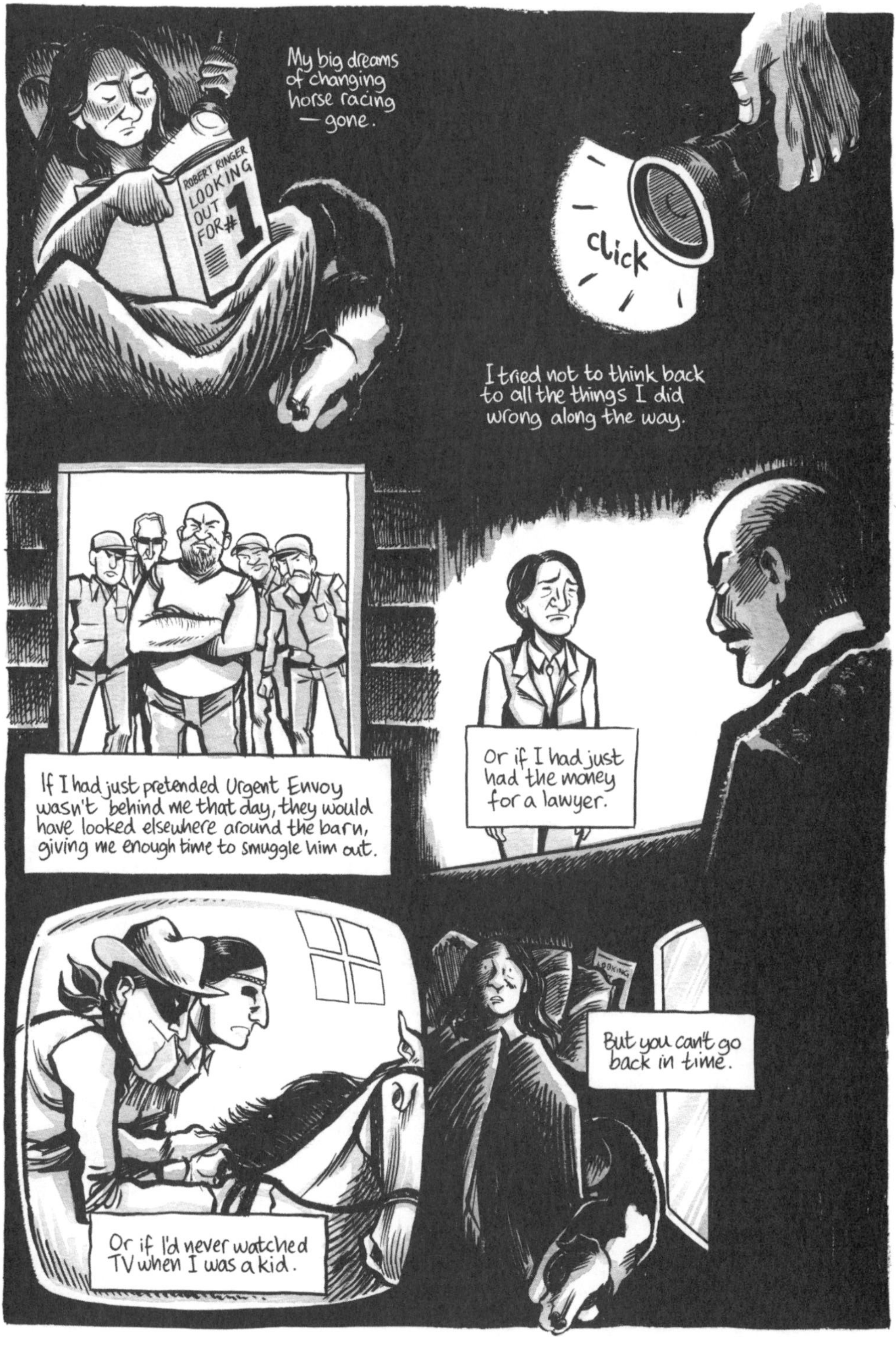
My big dreams of changing horse racing —gone.
ROBERT RINGER LOOKING OUT FOR #1
CLICK
I tried not to think back to all the things I did wrong along the way.
If I had just pretended Urgent Envoy wasn't behind me that day, they would have looked elsewhere around the barn, giving me enough time to smuggle him out.
Or if I had just had the money for a lawyer.
Or if I'd never watched TV when I was a kid.
LOOKING
But you can't go back in time.

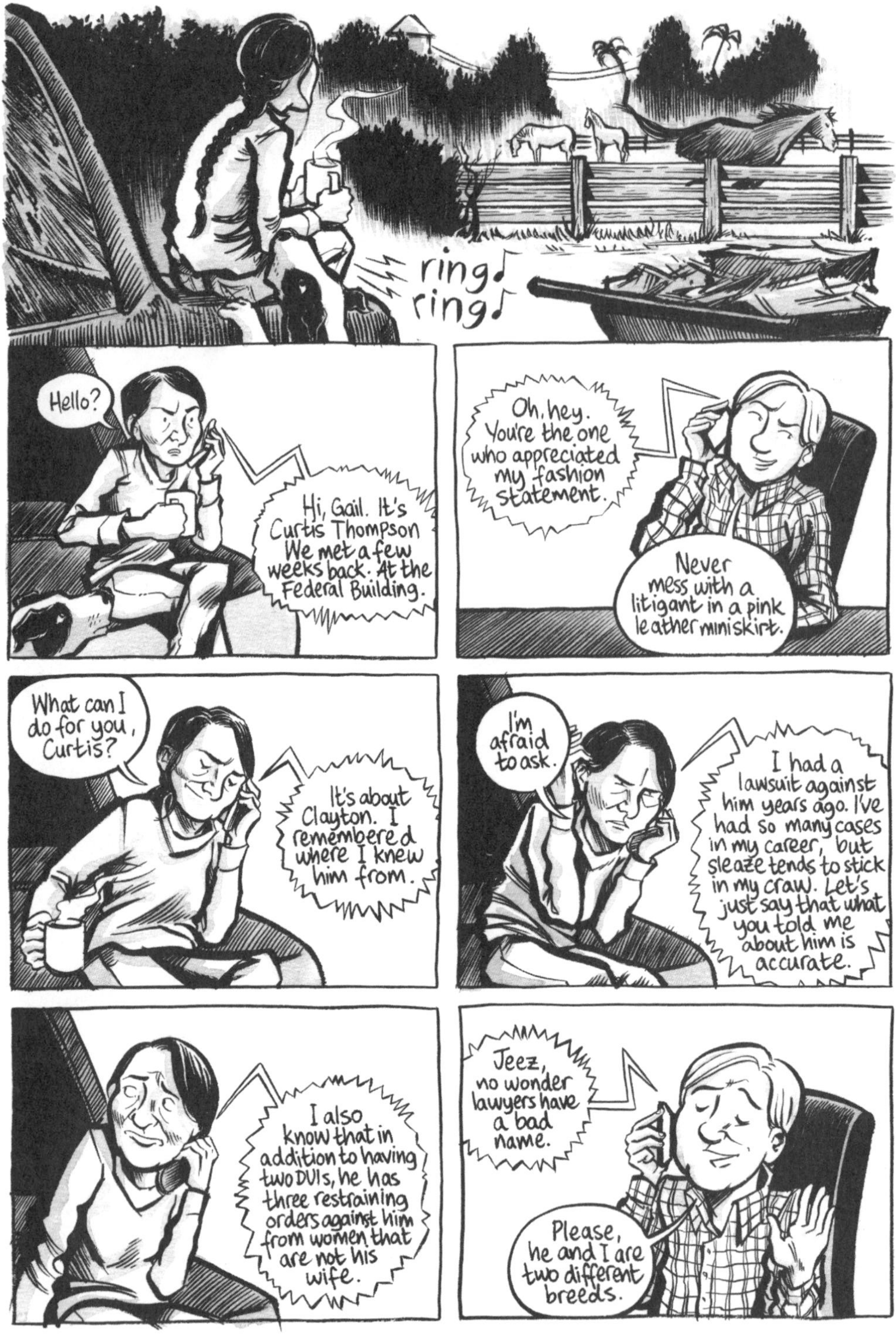
ring♪
ring♪
Hello?
Hi, Gail. It's Curtis Thompson We met a few weeks back. At the Federal Building.
Oh, hey. You're the one who appreciated my fashion statement.
Never mess with a litigant in a pink leather miniskirt.
What can I do for you, Curtis?
It's about Clayton. I remembered where I knew him from.
I'm afraid to ask.
I had a lawsuit against him years ago. I've had so many cases in my career, but sleaze tends to stick in my craw. Let's just say that what you told me about him is accurate.
I also know that in addition to having two DUIs, he has three restraining orders against him from women that are not his wife.
Jeez, no wonder lawyers have a bad name.
Please, he and I are two different breeds.

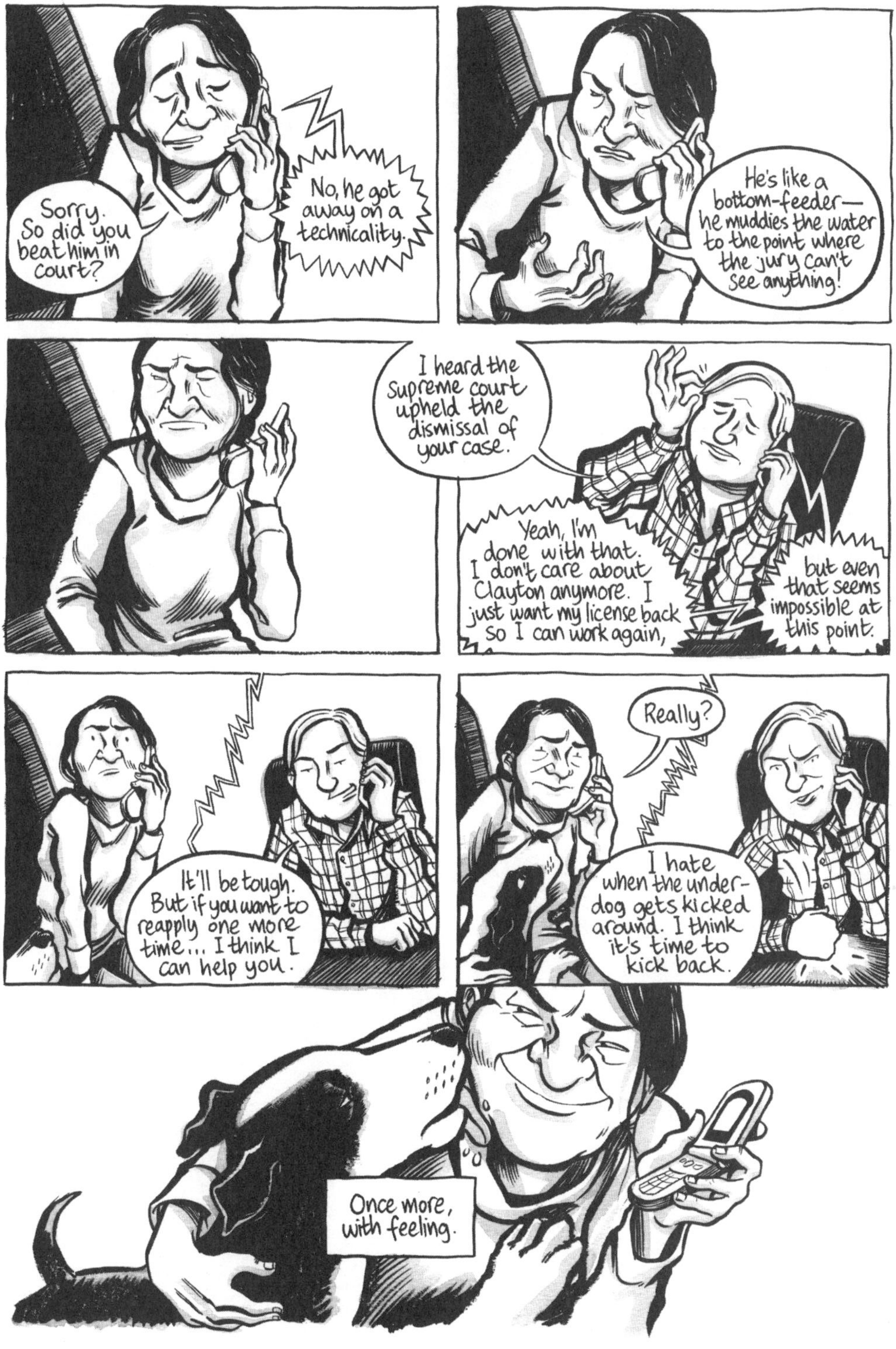
Sorry. So did you beat him in court?
No, he got away on a technicality.
He's like a bottom-feeder— he muddies the water to the point where the jury can't see anything!
I heard the supreme court upheld the dismissal of your case.
Yeah, I'm done with that. I don't care about Clayton anymore. I just want my license back so I can work again,
but even that seems impossible at this point.
It'll be tough. But if you want to reapply one more time... I think I can help you.
Really?
I hate when the under-dog gets kicked around. I think it's time to kick back.
Once more, with feeling.

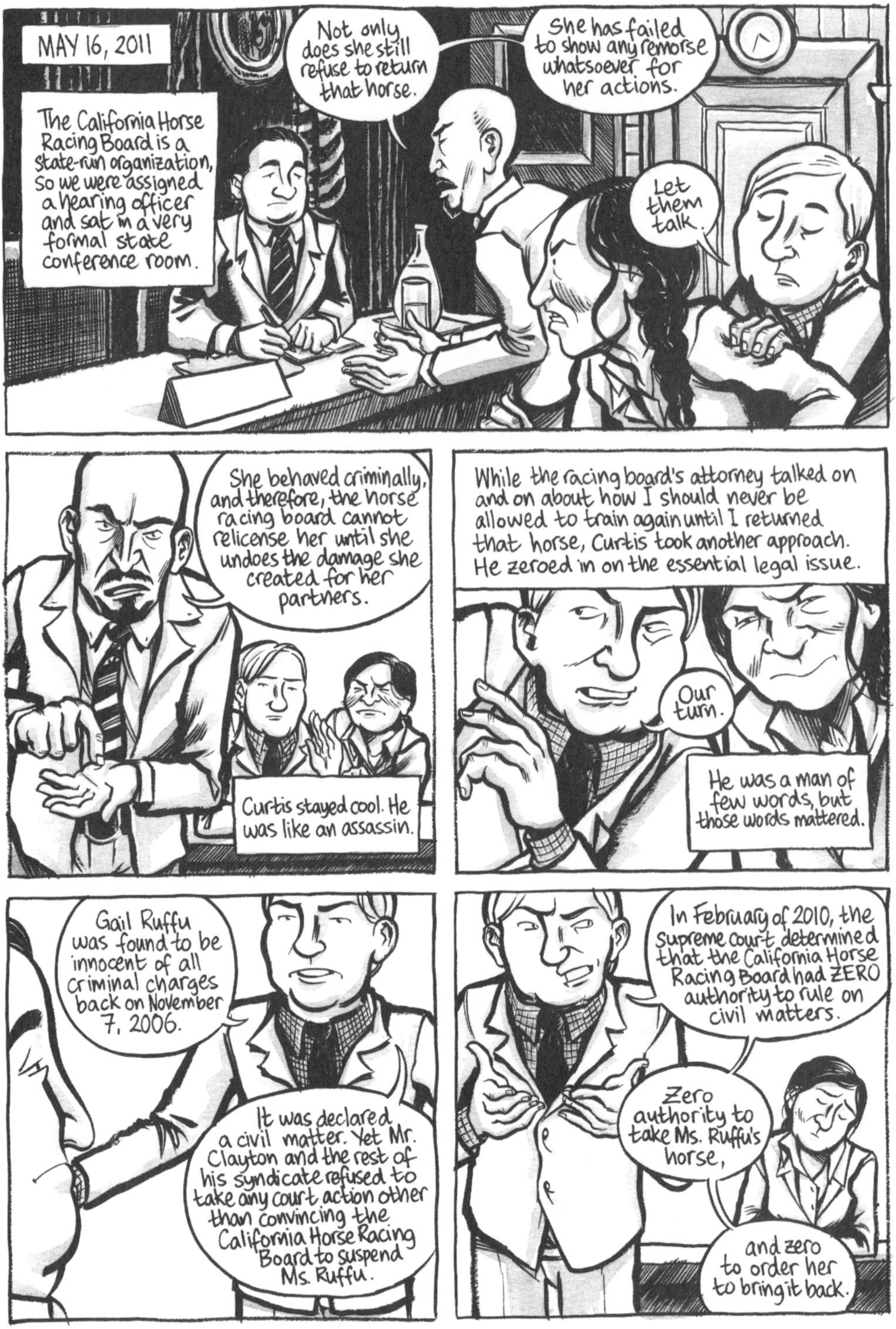
MAY 16, 2011
The California Horse Racing Board is a state-run organization, so we were assigned a hearing officer and sat in a very formal state conference room.
Not only does she still refuse to return that horse.
She has failed to show any remorse whatsoever for her actions.
Let them talk.
She behaved criminally, and therefore, the horse racing board cannot relicense her until she undoes the damage she created for her partners.
Curtis stayed cool. He was like an assassin.
While the racing board's attorney talked on and on about how I should never be allowed to train again until I returned that horse, Curtis took another approach. He zeroed in on the essential legal issue.
Our turn.
He was a man of few words, but those words mattered.
Gail Ruffu was found to be innocent of all criminal charges back on November 7, 2006.
It was declared a civil matter. Yet Mr. Clayton and the rest of his syndicate refused to take any court action other than convincing the California Horse Racing Board to suspend Ms. Ruffu.
In February of 2010, the supreme court determined that the California Horse Racing Board had ZERO authority to rule on civil matters.
Zero authority to take Ms. Ruffu's horse,
and zero to order her to bring it back.

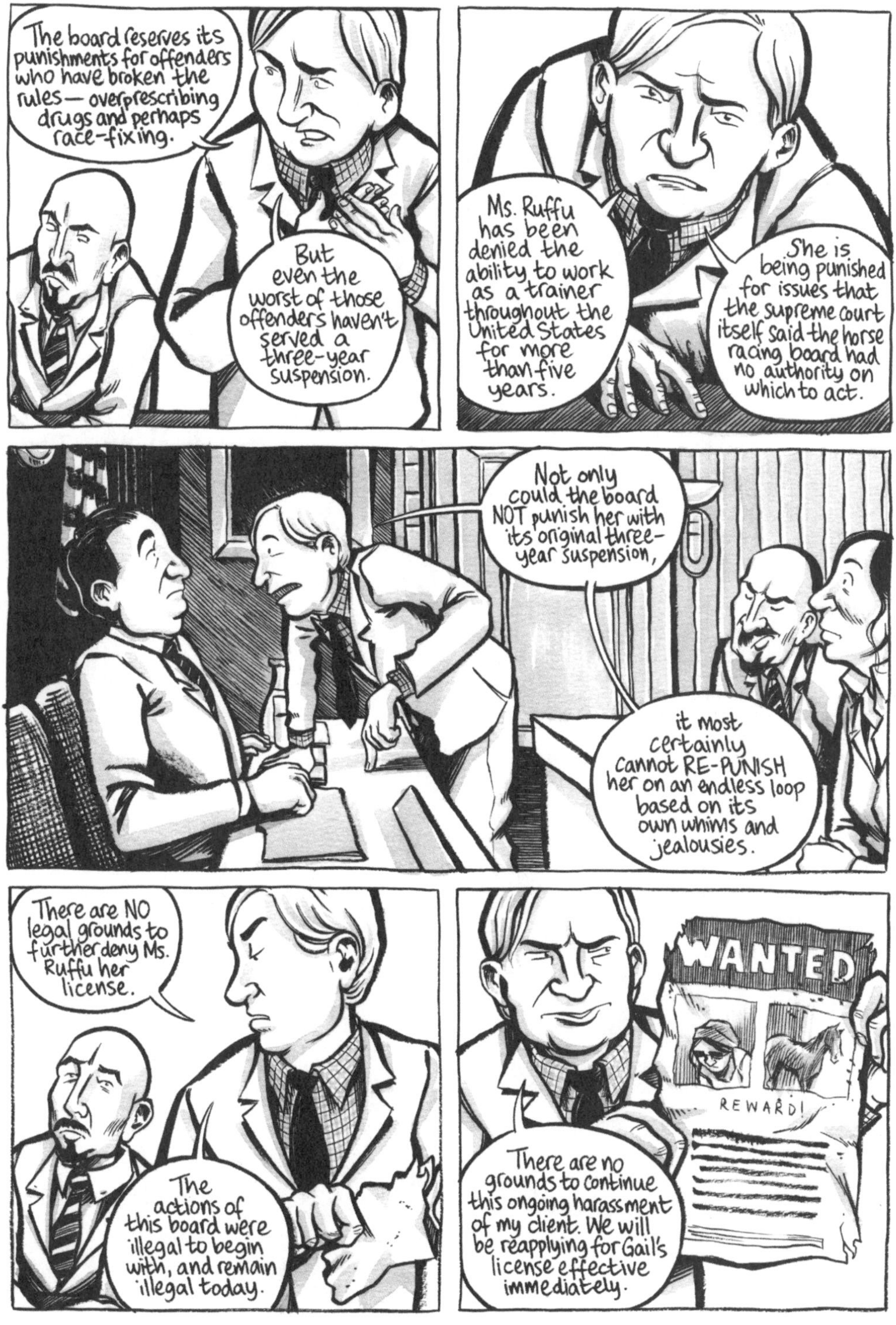
The board reserves its punishments for offenders who have broken the rules— overprescribing drugs and perhaps race-fixing.
But even the worst of those offenders haven't served a three-year suspension.
Ms. Ruffu has been denied the ability to work as a trainer throughout the United States for more than five years.
She is being punished for issues that the supreme court itself said the horse racing board had no authority on which to act.
Not only could the board NOT punish her with its original three-year suspension,
it most certainly cannot RE-PUNISH her on an endless loop based on its own whims and jealousies.
There are NO legal grounds to further deny Ms. Ruffu her license.
The actions of this board were illegal to begin with, and remain illegal today.
WANTED
REWARD!
There are no grounds to continue this ongoing harassment of my client. We will be reapplying for Gail's license effective immediately.

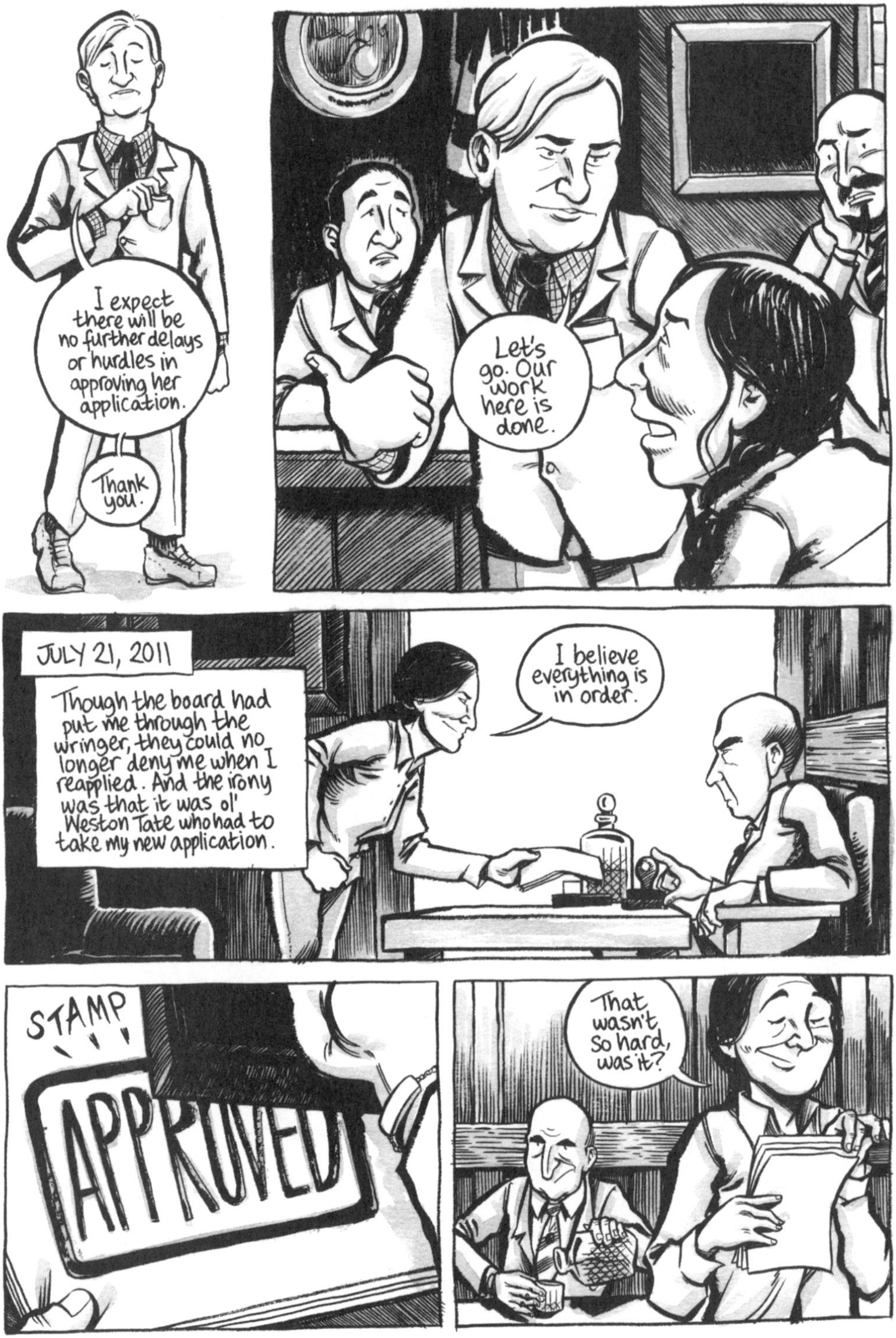
I expect there will be no further delays or hurdles in approving her application.
Thank you.
Let's go. Our work here is done.
JULY 21, 2011
Though the board had put me through the wringer, they could no longer deny me when I reapplied. And the irony was that it was ol' Weston Tate who had to take my new application.
I believe everything is in order.
STAMP
APPROVED
That wasn't so hard, was it?

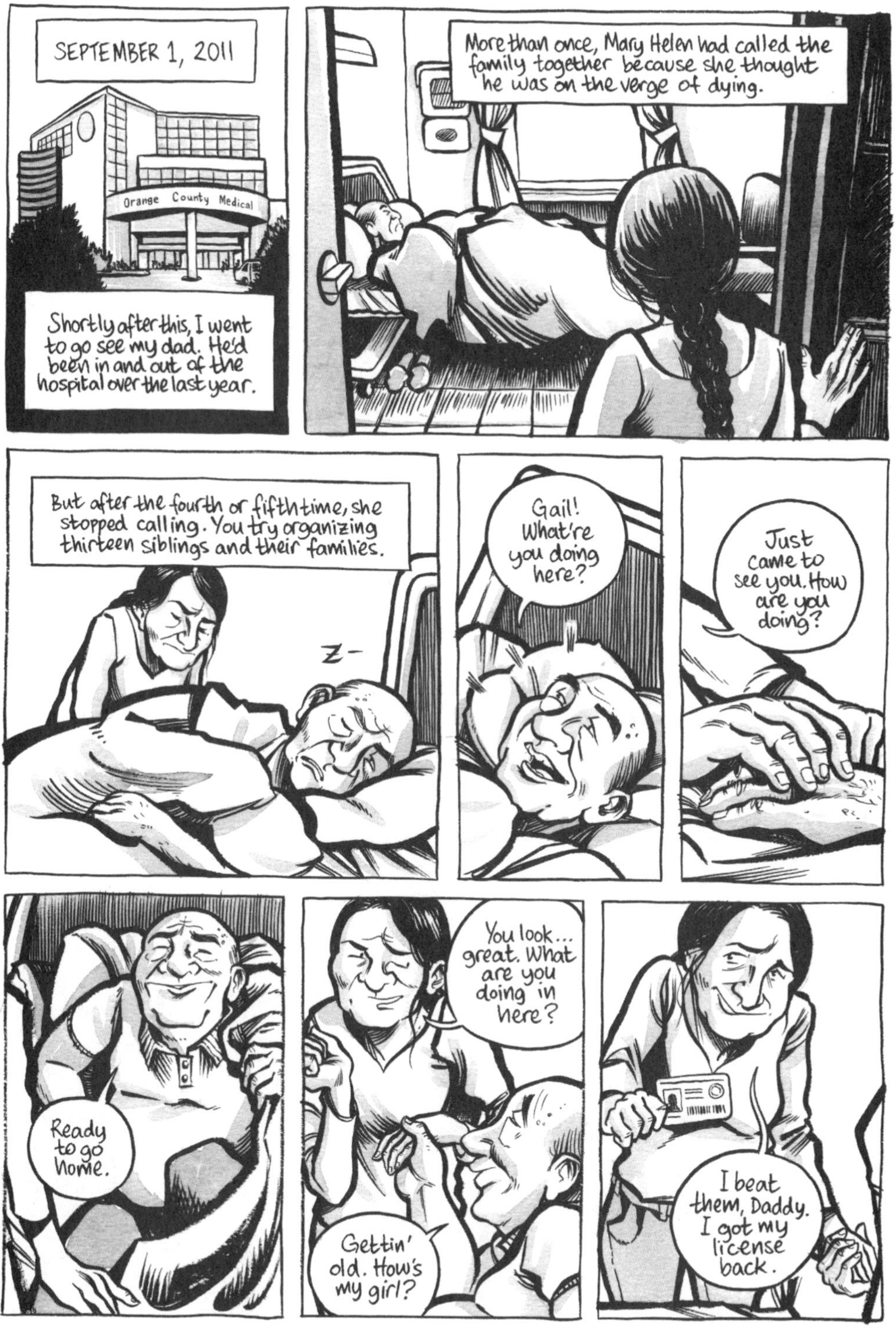
SEPTEMBER 1, 2011
Orange County Medical
Shortly after this, I went to go see my dad. He'd been in and out of the hospital over the last year.
More than once, Mary Helen had called the family together because she thought he was on the verge of dying.
But after the fourth or fifth time, she stopped calling. You try organizing thirteen siblings and their families.
Z-
Gail! What're you doing here?
Just came to see you. How are you doing?
Ready to go home.
You look... great. What are you doing in here?
Gettin' old. How's my girl?
I beat them, Daddy. I got my license back.

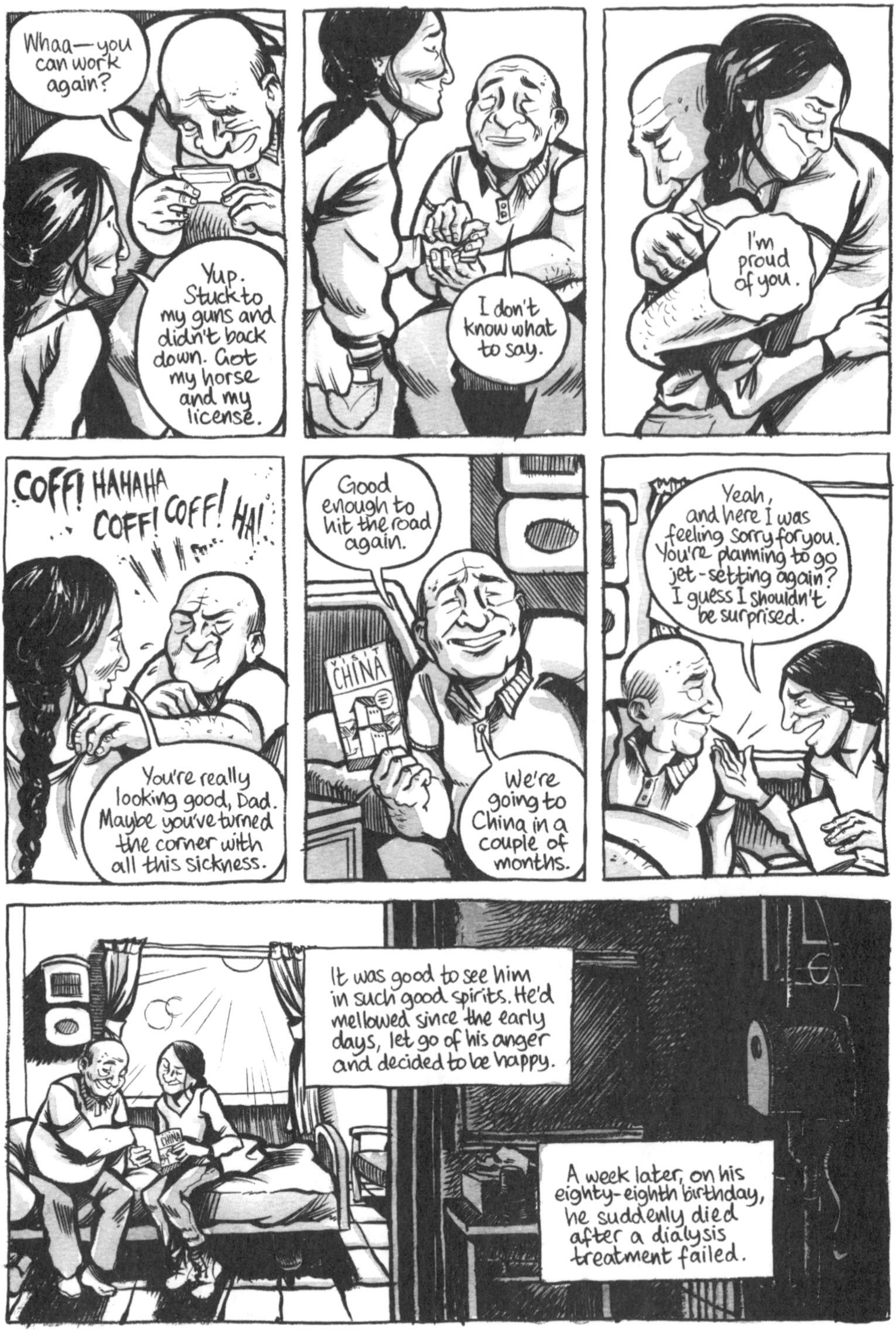
Whaa—you can work again?
Yup. Stuck to my guns and didn't back down. Got my horse and my license.
I don't know what to say.
I'm proud of you.
COFF! HAHAHA COFF! COFF! HA!
You're really looking good, Dad. Maybe you've turned the corner with all this sickness.
Good enough to hit the road again.
VISIT CHINA
We're going to China in a couple of months.
Yeah, and here I was feeling sorry for you. You're planning to go jet-setting again? I guess I shouldn't be surprised.
It was good to see him in such good spirits. He'd mellowed since the early days, let go of his anger and decided to be happy.
CHINA
A week later, on his eighty-eighth birthday, he suddenly died after a dialysis treatment failed.

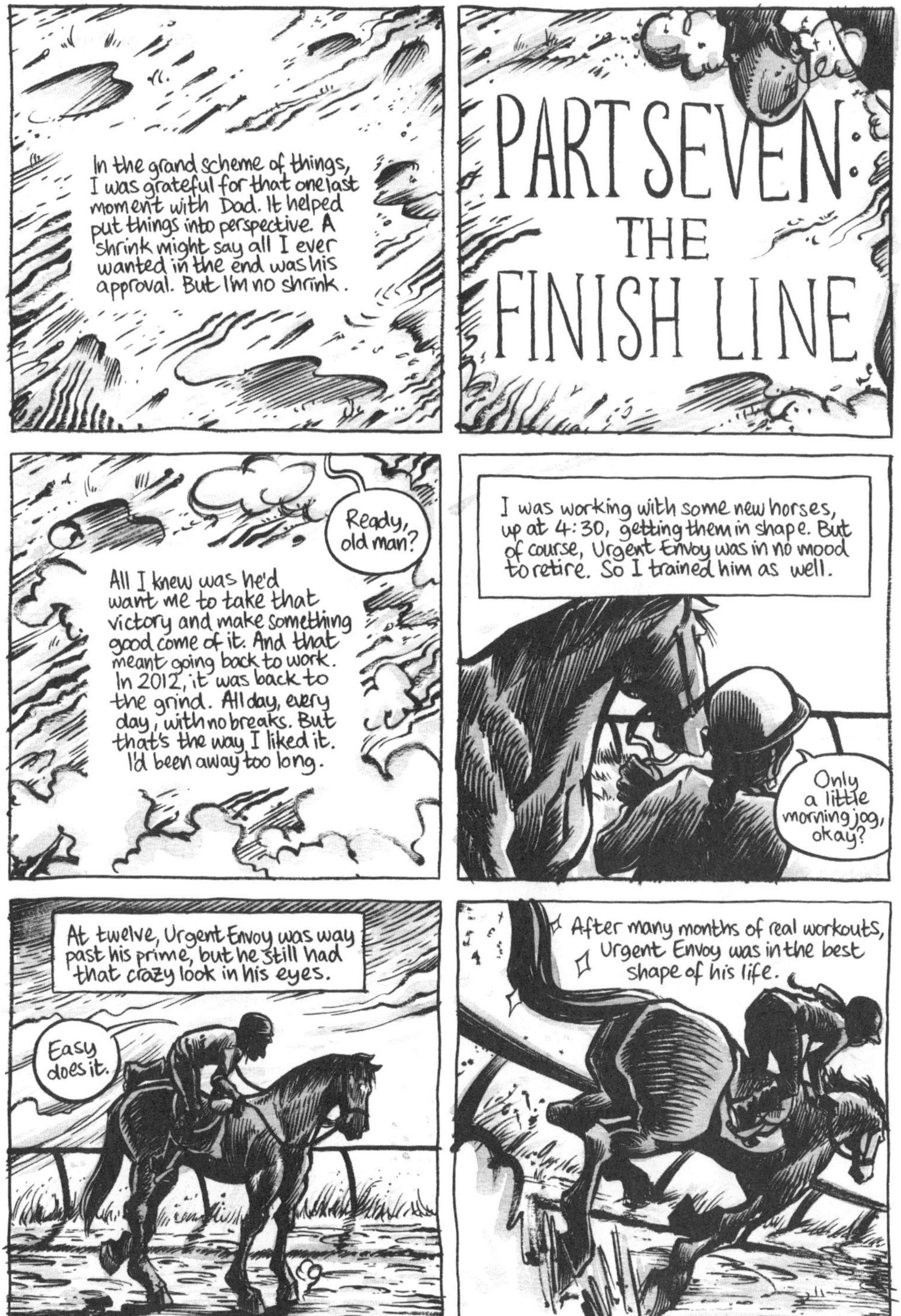
In the grand scheme of things, I was grateful for that one last moment with Dad. It helped put things into perspective. A shrink might say all I ever wanted in the end was his approval. But I'm no shrink.
PART SEVEN: THE FINISH LINE
Ready, old man?
All I knew was he'd want me to take that victory and make something good come of it. And that meant going back to work. In 2012, it was back to the grind. All day, every day, with no breaks. But that's the way I liked it. I'd been away too long.
I was working with some new horses, up at 4:30, getting them in shape. But of course, Urgent Envoy was in no mood to retire. So I trained him as well.
Only a little morning jog, okay?
At twelve, Urgent Envoy was way past his prime, but he still had that crazy look in his eyes.
Easy does it.
After many months of real workouts, Urgent Envoy was in the best shape of his life.

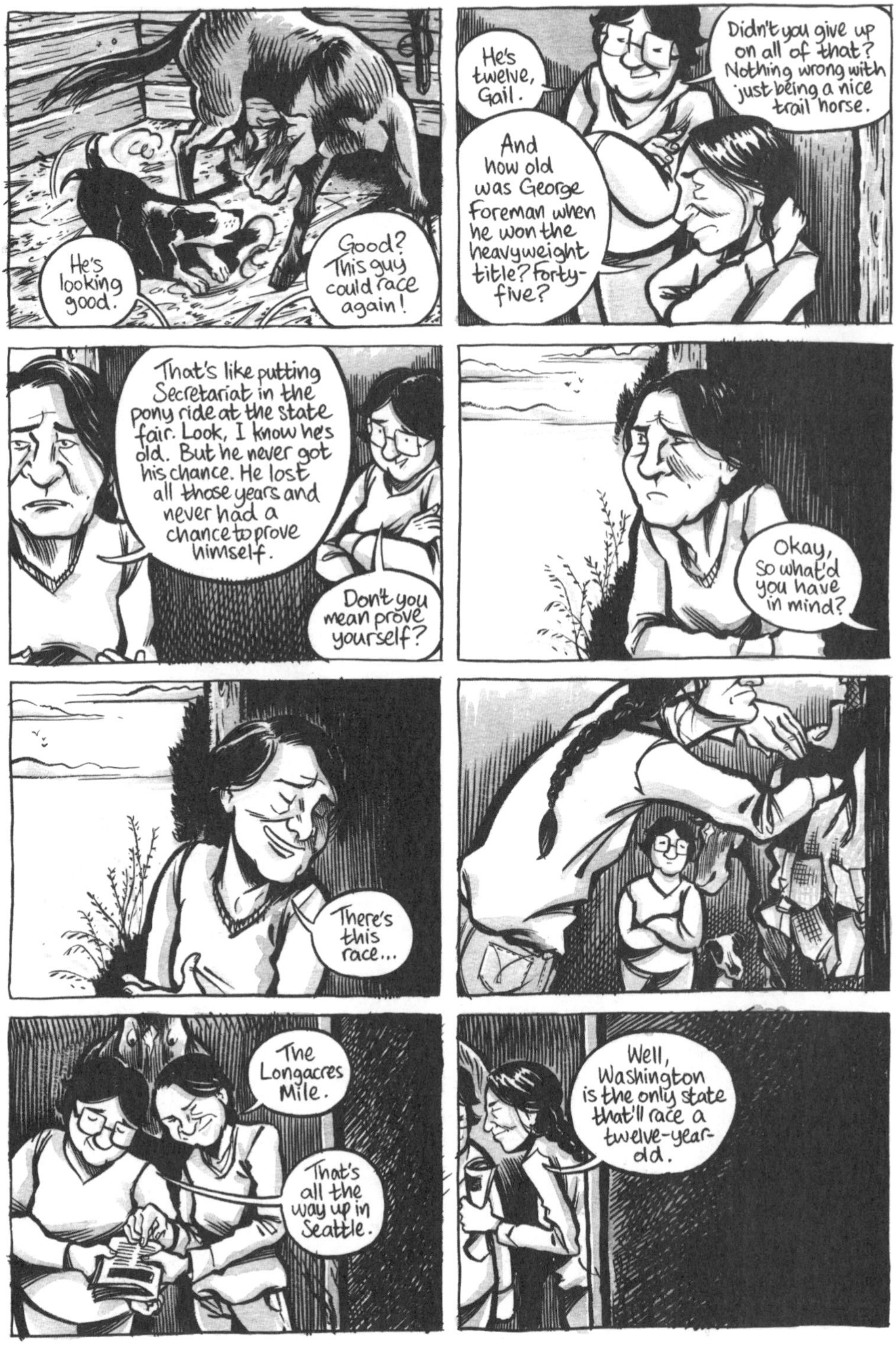
He's looking good.
Good? This guy could race again!
He's twelve, Gail.
Didn't you give up on all of that? Nothing wrong with just being a nice trail horse.
And how old was George Foreman when he won the heavyweight title? Forty-five?
That's like putting Secretariat in the pony ride at the state fair. Look, I know he's old. But he never got his chance. He lost all those years and never had a chance to prove himself.
Don't you mean prove yourself?
Okay, so what'd you have in mind?
There's this race...
The Longacres Mile.
That's all the way up in Seattle.
Well, Washington is the only state that'll race a twelve-year-old.

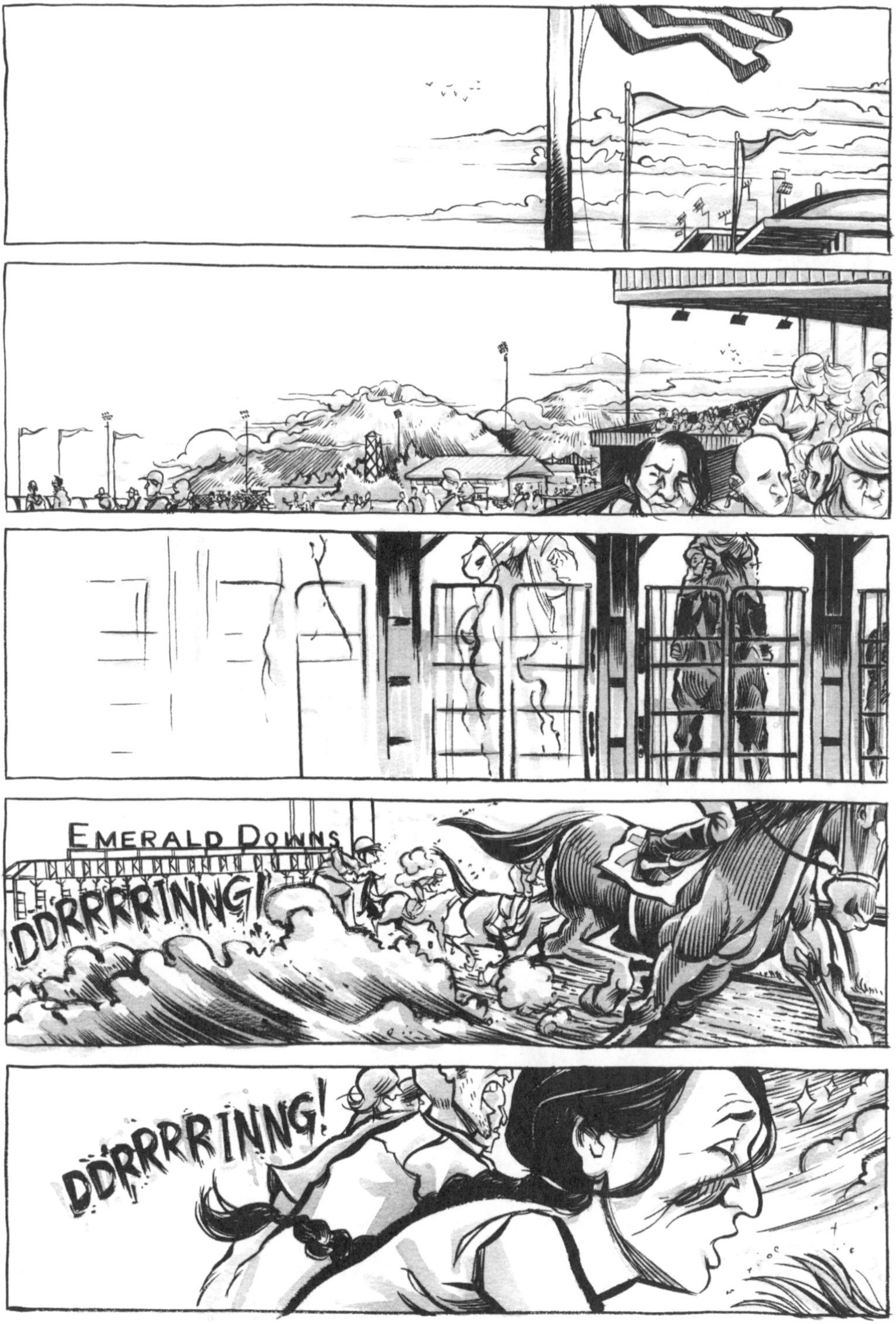
EMERALD DOWNS
DDRRRRINNG!
DDRRRRINNG!

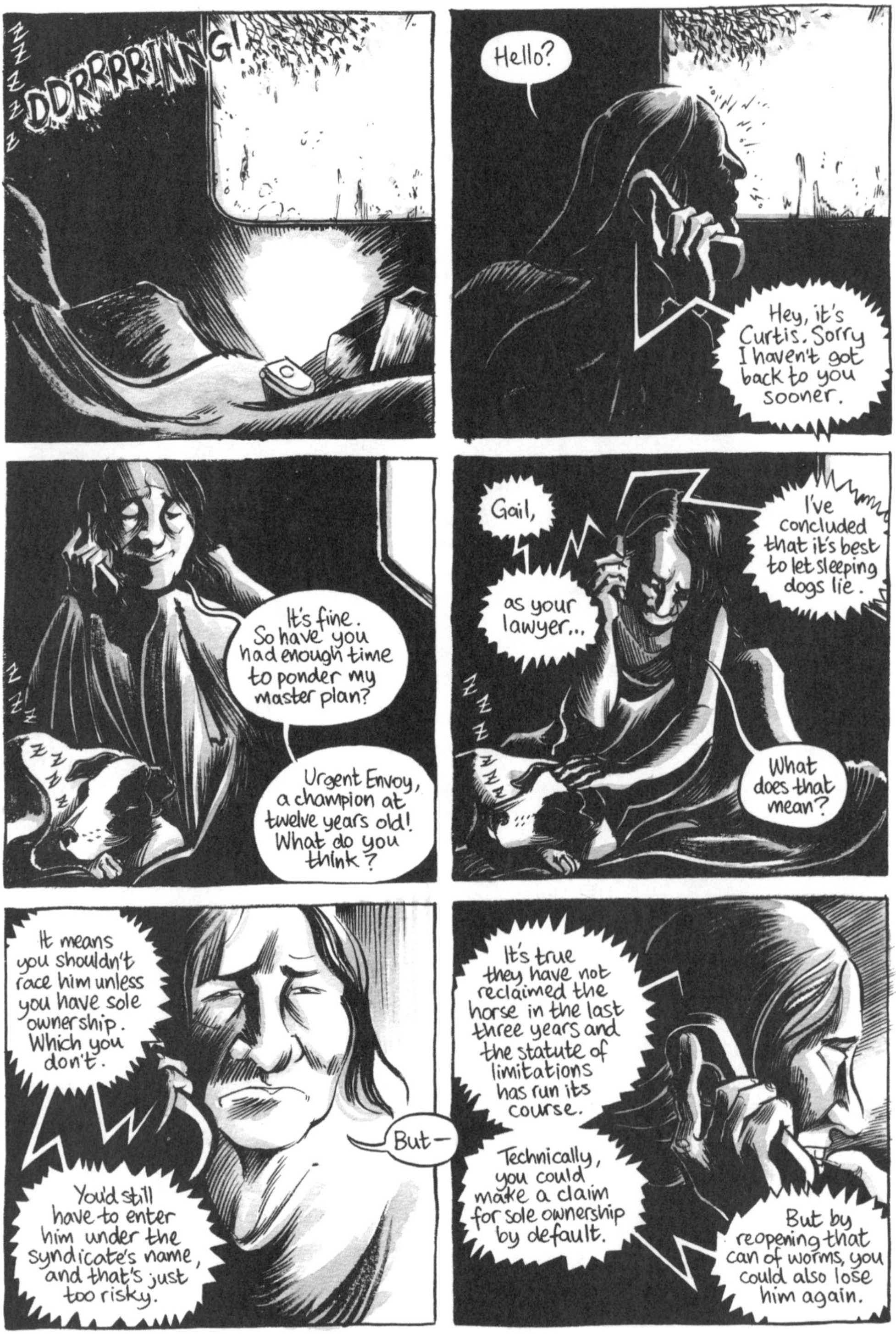
ZZZZZ
DDRRRRING!
Hello?
Hey, it's Curtis. Sorry I haven't got back to you sooner.
It's fine. So have you had enough time to ponder my master plan?
Urgent Envoy, a champion at twelve years old! What do you think?
ZZZ
ZZZZ
Gail,
as your lawyer...
I've concluded that it's best to let sleeping dogs lie.
What does that mean?
ZZZ
ZZZ
It means you shouldn't race him unless you have sole ownership. Which you don't.
But—
You'd still have to enter him under the syndicate's name, and that's just too risky.
It's true they have not reclaimed the horse in the last three years and the statute of limitations has run its course.
Technically, you could make a claim for sole ownership by default.
But by reopening that can of worms, you could also lose him again.

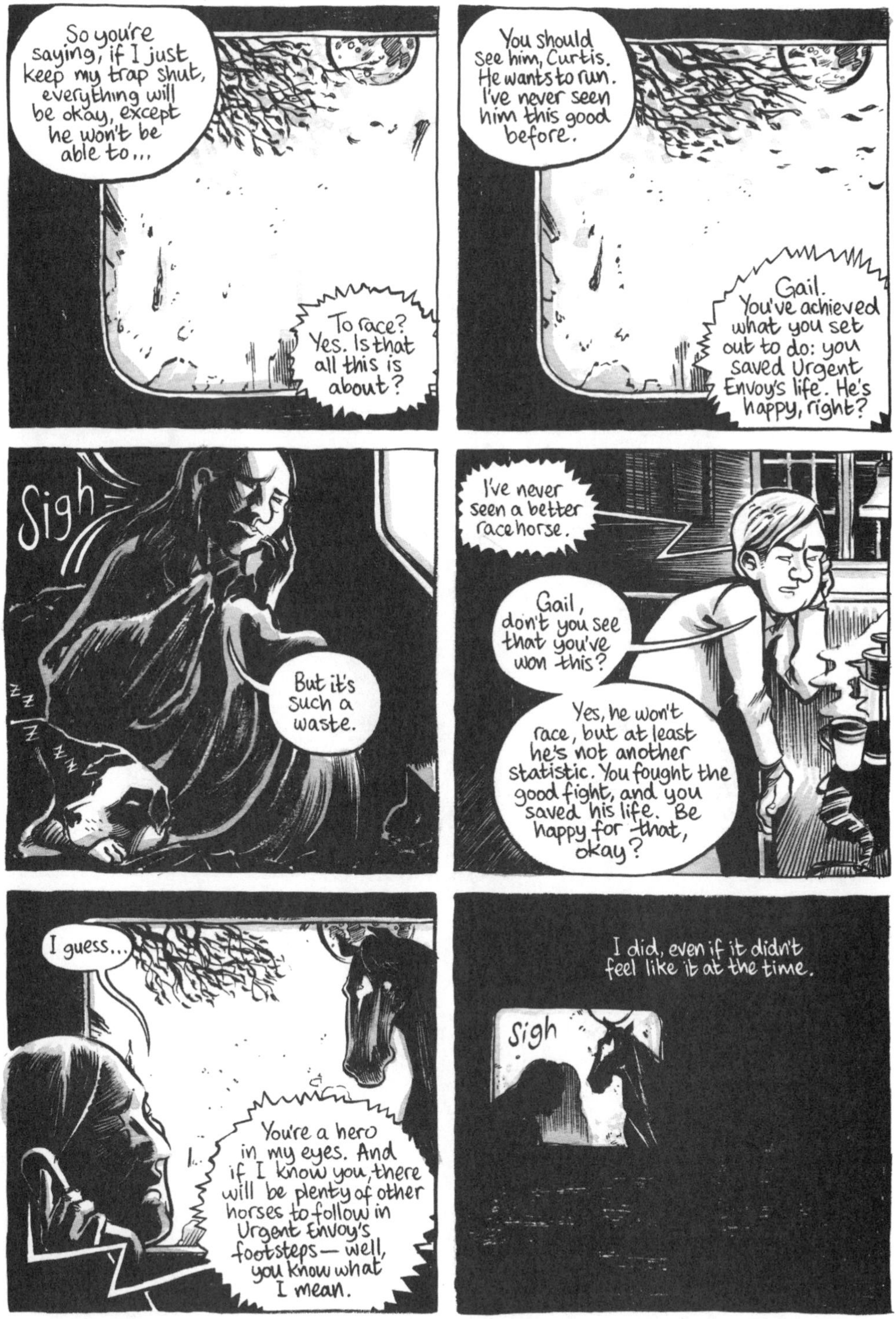
So you're saying, if I just keep my trap shut, everything will be okay, except he won't be able to...
To race? Yes. Is that all this is about?
You should see him, Curtis. He wants to run. I've never seen him this good before.
Gail. You've achieved what you set out to do: you saved Urgent Envoy's life. He's happy, right?
Sigh
But it's such a waste.
I've never seen a better race horse.
Gail, don't you see that you've won this?
Yes, he won't race, but at least he's not another statistic. You fought the good fight, and you saved his life. Be happy for that, okay?
I guess...
You're a hero in my eyes. And if I know you, there will be plenty of other horses to follow in Urgent Envoy's footsteps— well, you know what I mean.
I did, even if it didn't feel like it at the time.
Sigh

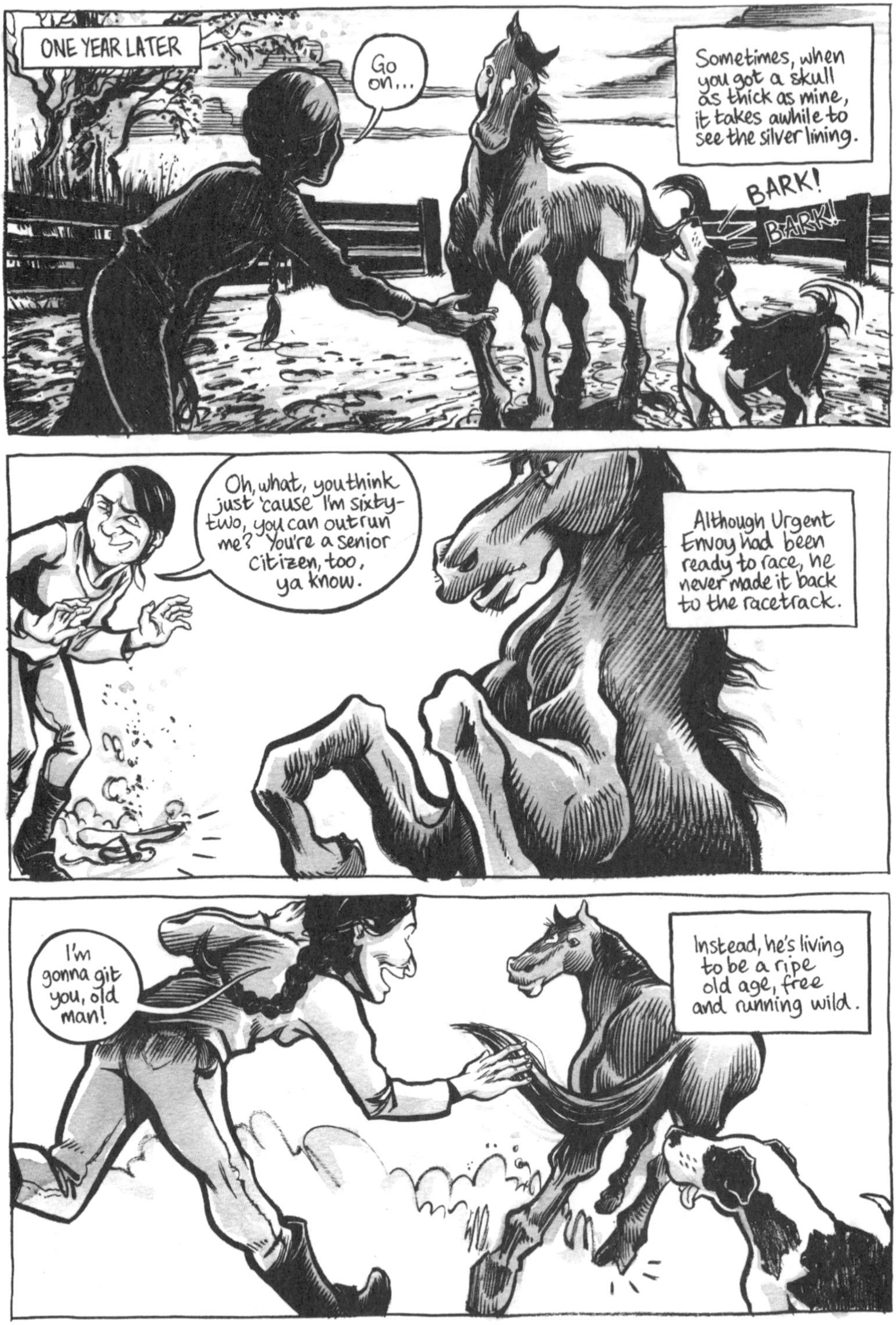
ONE YEAR LATER
Go on...
Sometimes, when you got a skull as thick as mine, it takes awhile to see the silver lining.
BARK!
BARK!
Oh, what, you think just 'cause I'm sixty-two, you can outrun me? You're a senior citizen, too, ya know.
Although Urgent Envoy had been ready to race, he never made it back to the racetrack.
I'm gonna git you, old man!
Instead, he's living to be a ripe old age, free and running wild.

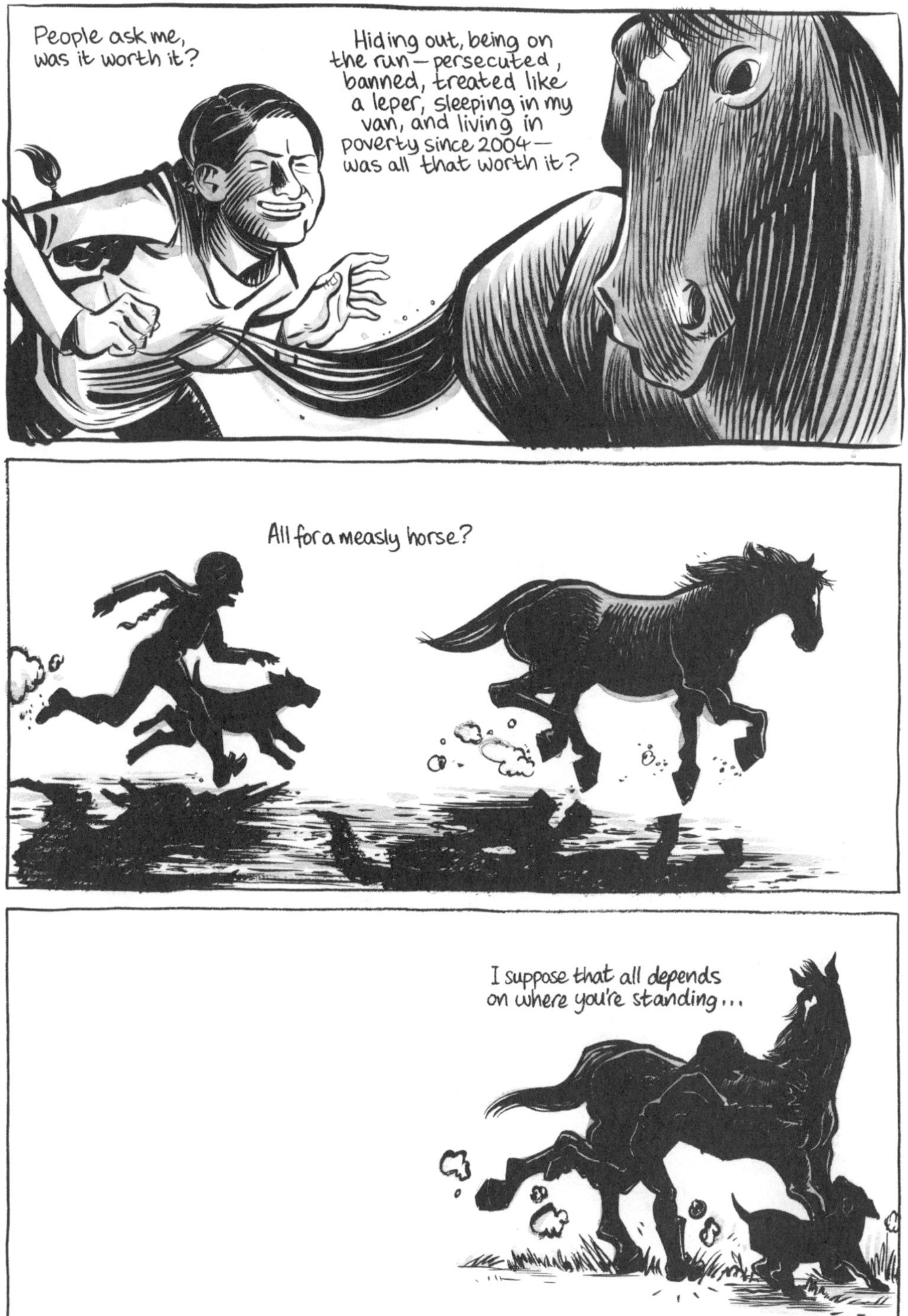
People ask me, was it worth it?
Hiding out, being on the run—persecuted, banned, treated like a leper, sleeping in my van, and living in poverty since 2004—was all that worth it?
All for a measly horse?
I suppose that all depends on where you're standing...

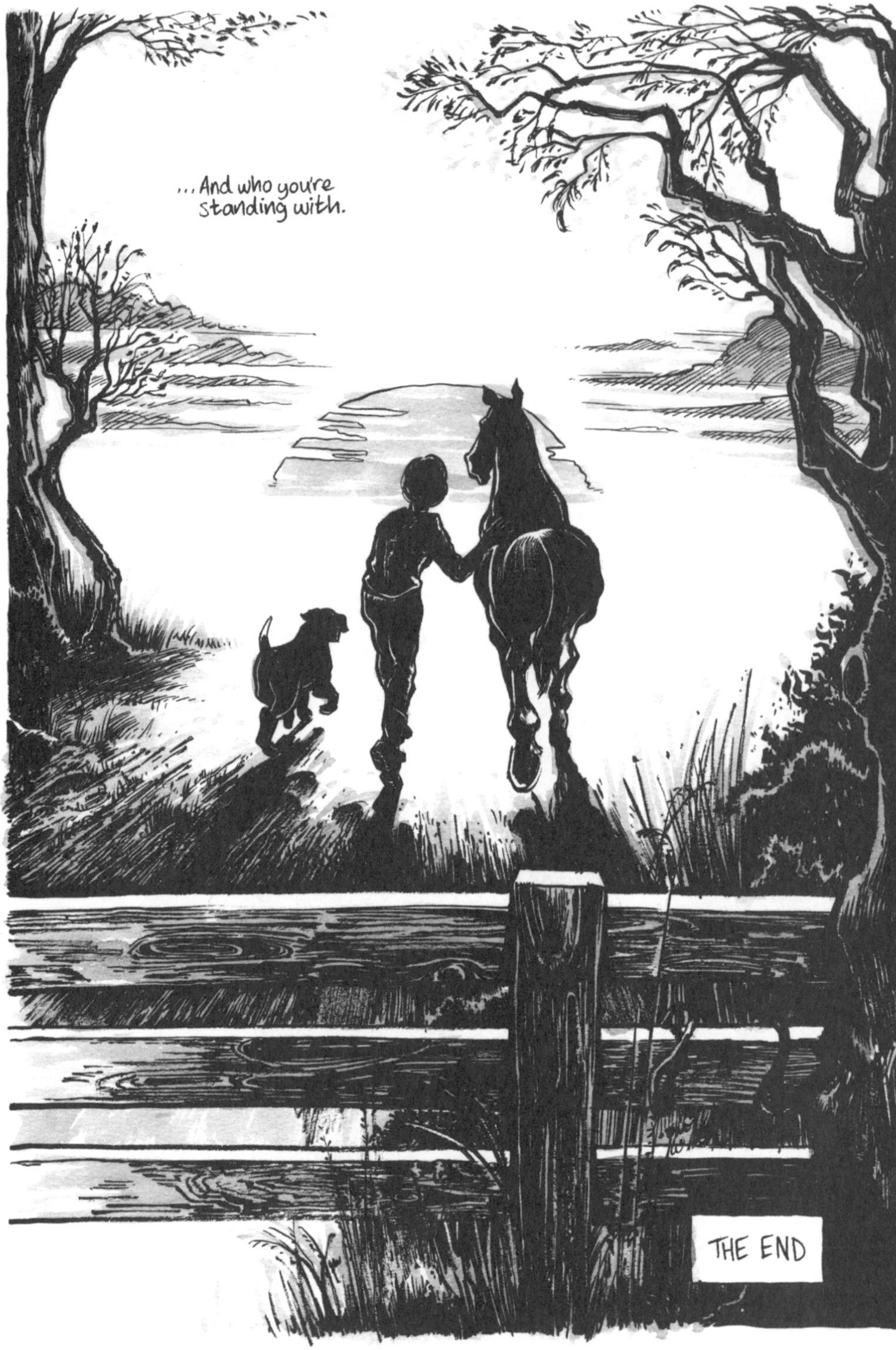
...And who you're standing with.
THE END

From top left: Shots of young Gail, ages 10-21. Our grandpa on Spice, Gail and her father Sid in the 70s, one of Gail's wanted posters. *Opposite page:* Gail galloping at Del Mar, various shots of Gail and Urgent Envoy in recent years.

FOR LAW ENFORCEMENT USE ONLY
CONFIDENTIAL

Call Security
DENIED ACCESS

CHP-B OK TO ENTER 6/30/11

GAIL ELIZABETH RUFFU
LICENSE: 231628

(K) EXERCISE RIDER

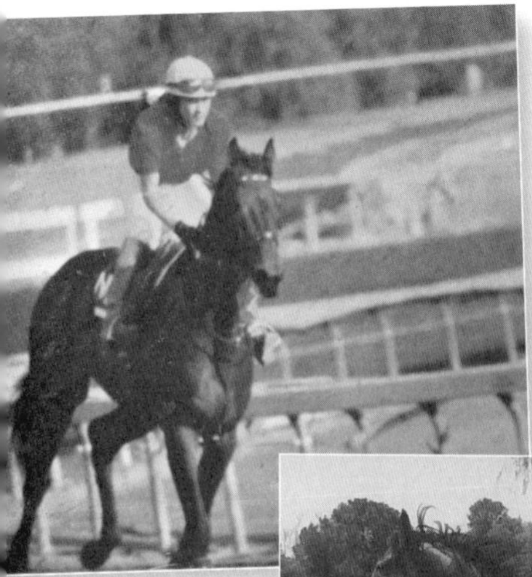

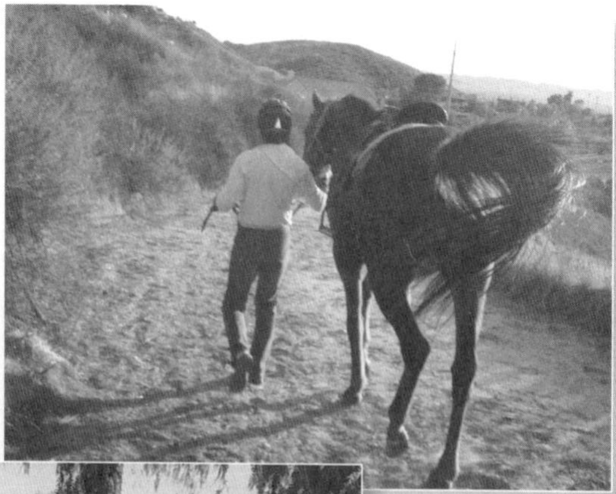

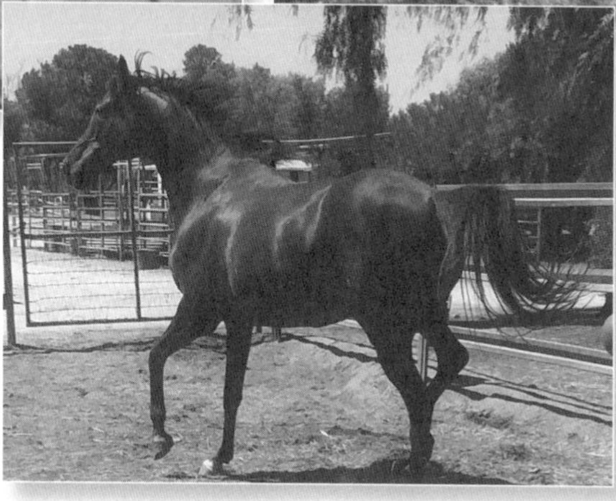

© Jamie Snyder

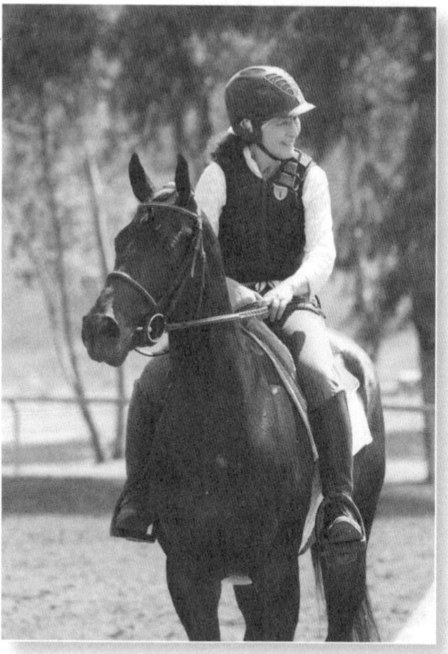

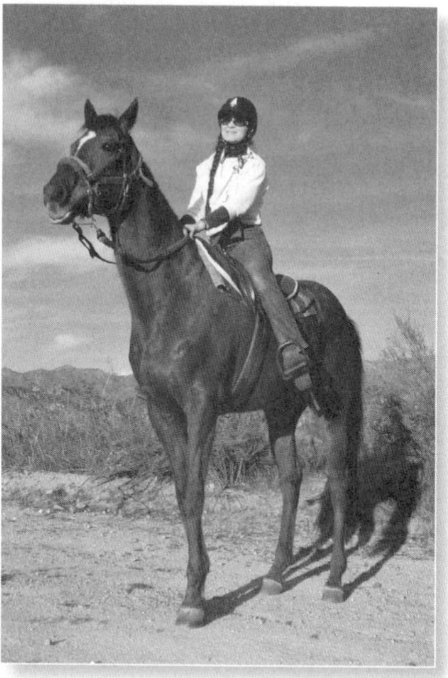

AFTERWORD

The path of human progress is lined with the bones of millions of horses who died along the way. We humans are indebted to these animals for their sacrifice in getting us to where we are. In small payment of that debt, I have made it my mission to advance reforms which will end some of the avoidable suffering of thousands of horses used for racing.

I grew up barrel racing and pole-bending in North Texas. During my teenage years, my parents "forced" me to move with them to Europe, where I studied dressage and stable management in Spain, England, Scotland, and Germany. In 1972, I returned to the United States, and for twenty years, I took part in dressage, jumping, competitive trail riding, and other competitions. When I entered the horse racing industry in the 1990s, I found my way to Hollywood Park, where I galloped horses as a freelance exercise-rider until I passed the California Horse Racing Board trainer exams in 1997. By then, I had seen enough to affect me for the rest of my life.

In American horse racing, twenty-four racehorses (on average) die every week on racetracks.[1] About 3,600 horses died racing or training inside state-regulated race track enclosures over the three years leading up to 2012.[2] Thousands more died in slaughterhouses due to injuries caused by reckless trainers and breeders. The practices of inbreeding and line breeding (selective mating within a horse's extended family) are both widespread. Because of these practices, the modern racehorse's bones mature more slowly and are therefore more fragile than those of the raw-boned racehorses of yesteryear. Even so, these horses often race as early as the age of two. The results are heartbreaking. One example of the nationwide decline in horse health: yearly starts for young racehorses have dropped from twelve (on average) in 1960 to fewer than seven (on average) in 2013.[3]

Then there's the unabated tradition of forcing yearlings and two-year-olds to perform repeated, maximum effort workouts in order to be sold for huge

---

[1] "Why Do So Many Horses Die in Races?" by Sam Dangremond, Town & Country Magazine, May 26, 2016

[2] "Mangled Horses, Maimed Jockeys" by Walt Bogdanich, Joe Drape and Rebecca R. Ruiz, *New York Times*, March 24, 2012

[3] "Today's Thoroughbred — What Animal Are We Dealing With?" presented by Edward L. Bowen at The Welfare and Safety of the Racehorse Summit, 2014

prices at auction or to race for million dollar Breeders' Cup purses, which is widely known to be destructive. Only one out of hundreds of two-year-old BC winners has ever been able to go on to win again as a BC three-year-old or older horse. This fact alone should have mandated an end to the BC two-year-old Division long ago. Instead, Breeders' Cup leadership has *expanded* the two-year-old Division to include baby fillies. In sharp contrast, the minimum age for Olympic athletes has been raised from thirteen years old to sixteen because repeated maximum stress efforts are less destructive to more mature bodies.

The pressure to produce a winning horse has *not* declined. There is a huge failure rate in horse racing: between 5% percent and 17 percent of racehorses earn enough for owners to recoup their training costs.[4] To increase the odds of winning, owners and trainers turn to drugs. The drug use is not hidden. Every edition of the *Daily Racing Form* lists the drugs each horse is taking before a race, showing that 95 percent of American racehorses train on powerful drugs. Those are the so-called "legal" drugs (which they're not allowed to use on the day of the race). However, between 2009–2012, trainers at tracks in the US had been caught illegally drugging horses 3,800 times (in a system where they are not tested very often).[5] Trainers often use chemicals designed to bulk up pigs and cattle before slaughter: cobra venom, Viagra, blood doping agents, stimulants, and cancer drugs.[6] Meanwhile, veterinarians sometimes act as both doctors and pharmacists. The more drugs vets prescribe, the more money they make.[7]

Virtually all the people in the racing community will tell you that they love horses. However, this community is made up of two very different groups of horse lovers. People in the first group sincerely love their animals and care deeply about their welfare. Taking care of horses is their primary motive and pay-off for being in the game. People in the second group love what horses *do* for them: create profit, excitement, and prestige. Unfortunately, this second group controls the sport. The first group has been unable to change horse racing because its members fear (as proven in my case) that they will be blackballed and bullied if they fail to conform to the majority's wishes. Few

---

[4] *Equine Veterinary Journal*, Equine vet. J. (2006) 38 (2) 113–118

[5] "Mangled Horses, Maimed Jockeys" by Walt Bogdanich, Joe Drape and Rebecca R. Ruiz, *New York Times*, March 24, 2012

[6] "Mangled Horses, Maimed Jockeys" by Walt Bogdanich, Joe Drape and Rebecca R. Ruiz, *New York Times*, March 24, 2012

[7] "Racing Economics Collide With Veterinarians' Oath" by Walt Bogdanich, Joe Drape and Rebecca R. Ruiz, *New York Times*, September 21, 2012

true horse lovers can afford lawyers to protect them from such consequences.

After years of witnessing these horrors and waiting for change to happen, I decided to experiment with a more humane training approach. I believe the only real way to effect change is to prove a more profitable, more humane way to win. Produce racehorses that are drug-free, healthy, and profitable, then other trainers might begin to copy these winning methods. Success breeds imitators.

I choose to treat a horse as I would a child. If you wouldn't start your kid in extreme sports as a toddler, don't do it to your horse! I also choose not to do maximum-speed workouts or to race horses under thirty-six months of age. Most importantly, I refuse to drug my animals. If the British Horse Racing Authority successfully banned harmful drugs, so can members of the United States horse racing community.

Because horses cannot speak for themselves, your voice is needed as well. Both the horse racing and animal welfare industries have proven for decades that it is unable—without significant public pressure—to end those destructive traditions. Pressure must come from the true horse lovers in America who stand outside of the horse racing industry. Please act. Contact Breeders' Cup Inc. and the sponsors of races that involve two-year-old horses. Protest by email, telephone, or social media. Ask your horse-loving friends to also participate in this grassroots protest.

People in racing say ending two-year-old Breeders' Cup events are impossible. But thirty years ago, who could have imagined the banning of smoking in public places or the legalization of gay marriage? These shifts are beginning to happen in horse racing as well. Just look at champion Thoroughbred Justify, who skipped the Breeders' Cup altogether, never racing as a two-year-old, and just won the Triple Crown—a feat thought impossible until now. Proof positive that horses do not need to race as two-year-olds to become champions. I choose to be part of the solution, not the problem. So can you.

—Gail Ruffu, 2018

THE TALENT

G. NERI is the Eisner-nominated, Coretta Scott King Award Honor-winning author of *Yummy: the Last Days of a Southside Shorty*, which Flavorwire hailed as one of the top 20 essential graphic novels of all time. He has written ten books for young people, including the Lee Bennett Hopkins Promising Poet Award-winner, *Chess Rumble*, and his books have been translated into multiple languages in more than 25 countries. Mr. Neri lives on the Gulf coast of Florida. For more information, visit gneri.com.

CORBAN WILKIN is the recipient of the 2012 Cape/Observer/Comica Graphic Short Story Prize for his comic *But I Can't* and was nominated for the 2014 British Comics Awards in the Emerging Talent category for the graphic novel *Breaker's End*. He lives in London, England. For more information, visit corbanwilkin.com.

GAIL RUFFU grew up in Texas, where she fell in love with horses. When she was a teen, her family moved to Spain and each fall and winter, she went to England and Scotland to learn and eventually pass the British Horse Society Exam. A few years later, she married and moved to Germany, where she studied dressage and teaching techniques.

She returned to the US in the 70s, and by the 90s, she was living at Hollywood Park and working with countless trainers in California and Texas. She has recently regained her CHRB license and is actively training horses and future trainers.

Urgent Envoy remains at large.